Creative Literacy in Action
Birth through Age Nine

JANET L. TOWELL
Florida Atlantic University

KATHERINE C. POWELL
Florida Atlantic University

SUSANNAH L. BROWN
Florida Atlantic University

CENGAGE
Learning·

Australia • Brazil • Mexico • Singapore • United Kingdom • United States

Creative Literacy in Action:
Birth through Age Nine
Janet L. Towell, Katherine C. Powell,
and Susannah L. Brown

Senior Product Director: Marta Lee-Perriard

Senior Product Manager: Cheri-Ann Nakamaru

Associate Product Manager: Brady Golden

Content Developer: Kate Scheinman

Product Assistant: Kimiya Hojjat

Marketing Manager: Andrew Miller

Senior Content Project Manager: Samen Iqbal

Senior Art Director: Helen Bruno

Manufacturing Planner: Doug Bertke

Intellectual Property Analyst: Jennifer Bowes

Intellectual Property Project Manager:
Nick Barrows

Text Perm Researcher: Kanchana Vijayarangan

Image Perm Researcher: Sathya Pandi

Production Service/Project Manager: Jill Traut,
MPS Limited

Copy Editor: Heather McElwain

Cover and Text Designer: Jennifer Wahi

Cover Image Credit: Illustrated by Jen Wahi Design

Compositor: MPS Limited

For product information and technology assistance, contact us at
Cengage Learning Customer & Sales Support, 1-800-354-9706
For permission to use material from this text or product,
submit all requests online at **www.cengage.com/permissions**
Further permissions questions can be e-mailed to
permissionrequest@cengage.com

Library of Congress Control Number: 2016936075

Student Edition:
ISBN: 978-1-285-17127-2

Loose-leaf Edition:
ISBN: 978-1-337-09596-9

Cengage Learning
20 Channel Center Street
Boston, MA 02210
USA

Cengage Learning is a leading provider of customized learning solutions with employees residing in nearly 40 different countries and sales in more than 125 countries around the world. Find your local representative at **www.cengage.com**

Cengage Learning products are represented in Canada by Nelson Education, Ltd.

To learn more about Cengage Learning Solutions, visit **www.cengage.com**

Purchase any of our products at your local college store or at our preferred online store **www.cengagebrain.com**

Printed in the United States of America
Print Number: 02   Print Year: 2019

We dedicate this text to
future teachers in the hope
that they will develop a love
of literacy and change the
world, one child at a time.

Brief Contents

Contents

PART 3

INTERACTING CREATIVELY WITH LITERACY

Our vision for writing this early literacy textbook is to provide a unique perspective for literacy instruction by combining the voices of a literacy professor, a psychology professor and an art professor into one voice. Each chapter in this book was written by all three of us, with much collaboration and negotiation. Our teaching experiences throughout the years—in elementary, secondary, and university classrooms—have contributed to concepts and ideas integrated into *Creative Literacy in Action*. To represent our three disciplines, we created a holistic model of literacy (HML), which incorporates the whole child—the cognitive, socioemotional, and physical parts of self. Refer to Figure 1.2 on p. 7, in which you will see that:

- The yellow head (hair) represents the cognitive domain;
- The red heart symbolizes socioemotional development; and
- The blue arms and legs signify the physical aspects of self.

Our visual model is infused throughout the text and adapted to symbolize different components of literacy instruction, such as a paintbrush for the arts, a lightbulb for ideas, and a book for reading comprehension. These aspects of self relate to executive function, which is a critical cognitive skill that includes self-regulation (Kray & Ferdinand, 2013). We envision children learning in an open, creative, accepting, and inspiring environment, experiencing reading and writing with passion and enthusiasm. When young children learn with passion, they gain confidence and independence, which instills a love of literacy that continues for their entire lives. A joy of reading continues to increase self-confidence and build self-esteem. The goal of literacy instruction is to develop independent, lifelong readers and writers who become critical thinkers and problem solvers in a diverse world.

AUDIENCE AND PURPOSE

The focus of this text is on creative literacy instruction through active participation of teachers, parents, and children. The purpose is to provide a comprehensive view of literacy development and instruction. including assessment, phonemic awareness and emergent literacy, phonics, vocabulary, reading, writing, and arts integration in diverse classrooms, for children from birth through age 9. Each child has a mental or cognitive perspective and a socioemotional view, and learns literacy through active engagement. We present this holistic approach to literacy to explain why and how reading/language arts should be taught from the perspective of the whole child—mind, heart, and body, and with an emphasis on creativity in a nurturing learning environment. A recurring theme throughout the text is the importance of a child's sense of self, self-efficacy, self-motivation, and self-expression.

Strategies and approaches for teaching literacy through children's literature that incorporate the six language arts (reading, writing, speaking, listening, viewing, and visually representing), are especially relevant for children in diverse classrooms. This text includes many interactive features (for example, *Apply and Reflect* and *Consider This*) to reinforce concepts as a review for preservice teachers. Our goal is to create dynamic teachers who know the principles of effective literacy instruction, have a repertoire of creative strategies and activities, understand the importance of getting to know each child individually, and teach by example, demonstrating a love of literacy every day.

STYLE AND APPROACH

The style of presentation and writing is interactive and conversational. This enables diverse readers to clearly and easily comprehend text. Practical teaching examples support theories presented in the text through features such as *Vignettes*, *Lesson Ideas*, and *Teacher Toolbox*. Exercises at the end of chapters provide opportunities for additional practice with important concepts related to standards and objectives. To address diverse learning styles, we include photographs, diagrams, charts, and tables along with *Diversity* features. We provide a broad theoretical foundation that is supported with practical teaching examples throughout the text to reinforce the understanding and application of new concepts.

ORGANIZATION

Young children learn from experiences through cognitive, socioemotional, and physical activities that promote engagement. Teachers need to provide an encouraging learning environment where children can explore their imagination and creativity. This text emphasizes active engagement (physical), providing strategies for cognitive (critical thinking/understanding) and emotional sharing (socioemotional).

This book includes 10 chapters that feature topics in the literacy curriculum, based on national standards in literacy (*Common Core State Standards in English Language Arts*, 2010) and the arts (*National Core Arts Standards for Dance*,

Music, Theater and Visual Arts, 2014). We also incorporated the NAEYC standards (*National Association for the Education of Young Children for Initial & Advanced Early Childhood Professional Preparation Programs*, 2010, and *Early Childhood Program Accreditation Standards*, 2009). The many features help readers to study throughout the textbook and meet the guidelines provided in the Institute of Education Sciences Practice Guide, *Organizing Instruction and Study to Improve Student Learning* (Pashler et al., 2007). Chapter 1 consists of theoretical foundations in literacy, psychology, and the arts. Chapters 2 through 8 focus on literacy instruction, and Chapter 10 describes arts integration in the literacy curriculum. Each chapter begins with a list of six objectives related to the area of emphasis and an introduction of important concepts. Each chapter ends with a table of literacy strategies and practices, arranged according to specific age groups: 0 to 3, 3 to 6, and 6 to 9. Recommendations are listed in the following categories: cognitive, socioemotional, physical, children's books, and family involvement. This text reflects our integrated perspectives on early literacy, and is organized to closely follow current syllabi used for teaching early literacy in many colleges and universities. The Appendix contains five integrated lesson plans for literacy instruction that preservice teachers can use as seed ideas or inspiration for future lessons.

UNIQUE CHAPTER FEATURES

This text integrates literacy, psychology, and the arts for the purpose of preparing preservice educators to effectively teach children (birth through age 9) using developmentally appropriate practices (DAP). The text builds a flexible foundation of curriculum design that can easily be adapted for select groups of children. Sample activities by age groups (0 to 3, 3 to 6, and 6 to 9) facilitate this process. A chapter introduction describes the main objectives and guides readers. A strong thread of children's literature is integrated throughout the text. Practical tools, lesson ideas, vignettes, and learning strategies are discussed in each chapter such as:

- A beginning *Quote* inspires readers to anticipate the chapter content;
- The *Standards* and *Learning Objectives* serve as guides to chapter content;
- The *Introduction* includes an overview of main ideas and serves as an anticipation guide to chapter content;
- A *Vignette* (linked to Standards) with adaptations for children 0 to 3, 3 to 6, and 6 to 9, and a *Classroom Connection*;
- *Lesson Ideas* feature brief literacy lessons with technology, DAP, executive function, and classroom links;
- *Brain Briefs* are snapshots of recent research linked to brain development;

- *Diverse Learners* feature boxes have strategies for teaching children with different learning styles and abilities;
- *Consider This* feature boxes are short prompts to spark discussion of each section that matches a learning objective;
- *Apply and Reflect* feature boxes are activities for preservice teachers to complete and apply what was read and learned;
- *Literacy Assessment* feature boxes are sample assessments that measure skills related to the chapter topic;
- *Professional Resource Downloads* offer customizable content for immediate use;
- *Literacy Strategies and Practices* tables are divided into three age groups: birth to 3, 3 to 6, and 6 to 9;
- The *Summary* includes a synopsis of the main topics in the chapter related to the core objectives;
- *Chapter Exercises* align with the Learning Objectives and provide extension activities that can be completed individually, with a peer, or in a small group;
- *Teacher Toolbox* describes a practical lesson idea for reading or writing with a children's literature link and related anchor chart; and
- *Key Terms* are included in a running glossary in each chapter, listed at the end of each chapter, and defined in the *Glossary* at the back of the book.
- *MindTap for Education* is a first-of-its-kind digital solution with an integrated eportfolio that prepares teachers by providing them with the knowledge, skills, and competencies they must demonstrate to earn an education degree and state licensure, and to begin a successful career. Through activities based on real-life teaching situations, MindTap elevates students' thinking by giving them experiences in applying concepts, practicing skills, and evaluating decisions, guiding them to become reflective educators.

We anticipate that preservice teachers will use the ideas presented in our text as a springboard for developing their own unique styles and methods of literacy instruction through application and critical thinking. Reflective practices are key components in preservice teacher preparation and certification. We ask readers to analyze strengths and areas of improvement for the *Lesson Ideas* feature box, by responding to the following questions:

- What is successful?
- What would you change to improve the lesson?
- What did you learn about teaching literacy?

Opportunities for reflection (*Think about It* prompts) are included in the following features: *Brain Briefs*, *Diverse Learners*, and *Literacy Assessment*. In addition, *Consider This* and *Apply and Reflect* features stimulate readers to expand their thinking and make personal connections "outside the box." *Creative Literacy in Action* emphasizes reflection, active engagement, and the visual and performing arts. Preservice teachers learn how to support children in their journeys to becoming lifelong readers and writers as global citizens in a diverse world.

SUPPLEMENTS

MindTap™: The Personal Learning Experience

MindTap for Towell, Powell, Brown, *Creative Literacy in Action*, represents a new approach to teaching and learning. A highly personalized, fully customizable learning platform with an integrated eportfolio, MindTap helps students to elevate thinking by guiding them to:

- Know, remember, and understand concepts critical to becoming a great teacher;
- Apply concepts, create curriculum and tools, and demonstrate performance and competency in key areas in the course, including national and state education standards;
- Prepare artifacts for the portfolio and eventual state licensure, to launch a successful teaching career; and
- Develop the habits to become a reflective practitioner.

As students move through each chapter's Learning Path, they engage in a scaffolded learning experience, designed to move them up Bloom's taxonomy, from lower- to higher-order thinking skills. The Learning Path enables preservice students to develop these skills and gain confidence by:

- Engaging them with chapter topics and activating their prior knowledge by watching and answering questions about authentic videos of teachers teaching and children learning in real classrooms;
- Checking their comprehension and understanding through *Did You Get It?* assessments, with varied question types that are autograded for instant feedback;
- Applying concepts through mini-case scenarios— students analyze typical teaching and learning situations, and then create a reasoned response to the issue(s) presented in the scenario; and
- Reflecting about and justifying the choices they made within the teaching scenario problem.

MindTap helps instructors facilitate better outcomes by evaluating how future teachers plan and teach lessons in ways that make content clear and help diverse students learn, assessing the effectiveness of their teaching practice, and adjusting teaching as needed. MindTap enables instructors to facilitate better outcomes by:

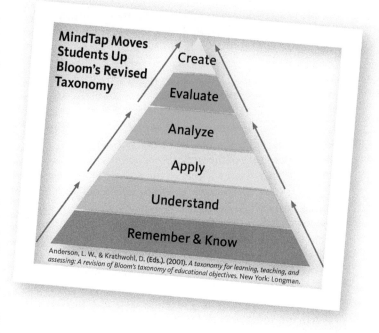

Anderson, L. W., & Krathwohl, D. (Eds.). (2001). *A taxonomy for learning, teaching, and assessing: A revision of Bloom's taxonomy of educational objectives.* New York: Longman.

- Making grades visible in real time through the Student Progress App so students and instructors always have access to current standings in the class.
- Using the Outcome Library to embed national education standards and align them to student learning activities, and also allowing instructors to add their state's standards or any other desired outcome.
- Allowing instructors to generate reports on students' performance with the click of a mouse against any standards or outcomes that are in their MindTap course.
- Giving instructors the ability to assess students on state standards or other local outcomes by editing existing or creating their own MindTap activities, and then by aligning those activities to any state or other outcomes that the instructor has added to the MindTap Outcome Library.

MindTap for Towell, Powell, Brown, *Creative Literacy in Action*, helps instructors easily set their course since it integrates into the existing Learning Management System and saves instructors time by allowing them to fully customize any aspect of the learning path. Instructors can change the order of the student learning activities, hide activities they don't want for the course, and—most importantly—create custom assessments and add any standards, outcomes, or content they do want (e.g., YouTube videos, Google docs). Learn more at www.cengage.com/mindtap.

Online Instructor's Manual with Test Bank

An online Instructor's Manual accompanies this book. It contains information to assist instructors in designing courses, including sample syllabi, discussion questions, teaching and learning activities, field experiences, learning objectives, and additional online resources. For assessment support, the updated test bank includes true/false, multiple-choice, matching, short-answer, and essay questions for each chapter.

PowerPoint Lecture Slides

These vibrant Microsoft PowerPoint lecture slides for each chapter assist you with your lecture by providing concept coverage using images, figures, and tables directly from the textbook.

Cognero

Cengage Learning Testing Powered by Cognero is a flexible online system that allows you to author, edit, and manage test-bank content from multiple Cengage Learning solutions; create multiple test versions in an instant; and deliver tests from your LMS, your classroom, or wherever you want.

ACKNOWLEDGMENTS

We thank our family and friends for their support throughout this endeavor. We thank everyone at Cengage Learning whose assistance made publishing this book possible. We especially thank Kate Scheinman, our incredible editor and Jill Traut, our senior project manager whose vision guided us throughout the process. The wonderful images come from a variety of schools, centers, and homes through the creativity of photographers at Cengage Learning, the authors, and Josh Weinberger (colleague of Katherine Powell). Many family members contributed children's drawings and writing samples, including Austin Brown, Hampton Newman, Timothy Weinberger, and Penelope Weinberger. We appreciate the parents' permissions to use the images and artwork of their children in our book.

We would like to thank the many reviewers of this first edition text:

Cecile Arquette, Bradley University
Kerry Belknap Morris, River Valley Community College
Johnny Castro, Brookhaven College
Jackie Covault, Purdue University North Central
Christine Draper, Georgia Southern University
Sherry Fairfield-Tagle, Muskegon Community College
Kristen Flesher, Ivy Tech Community College
Margaret Freedson, Montclair State University
Randa Gamal, Central New Mexico Community College
Rosemary Geiken, East Tennessee State University
April Grace, Madisonville Community College
Caroline Hagen, University of Jamestown
Lori Hamilton, East Tennessee State University
Virginia Harmelink, Pima Community College
Ruth Hasseler, University at Buffalo
Beverly J. Hearn, University of Tennessee–Martin
Keith Higa, University of Central Oklahoma

Kelly Hoover, Regis University
Holly Hullinger-Sirken, Ball State University
Jennifer Kaywork, Dominican College
Jane Kelley, Washington State University
Ritchie Kelley, Summit University of Pennsylvania
So Jung Kim, University of Texas at El Paso
Ellen Koitz, Hood College
Roxane Moore, California State University, Fullerton
Michelle Morris, Wor-Wic Community College
Susan Morrison, Southeastern Oklahoma State University
Carol J. Nelson, Lewis-Clark State College
Lucia Obregon, Miami Dade College
Jennifer Oswald, Northwestern Oklahoma State University
Nancy Peterson, Utah Valley University
Julia Postler, Nazareth College–Rochester
Audrey Quinlan, Seton Hill University
Jennifer Quong, Grayson County College
Robyn Ridgley, Middle Tennessee State University
Lindsey Russo, SUNY New Paltz
Kathryn Sharp, East Tennessee State University
LaTonya Slater, Mississippi State University
Nancy Stackhouse, Northern Arizona University and Paradise Valley Community College
Kristine Still, Cleveland State University
Pamela Sullivan, James Madison University
Holly Tower, Lewis-Clark State College
Catherine Twyman, Daytona State College
Susan Vanness, Manchester Community College
Doris Walker-Dalhouse, Marquette University
Barbara Ward, Washington State University
Angela Williams, Alabama A&M University
Linda Williams, Purdue University North Central
Cristal Dawn Wilson, Central New Mexico Community College
Clover Wright, California University of Pennsylvania
Melanie Yeschenko, Community College of Allegheny County

Colleagues and students in the Teaching and Learning Department at Florida Atlantic University supported us in this writing endeavor. It takes a team to produce a text, and as authors, we collaborated in all tasks: brainstorming ideas, researching concepts, drafting sentences, writing chapters, revising, and editing text to reach final publication. This text would not have been possible without the support of our families and friends during the writing process.

ABOUT THE AUTHORS

DR. JANET L. TOWELL

Dr. Janet L. Towell, professor of reading/language arts and children's literature for the Department of Teaching and Learning in Florida Atlantic University (FAU)'s College of Education (COE), joined the university in 2004. She teaches undergraduate and graduate courses in reading/language arts and children's literature. Dr. Towell's doctorate in *Curriculum & Instruction: Reading* is from the University of Maryland, College Park. She is professor emerita from California State University, Stanislaus, in Turlock, California, where she taught reading education courses for 14 years. Prior to teaching at the university level, Dr. Towell worked as a preschool teacher, elementary teacher, and reading specialist in North Carolina. One of Dr. Towell's greatest honors was receiving the Constance McCullough Award from the International Reading Association for her literacy work with teachers in Jamaica. While teaching as a professor at CSU, Stanislaus, she was principle investigator of the ABC Project, which distributed books to over 1,000 children from birth to age 5 as part of Dolly Parton's Imagination Library. As an executive member of the California Reading Association, the author served as editor of *The California Reader* for three years.

Hooked on Books: Language Arts and Literature in Elementary Classrooms, PreK–Gr. 8, was Dr. Towell's first textbook (2010) and is currently in its second edition with Kendall Hunt (2013). The author has published articles in professional journals and is the principal investigator of a research project called "Reading Aloud to Babies: The Impact on Language Development." In her spare time, Dr. Towell enjoys visiting her family in North Carolina, walking on the beach, playing with her grandchildren, and watching Marlins' baseball games.

DR. KATHERINE C. POWELL

Dr. Katherine C. Powell has dedicated her life to research on the development of self, creativity, and reaching one's highest potential. She received her educational doctorate (EdD) in human development from the University of Massachusetts at Amherst; her MA in psychology from Boston College; and her BA in biochemistry from Syracuse University. Dr. Powell has taught English, literature (American/British), and Spanish in private schools. She is an adjunct professor for Florida Atlantic University and conducts workshops on creative writing. She has written several books and articles on early childhood relationships, self-confidence, secondary language acquisition, constructivism learning methods, and nonverbal communication.

Dr. Powell has presented several published papers to international and national audiences, such as on early gender issues to Oxford University in England, and on identity conflicts for Athens Institute for Education and Research in Greece. Dr. Powell has published two texts: *Educational Psychology of the Self: An Inter-Active Workbook* (Kendall Hunt, 2005); and *Educational Psychology of the Self and*

Learning (Pearson, 2012). She has also written a series of books on the psychology of the self, including achieving self-confidence and high self-esteem, as well as social connections. She has completed certificates in health education and meditation to teach others how to live in a less stressful environment. Dr. Powell is currently writing a book on finding and being your happy self. She believes that each person has gifts and talents that can be discovered through social interaction, self-reflection, gaining confidence, trusting in self, and perseverance for truth and honesty. Dr. Powell enjoys life and teaches with humor. Her research projects, quest for truth, and improving the state of human beings has encouraged her to travel extensively. Her enthusiasm is evident in her written work.

DR. SUSANNAH L. BROWN

Dr. Susannah L. Brown, an associate professor of art education in the Department of Teaching and Learning in Florida Atlantic University (FAU)'s College of Education (COE), joined the university in 2004. She has been inspiring creativity throughout her teaching career beginning in 1989 after earning her bachelor's in fine arts degree from FAU with art K–12 teaching certification. For 11 years, she worked as an elementary art specialist before completing her master's and doctoral work at Florida State University and beginning her journey at the university level. She recently completed her master's in reading education degree at FAU. Prior to working at FAU, Dr. Brown held a similar position at the University of North Carolina at Charlotte in the Department of Art, College of Arts and Sciences. Dr. Brown has published *Teaching Art Integration in the Schools* (2013) with Cengage Learning, and has used this textbook in her art education courses. She has published several book chapters in edited textbooks and numerous articles in scholarly reviewed journals.

Her dedication to her students has resulted in several awards, including FAU Excellence and Innovation in Undergraduate Teaching, Florida Higher Education Art Educator of the Year, and FAU Owl Award for Organization Advisor of the Year. She actively served as co-counselor for five years for the Rho Omega Chapter of Kappa Delta Pi (KDP), an International Education Honor Society, and continued her leadership role in KDP as elected vice president (2014–16). She has also been an active member and served on the board of directors of the Florida Art Education Association. As a watercolor artist who loves to also sculpt with clay, she displays her artwork in numerous juried exhibitions. Her areas of research include arts integration, environmental art education, and literacy development. Sharing her passion for the arts drives her teaching and personal work.

LWA/Dann Tardif/Blend Images/Getty Images

STANDARDS ADDRESSED IN THIS CHAPTER

The standards from the following organizations will be used throughout the chapter: Common Core State Standards for English Language Arts, the National Association for the Education of Young Children (NAEYC), and National Core Arts Standards. These standards are discussed further in the chapter as appropriate.

Common Core State Standards for English Language Arts

Anchor Standards for Reading
Reading Standards for Literature/Informational Text K–5
- Key Ideas and Details
Reading Standards: Foundational Skills (K–5)
- Print Concepts
- Phonological Awareness

Anchor Standards for Writing
- Range of Writing

Anchor Standards for Speaking and Listening
- Comprehension and Collaboration

Anchor Standards for Language
- Knowledge of Language

2010 NAEYC Standards for Initial and Advanced Early Childhood Professional Preparation Programs
- *Standard 1.* Promoting Child Development and Learning

NAEYC Early Childhood Program Standards and Accreditation Criteria
- *Standard 1:* Relationships

National Core Arts Standards (Dance, Media Arts, Music, Theater, Visual Arts)
Creating
- *Anchor Standard 1:* Generate and conceptualize artistic ideas and work.
- *Anchor Standard 2:* Organize and develop artistic ideas and work.
- *Anchor Standard 3:* Refine and complete artistic work.

Theoretical Foundations in Literacy, Psychology, and the Arts

1

> *Any book that helps a child to form a habit of reading, to make reading one of his deep and continuous needs, is good for him.* — Maya Angelou

From birth to age 9, emotions, social interaction, and creativity play key roles in children's literacy development. The integration of literacy, psychology, and the arts enhances children's learning processes, which involve active engagement of children with their environment. Understanding the language acquisition process for young children includes understanding how literacy theory relates to the lives of children, parents, teachers, and others in the community. By connecting literacy with educational psychology and the arts, our approach to literacy is influenced by language, culture, and real-world experiences.

The purpose of this text is to explain why and how language arts can be integrated with visual arts and psychology. We present literacy development and instruction through a holistic perspective, with an emphasis on creativity and self-development, including self-motivation and self-expression. Our holistic model of literacy (HML) includes cognitive, socioemotional, and physical aspects of self. A variety of theorists inspired the development of the HML, including Maria Montessori (1914) and Jean Piaget (1953). Montessori emphasized independence, play, and respect for a child's natural, psychological, physical, and social development. Jean Piaget is the founder of constructivism, focusing on children's learning through discovery. Piaget (1953) believed that children learn best from individual and social activities such as playing games. Our theory of integrating literacy, psychology, and the arts is relevant for children in diverse classrooms because different learning styles require multiple ways of knowing. In a holistic literacy model, the needs of the whole child are important, addressing their cognitive, socioemotional, and physical development. It is imperative in today's classroom for children to interact and creatively engage in the language and learning process.

We are looking at literacy from a broad perspective acknowledging that community, parents, teachers, and children communicate and collaborate to help children achieve their literacy goals. Creative thinking, higher-order thinking, and problem-solving skills are emphasized from a global perspective of literacy. Our primary goal is to help children become more effective readers and writers. This goal involves teaching parents and educators how to become active participants in the collaborative learning process. Young children need connection, love, respect, and understanding to be open to learning. Literacy activities are integrated with creative learning experiences to promote our holistic model of literacy.

LEARNING OBJECTIVES:

After you have read this chapter, you should be able to:

- 1-1 Describe integration of literacy, psychology, and the arts.
- 1-2 Explain literacy theories for teaching young children.
- 1-3 Analyze psychological theories related to early childhood.
- 1-4 Compare theories of the arts for a literacy foundation.
- 1-5 Summarize interrelated theories of literacy, psychology, and the arts.
- 1-6 Apply strategies and practices for the holistic model of literacy.

STANDARDS CONNECTION TO THE VIGNETTE

NAEYC Early Childhood Program Accreditation Standards

Standard 1: Relationships

1.B.08 Teaching staff support children's competent and self-reliant exploration and use of classroom materials.

Common Core State Standards for English Language Arts

Key Ideas and Details

Kindergarten

1. With prompting and support, ask and answer questions about key details in a text.

The enjoyment of reading and writing encourages children to identify new words and comprehend text. This vignette paints a picture of how the arts inspire a passion for reading.

A group of young children are sitting on stuffed pillows in a corner of a classroom with a basket of books. After listening to the teacher read the book, *Pearl Paints* (Thomas, 1994), Joey walks over to the art section of the classroom where an easel with paper, brushes, and tempera paints invites him to create. Joey begins to paint images of cats and dogs using a variety of colors (see Photo 1.1). Joey and Maria (another child who is also painting) discuss the colors, the images of cats and dogs in his painting, and the story, *Pearl Paints*. The teacher, Mrs. Gonzales, comes over and asks Joey to tell her about the story. After discussing the story's main character and events, she brings Joey a new book with colorful illustrations (text-to-text connection), *When Pigasso Met Mootisse* (Laden, 1998). Joey finishes cleaning up his painting supplies, takes the book from Mrs. Gonzales, and quickly walks to the reading area.

We hope that children never run out of paint as the creative self will always find ways to ensure a steady supply of materials and resources supported by teachers, family, and friends.

Developmentally appropriate practice (DAP) is featured in the vignette and can be adapted for younger children (birth to age 5) and older children to age 9. Suggested adaptations include:

- Ages 0 to 3: Infants and toddlers can explore texture through various materials relating to a story that is read aloud. For example, infants and toddlers can touch objects that correspond with letters of the alphabet such as an apple, a stuffed teddy bear, and a carrot. Toddlers can paint using a brush on paper positioned on a child-sized easel or use finger paint on paper.
- Ages 3 to 6: Three- and four-year-olds love to use safe art materials such as washable paint, markers, and crayons. Children can share photographs of their pets or favorite animals and create illustrations for a class book.
- Ages 6 to 9: Children can read informational text about favorite animals and create a graphic organizer that compares different animals and their habitats. Children can create a collage of images of different animals cut from magazines and label characteristics.

holistic model of literacy (HML)
Becoming literate includes the cognitive, socioemotional, and physical aspects of self.

developmentally appropriate practices (DAP) Involves an understanding of child development, the specific strengths and needs of a child, and the cultural context in which the child lives.

language development The process through which a child learns expressive and receptive language.

Classroom Connection

How can you integrate the arts into your literacy curriculum to inspire a passion for reading?

1-1 Integration of Literacy, Psychology, and the Arts

When working with young children, it is important to understand a variety of foundational theories that connect to language development. As children grow in the early years, their brains adjust quickly to their surroundings, picking up language as it is spoken. Children build vocabulary continually through play and exploration (see Photo 1.2).

Learning to read includes the cognitive, socioemotional, and physical aspects of the child (HML). Literacy is about connecting and communicating thoughts and feelings and expressing creativity.

Connecting literacy, psychology, and the arts provides a unique view of child development. Literacy development occurs through active engagement. Figure 1.1 illustrates this integrated and holistic approach by including selected theorists in literacy, psychology, and the arts. In this figure, we identify individual theorists for each discipline, as well as some theorists often associated with child development. Our goal is to provide a solid foundation for literacy instruction, which involves the development of the whole

BRAIN INTERACTION FOR LITERACY

Robert Sternberg (1990) believed that intelligence involves the creative, analytic, and practical parts of the brain. Using new technological advances, researchers recognize that both hemispheres of the brain interact during literacy development (Woolfolk, 2011). The left and right hemispheres connect with the emotional side of the brain (amygdala) to learn language. Speech resides in the left side of the brain, and visual language is stimulated by the right side of the brain. A bridge interacts between the two hemispheres when learning to read and write. The emotional part of the brain (limbic) also participates in language development. Interaction of all parts of the brain is simultaneous and spontaneous (Chopra & Tanzi, 2013).

Think about It

What activities can children participate in that will support language development, including speech and visual representation? For example, children can draw a picture of the main character in a story. While each child describes his or her drawing, the teacher can write (verbatim) what the child explains. Then the teacher reads the dictated sentence(s) to the child, pointing to the words as the child follows along.

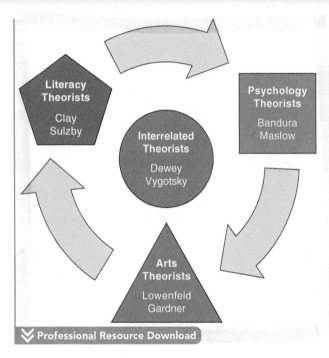

Figure 1.1
Interrelated Theories in Literacy, Psychology, and the Arts

executive function A critical cognitive skill that includes self-regulation, which focuses attention, builds working memory, and controls socioemotional behaviors through creative play, games, and active engagement (Kray & Ferdinand, 2013).

child. Figure 1.1 provides the organizational structure for the theorists, which support our holistic model of literacy.

Our text introduces the holistic model of literacy (HML), which utilizes concepts from the featured theorists. Figure 1.2 provides a metaphor for how children are involved in literacy. Literacy for young children involves developing a balanced self. The three parts of self are:

1. Cognitive self (mind)—in yellow;
2. Socioemotional self (heart)—in red; and
3. Physical self (legs and arms)—in blue.

Cognition assists children in focusing and concentrating on learning tasks. The socioemotional self allows children to positively interact and encourage others. Children use all five senses to enhance understanding and comprehension through the physical self. A child's whole self interacts with his or her environment along the path to literacy. Our HML supports the concept of executive function, a critical cognitive skill that includes independence and self-regulation in the early literacy classroom. Children learn how to control socioemotional behaviors while engaged in creative play (Kray & Ferdinand, 2013). We will be revisiting this figure multiple times and adding to it in subsequent chapters.

 CONSIDER THIS...

Consider how you can implement the holistic model of literacy in your classroom. For example, teachers can connect physical movement activities and dramatic play while reading common nursery rhymes aloud to a group of children.

JIGSAW PUZZLE ACTIVITY FOR PRESERVICE TEACHERS TO DO WITH CHILDREN

Purpose: To illustrate a holistic model of literacy (parts to whole)

Procedure: Read *Seven Blind Mice* by Ed Young (2002) to a group of children (age group 3 to 6). This story is a variation of the fable about blind mice trying to identify an elephant. Discuss the moral of the story in a way that the children can understand and contribute to the discussion. Assign each child to work with a partner, and ask the children to select a picture (perhaps from an old calendar) to eventually cut apart into 10 jigsaw pieces. Before the cutting begins, draw shapes on the back of the picture to trace out the jigsaw pieces. Help the children do the cutting, if age appropriate. Then once the picture has been cut into 10 pieces, ask each group to mix up their own pieces and to put them back together to complete the puzzle—to better understand the concept of parts to whole. After the pictures have been reassembled, glue the finished puzzle onto a piece of construction paper.

Teaching Analysis: Reflective practices are a necessary part of the *literacy assessment cycle* and are key components in preservice preparation and certification such as edTPA, an assessment for candidates in teacher education programs. Analyze the strengths and areas of improvement in this lesson idea. Answer the following:

- What is successful?
- What would you change to improve the lesson?
- What did you learn about teaching literacy?

Links: Making connections to technology and developmentally appropriate practices (DAP) supports lesson planning and literacy instruction. Adaptations of this lesson idea are provided through the following:

- **Technology Link:** Part of the literacy process is sharing and publishing. Take a photo of the finished product and post it on Instagram.
- **DAP Link:** Using manipulatives (puzzle pieces) when learning a new concept is important for young children.
- **Executive Function Link:** Creative play and active engagement during an interactive read-aloud develop children's self-regulation skills in social settings as reflected in the holistic model of literacy (cognitive, socioemotional, and physical).
- **Classroom Link:** For infants and toddlers (0 to 3), a toy elephant can be used while reading the story to identify animal parts.
- **Classroom Link:** Children (3 to 6) can draw a picture of an elephant and label the different parts (trunk, tail, ears). A nonfiction book about elephants can be read aloud to learn more about this animal.
- **Classroom Link:** The puzzle activity can be adapted for ages 6 to 9 for any learning concept. For example, when studying habitats in science, students can select magazine pictures of different landscapes and identify the type of habitat when assembling the puzzle. Student groups could trade puzzles and identify or list the details of each habitat on the different puzzle pieces to predict the type before assembling the whole puzzle.

1-2 Literacy Theories for Teaching Young Children

In this section we want to introduce you to two important theorists in the field of literacy, whose approaches to teaching literacy are foundational to all active learning approaches—Marie Clay and Elizabeth Sulzby:

- Marie Clay (1979) changed what we know and believe about emergent literacy and the reading process.
- Elizabeth Sulzby (1985) taught us how children develop their literacy skills in sequential stages as they learn to read and write.

1-2a Marie Clay and the Reading Process

Marie Clay is well known for her research on emergent literacy in New Zealand schools (Clay, 2006). Clay first coined this term in 1966. Emergent literacy means that children learn to read and write gradually (see Photo 1.3). Literacy begins at birth and is ongoing. Emergent literacy is a child-centered approach with an

Figure 1.2
The Holistic Model of Literacy (HML)

Photo 1.3 *Young boy practicing writing*

emphasis on social learning and problem solving. Exploration and play through dance, music, drama, and the visual arts is encouraged. Children's approximations (scribble writing and pretend reading) are important stages in their literacy development. Clay researched the reading process and the language cueing systems: semantic, syntactic, graphophonic, and pragmatic. These terms will be discussed further throughout the text. She developed *The Observation Survey* (1993) for beginning readers (kindergarten), which includes the following assessments: letter identification, sentence dictation, sight words, concepts about print, and running records. Clay's *Reading Recovery* early intervention program for first grade readers has been widely adopted in the United States.

emergent literacy Children learn to read and write gradually, as they progress in their literacy development (Clay, 1966).

approximations Scribble writing and pretend reading, early stages in literacy development.

language cueing systems Systems of language that are used during the reading process: semantic, syntactic, graphophonic, and pragmatic.

concepts about print An awareness of how print works (Clay, 2006).

running records An oral reading assessment that is used to determine if a child is reading on his or her correct instructional reading level, used in Marie Clay's *Observation Survey of Early Literacy Achievement* (1993).

Reading Recovery An intensive early intervention program for first graders that was designed by Marie Clay (2006).

1-2b Elizabeth Sulzby and Emergent Literacy Development

Elizabeth Sulzby (1985) has widely researched stages of reading and writing development in emergent literacy. She studied children between the ages of 2 and 6 "pretend reading" favorite storybooks (Morrow, 2009). It was obvious that these stories had been read to them multiple times because they knew the stories so well. The children's speech during emergent reading was clearly different in structure and intonation from their speech in everyday conversations. Sulzby distinguishes between picture prompts and text prompts. In other words, children pretend to read first with pictures and then with written words.

In the beginning, children pretend to read using single words and phrases. Later, children are able to tell a complete story, with a beginning, middle, and end (see Figure 1.3).

Sulzby used children's attempts at storybook reading to determine characteristics of early reading behavior. She documented how "pretend reading" is an important step in the journey to learning how to read.

The work of Marie Clay and Elizabeth Sulzby provides a solid foundation for early literacy instruction. Engaged learning focuses on developing the creative problem-solving abilities of young children in order to be independent and self-sufficient.

EMOTIONS, MEMORY, AND THE BRAIN

All parts of the brain, especially the limbic system and short-term memory, are interactively involved in literacy development (Woolfolk, 2011). Educators must understand the important role that the emotional brain (limbic system and associated brain functions in the temporal region/right lobe) plays in the literacy development of young children. Recognition and memory rely on the limbic system through emotional experiences (Chopra & Tanzi, 2013). Learning to read and write involves complex brain synapses and connections. Understanding these processes in detail helps us realize that the visual, verbal, and emotional parts of brain are intertwined in literacy development.

Think about It

How can you utilize emotional memories to enhance children's connection to the text they are reading? Discuss how children can write, speak, and visually represent their emotional state using recalled experiences (memories). For example, when discussing memories, you could read *Wilfrid Gordon McDonald Partridge* by Mem Fox (1989).

Stage 1: Child looks at pictures but is not able to tell stories.

Stage 2: Child looks at pictures and tells oral stories but the stories may not make sense.

Stage 3: Child looks at pictures and alternates between telling and "reading" oral stories.

Stage 4: Child looks at pictures and words to "read" the stories, sometimes quoting from the text.

Stage 5: Child looks primarily at words to read the stories in a somewhat traditional manner. Pictures may be used occasionally to tell the stories.

Figure 1.3
Sulzby's Stages of Emergent Reading

✔ CONSIDER THIS...

Consider how your teaching in a future classroom can reflect the concepts you have learned in this section. For example, how can you make your language arts lessons multisensory and interactive? Why is it important for children to become independent readers and writers?

1-3 Psychological Theories Related to Early Childhood

Next we want to introduce you to two important theorists in the field of psychology—Albert Bandura and Abraham Maslow:

- Albert Bandura (1986) guided educators to understand the critical role of observation, self-motivation, and self-regulation in education.
- Abraham Maslow (1954) created a hierarchy of needs leading to self-actualization.

Apply & Reflect

Ask a child (age range of 4 to 6) to draw a picture. Discuss the artwork with the child. Have the child write a sentence about his or her artwork. Consider the child's writing sample and how it relates to Sulzby's (1985) writing stages. Share your ideas with a colleague and discuss individual learning differences.

1-3a Albert Bandura and Learning through Observation

Albert Bandura (1986) was a behaviorist theorist who focused not only on the influences of a nurturing environment on behavior and learning but also on how the personality affects psychological growth and motivation. Bandura theorized that motivation is connected to self-regulation. Self-motivation is the best type of motivation because it is internal or intrinsic and not dependent on external influences. Bandura believed children have an innate desire to learn (see Photo 1.4).

The observational learning theory explains that the behavior to be imitated and the learning of that behavior do not have to occur at the same time. Bandura's observational theory describes four steps necessary for modeling behavior:

1. Attention—the individual notices something in the environment, either through the senses or perception, and has to pay attention to learn.
2. Retention—the individual remembers what was noticed and is able to recall or memorize well enough to use it again.
3. Motor reproduction—the individual produces an action or uses motor skills that are a copy of what has been witnessed in order to reproduce what was learned.
4. Motivation—the environment delivers a consequence that makes the individual want to model the behavior, driven by self-reinforcing terms such as "well done" (see Photo 1.5).

Photo 1.4 *Stimulating learning environment*
Josh Weinberger

Photo 1.5 *Young children discover the outdoor garden*

observational learning theory This theory (Bandura, 1986) states that behavior is imitated and learning occurs through the observation of role models.

Bandura (1986) believed that externally controlled punishment does not work well, and he claimed that preparing students for controlling their own behavior—rather than external motivation—is more effective.

1-3b Abraham Maslow and Self-Actualization

Abraham Maslow (1954) believed that educators should view children as whole entities and not neglect their personal growth. He developed a hierarchy of levels or tiers reflecting the needs of a total person, which are: (1) Physiological needs or survival (including shelter, food, and water); (2) safety needs or a safe environment (including physical or emotional safety); (3) belonging and love needs or approval (acceptance from friends and family); (4) self-esteem needs or self-respect (including approval and high regard of self); and (5) self-actualization needs or reaching one's potential (including aesthetic and intellectual achievement) (Maslow, 1954). Our literacy adaptation of Maslow's hierarchy of needs is modified into three sections for young children (see Figure 1.4).

Literacy is dependent on the ability to comprehend information as received and the ability to retrieve it when writing, reading, or speaking. Young children need to develop good habits and routines when learning to read and comprehend text. For example, children may dedicate a specific time each day to read and write (see Photo 1.6).

Figure 1.4
Literacy Adaptation of Maslow's Hierarchy of Needs

Self-Realization
Potential of Creative Self

Connecting Needs and Relationships
Collaborative Storytelling
Experiencing Reading/Writing

Comfort Needs (food, shelter, water)
Read-alouds, Lap Reading, Listening

Photo 1.6 *Immersed in reading*

self-actualization Reading one's potential, including aesthetic and intellectual achievement (Maslow, 1954).

The psychological theories discussed in this section provide a foundation to support literacy development.

✔ CONSIDER THIS...

In your future classroom, consider how you will motivate your students to reach their full potential. Knowing your students well—their interests, academic strengths and needs, learning styles, and cultural/linguistic backgrounds—is necessary to help them achieve their learning goals. How can you use reading interest and attitude surveys to better know your students? One example is the *Elementary Reading Attitude Survey* (McKenna & Kear, 1990).

1-4 Theories of the Arts for a Literacy Foundation

Finally, we want to introduce you to two key theorists/approaches in the field of the arts—Viktor Lowenfeld and Howard Gardner:

- Viktor Lowenfeld (1968) delineated the stages of artistic development and theories about creativity.
- Howard Gardner (1983) connects multiple ways of learning and demonstrating knowledge (arts integrated learning).

1-4a Viktor Lowenfeld and Creative Intelligence

Viktor Lowenfeld, an Austrian art educator, immigrated to the United States, where he aligned with the child-centered creativity movement in American schools. According to Lowenfeld (1968), creative intelligence is unique to each individual and is developed through imagination, application of knowledge, and adaptation. Self-development is the goal of the creative endeavor as children become one with the creative act through immersion and seamlessly bonds their self into the artistic creation. In other words, the self becomes an extension of the creative work (Lowenfeld, 1968).

Lowenfeld, through many years of observing children of all ages into adulthood creating artwork, developed a theory concerning the stages of artistic development. The first three age groups he described are appropriate for this textbook:

1. The *scribbling stage* (ages 2 to 4) begins once a child has the motor skills to hold a drawing instrument such as a crayon. Children make marks on paper as a precursor to writing. At age 2, children make random marks that they can verbally describe. Nearing the age of 4, children tend to draw circular shapes that represent people, which leads to the next artistic stage of development.

Photo 1.7 *Four-year-old girl drawing*

creative intelligence Developed through imagination, adaptation, and application of knowledge (Lowenfeld, 1968).

schemata The plural form of schema.

2. The *preschematic stage* (ages 4 to 7) begins as children conceptualize forms into their drawings. Drawings become representational and more realistic with images or icons (schemas) that are recognized by adults.
3. The *schematic stage* (ages 7 to 9) is the stage that adults consider the "golden age" of children's art. Children have developed detailed schemata that represent and clearly communicate the meaning of the artwork (see Photo 1.7).

Children develop in unique ways, and the teacher's role is to guide the unfolding of students' creative selves. This process-based approach celebrates the joy of discovery through creative learning (Lowenfeld & Brittain, 1987).

MULTIPLE INTELLIGENCES AND LITERACY

Children with varying abilities are able to learn words through multiple intelligences by coordinating their strengths and learning styles (that is, visual, verbal, musical, mathematical, and kinesthetic). When children in diverse classrooms read text (fiction/nonfiction), they can select key words and demonstrate comprehension through multiple intelligences, such as dramatizing meaning or illustrating concepts (Gardner, 1983, 1999b).

Think about It

Teachers can use children's literature to value the uniqueness, as well as cultural similarities and differences, of individual children. One possibility that relates to the arts is *Giraffes Can't Dance* by Giles Andreae (2001). How can children demonstrate their understanding of key vocabulary terms through visual, musical, and kinesthetic intelligences? For example, children can dramatize action-oriented vocabulary through music and dance.

1-4b Howard Gardner and Multiple Intelligences

Howard Gardner (1983, 1999a) is a prominent developmental psychologist. Gardner claimed that academic concepts should be taught using a variety of multiple intelligences. Gardner found that measuring children's cognitive ability in narrow dimensions, as was the case with IQ testing, was not reflective of the many talents and skills that children demonstrate (Gardner, 1983, 1999b). Gardner proposed a theory of multiple intelligences encompassing many aspects of the educational experience and that teachers need to use a variety of activities to stimulate early primary grade students' skills. His theory (1983) includes logical, verbal, visual, kinesthetic, musical, interpersonal, intrapersonal, and naturalistic skills. Gardner developed his eight multiple intelligences theory (1983) as a response to the narrow view that intelligence is only verbal, mathematical, or abstract thought.

Visually representing thoughts and ideas assists children in comprehension of text. The arts are a form of communication that young children often use to demonstrate their understandings. We believe that the approaches and theories described in this section contribute significantly to a child's literacy development.

✔ CONSIDER THIS...

Consider how you can integrate the visual and performing arts in your future classroom. Giving children the opportunity to express their learning in multiple ways (through dance, drama, music, or the visual arts) will enhance their ability to succeed in all subjects. How can you use picture books that feature songs to inspire musical dramatic play?

1-5 Interrelated Theories of Literacy, Psychology, and the Arts

Now that you are familiar with theories and approaches unique to literacy, psychology, and the arts, we want to introduce you to two interrelated theorists who represent a combined view of literacy development. John Dewey and Lev Vygotsky paved the way for an integrated approach that supports the holistic model of literacy, that children's

process-based approach The process of creating where children immerse themselves in the learning experience rather than the end result.

multiple intelligences A theory developed in 1983 by Dr. Howard Gardner that suggests there are eight different kinds of intelligence: linguistic, logical-mathematical, spatial, bodily-kinesthetic, musical, interpersonal, intrapersonal, and naturalist.

literacy development depends on the interconnection of the cognitive, socioemotional, and physical selves:

- John Dewey's (1938) theory supports active engagement, which involves the physical self (active learning).
- Lev Vygotsky (1978) encourages social interaction to support the emotional self (collaborative learning).

1-5a John Dewey and Progressive Education

In the early 20th century, John Dewey was considered a progressive educator because of his philosophy that children "learn by doing." Children acquire knowledge through real-world experiences. He was the grandfather of constructivism, preceding Piaget and Vygotsky. John Dewey's progressivism (1938) changed our educational system through experiential learning. Education became more child-centered through his work, and creative applications were enhanced through a variety of real-world experiences. Progressivism involves two essential elements: a respect for the diversity of the children (a child-centered approach that recognizes each child's abilities, interests, needs) and the development of critical, socially engaged intelligence (a social reconstruction approach involving collaboration for the common good). Children were allowed to make choices in their education, thus democracy and active learning were brought to the classroom. Teachers began to design classroom spaces to mimic situations in the community and to provide practice in problem solving. Children worked individually and in collaborative groups to solve real-world problems (Dewey, 1934, 1966).

Photo 1.8 Thinking and listening support cognitive growth.
Josh Weinberger

1-5b Lev Vygotsky and Social Interaction

Lev Vygotsky, a cultural-historical psychologist, theorized that knowledge was a collaborative process and that cognitive functioning had social origins. His theory incorporated social constructivism, which implies that knowledge can be mutually built and constructed by young children. Vygotsky's (1962) theory consists of six major aspects of learning:

1. Social interaction or collaborative learning;
2. Cultural or background influences;
3. Zone of proximal development (ZPD) where learning occurs;
4. Scaffolding or assisted learning;
5. Inner speech or talking to oneself to resolve ideas; and
6. Cognitive dialogue, or discussions between students or with teachers.

Vygotsky (1978) viewed language as an important process of cognitive growth (see Photo 1.8).

Language starts at birth with sounds and cries, and develops more extensively for children during the early years. Reading aloud to children develops their speaking and listening skills. When a caring adult models reading behavior, the physical aspect of the reading environment, such as lap reading and cuddling, allows children to associate reading with love and attention. This helps children to bond and create a positive psychological response to reading (Vygotsky, 1978). When children are engaged, learning

progressivism John Dewey's philosophy of education (1916) that consists of two essential elements: a respect for the diversity of children and the development of critical, socially engaged intelligence.

social constructivism Knowledge can be mutually learned and constructed by young children in social contexts (Vygotsky, 1962).

zone of proximal development (ZPD) The zone where a child learns best, with assistance from a peer or teacher (Vygotsky, 1962).

scaffolding Assisted learning that links prior learning to new learning.

cognitive dialogue Discussions between students and teachers that encourage thinking.

Table 1.1 *Theorists of Literacy, Psychology, and the Arts*

Theorists	Main Points of Theory	Application to Early Literacy
Literacy Marie Clay	Importance of the language cueing systems in the reading process Observation survey for assessing foundational skills in early reading, which includes a running record for assessing oral reading	Clay's research in beginning reading led to the development of an early intervention program for first graders called Reading Recovery.
Elizabeth Sulzby	Five stages of emergent reading Studied children "pretend" reading between the ages of 2 and 6 Stages of emergent writing	Sulzby carefully documented how children learn to read, distinguishing between pictures and print.
Psychology Albert Bandura	Observational theory Learning through observation and imitation of behaviors	Children learn by watching others. Literacy is enhanced when reading aloud to children. They imitate the actions of reading.
Abraham Maslow	Self-actualization theory Hierarchal theory involving meeting needs starting with the first tier (physiological, safety, belonging) and then moving toward self-esteem building and culminating with self-actualization	Children learn to read and write when they feel accepted, loved, and have high self-esteem.
Arts Viktor Lowenfeld	Artistic development A developmental theory for children's drawings with three stages—*scribbling stage* (ages 2–4); *preschematic stage* (ages 4–7); and *schematic stage* (ages 7–9)	Children learn to read and write by recognizing shapes in letters. Allowing children to draw their ideas helps to develop language.
Howard Gardner	Multiple intelligence theory Interpersonal, intrapersonal, verbal, mathematical, musical, visual/spatial, naturalistic, and kinesthetic	This involves teaching through a variety of avenues of learning and perspectives.
Interrelated Lev Vygotsky	Social constructivism: scaffolding, zone of proximal development (ZPD), inner speech, cognitive dialogue, and sociocultural interaction	Literacy learning is taught through interaction and group work with assistance from peers and teachers.
John Dewey	Progressivism Real-world application of knowledge (learning by doing)	Making connections Text-to-self, text-to-text, and text-to-world

can occur. Our holistic model of literacy (HML) illustrates that the cognitive, socioemotional, and physical aspects promote effective learning.

The theories of literacy (Clay and Sulzby), psychology (Bandura and Maslow), the arts (Lowenfeld and Gardner), and integrated theories (Dewey and Vygotsky) are important to guide teaching and learning. Table 1.1 summarizes the literacy, psychology, arts, and interrelated theorists/approaches discussed in this chapter. The concepts presented in this section can guide educators to implement effective teaching practices and learning strategies.

Teachers, parents, siblings, relatives, friends, and the community must work together to provide a successful learning environment.

Consider how you can incorporate social interaction and real-world connections in your literacy curriculum. How can you design learning stations (that is, housekeeping, dramatic play areas) to promote collaboration?

1-6 Strategies and Practices for the Holistic Model of Literacy

As teachers of early literacy, our goal is to "ignite a passion for reading" (Gambrell, 1996; Layne, 2009) in each and every child. We must teach our children how to read and write, but we must also teach them to love reading and writing. Reading aloud can motivate children to have a passion for literacy (Trelease, 2013). Reading a story and discussing main ideas helps children to comprehend text. Comprehension strategies, such as predicting, summarizing, inferencing, and visualizing, can be taught through read-alouds. The importance of read-alouds in the classroom cannot be underestimated. See Figure 1.5 for additional strategies on motivating readers.

Figure 1.5
Motivating Readers

1. *Knowing your students*

We must get to know our students—their interests, passions, language and culture, strengths, needs, and learning styles, if we expect them to reach their maximum potential. Young children must know that we love them and care about them. When you stock your classroom library with books related to your students' interests, your students will know that you truly care about them and that you will do everything you can to meet their needs.

2. *Celebrating books*

We should create a special shelf in our classroom libraries that includes specific content-appropriate books, autographed copies of books, book gifts from friends, and favorite childhood books.

3. *Book chats*

If you want to get your students excited about reading, you can chat about new children's books from your school library, public library, or bookstore. It's a good idea to record notes from book chats on forms for future use. Use a "hook" to help students remember the book. It might be an interesting question, a costume, a dialect, or a prop.

4. *Book discussions*

Children are motivated when they are allowed to talk about the books they are reading. They learn from each other when they are exposed to multiple perspectives. Book clubs (a group of four students) can meet for 15 minutes to discuss books. Free writing may occur after the book discussion.

5. *Reading with students*

Reading with students is all about modeling. Students need to know that their teachers are readers. You can place a book that you are currently reading (age-appropriate for your students) on a special stand by your desk. It's not a book that you are currently using in the classroom for anything else. It's a book that will get your students excited about reading, just because you are excited about reading it.

6. *Effective read-alouds*

During read-alouds you can use exaggerated voices and animated gestures to engage your audience. Effective storytelling techniques include the use of costumes, props, masks, puppets, music, and sound effects.
(Layne, 2005)

1-6a Age-Appropriate Strategies for Literacy Development

Children begin their literacy development the day they are born. Some mothers begin reading to their babies even before they are born, when their babies are in the womb. Lap reading is a precious bonding experience between parent and child. Children associate reading with the love of a parent. This love typically translates into a love of reading that lasts for a lifetime. There are sequential stages of development in a child's journey to literacy (McGee & Richgels, 2011). We organized this section on literacy development into three major age groups: (1) birth to 3 years, (2) 3 to 6 years, and (3) 6 to 9 years.

Birth to 3 Years

When babies are born, they learn many new concepts or schemas every day. Parents provide visual stimulation in their babies' cribs through musical mobiles, cloth books, and stuffed toys. Babies love listening to a story, and may be attracted to illustrations that have bright colors and interesting shapes. Infants and toddlers learn to understand oral language and speech patterns at an amazing rate. They begin recognizing environmental print—stop signs and advertisements. Children between 1 and 3 years of age are in the scribbling stage of spelling development (Sulzby & Teale, 1985). They experiment with lines and squiggles, coloring all over the page. This occurrence aligns with Lowenfeld's (1968) theory of children's artistic creativity, which correlates with Sulzby's (1985) first emergent writing stage.

Durable board books, washable cloth books, plastic books for the bathtub, or books with textures like *Pat the Bunny* by Dorothy Kundardt (2001) are recommended. Books with rhyme, rhythm, and repetition are ideal for babies and children.

3 to 6 Years

In this phase of awareness and exploration, children pretend to read and develop proper reading habits (McGee & Richgels, 2011). Children learn the alphabet and how to write their names and other common words they encounter on a daily basis. They recognize concepts of print and distinguish between capital and lowercase letters when spelling. Preschoolers learn the concept of rhyme and other elements of phonemic and phonological awareness, such as blending, segmenting, and manipulating sounds in words (oral and written). They become aware of the alphabetic principle, that letters represent sounds. Children in this stage have a concept of a word and a sentence. They begin to use grammar, such as simple punctuation in their writing. Writing may look like "symbol soup," consisting of a combination of letters, symbols, numbers, and letterlike formations. However, if you ask a child to read what they have written, they may be able to explain the story.

Story grammar (the parts of a story—setting, characters, events, problem, and solution) becomes important. Emergent readers and writers have a concept of story—beginning, middle, and end. They begin learning sight words or high-frequency words, like color words, number words, days of the week, and months of the year. Predictable, patterned books, such as *Goodnight Moon* by Margaret Wise Brown (1947), *Brown Bear, Brown Bear, What Do You See?* by Bill Martin Jr. (1967), or *Green Eggs and Ham* by Dr. Seuss (1960), are excellent choices for children in this stage of literacy development. Labeling objects in the environment, language experience stories, word walls, and manipulatives such as letter tiles or magnetic letters are ideal for early readers and writers. Children in this stage of literacy need lots of practice reading and writing in a risk-free, playful, print-rich environment.

6 to 9 Years

Children in this stage of literacy development are more advanced in their reading and writing skills. They are learning basic decoding and phonics skills, such as consonant blends, short and long vowel sounds, and the silent "e." Invented spelling is common in this stage of literacy development (McGee & Richgels, 2011).

scribbling stage of spelling development The first stage of writing when children between one and three years of age experiment with lines and squiggles (Sulzby & Teale, 1985).

story grammar Components of a story and the relationship between the parts (setting, theme, plot, and resolution).

sight words High-frequency words that must be memorized for instant recognition.

word wall Class display of key words.

Table 1.2   *Strategies and Practices for the Holistic Model of Literacy*

Age Groups	Cognitive	Socioemotional	Physical
0–3	Manipulating puzzles, blocks, toys Differentiating between objects in number, color, type Learning letters and words through alphabet books Repeating a refrain while listening to a story	Responding to music (singing, humming) Clapping hands and verbalize sounds to express emotion Repeating sounds (animals, birds) Caring for pets and plants Experiencing read-alouds with a caring adult	Interacting with nature and the environment through the five senses Dancing with simple props (rattles, scarf, hat) Performing finger plays about nursery rhymes Creating finger paintings to music
3–6	Learning how to write names in different media Asking and answering questions about what they are reading Creating a story map labeling the parts of the narrative Recognizing the features of nonfiction text	Acting out character roles in fairy tales Verbalizing emotions in their artwork Identifying emotions in poetry Analyzing emotions in book illustrations Discussing morals in popular fables and folktales	Experimenting with movement and creative dance Dancing in rhythm and sequence according to lyrics Singing folk songs and performing multicultural dances Visiting parks, zoos, gardens to experience natural habitats
6–9	Writing a variety of genres (narrative, persuasive, and informational) Reading and comparing different forms of text on the same topic Using technology to present information on a selected research topic	Changing plot and character development to express different emotions Role-playing favorite characters Creating and using masks depicting emotions of story characters Debating historical events	Interpreting stories through the visual and performing arts Creating and using dioramas as miniature scenes in a play Observing an event and writing or drawing in a journal or sketchbook

⌄ Professional Resource Download

Beginning readers can read predictable text with repetitive patterns as well as beginning chapter books. More advanced readers read a variety of genres, such as poetry, historical fiction, fantasy, science fiction, and traditional literature. Children learn to comprehend at literal, inferential, and critical levels. They are able to write an assortment of text forms, including narrative, descriptive, persuasive, and informational writing. Using technology, children in this age group can create research reports, graphic organizers, digital storybooks, presentations, and blogs. Choices for reading, writing, listening, speaking, and visually representing will inspire children to use their creativity in demonstrating their understanding of the world around them.

1-6b Age-Appropriate Activities for the Holistic Model of Literacy

The integration of the cognitive, emotional, and physical parts of self are integral in literacy development. Table 1.2 depicts activities that promote literacy development by age group. Our holistic model of literacy, introduced earlier in this chapter, is used throughout the textbook to illustrate strategies and practices for an integrated literacy approach and to provide engagement for various age groups. Although we separately discuss the cognitive, socioemotional, and physical concepts, in reality, these aspects of self are intertwined. Chapters 2 through 10 contain tables that focus on active engagement in all three aspects, children's books, and ideas for family involvement, expanding the concepts introduced in Table 1.2. These chapter tables offer inspiration for further adaptation of literacy strategies and practices. As educators, you can expand the following concepts to promote imagination and a passion for literacy.

End-of-Chapter Study Aids

Summary

A variety of literacy strategies and practices are described throughout this textbook. As you continue reading, you will discover ways to integrate literacy, psychology, and the arts in early childhood classrooms. Each of the three disciplines has primary theorists that were selected because of their individual contributions to the field of education. Interrelated theorists formulate the core of literacy development. In addition to the theoretical foundation in this chapter, we introduce literacy strategies and practices that reflect our holistic model of literacy (the cognitive, socioemotional, and physical aspects of self).

Integration of literacy, psychology, and the arts forms a foundation for innovative early childhood education. Ultimately, however, teachers are the key to success, rather than the literacy program. Teachers must have high expectations for their students, encouraging them to take risks, learn from their mistakes, explore their passions, and follow their dreams. They must believe in their students, and the children must believe in themselves. Teachers can truly make a difference, one child at a time.

Chapter Exercises

1. Describe a reading or writing activity for preschool children (ages 2 to 4) that integrates collaboration and drawing.
2. With a partner, select a picture book and role-play Sulzby's five stages of emergent reading.
3. Choose a picture book on the theme of self-esteem or self-respect. Model or record a read-aloud and share with a small group of your peers.
4. Collect children's drawings (ages 2 to 4, 4 to 6, 6 to 9) and organize into Lowenfeld's (1968) artistic stages.
5. As a whole class, predict what a picture book will be about based upon the cover illustration, and collaboratively read the book aloud (each person reads one page before passing to the next person).

Teacher Toolbox

READING AND WRITING IN THE CONTENT AREA

Appropriate for Ages 7 to 9

Teaching vocabulary and concepts in the content areas (science, math, and social studies) is an important part of the early literacy curriculum. Teachers can begin by collecting a text set of fiction and nonfiction books on a specific topic such as the ocean, with an emphasis on sea creatures, such as *Flotsam* by David Wiesner (2006), *Big Al* by Andrew Clements (1997), *The Ocean Alphabet Book* by Jerry Pallotta (1989), and *Sea Turtles for Kids* by Catherine Wilder (2014). After sharing several books with the class as read-alouds or literature circles, ask the children to individually research a sea creature, answering questions (written on an anchor chart), such as the following questions. Drawings of the sea creatures painted by the children can be labeled and added to a class mural of the ocean on the classroom wall. Research reports could be presented and posted on a class bulletin board or bound into a class book. A field trip to a local aquarium would be an interesting culminating activity.

THINKING QUESTIONS FOR RESEARCH REPORT ABOUT SEA CREATURES

1. What does this sea creature look like?
2. What does it eat?
3. Where does it live in the ocean?
4. Who are the sea creature's enemies?
5. How long does it live?

Key Terms and Concepts

approximations

cognitive dialogue

concepts about print (CAP)

creative intelligence

developmentally appropriate practice

emergent literacy

executive function

holistic model of literacy (HML)

language cueing systems

language development

multiple intelligences

observational learning theory

process-based approach

progressivism

Reading Recovery

running records

scaffolding

schemata

scribbling stage of spelling development

self-actualization

sight words

social constructivism

story grammar

word walls

zone of proximal development (ZPD)

Olesya Feketa/Shutterstock.com

STANDARDS ADDRESSED IN THIS CHAPTER

The standards from the following organizations will be used throughout the chapter: Common Core State Standards for English Language Arts, the National Association for the Education of Young Children (NAEYC), and National Core Arts Standards. These standards are discussed further in the chapter as appropriate.

Common Core State Standards for English Language Arts

Anchor Standards for Reading

Reading Standards: Foundational Skills (K–5)
- Print Concepts
- Phonological Awareness
- Phonics and Word Recognition

Anchor Standards for Speaking and Listening
- Comprehension and Collaboration
- Presentation of Knowledge and Ideas

Anchor Standards for Language
- Knowledge of Language
- Vocabulary Acquisition and Use

2010 NAEYC Standards for Initial and Advanced Early Childhood Professional Preparation Programs
- *Standard 1:* Promoting Child Development and Learning

NAEYC Early Childhood Program Standards and Accreditation Criteria
- *Standard 2:* Curriculum
- *Standard 3:* Teaching

NCA

National Core Arts Standards (Dance, Media Arts, Music, Theater, Visual Arts)

Creating
- *Anchor Standard 1:* Generate and conceptualize artistic ideas and work.

Presenting
- *Anchor Standard 6:* Convey meaning through the presentation of artistic work.

Responding
- *Anchor Standard 7:* Perceive and analyze artistic work.

Connecting
- *Anchor Standard 10:* Synthesize and relate knowledge and personal experiences to make art.

Emergent and Early Literacy

2

Children are made readers on the laps of their parents. — Emilie Buchwald

Emergent literacy is a process involving the development of language and concepts, especially when connected with young children's experiences starting at birth. Communication and the expression of ideas are first steps on the journey to literacy. This process may include listening, speaking, signing, writing, using gestures, and any other ways in which children comprehend and communicate their experiences and knowledge of the world (DeVries, 2011).

Language development is a key factor in establishing a foundation for literacy, and young children need a safe, nurturing, healthy, and print-rich environment to learn. Interaction at an early age with caring adults prepares children for successful oral language development. Reading aloud, discussions, singing, dramatic play, and story time are strategies to develop language and literacy skills. Children should be guided and supported by caring adults, starting at birth, to eventually become independent readers and writers. The International Literacy Association (formerly the International Reading Association) and the National Council of Teachers of English (NCTE) published *Standards for the English Language Arts* (2012), which describe the six language arts: reading, writing, speaking, listening, viewing, and visually representing. Visual representation and viewing have increased dramatically due to digital media as accessed through electronic devices such as phones, computers, cameras, and tablets.

Learning occurs through active engagement of the child's cognitive, socioemotional and physical aspects of self as noted in the holistic model of literacy (HML):

- The cognitive aspect of self is enhanced through critical thinking (analysis and evaluation), problem solving, play, decision making, and expression of ideas.
- The socioemotional bond between a caring adult and a child is strengthened during activities such as lap reading and the **cuddle read** (when a child snuggles in an adult reader's arms during read-aloud sessions).
- Physical development is supported through the manipulation of objects using the five senses, such as making words with magnetic letters or writing letters in sand.

Effective and appropriate literacy practices for each age group (0 to 3, 3 to 6, and 6 to 9) guide children's literacy development.

LEARNING OBJECTIVES

After you have read this chapter, you should be able to:

- 2-1 Identify concepts of emergent and early literacy.
- 2-2 Describe language acquisition and development.
- 2-3 Explain stages of the reading process.
- 2-4 Summarize family literacy strategies.
- 2-5 Explore components of effective literacy instruction.
- 2-6 Apply early literacy strategies and practices.

STANDARDS CONNECTION TO THE VIGNETTE

NAEYC Early Childhood Program Accreditation Standards

Standard 2: Curriculum

2.J.04 Children are provided varied opportunities to learn new concepts and vocabulary related to art, music, drama, and dance.

Common Core State Standards for English Language Arts

Key Ideas and Details

First Grade

2. Retell stories, including key details, and demonstrate understanding of their central message or lesson.

My Many Colored Days by Dr. Seuss (1996) connects emotions with colors and animals. Children explore imaginary movement and sound described through the illustrations and rhythmic text. For young children, especially toddlers, color expression is an important part of their emotive communication process.

First grade students listen to their teacher, Mrs. Valdez, read *My Many Colored Days* by Dr. Seuss (1996), illustrated by Steve Johnson and Lou Fancher. After reading, a class discussion ensues where the children identify the emotion and the emotional response in the story and discuss other colors and associated emotions and responses. Next, they share words that describe emotional responses or action words that rhyme with colors while Mrs. Valdez writes these on a chart for the children to use in their writing and artistic work.

Mrs. Valdez displays the color wheel for the children to use when selecting colors. The children, with the teacher's guidance, select one color and complete these sentence frames, imagining that they are animals that exhibit these traits:

- When I feel (color), I'm (emotion).
- I (emotional response or action), (emotional response or action), and (emotional response or action word that rhymes with the color).

Children then draw the animal using only the color they have selected (see Photo 2.1). During the sharing session, Joshua reads his sentence to the class, "When I feel blue, I'm calm and cool. I relax in my shell, sit still, and stay quiet in school." Joshua shares his drawing of a blue turtle, and the other children compliment him on his color selection and use of rhyming words.

When children develop an understanding of their emotions, their self-awareness and self-acceptance are nurtured. Understanding their own emotions leads children to better comprehend storybook characters. Using children's literature is an effective way to explore, accept, and manage emotions.

Developmentally appropriate practice (DAP) is featured in the vignette and can be adapted for younger children (birth to age 5) and older children to age 9. Suggested adaptations include:

- *Ages 0-3:* When caring adults cuddle read with infants and toddlers, an emotional bond is strengthened, promoting a love of literacy. Books with bright colors and shapes, such as *The Artist Who Painted a Blue Horse* by Eric Carle (2011), engage babies and toddlers.
- *Ages 3-6:* Preschool and kindergarten children can discuss emotions using Eric Carle's *Friends* (2013). Children can draw a picture of themselves with a friend and discuss things they like to do together.
- *Ages 6-9:* Children can read Dan Santat's *The Adventure of Beekle: The Unimaginary Friend* (2014) and create a drawing of an imaginary friend. A written description, including the friend's name and characteristics, can be shared with the class or small group.

cuddle read When a child snuggles in the adult reader's arms during read-aloud sessions.

Photo 2.1 *Calm, blue turtle*
Courtesy of the authors

Classroom Connection

How can you integrate picture books that describe different emotions and relationships into your literacy curriculum?

Concepts of Emergent and Early Literacy

Emergent literacy implies that children learn to read while they are developing their foundational literacy skills such as alphabet knowledge, *sight words,* and *concepts about print* (Clay, 1966). Early literacy refers to beginning stages of reading and writing (Clay, 1979). Young children must learn to recognize the 26 letters in the English alphabet (alphabet knowledge), including capital and lowercase letters, as well as individual consonant and vowel sounds. They must also memorize over 300 sight words, which are words that appear frequently in all beginning readers. These words cannot be decoded and have no meaning of their own (that is, *a, and,* and *the*). A concept of print (print awareness) is an understanding of print and how print works. Figure 2.1 features additional tools that provide a foundation for beginning readers and writers.

An important concept in early literacy is constructivism, a theory where individuals build their own understandings and personal perspectives when introduced to new ideas (Dewey, 1938; Piaget, 1953). When children are learning to read and write, they create meaning using imagination, background knowledge, and experiences. *Social constructivism* promotes collaborative and interactive learning. Children create meaning through interactions with each other and the learning environment (Piaget, 1953; Vygotsky, 1978).

Emergent Literacy Skills:

- Oral language
- Concepts about print
- Environmental print
- Alphabet knowledge
- Phonemic awareness
- Sight vocabulary
- Emergent or "pretend" reading
- Emergent or "pretend" writing

Figure 2.1
Skills for Beginning Reading and Writing
Adapted from DeVries (2011).

alphabet knowledge Knowing the names and sounds of the English alphabet, including capital and lowercase letters as well as individual consonant and vowel sounds.

constructivism Includes the idea that all learning should flow from the students' desires and connections to the real world.

Constructivist perspectives to early literacy include the Reggio Emilia (Gandini, Etheredge, & Hill, 2008) and Montessori (1914) approaches based on Vygotsky's (1962) theory of social constructivism and collaboration. The Reggio Emilia approach emphasizes group and individual art and sensory-based activities that lead to self-discovery to build independence and self-esteem. The Montessori approach also leads to children's independence in a more structured and curriculum-based environment focusing on real-life skills. Both approaches nurture individual strengths and talents through play in a creative and risk-free environment. "Play awakens the creative energy needed for intellectual development and for healthy human development as a whole" (Nell, Drew, and Bush, 2013, p. 29). Teachers of young children using these approaches guide and facilitate each child's journey to literacy. Children's ideas and dialogues are valued and respected within the classroom community. The social constructivist environment supports guided conversations and inquiry for children to pursue their personal interests (Vygotsky, 1978).

As children become more proficient in learning to read or write, their confidence soars after each step until they become comfortable with the their new skills such as, alphabet knowledge and sight vocabulary. When beginning to read and write, children use these skills as a literacy toolbox (DeVries, 2011). The goal for literacy teachers is to build a love of learning and curiosity so that each child is motivated to read and write independently. Parents need to help children in their literacy adventure by validating their accomplishments and providing the support for their children to succeed.

Photo 2.2
Learning with pictures

scientifically based reading
research Reading skills, such
as phonemic awareness, are
taught through systematic, explicit
instruction.

2-1a Emergent Literacy Perspectives

What does it take to raise a lifelong reader—a child who can read and who enjoys reading just for the sake of reading? There are two distinct views on early reading and writing instruction—*emergent literacy* and scientifically based reading research (SBRR). Proponents of emergent literacy believe that teaching phonemic awareness is unnecessary because children learn the skills best from being read to, listening to poems and stories by Dr. Seuss and Mother Goose with lots of rhyme, rhythm, and repetition, whereas SBRR advocates insist that children should be taught how to rhyme, segment, blend, and manipulate sounds through systematic, explicit instruction (Vukelich & Christie, 2009).

Marie Clay introduced the emergent literacy perspective in 1966, implying that learning to read is a natural process that evolves over time (see Photo 2.2). Both theories should be incorporated into early literacy curriculum and instruction. The first approach, emergent literacy, is defined as:

A perspective on early literacy development that contends that children construct their own knowledge about reading and writing as a result of social interaction and meaningful engagements with print. (Vukelich and Christie, 2009, p. ix)

Why do some children become early readers and others do not? Durkin's (1966) seminal research on early readers indicated that children who learned to read before attending kindergarten came from a print-rich home environment with many reading and writing materials. The parents read to their children frequently, from a very early age. The preschoolers learned to read naturally, from being read to on a regular basis. The parents talked to their children about books and answered their questions about reading, writing, and the world. The children's head start in reading did not last, however, in this study (Durkin, 1966). By the end of third grade, Durkin found that there was essentially no difference in the reading levels between those who are and are not early readers.

Vukelich and Christie's research (2009) on early reading focused primarily on four major strands: concepts of print, environmental print, developmental trends, and home environment. Young English-speaking children learn that a book is read from top to bottom, left to right, and front to back. Eventually, they understand the concepts of a letter, a word, a sentence, and a story. When they learn the alphabetic principle, that letters represent sounds, children usually begin to learn to read. Environmental print is print that is found in the real world, such as street signs (STOP), billboards, restaurant signs (McDonald's), and labels on cereal boxes or other food products. Children also begin to recognize letters in their names and brand names on toys such as "Hot Wheels" from the ages of 2 or 3. Developmental trends are also considered in early reading development as children gravitate toward the reading process when modeled by others around them. The home environment is particularly important in developing early readers. Providing reading materials at home and discussing what was read with parents assist early reading development (Vukelich & Christie, 2009).

Part of the emergent literacy perspective involves writing development. Children progress through predictable stages of writing (Sulzby & Teale, 1985). Sulzby's research on writing development (1990) proposed seven stages:

1. Drawing as writing,
2. Scribble writing,
3. Letter-like units,
4. Nonphonetic letter strings,
5. Copying from environmental print,
6. Invented spelling, and
7. Conventional writing.

At first, children draw shapes or figures and write letters randomly on a page. Children's early writing typically reflects letters in their names. Later, they progress to lines and squiggles imitating words and sentences. Letter strings may contain only consonants or a mixture of consonants and vowels (semiphonetic writing). The writing during this stage usually goes from left to right on the page. The next stage is invented or temporary spelling. Children learn to spell words the way they sound (phonetic writing). Although one or more sounds may be omitted or spelled differently, the writing can be easily understood. Research on early literacy (National Early Literacy Panel, 2008) indicated that access to print and books, storybook reading, and adults' modeling of reading behaviors are important to children's later success in reading and writing.

A different point of view is scientifically based reading research (SBRR). Using the SBRR approach, children learn a series of skills to achieve reading readiness, and these skills are taught using specific strategies through explicit instruction. Marilyn Adams's *Beginning to Read: Thinking and Learning about Print* (1990) formed the basis of SBRR. Phonological or phonemic awareness, alphabet knowledge, and oral language are essential skills for later success in reading according to a study by Snow, Burns, and Griffin (1998) entitled, *Preventing Reading Difficulties in Young Children*. Reading researchers have different perspectives on how to effectively teach beginning reading.

One perspective is that phonemic awareness (the awareness of sounds in spoken words) should be taught through explicit instruction (SBRR point of view). Phonemic awareness skills include rhyming, blending (putting sounds together), segmenting

environmental print Print that is found in the real world, such as street signs, billboards, restaurant signs, and labels on cereal boxes or other food products.

explicit instruction Systematic, explicit instructional strategies are used for teaching a variety of emergent literacy skills.

phonemic awareness An awareness of letters and sounds in spoken words.

blending Putting sounds together (phonemic awareness skill).

segmenting Breaking sounds apart (phonemic awareness skill).

LIFT THE FLAP BOOK ACTIVITY FOR PRESERVICE TEACHERS TO DO WITH CHILDREN

Purpose: Practice sequencing activities using narrative text.

Procedure: Complete a picture walk of *Flora and the Flamingo* by Molly Idle (2013). Ask the children to describe what is happening on each page while "reading" the wordless picture book (lifting the flaps to expose what is underneath). Children share their feelings about the story. Children can listen to music and practice ballet poses to deepen their comprehension of the text. Children use simple shapes to draw pictures of the beginning, middle, and end of the story and create their own flap book (see Photo 2.3).

Directions: Fold a sheet of paper in half lengthwise. Divide into three equal parts (beginning, middle, and end). Label top of flaps: 1, 2, and 3. Cut each flap to the fold. Illustrate a scene underneath the appropriate flap.

Teaching Analysis: Reflective practices are a necessary part of the *literacy assessment cycle* and are key components in preservice preparation and certification such as edTPA. Analyze the strengths and areas of improvement in this lesson idea. Answer the following:

- What is successful?
- What would you change to improve the lesson?
- What did you learn about teaching literacy?

Links: Making connections to technology and developmentally appropriate practices (DAP) supports lesson planning and literacy instruction. Adaptations of this lesson idea are provided in the following:

- **Technology Link:** Children view online video clips of children in a ballet performance.
- **DAP Link:** Age-appropriate arts integration strategies are used including dance, drama, music, and visual art.
- **Executive Function Link:** Creative play and active engagement during

an interactive read-aloud develop children's self-regulation skills in social settings as reflected in the holistic model of literacy (cognitive, socioemotional, and physical).

- **Classroom Link:** Children (0 to 3) can listen to music while a caring adult guides the movement of their arms and legs to mimic the illustrations in the book.
- **Classroom Link:** Children (3 to 6) can dictate their interpretation of the illustrations while the teacher writes using the children's language on chart paper.
- **Classroom Link:** Children (6 to 9) can create more illustrations (up to eight flaps) and write sentences and paragraphs to describe their drawings. Children can also research topics related to the book, such as flamingos and ballet.

Photo 2.3 *Story illustrations in sequence*
Courtesy of the authors

VISUAL DISCRIMINATION OF LETTERS AND WORDS

According to Richard Gentry (2010), the critical period for brain development occurs between birth and 6 years of age. The more senses involved during learning, the more likely the brain will receive and process information. Within the brain, the dorsal stream connects the visual cortex with the spatial attention area, allowing for locating objects in space. When children learn letters and words, they recognize shapes and forms through visual discrimination.

Think about It

How can teachers help children develop visual discrimination skills? For example, using word walls and word labels on objects in your classroom assists children in visually recognizing key vocabulary. Teachers can cut out words into contour shapes and place these on the classroom word wall.

(breaking sounds apart), and manipulating sounds in words (changing the first, middle, or final sound in a word to a different sound, such as "dog" to "log"). A counter perspective is that children learn phonemic awareness naturally through reading experiences at home and in school (emergent literacy point of view). Different systematic, explicit instructional strategies are used in the SBRR approach for teaching a variety of emergent literacy skills. For example, "Elkonin" or sound boxes may be used in an activity to teach children how to segment sounds. Three boxes are drawn for the phonemes in the word *cat*. As the teacher says each letter sound, the child is asked to move a chip into each box, from the left to the right. This activity is based on the work of D. B. Elkonin, a Russian psychologist, as described in Marie Clay's *The Early Detection of Reading Difficulties* (1979). By completing a series of explicit instruction exercises, SBRR supports that reading development is strengthened in children. Effective reading instruction uses many different approaches to meet the needs of individual children.

Apply & Reflect

Create an example for one stage of writing development (Sulzby & Teale, 1985). Share your writing example with peers to compare characteristics of writing at different stages of development.

 CONSIDER THIS...

Consider which of these early literacy perspectives best relates to your personal philosophy of teaching and learning: SBRR or emergent literacy. How can you integrate one concept from your perspective into a literacy lesson?

2-2 Language Acquisition and Development

The aspects of language development integrate all three parts of the self (cognitive, socioemotional, and physical) as illustrated in our HML. Oral language develops in a nurturing environment that promotes reading, writing, speaking, and listening (see Photo 2.4). Children imitate adults and peers when they hear words read from a book or hear others telling a story or through dialogue.

Language acquisition involves purposeful communication. Many variables impact language acquisition, including family structure, cultural and linguistic diversity, sociocultural heritage, and physical abilities (Vukelich, Christie, & Enz, 2011). Children use language for various reasons to express their ideas, communicate their feelings,

manipulating sounds Changing the first, middle, or final sound in a word to a different sound (phonemic awareness skill).

Table 2.1	The Functions of Children's Oral Language

Stages	Functions
1. Instrumental Stage	Uses language to achieve basic needs Says concrete nouns and verbs
2. Regulatory Stage	Uses language to obtain goals Speaks words, phrases, and commands
3. Interactional Stage	Uses language to develop social relationships Expresses emotions and caring
4. Personal Stage	Uses language to share attitudes and emotional responses Conveys personal preferences
5. Informative Stage	Uses language to communicate information Relays or requests information
6. Heuristic Stage	Uses language to discover the environment Questions and comments on actions or observations
7. Imaginative Stage	Uses language to reveal imaginative thoughts Engages in playful conversations

Adapted from Halliday (1978).

receptive language Involves listening and reading.

expressive language Communication involving speaking and writing.

Photo 2.4 *Conversation at home*
Josh Weinberger

or gain information. Halliday (1978) developed seven stages to describe the functions or purposes of a child's oral language (see Table 2.1).

Children acquire language in predictable stages, absorbing the speech they hear in the world around them. Receptive language (when children understand the meanings of words and can follow directions) comes before expressive language (when they can repeat words, express their ideas and feelings, or answer questions). Children learn words through social interaction and by playing with language. Their first words are meaningful and usually relate to basic needs, such as *home*, *milk*, or *snack*. For example:

- A toddler may say "milk" when thirsty (instrumental stage).
- A preschooler might string words into phrases or commands and state "I want milk" (regulatory stage).
- A kindergarten child may explain that he or she wants chocolate milk (personal stage).

Depending upon the sociocultural context and purpose/function, children communicate through different stages of oral language. Young children's language expands dramatically after they learn to combine words into sentences, around the age of 2. During the years between 2 and 4, a child's oral vocabulary grows at an even faster rate (expressive and receptive language). Children's conversations begin to mimic adult dialogue during play (that is, talking on a phone with a friend, real or imaginary). Sentence structure becomes more complex with increased vocabulary. Children, ages 5 and 6, expand their language patterns to express ideas in creative ways, blending fantasy and reality. Grammar use and vocabulary continue to improve for older children, ages 7 to 9 (Krashen, 2004). Caring adults should model discussion with children to demonstrate proper language use and stimulate curiosity about the world. Engaging children in collaborative dialogue creates a dynamic, inquiry-based learning environment.

2-2a The Language Experience Approach

Early literacy strategies are used to further develop reading and writing skills in young children, such as shared reading or writing, based on the language experience approach or key word approach (Ashton-Warner, 1963). This approach can be expanded to synthesize learning through the integration of reading, writing, speaking, viewing, visually representing, and listening skills (see Figure 2.2). The premise of the language experience approach (LEA) is that children learn to read from text that consists of their own words or language. Children dictate a story to the teacher, who records it on a chalkboard or whiteboard as the children observe. The teacher reads the story to the children and then they read it together in unison. Finally, the children read the story on their own. This strategy encourages self-esteem and self-efficacy as the children develop their own reading and writing style at the same time. Children can illustrate their story to encourage visually representing their ideas and to expand their communication skills. English learners benefit from this strategy, as it allows children to express more clearly what they are thinking and feeling.

The language experience approach is an authentic and meaningful way for children to become literate because of the emphasis on personal experience. Children use language arts skills (reading, writing, speaking, listening, viewing, and visually representing) during the literacy process. When young readers and writers become more independent, they can co-write stories with their peers or the teacher. The writing process becomes interactive, when the teacher and students share the pen (shared writing). This collaboration, with appropriate scaffolding by the teacher, builds confidence and motivation, which is especially important for English learners and struggling readers.

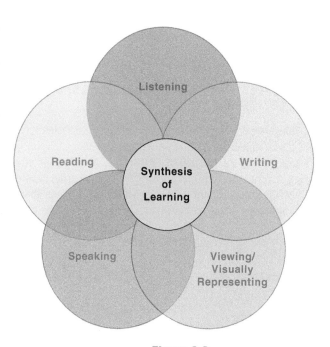

Figure 2.2
Language Experience Model with the Six Language Arts

 CONSIDER THIS...

Consider how a child's oral language impacts his or her ability to read and write. How can you meet the needs of individual children using the language experience model?

2-3 Stages of the Reading Process

Emergent literacy, when children develop an understanding of letters and sounds, is the beginning of the reading process, which involves decoding (phonological awareness) and comprehension skills (semantics and syntax). When children are reading, they construct meaning to comprehend text. Reading is a multifaceted negotiation between the text, the readers, and their purpose for reading. The readers' interpretation of the text is based on many factors, including knowledge of the topic, language and culture, language of the text, social context, knowledge about reading and print, as well as expectations about reading based on the readers' *schemata* or experiences in the world (Weaver, 2002). Understanding the connection between children's individual

shared reading The teacher and children read together, typically using a big book, in a whole class setting.

shared writing An interactive writing experience when a teacher and students share the pen.

language experience approach A method (consisting of dictated stories and word banks) for teaching children how to read that uses their own language as the primary text.

key word approach A form of the language experience approach that begins with a word and ends with a story (Ashton-Warner, 1963).

ASSESSING ORAL LANGUAGE DEVELOPMENT THROUGH THE LANGUAGE EXPERIENCE APPROACH

Language experience approach is an authentic assessment using the child's language as a tool for learning how to read. First, children have a common experience such as making popcorn or going to the zoo on a field trip. After the experience, the children as a whole group discuss their perspectives and feelings about what happened. Using a recording device, each child tells her or his own version of the events. Later, the teacher listens to each child's recording and determines use of key vocabulary words, description of key details, proper sentence structure, and proper sequencing of events.

Oral Language Guide

Directions: Listen to an audio recording of a child retelling an event. Record anecdotal notes on the guide to assist in identifying learning behavior/strategies. Strengths and areas of improvement are identified and written in the guide to plan future instruction.

Teacher Reflection Prompts	Oral Language Response	Use of Sentence Structure	Use of Event Sequencing	Use of New Vocabulary
Strengths of the child to guide future instruction				
Areas of improvement based upon child's needs				
Strategies and practices to support child's development				

Think about It

When assessing oral language, how can you identify a child's strengths and areas of improvement? For example, if your observations indicate that a child has difficulty using new vocabulary words, design a storytelling activity that emphasizes unfamiliar words.

⌄ Professional Resource Download

backgrounds and how they learn helps teachers prepare their students to become independent, strategic readers.

The reading process consists of five stages: prereading, reading, responding, exploring, and applying as shown in Table 2.2.

Young readers experience all five stages of the reading process in their journey to becoming fluent readers. Teachers can design literacy lessons to incorporate many of the ideas listed in Table 2.2. For example, to incorporate level four, teachers may select children's books that include themes for analysis and drawing conclusions. The theme of relationships is explored in *The Year of Billy Miller* by Kevin Henkes (2013), a funny story about a second-grade boy who learns how to get along with others. Book talks by teachers and peers inspire children to read more at home and in school. Book clubs and literature circles (Daniels, 2002) motivate children through discussion to better understand and analyze a common text.

2-3a Language Cueing Systems

During the reading process, children use their decoding skills and vocabulary to read and comprehend the text. Fluent readers are better able to comprehend the text because of their word identification and decoding skills.

Table 2.2 *Stages of the Reading Process*

Lower Level Cognition

Level 1: Pre-reading—Setting the Stage

- Making predictions and introducing new concepts
- Activating prior knowledge
- Making personal connections

Level 2: Reading—Performance

- Applying skills and strategies
- Reading independently with a partner or small group
- Interpreting and reading pictures, charts, diagrams, and other text features

Level 3: Responding—Interactive Dialogue

- Reading for information (brain) and feelings and emotions (heart)
- Discussing stories through book clubs, role playing, and storytelling
- Learning vocabulary through context clues, listening, and interactive activities

Higher Level Cognition

Level 4: Exploring—Improvisation

- Analyzing themes and drawing conclusions
- Making connections through inferences
- Examining authors' craft and style of writing

Level 5: Applying—New Productions

- Creating artistic expression through the arts
- Evaluating your reading experience and applying to new reading material
- Infusing the new skills and strategies across disciplines

Adapted from Tompkins (2013).

When readers are struggling with text, they may need to slow down or back up and reread a passage until it makes sense. They may cross-check or use multiple decoding strategies with unfamiliar words using their *language cueing systems* (Halliday, 1978). English has four language cueing systems that are based on creating meaning through socially shared conventions:

- graphophonic or phonological,
- semantic,
- syntactic, and
- pragmatic.

The graphophonic cueing system refers to word spellings (graphic symbols) and sounds (phonics); the semantic cueing system is the meaning of the word; and the syntactic cueing system is the syntax (word order or sentence structure). The pragmatic cueing system deals with the social aspects of language use, which vary among ethnic groups and geographic regions. These language variations are known as dialects. Good readers use all four cueing systems automatically when they read and write. They read fluently, decode words into meaningful chunks, make personal connections, use picture and context clues, reread for understanding, and ask questions during the reading process.

cross-check Using multiple strategies for decoding unknown words.

graphophonic cueing system One of the language cueing systems that represents how a word looks (graphic symbols) and how a word sounds (phonics).

semantic cueing system One of the language cueing systems that represents meaning.

syntactic cueing system One of the language cueing systems that represents word order or sentence structure.

pragmatic cueing system One of the language cueing systems that deals with the social aspects of language use.

dialects Language variations within geographic regions.

Consider how you can model the various levels of the reading process using a picture book (see Photo 2.5) during an interactive read-aloud, such as *Olivia* by Ian Falconer (2004). How can you set the stage for reading the book? What interactive strategies can you use to interpret the illustrations?

2-4 Family Literacy Strategies

Early literacy development is guided by initial reading experiences and therefore it is critical that parents participate in this process for young children's future success in reading. "Reading aloud to children is the single most important activity in building a foundation for learning to read" (Adams, 1990, p. 4). In *The Read-Aloud Handbook*, Jim Trelease (2013) gives parents advice on how to raise a reader. His reading kit for parents (other than a free library card) is called the "three Bs" (Trelease, 2013, pp. 37–38).

- *The first B is books:* It is very important for children to have books of their own that they don't have to share or return to the library.
- *The second B is book basket:* A book basket or magazine rack full of books should be placed in the home where it is handy, such as in a bathroom or near a kitchen table.
- *The third B is bed lamp:* A small reading lamp should be placed on a bedside table to encourage children to stay up a little longer (15 minutes or more, depending on the age of the child) and read in bed.

Reading is central to a child's life, and therefore should have a prominent place a child's home and classroom (Codell, 2003). Pam Allyn (2009) emphasizes why reading aloud to children is so critical in the life of a reader; it helps children to:

1. Develop shared values
2. Fall in love with language
3. Build comprehension
4. Learn the power of story
5. Be exposed to a variety of genres
6. Learn about text structures
7. Find comfort
8. Build critical thinking skills
9. Shape a lifelong reading identity
10. Visit many worlds and hear many voices (pp. 11–15)

Photo 2.5 *Young minds using their curiosity and imagination*
Josh Weinberger

A literacy-rich home environment that nurtures young readers promotes early motivation for reading and writing (see Photo 2.5). Reading motivation through a supportive home environment encourages young children to read what they love and love what they read.

2-4a The Four Keys to Reading

Allyn (2009) uses READ as an acronym to explain the four keys to reading: ritual, environment, access, and dialogue.

- *Ritual* means that families must set aside a special time for reading every day, such as bedtime, bath time, during breakfast, or after dinner. She suggests that parents set aside time to read individually with each child whenever possible, because each child has different needs and interests (see Photo 2.6). The idea is that reading becomes a routine or habit, just as important as taking a bath or brushing teeth.
- *Environment* means that special places for reading and writing should be designated in the home. Perhaps a child-sized writing table could be set up in the living room or a cozy beanbag chair in the bedroom with a basket of books.
- *Access* is probably the most important key, having plenty of books available that match the children's reading levels and interests. Parents should make sure that the books are readily available, in baskets or on low bookshelves in different areas of the house. There should be a range of difficulty in reading levels, including "uphill" books for reading aloud, "just right" books for reading together, and "downhill" books for children to read on their own. "A study by the National Endowment for the Arts found that homes with ten or more children's books have a profound influence on kids' lives and how well they do in school" (Allyn, 2009, p. 23).
- Finally, *dialogue* means that parents talk to their children about what they are reading, discussing personal connections that are meaningful and relevant, rather than just asking questions about the story. As children get older, the dialogue will change, but the doors should remain open. Allyn states, "Our goal is lifelong dialogue with our children" (2009, p. 25). What we should do is talk about what really matters to our children and what better way to do this than through the pages of a book?

Photo 2.6 *Father reading to his daughter.*

 CONSIDER THIS...

Consider how you can motivate the parents or guardians of students in your class to understand the importance of family literacy. How can you discuss the significance of a print-rich environment with the families of children in your class? How can daily reading be encouraged in the home?

2-5 Components of Effective Literacy Instruction

Children in the developmental stages of literacy need to experience engaging storytelling, reading environments, interactive picture books, and literacy-supported technology. Toddlers learn to recognize letters and words when interacting with sounds, colors,

1. *Early language and literacy education should focus on core content—the knowledge, skills, and dispositions that are predictive of later success in learning to read and write (that is, oral language, phonological awareness, alphabet knowledge, and print awareness).* These skills are the building blocks of early literacy.

2. *Oral language lays the foundation for early literacy development.* Teachers and parents should engage children in rich experiences and conversations to build schema and vocabulary through children's literature, project-based learning, and field trips.

3. *Storybook reading is the cornerstone of early literacy instruction.* Children must be read to often, from a variety of genres, in age-appropriate books related to curricular themes and topics. These include narrative and expository text (information books), poetry, and biographies, and big books. Teachers should select children's literature that is relevant to their students' interests and cultures whenever possible.

4. *A carefully planned classroom environment enables literacy development to flourish.* A print-rich environment consists of literacy centers such as a diverse classroom library with a cozy area for reading, a writing center, dramatic play area, science corner, and listening center. Teachers should encourage their students to create their own books for the classroom library.

5. *Children need opportunities to engage in emergent forms of reading and writing.* Children can tell their own stories using wordless picture books. They can draw or paint pictures and words, using alphabet books to learn their letters and sounds. After reading *My Many Colored Days* by Dr. Seuss, children can be encouraged to paint with colors representing their feelings and emotions.

6. *Developmentally appropriate forms of explicit instruction should be used to teach core literacy concepts and skills.* Teachers can teach concepts about print through shared reading and writing using the language experience approach. Familiar songs such as "Old McDonald" or "Skip to My Lou" can be used to teach phonemic awareness skills.

7. *Teachers need to help parents support their children's language, reading, and writing development.* Parents can be taught effective read-aloud techniques and how to select appropriate books for their children. "Parents" may include fathers, mothers, and grandparents, as well as other relatives or caregivers.

8. *Oral language and early literacy instruction and assessment should be guided by standards that define the knowledge and skills young children need to become successful readers and writers.* Teachers must integrate national and state early learning standards into their preschool curriculum.

Figure 2.3
Principles of Effective Early Literacy Instruction
Adapted from Vukelich and Christie (2009, pp. 12–13).

Photo 2.7 *Learning through play*
Janet Towell

shapes, forms, and textures through the five senses. Children use sounds, colors, and shapes for building their literacy foundation (see Photo 2.7). Educators of young children (birth to age 5) should be familiar with the principles of effective literacy instruction (see Figure 2.3).

Vukelich and Christie (2009) suggest an integrated approach incorporating eight principles as the ideal philosophy for preschool literacy. Teachers should develop their own strategies and activities for implementing the principles of effective literacy instruction based upon each child's specific strengths and needs.

2-5a Storytelling Strategies for Young Children

There are many literacy strategies that can be implemented to engage young readers. Storytelling is an effective way to promote oral language development in the primary grades (Towell, 2013). Collaborative stories work well in the beginning because the children can support one another. Storytelling is an interactive process among children and teachers to build self-identity. At-risk learners, such as English learners and students with

MULTICULTURAL STORYTELLING

Storytelling allows children from all cultures and abilities to share their ideas and emotions. English language learners (ELLs) and at-risk learners can tell stories successfully, which builds their confidence and self-esteem. Children and teachers can retell stories they have read or heard such as family stories, multicultural fables, fairy tales, and folktales (Galda, Sipe, Liang, & Cullian, 2013).

Think about It

How can multicultural storytelling be used to promote cultural understanding? For example, children can share their stories about different artifacts, relics, food items, and photographs that illustrate a cultural practice or event. A patchwork quilt made from clothing of family members could begin a discussion of Patricia Polacco's (2001) _The Keeping Quilt._

disabilities, benefit from this process because it facilitates their cognitive abilities when they are participating. The eclectic and interactive atmosphere appeals to all types of learners because storytelling uses their cognitive, emotional, and psychomotor skills (see Figure 2.4). Individual children use a variety of learning styles during their literacy development.

Children learn appropriate language usage in a creative and motivating way through storytelling. Reading skills, including speaking and listening, are demonstrated through student storytelling performance. As children are exposed to storytelling, they develop and apply literacy skills in meaningful ways that build their self-esteem and self-confidence.

2-5b Reading Environments

Storytelling strategies are enhanced through a colorful and comfortable reading environment. Having a colorful rug area that invites children to sit for story time encourages and excites young readers. Reading areas within your classroom are important. Teachers can create spaces with colorful pictures, interesting chairs (the chairs can be hand-painted with colorful designs), a variety of books, and inspirational props or objects. These areas invite children to actively engage in reading and discussion, which encourages independent reading behaviors.

A classroom management system called the "Daily 5" evolved from the Literacy CAFÉ (Boushey & Moser, 2006). This organization system is designed to give children

Apply & Reflect

Design a reading area for the classroom utilizing the concepts highlighted in this section. Sketch your floor plan to include seating areas, books, bookshelves, carpets, puppets, stuffed animals, and other items of your choice. Share your plan for an interactive reading area with a small group of peers.

1. Select a short, personal, and familiar story (relevant to students' lives).
2. Repeat key words and phrases and substitute students' names for characters.
3. Use sound effects, role playing (villains and heroes), and surprise endings.
4. Use flash cards and theatrics to help remember the key words, structure, and sequence of a story.
5. Tell stories with props (dramatic masks, hats, costumes) or puppets to promote self-esteem, interaction, and praise.

Figure 2.4
Storytelling Techniques for Early Learners

options when they finish their independent work. CAFÉ is an acronym for comprehension, accuracy, fluency, and expanding vocabulary. The "Daily 5" consists of literacy activities that children complete independently while their teacher works with another child or small groups for guided reading. The activities are:

1. Read to self;
2. Read to someone;
3. Listen to reading;
4. Work on writing; and
5. Word work.

For example, children can read independently in beanbag chairs or read aloud with a friend. Children can listen to recorded books in a study carousel. A writing center can be designed with creative materials such as a variety of papers, writing tools, and props to inspire independent writing. Other literacy centers can include games and activities to practice decoding, phonics, and vocabulary skills. The element of choice appeals to young readers and writers. Children are more engaged when they can decide which activities they are most interested in during independent work time.

2-5c The Power of Picture Books

Children are attracted to colorful visual imagery (see Photo 2.8). Before learning to recognize letters and words, children comprehend the meaning of pictures. Picture books are a powerful tool in early literacy and promote early and emergent language development. "Picture books are a marriage of literature and the fine arts in a unique literary form" (Kasten, Kristo, & McClure, 2005, p. 147).

Readers are attracted to bright, bold, colorful, and moving visual imagery. Often the illustrations are what attract children to read the book. Details in the illustrations may extend concepts and story lines apparent in the text. Age-appropriate text helps ensure successful

Photo 2.8 *Baby enjoying illustrations*

reading development, but books must excite and motivate young readers. Identifying with book characters and plot situations validates the readers' feelings and emotions. When children identify with characters and events in a story, they realize that their circumstances and feelings are not unique. Visual imagery enhances the recognition of letter, words, and sentences in text. Illustrations are bridges connecting action and images to text. The path to literacy success is embellished through the art in picture books.

2-5d Technology in Early Reading and Writing Instruction

Young children are drawn to technology in today's society. People smile when a young child plays "telephone" on a locked cell phone while waiting in the grocery store line or uses a digital camera to snap pictures of the world as they see it. Technology surrounds young children, and it is a very real part of their lives. The computer keyboard or an iPad invite small hands to push and prod, inviting a response in sound, color, and animation on the screen. Most early childhood software programs invite preschoolers to push any button on the keyboard or move the mouse in any direction to create a response on the screen.

As children gain an understanding of letters and sounds associated with letters/words, software programs lead them to correct answers. New programs for young children are constantly being developed, and keeping up with the latest technology is important for both teachers and parents. With the many types of handheld devices in our modern times, technology can be used anywhere at any time. There are a variety of applications for young children, but be cautious before handing a device to young children. Always supervise children who are using technology.

There are many free downloads for children of all ages and stages of reading and writing development. Television shows (for example, Nick Jr. and PBS Kids) have expanded into a vast online world where children can learn, with their favorite television characters, skills like letter/word recognition, image-to-word matching, and memorization of a sequence in a story line.

Northrop and Killeen (2013) have developed a framework for introducing apps using iPads with young children. Some of the recommended apps for teaching letter identification and phonics are iWriteWords, Little Matchups ABC, and ABC Pocket Phonics. The framework includes the following four steps: (1) Teach the targeted literacy skill without the app; (2) explain and model the app; (3) give guided practice with the app and the targeted literacy skill; and (4) provide independent practice with the app (Northrop & Killeen, 2013). Teachers should be careful to preview new apps before introducing them to young children.

The list and availability of technology-based programs that support reading and writing skills is endless, and new concepts and devices are being developed at a fast pace. Teachers and parents are responsible for keeping updated with changing technology and making decisions that are developmentally appropriate for the children.

Collaboration and inquiry dialogue augment early literacy development and guide readers toward deeper comprehension. Sharing stories about reading experiences builds a community of learners.

 CONSIDER THIS...

Consider how you can use technology in your daily literacy instruction. For example, how can social media be used to share different perspectives of characters and events during a book discussion?

2-6 Early Literacy Strategies and Practices

Classroom practice guidelines are keys in developing early reading instruction. In your classroom, you will discover the interests of each child and use this information to help promote early childhood language development through children's literature. Active engagement of your students is important and can be accomplished in many ways, including arts integration. Allow your students time to demonstrate their understanding through a variety of arts disciplines, including visual arts, music, creative movement, and drama. Together the children in your classroom will develop self-confidence in their reading and writing abilities through a variety of learning activities. Early literacy strategies include creating a caring environment to help children gain comprehension on their own.

Curriculum development and instruction for young children involve sensory and hands-on engagement activities. Children acquire learning on their own by building schema (organized data) into what they already know (Piaget, 1953). Vygotsky (1978)

Table 2.3

Literacy Strategies and Practices Supporting Early Literacy

Age Groups	Cognitive	Socioemotional
0–3	Colorful displays with shapes to encourage sensory experiences Picture books, cloth books, sound books, and texture books	Social interaction with other infants and toddlers Stuffed animals to cuddle and interact with when exploring colorful books
3–6	Classroom library organized and accessible Circle time and group interaction for literacy activities Interactive and electronic word play and letter/sound recognition games	Displays of work to celebrate achievement Music played to promote quiet reflection Special events to celebrate literacy development
6–9	Literacy centers designed to use technology, iPads, interactive games, and writing (character/story maps) Creating characters and performing the story dramatically	School gardens for caring for all living things Collaborative literacy centers that promote vocabulary and comprehension development Formal literacy awards ceremony

⌄ Professional Resource Download

promotes social interaction and connecting the known to the unknown. By providing an external caring environment that promotes internal awareness and comprehension, teachers facilitate constructivist learning activities, such as storytelling, dramatic play, bookmaking, and music (dancing, singing, and playing instruments) as shown in Table 2.3.

End-of-Chapter Study Aids

Summary

Early literacy is important because children are building their literacy foundations as a developmental process through the six language arts (reading, writing, speaking, listening, viewing, and visually representing). Children develop knowledge (through the cognitive aspect of self), a passion for reading and writing (the socioemotional aspect), and interactive play (the physical aspect) through effective literacy practices, as illustrated in our holistic model of literacy (HML). They learn literacy skills by expanding their prior knowledge and developing their speaking and listening vocabularies. Children develop their own understandings based upon their cultural and linguistic backgrounds, imagination, prior knowledge, and experiences.

Physical	Children's Books	Family Involvement
Manipulative toys such as rattles, mobiles, and squeaky toys in play areas Reading centers, dress-up areas, art/music/dance Finger plays and rhymes, songs with creative movement	*The Movable Mother Goose pop-up book* by Robert Sabuda (1999) *Max's Chocolate Chicken* by Rosemary Wells (1989)	Organize a play group with board books Use a cardboard box with a cutout window to perform a puppet show of nursery rhymes Read aloud daily all types of print while holding your child
Wooden blocks, puzzles, literacy centers that involve physical skills (magnetic letters) Library visits that include books for toddlers, dramatic activities, and dance	*My Brave Year of Firsts: Tries, Sighs, and High Fives* by Jamie Lee Curtis and Laura Cornell *Warthogs in the Kitchen: A Sloppy Counting Book* by Pamela Duncan Edwards (1998)	Organize a karaoke play group complete with props and costumes Make and decorate special reading hats, eyeglasses, T-shirts, or other items to wear during reading groups Go to the library for story time and special events
Group activities that connect listening, speaking, reading, and writing (word and story play) Art making centers (painting, sculpture, puppet making, dramatic role play)	*Bink & Gollie* by Kate DiCamillo & Alison McGhee (2010) *Wonderstruck* by Brian Selznick (2011)	Read chapter books at night before bed Fill a backpack with favorite books and writing materials for car rides Download e-books on technology devices so children can read anytime, anyplace

Family involvement and effective instructional strategies support language development and acquisition in the reading process. Language development is affected by issues such as family structure, cultural and linguistic diversity, sociocultural heritage, and physical abilities. Early literacy skills are developed through nurturing classrooms and home environments. Children are supported during the reading process to become fluent readers who use all four language cueing systems: graphophonic or phonological (visual), semantic (meaning), syntactic (structure), and pragmatic (prior knowledge). Storytelling and reading at home and at school provide practice with oral language. Interactive experiences such as visiting libraries, museums, or parks expose children to new environments that build knowledge and connections to the world. Parents and family members should take an active role in their children's literacy development through these activities. Caring adults (teachers and family members) who are engaged readers and writers provide invaluable role models for young children.

Chapter Exercises

1. Choose a picture book that is appropriate for a 4- or 5-year-old. Plan an integrated lesson with a partner that includes three of the six language arts: reading, writing, speaking, listening, viewing, and visually representing.
2. Design a lesson idea for teaching one of the following phonemic awareness skills to a kindergartner or first-grader: rhyming, blending, segmenting, or manipulating sounds in spoken words.
3. Select a nonfiction picture book on a topic of your choice. Introduce this book to a peer, using strategies described in the first stage of the reading process (prereading).

4. Using a familiar fairy tale, such as "Goldilocks," "Cinderella," or "Little Red Riding Hood," retell the story in small groups to the whole class, incorporating some of the storytelling techniques described in this chapter.

5. With a partner, study the illustrations in a Caldecott Medal winner or honor book. Discuss why you think the illustrator of this book won this prestigious award.

Teacher Toolbox

TEACHING WORD CHOICE THROUGH PICTURE BOOKS

Appropriate for Ages 6–9

Award-winning children's authors select specific words to create vivid images, using descriptive adjectives and strong verbs in their writing. This skill, included in the Common Core State Standards, is known as "author's craft," and the writing trait is called word choice. Selecting vocabulary to convey specific thoughts and ideas is an art that develops over time for experienced authors. For example, Newbery medalist Karen Hesse (1999) wrote about the comfort of a quenching rain on a hot summer day in her picture book, *Come On, Rain!* To introduce the book, children could dramatize what they would do if they were outside playing in the rain on a hot summer day. During the read-aloud, they can write down some of their favorite words on sticky notes or draw a sketch of how they feel as they are listening to the story. The teacher should stop several times during the reading to let the class talk about these words (in pairs) and to check for understanding. After retelling the story, the children's favorite words (that is, the strong verbs) can be posted on an anchor chart and discussed. The teacher and children can create sentences using the new vocabulary words. These words may be copied in writing notebooks as a resource for writing workshop.

Sample Words and Sentences

- Sprouted—The seed <u>sprouted</u> from the ground.
- Sizzling—The bacon was <u>sizzling</u> in the pan.
- Trickles—Sweat <u>trickles</u> down my cheek.
- Sway—Branches <u>sway</u> in the wind.
- Glisten—Raindrops <u>glisten</u> on the flower petals.
- Squealing—Children are <u>squealing</u> on the playground.
- Whooping—Sports fans were <u>whooping</u> and hollering during the game.

Key Terms and Concepts

alphabet knowledge	graphophonic cueing system	scientifically based reading
blending	key word approach	research
constructivism	language experience	segmenting
cross-check	approach	semantic cueing system
cuddle read	manipulating sounds	shared reading
dialects	phonemic awareness	shared writing
environmental print	pragmatic cueing system	syntactic cueing system
explicit instruction	receptive language	word choice
expressive language		

word choice Vocabulary a writer uses to convey specific thoughts and ideas.

Monkey Business Images/Shutterstock.com

STANDARDS ADDRESSED IN THIS CHAPTER

The standards from the following organizations will be used throughout the chapter: Common Core State Standards for English Language Arts, National Association for the Education of Young Children (NAEYC), and National Core Arts Standards. These standards are discussed further in the chapter as appropriate.

 COMMON CORE STATE STANDARDS

Common Core State Standards for English Language Arts

Anchor Standards for Reading

Reading Standards for Literature/Informational Text K–5
- Range of Reading and Level of Complexity

Anchor Standards for Writing
- Range of Writing

Anchor Standards for Speaking and Listening
- Comprehension and Collaboration

Anchor Standards for Language
- Knowledge of Language
- Vocabulary Acquisition and Use

naeyc

2010 NAEYC Standards for Initial and Advanced Early Childhood Professional Preparation Programs
- **Standard 3:** Observing, Documenting, and Assessing to Support Young Children and Families

NAEYC Early Childhood Program Standards and Accreditation Criteria
- **Standard 4:** Assessment of Child Progress

NCA

National Core Arts Standards (Dance, Media Arts, Music, Theater, Visual Arts)

Creating
- **Anchor Standard 3:** Refine and complete artistic work.

Presenting
- **Anchor Standard 4:** Select, analyze, and interpret artistic work for presentation.
- **Anchor Standard 5:** Develop and refine artistic techniques and work for presentation.

Responding
- **Anchor Standard 7:** Perceive and analyze artistic work.
- **Anchor Standard 9:** Apply criteria to evaluate artistic work.

Connecting
- **Anchor Standard 10:** Synthesize and relate knowledge and personal experiences to make art.

Literacy Assessment

3

Assessment must promote learning, not just measure it. — Regie Routman

Assessment is the process of gathering information on student performance for instructional decision making. The word *assessment* comes from the Latin word *assidere,* which means "to sit beside." Assessment involves the evaluation of children's achievement through observation and conferencing to provide feedback and set learning goals. Individual evaluation guides children through literacy assessment to become aware of their own strengths and abilities. Young children need constant guidance and support from teachers, parents, and peers through collaboration, conversation, and conferencing to accomplish literacy goals. Children learn self-monitoring of reading and writing skills through assessment practices such as conferencing, peer collaboration, and self-assessment (Clay, 1993).Through **systematic assessment** (a frequent preplanned assessment cycle), teachers help children to be aware of their own literacy skills, learning goals and areas for improvement. Documentation of children's work is collected over time to show progress in a variety of literacy areas (**portfolio assessment**). Children need guidance and *scaffolding* (connecting prior learning to new learning) to become independent and strategic readers and writers. Teachers are role models for literacy enthusiasm, reading and writing strategies, self-awareness, and self-assessment.

Critical thinking is also an important part of assessment, and benefits individual learners (Dewey, 1938). **Informal assessments** include observation, miscue analysis, checklists, and running records, administered frequently throughout the year (focuses on the learning process). **Formal assessments** include norm-referenced and criterion-referenced tests, mastery learning, and standardized testing, and are usually administered two or three times per year (focus on product or end result). **Formative assessments** occur frequently and document a child's learning process. **Summative assessments** are records of a child's mastery of specific skills (DeVries, 2011).

Educators must understand the individual needs of each child to plan effective literacy instruction. Continuous assessment is necessary because a child's strengths, needs, and perspectives change often throughout the early years. Teachers should build a respectful and trusting relationship with each child, so that the assessment process is natural and authentic. Positive feedback and sincere praise from the teacher and peers are essential to building the self-esteem of children.

LEARNING OBJECTIVES

After you have read this chapter, you should be able to:

3-1 Compare concepts of assessment.

3-2 Summarize the interactive assessment cycle.

3-3 Analyze authentic literacy assessment.

3-4 Explain readability and matching readers to text.

3-5 Interpret assessment of early literacy skills.

3-6 Apply literacy assessment strategies and practices.

STANDARDS CONNECTION TO THE VIGNETTE

NAEYC Early Childhood Program Standards and Accreditation Criteria

Standard 2: Curriculum

2.A.05 Curriculum goals and objectives guide teachers' ongoing assessment of children's progress.

2.A.06 The curriculum guides teachers to integrate assessment information with curriculum goals to support individualized learning.

Common Core State Standards for English Language Arts

Key Ideas and Details

Grade 2

1. Ask and answer such questions as who, what, where, why, and how to demonstrate understanding of key details in a text.

Text Types and Purposes

2. Write informative/explanatory texts in which they introduce a topic, use facts and definitions to develop points, and provide a concluding statement or section.

Giving immediate and interactive feedback to children in the early stages of writing helps establish confidence, support, and self-reliance. Children learn more when they can evaluate themselves. As they practice and understand the writing process, it becomes easier and less overwhelming.

assessment The process of gathering information on student performance for instructional decision making.

systematic assessment Teachers help children to be aware of their own literacy skills, goals, and needs through a frequent, preplanned assessment cycle.

portfolio assessment Planned continuous assessment that allows children to demonstrate their goals and skills in literacy development.

informal assessments Frequent assessments, such as observation, anecdotal records, criterion-referenced tests, and portfolio assessment, that are tied to instruction.

formal assessments Tests that systematically measure how well students have mastered learning outcomes, such as standardized testing, norm-referenced tests, and placement criteria.

formative assessments Assessments that occur frequently and document a child's learning process.

summative assessments Assessments are records of a child's mastery of specific skills.

After assessing writing samples and noting an overall misunderstanding by children in the class about how to organize a story, Mr. Miller decides to teach the narrative and expository writing process by using graphic organizers and drawing as prewriting activities. During the next classroom session, Mr. Miller discusses narrative writing and expository writing samples. The children create graphic designs, including cues that indicate the type of writing (narrative or expository).

Children begin to write a narrative story by graphing the story using a drawing of a "roller coaster," which is a simple line drawing of the "ups and downs" of the "roller coaster." (The Reading and Writing Project at Teachers College uses a similar idea called a "story mountain" to emphasize the story's climax.) Along the line, the children write notes to guide them when writing the story (see Photo 3.1). The children wrote their stories with ease after this visual emphasis of ideas. The children also used their drawings to help them self-assess their writing samples during the editing process to check for sequencing. For example, Joey wrote:

> I got in the house and shut the door. I walked in the backyard and saw my dog. My dog started to bark and play. I played ball with my dog. I love my dog.

When discussing his story with other children, he noticed that his sequence illustration included playing ball with the dog and then bringing the dog inside for a treat. Joey decided to add another sentence to his story to complete the sequence illustrated in his graphic organizer. Mr. Miller recognized that the revision process is strengthened by the prewriting exercises and incorporated this strategy into the assessment of his students' writing samples.

The children's writing could be assessed using the *K-8 Continuum for Assessing Narrative Writing,* available on the Teachers College Reading and Writing Project (TCRWP) website. The child's level of development can be determined as well as next steps for improving narrative writing. According to Lucy Calkins (1994), the point of the process is to teach to the writer, not the writing. Focusing on individual needs empowers children to become better writers.

Photo 3.1 *Journal writing*

Developmentally appropriate practice (DAP) is featured in the vignette and can be adapted for younger children (birth to age 6) and older children to age 9. Suggested adaptations include:

- Ages 0 to 3: Caring adults can read aloud *More, More, More Said the Baby: Three Love Stories* by Vera Williams (1997) to infants and toddlers to informally assess their interest and engagement. Under adult guidance, children can practice the beginning stages of writing, known as scribbling, using crayons, finger paints, markers, or chalk.
- Ages 3 to 6: Young children begin writing through drawing lines, shapes, and simple images. After listening to one of the books in Mo Willems's pigeon series, such as *Don't Let Pigeon Drive the Bus* (2003), the children draw a picture that reflects their understanding of the story.
- Ages 6 to 9: A mentor text, such as *If You Give a Dog a Donut* by Laura Numeroff (2011), can be used to assess cause and effect. After independently reading the story, children complete a graphic organizer of the story sequence. For example, children can write or illustrate events on a paper plate divided into eight pie shapes demonstrating the circular plot.

Classroom Connection

How can you use prewriting strategies such as graphic organizers in your writing workshop?

Photo 3.2 *A child exploring his community.*
Josh Weinberger

3-1 Concepts of Assessment

Assessment is an integral part of creative teaching and learning. Developmentally appropriate practices (DAP) are important parts of the assessment process. DAP involves understanding:

1. Child development;
2. The specific needs and strengths of a child; and
3. The cultural context (see Photo 3.2) in which the child lives. (National Association for the Education of Young Children and National Association of Early Childhood Specialists in State Departments of Education, 2003)

Teachers design curriculum and assessment responsive to DAP. For example, reading interests and attitude surveys provide information that teachers can use when planning units of study and building classroom libraries. Teachers learn about their students' development and cultural diversity through assessment practices such as teacher/parent interviews, conferencing, and home visitations/evaluations. Culturally relevant literature, based upon children's linguistic and cultural backgrounds, creates meaningful connections between school and home. Parents should be actively engaged in their children's assessment (DeVries, 2011).

Concepts of assessment related to Lev Vygotsky's (1978) theory of social constructivism implies that young children can collaboratively construct knowledge. Vygotsky promoted collaborative, social, and interactive learning influenced by culture and verbal reasoning (see Photo 3.3). He emphasized that learning occurs in the zone of proximal development (ZPD), where children progress to the next level of comprehension with assisted learning (peers and teachers). According to Vygotsky (1978), the ZPD is "the distance between the [child's] actual development as determined through problem solving and the level of potential development as determined through problem solving under adult guidance or in collaboration with more capable peers" (p. 86). For example, a child's instructional reading level is the range in which the child learns best (ZPD), usually situated between the child's independent reading level and his or her listening comprehension level (potential or capacity level) (Pinnell & Fountas, 2011).

Our approach to assessment for literacy includes three parts of self (cognitive, socioemotional, and physical) to fully understand the child's strengths and needs in all areas of growth and development. In Chapter 1 (Figure 1.2), we first introduced our holistic model of literacy (HML) consisting of the cognitive (yellow/mind), socioemotional (red/heart), and physical (blue/arms and legs) parts of self to promote creative thought and passion for literacy. Figure 3.1 shows an enhanced version of our HML illustration, where we added a light bulb to represent creative thought during the learning process.

The light bulb symbolizes the imaginative ideas that result in creative thought and action. Engagement begins with a challenged mind and a safe environment where imagination can flourish. Children are open to socioemotional aspects of learning experiences, and assessment is effective when children have secure and trusting relationships with others. The learning experience and assessment connect cognitive development with the socioemotional and physical development.

Photo 3.3
Social play and observation
Josh Weinberger

The National Council of Teachers of English (NCTE) and the International Reading Association (IRA), now known as the International Literacy Association (ILA), created the *Standards for the Assessment of Reading and Writing* (2010). These standards guide teachers while planning assessment. Standard 5 explains: "Assessment must recognize and reflect the intellectually and socially complex nature of reading and writing and the important roles of school, home, and society in literacy development" (NCTE & IRA, 2010). This assessment concept links directly to our HML by emphasizing the importance of cognitive and social engagement in children's reading and writing development.

3-1a Marie Clay's Early Literacy Assessment

Marie Clay, a significant theorist in the field of literacy and assessment, coined the term *emergent literacy* in her doctoral dissertation (1966), establishing a foundation for research-based assessment practices such as reading *running records* and *concepts about print* (Clay, 1993). Her Reading Recovery model, a short-term intervention of one-to-one tutoring for low-achieving first-grade readers, is well known throughout the world. Individual students receive a half hour of intensive tutoring daily from 12 to 20 weeks with a trained Reading Recovery teacher. The goal is for children to read independently on grade level. Clay developed the *Observation Survey of Early Literacy Achievement* (1993), which is a collection of emergent literacy informal assessments such as alphabet knowledge, concepts about print, reading running records, and sight words.

Clay's *Observation Survey* includes teachers assessing children's emergent literacy skills to evaluate their foundation for reading such as letter recognition and how print works in English (left to right, top to bottom, and front to back). Recognizing words, sentences, and spacing within text, and using picture clues, punctuation, and return sweep (how one line connects to the other) support the development of print concepts. Sight words are high-frequency words in beginning reading text such as *the, a, and, when,* and *why.* There are over 300 of these function words that appear in all beginning reading texts. These words have no meaning of their own and they cannot be decoded. Children learn to recognize these words instantly when reading text. Children are assessed on their recognition of these sight words by <u>periodic testing</u>. Reading running records are another informal assessment of a child's oral reading skills. For example, during small group guided reading, the teacher circulates to observe what the children are reading and records correctly read words, miscues (substitutions, insertions, omissions), and reading behaviors (self-correction, repetition). The purpose of these informal assessments is to determine the child's reading progress and strategies.

Student achievement must be effectively monitored in a variety of ways to provide a complete picture of a child's learning. Each teacher designs assessment plans according to the needs of each child. Assessment includes informal and formal testing.

 CONSIDER THIS...

Consider how sight words impact a child's early literacy skills. What strategies can you use to help a beginning reader learn sight words?

3-2 Interactive Assessment Cycle

Assessment is an integral part of any balanced literacy program that requires a continual inquiry process used by teachers to make informed instructional decisions (Glazer, 1998; Serafini, 2001). Effective teachers design instructional goals and objectives to coincide with their assessment plans. If assessments determine that students have not learned a particular

Figure 3.1
The Holistic Model of Literacy (HML) with Creative Thought (Light)

developmentally appropriate practices (DAP) Involves an understanding of child development, the specific strengths and needs of a child, and the cultural context in which the child lives.

return sweep A concept of print when a child understands that the end of one line of text connects to the beginning of the next line on a page.

miscue A response during oral reading that is different from the actual text.

reading behaviors Behaviors readers exhibit when they are reading orally, such as repetitions, self-corrections, and pauses that are not counted as reading errors.

Figure 3.2
Literacy Assessment Cycle

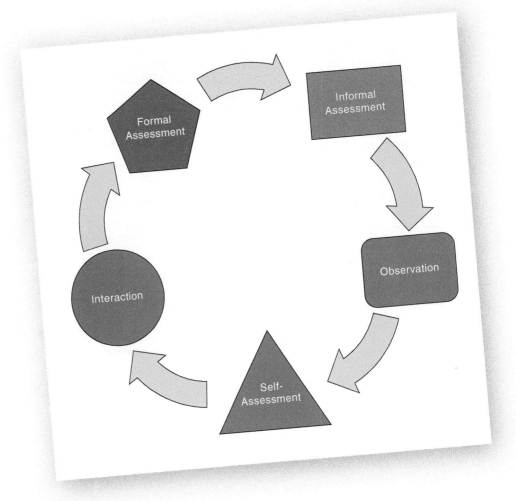

skill, the teacher must reteach the skill using a different approach or strategy. Assessing a child's strengths and needs in reading and writing is different from evaluation, which implies making a judgment on the quality of the work for a possible grade on a report card (Kasten, Kristo, & McClure, 2005). Children need to be able to self-assess their strengths and needs in the reading and writing process. Our assessment cycle (see Figure 3.2) includes a self-assessment stage to create independent, motivated, and strategic readers and writers.

Although there are many theories for the process of assessment, we recommend the following five-step process to be most effective in early childhood classrooms. Our interactive assessment process, as illustrated in Figure 3.2, involves:

1. Informal assessment of current knowledge and skills,
2. Observation (teacher),
3. Self-assessment (student),
4. Teacher-student-peer interaction (teacher scaffolding), and
5. Formal assessment to address literacy strengths and needs.

The informal (formative) process includes observation during the reading process and taking advantage of "teachable moments," and provides strategies for self-monitoring. When teacher-student-peer interaction occurs, a total picture of the child's reading ability is developed, and this leads to formal or summative assessment. Formal assessments systematically measure how well students have mastered learning outcomes. State or national standards guide formal assessment of individual literacy strengths and needs and/or the progress of the class in different skills areas, such as phonics and phonemic awareness, vocabulary, comprehension, and writing. The results of these formal assessments can be used to make adjustments in instruction, such as grouping children for guided reading. The assessment process is cyclical and continual.

Photo 3.4 *Engaged writers*

For example, a teacher who wants to assess a child's strengths and needs during oral reading may wish to *informally assess* the student's background knowledge of the topic (for example, birds) through observation. As a child reads the selection, the teacher *observes* reading behaviors and errors or miscues. The teacher praises the young reader for self-correcting and self-monitoring (*self-assessment*). After the reading, the teacher asks the child to do a retelling of the passage to check comprehension. This information is used to *formally assess* the child's reading strategies, strengths, and needs. This will help the teacher to determine if the student is reading material at the instructional level. Adjustments are made if necessary.

The interactive assessment process involves record keeping and organization. Whether using formal or informal assessment, the teacher is responsible for communicating learning results to the child and parent. Assessment is reflective of a child's holistic development (cognitive, socioemotional, and physical). Teachers are responsible for assessing each child daily (see Photo 3.4). For example, a child's portfolio may consist of progress reports, anecdotal records, his or her writing/artwork, photographs of actively engaged children, checklists, observation reports, emotional/physical reports, parent conference notes, and feedback from parents. Verbal and written communication with parents is especially important.

Educators need to utilize formal and informal assessment methods to evaluate their students as illustrated in Figure 3.2. Assessment is ongoing and tied to instruction. Teachers adapt their lessons according to individual needs based upon assessment. Assessment can be formal (diagnostic information, standardized tests, norm-referenced tests, and placement criteria) or informal (observation, anecdotal records, criterion-referenced tests, and portfolio assessment).

3-2a Informal Assessment

Informal ongoing assessment is an integral part of learning during early literacy development. Young children need various stimuli using all five senses to enhance their learning. Children engage in personal expression through the arts and literacy

STRATEGIES FOR ENGLISH LANGUAGE LEARNERS (ELLS)

ELLs often interact with classmates easily through gestures, smiles, and laughs (Ariza, Morales-Jones, Yahya, & Zainudden, 2010). Social interaction between children is supported by using cultural artworks, artifacts, dances, music, clothing, and food. Basic interpersonal skills are developed through opportunities to communicate not just through the written word but also through sensory-based experiences that allow children to explore new ideas.

Think about It

Celebrations (including special foods) are important to a child's cultural heritage. For example, you could eat tamales after reading the book *Too Many Tamales* by Gary Soto (1993) to provide a sensory-based experience. What other children's literature can connect with the cultural backgrounds of your students?

(storytelling, music, art, dance, and drama). Storytelling using costumes, masks, props, musical instruments, colorful patterned fabrics, and paper promotes creative interaction and expression. Creative interaction incorporates long-term memory effectiveness. Children need to interact, speak, listen, and express themselves to expand memory capacity, self-concept, self-esteem, and motivation. Promoting interaction through reading can involve multicultural children's literature, which promotes social relationship building and cultural connections. Listening to similarly themed folktales from various cultures expands children's understanding and respect of similar and different perspectives.

Teachers should consider a variety of genres to inspire children during reading, listening, and writing sessions. Informally evaluating reading, writing, and listening abilities of children involves using different types of assessments.

3-2b Observation

One form of observation (informal assessment) is called "kid watching," a naturalistic assessment technique promoted by Yetta Goodman and Gretchen Owocki (2002). They believed that kid watching is more authentic and valid than test scores for understanding and assessing learners' strengths and needs. There are two basic steps:

1. Observe students during daily literacy tasks; watch how they think and perform independently and with others.
2. Document how and where students are improving, and note areas of concern.

Examples of literacy tasks include the following:

- Writing development
- Miscues during oral reading
- Questioning/comprehension skills
- Reading fluency

- Oral language development
- Retelling skills
- Vocabulary knowledge (reading, writing)
- Decoding strategies for unknown words

Kid watching can be formal (preplanned, checklists, rating scales) or informal (unplanned, teachable moments). Observations, sometimes referred to as anecdotal records, may be recorded on sticky notes and later placed in students' folders. Notes are analyzed to determine patterns of learning development such as use of metacognitive strategies during oral reading.

kid watching A naturalistic assessment technique, based on observation.

3-2c Self-Assessment

Children recognize their own literacy development when interacting with others in daily activities such as reading and discussing books and illustrations. Parents and teachers assist in the self-assessment process by praising children with specific academic praise focusing on their strengths. This positive interaction promotes self-awareness and encourages repetition of successful literacy behaviors. Self-assessment allows children to be in control of the assessment process, which alleviates anxiety. Self-assessment can occur both formally and informally depending upon the children's strengths and needs.

Self-assessment begins informally at home with parents to promote confidence through engaging activities in varied environments. For example, learning through nature experiences, such as walks through the park and visits to the zoo, promotes sensory and perceptual development in young children and provides opportunities for parents and children to informally self-assess and discuss learning experiences. Self-awareness, self-identity, and the skills for self-assessment are promoted through cultural and social contexts. Social context includes activities with family members, peers, teachers, and other people in the community, such as a family visit to a cultural festival where children sample ethnic foods and observe traditional dances. Informally discussing what is learned through questioning before, during, and after the experience is an important part of the assessment process and leads to reflective self-assessment. An example of supporting self-assessment in a school setting could occur during a writing workshop where sitting in the author's chair (a special chair where writers sit to share their work in front of a group of peers) allows children to experience praise and positive feedback from classmates about written work. This recognition reinforces self-assessment and self-confidence in young writers while promoting literacy development. The young authors become more aware of their writing strengths through feedback from peers.

3-2d Interaction

Interaction in the classroom involves communication between teachers and students or peer to peer. Teachers interact with students every day, through guided reading groups, whole-class shared reading or read-alouds, teaching mini-lessons, or conferencing during reading or writing workshop. Students interact with each other daily through partner work, shared reading, buddy reading, discussions in literature circles, or *turn and talk* time during interactive read-alouds (see Photo 3.5).

Interactions may occur in the classroom environment or beyond through online chat rooms, social media such as Twitter, web-based resources, or on class-designed WIKI pages (Serafini & Youngs, 2013). First graders can become pen pals with other children in classrooms across their school district, nation, or in other countries around the world. For example, the *Blue Planet Writers Room* website sponsors a newsletter in which children from south Florida correspond with pen pals in Merida, Mexico, posting and sharing their creative writing and artwork online.

> Learning is a process that teachers and students engage in together. Both teachers and students must be able to answer and understand these questions: (1) Where am I going? (2) Where am I now? and (3) What do I need to do to move forward? (*Miller*, 2013, p. 361).

Establishing standards-based learning goals together on a regular basis during individual student-teacher conferences is essential. Specific teacher feedback, student self-reflection or assessment, appropriate scaffolding, and consistent documentation will allow students to be in control of their own learning. These components are important parts of the interactive assessment process.

3-2e Formal Assessment

Formal assessment can involve subjective or objective criteria for measurement, as well as standard and nonstandard testing. This stage in the assessment cycle may only be

specific academic praise This positive interaction promotes self-awareness and encourages repetition of successful literacy behaviors.

author's chair A special chair where writers sit to share their work in front of a group of peers.

Photo 3.5
Assessing comprehension through an interactive read-aloud

necessary once each grading period, or two to three times a year (beginning for screening, middle, and end), or near the end of the year for state-required tests. Standardized tests are administered by educators to measure student performance on a nationwide level. These norm-referenced tests compare one group of students to other students in the country who took the same test. Criterion-referenced tests are teacher-created assessments that measure student performance to determine learning mastery of specific content knowledge or skills (DeVries, 2011). Norm-referenced tests involve validity (Does the test measure what it is intended to measure?) and reliability (Are there consistent results over time?). The interpretation of test results can be used for many reasons; however, standardized tests generally compare test results to similar students who took the same tests throughout the school system, state, or nation. Standardized tests, such as end-of-year achievement tests, require students to pass minimum scores that can be used as diagnostic tools for placement in remedial programs.

✔ CONSIDER THIS...

Consider how a teacher can measure a student's work authentically and where to begin in the assessment cycle. For example, when you are assessing a child's vocabulary skills using a graded word list, you would begin in the informal stage of the assessment cycle. What would you do next, depending on the results of the assessment?

3-3 Authentic Literacy Assessment

Teachers need to evaluate students, as well as measure or assess their learning process using different methods or tools to procure students' understanding of facts or procedures. Assessment, quality teaching, and learning are seamlessly bound, as one is connected to the other to ensure achievement (authentic assessment). Evaluation involves judging or evaluating test results based on certain rules or rubrics (set criteria for measuring student learning) that determine a classroom value system that compares the amount of knowledge students have acquired. Student knowledge can be formally

standardized test Administered by educators to measure student performance on a nationwide level.

norm-referenced test Standardized assessments that involve validity (Does the test measure what it is intended to measure?) and reliability (Are there consistent results over time?).

criterion-referenced test Teacher-created assessments that measure student performance to determine learning mastery of specific content knowledge or skills.

authentic assessment Assessment, quality teaching and learning are seamlessly bound, as one is connected to the other to ensure achievement.

rubrics Set criteria for measuring student learning.

Table 3.1	*Sample Rubric*		
Criteria	Exceeds Expectations	Meets Expectations	Does Not Meet Expectations
Participation criteria (completing project, group collaboration, effort, and time)	All criteria are met	Most criteria are met	Little to none is met
Specific academic criteria (content driven, standards, benchmarks, and learning objectives)	Written criteria description to meet all criteria	Written criteria description to meet most of the criteria	Little to none of the criteria

and informally evaluated using a rubric or a means of standard measurement. When using subjective testing and assessment, such as essays and book reports, rubrics are necessary to provide an objective record and documentation of children's progress. Criteria are set and describe levels of mastery for specific learning objectives. A rubric is most important for subjective testing because students need to understand how they are being evaluated or measured for grades they have received. Rubrics are also used in objective testing because all assessments need to be valid, consistent, and reliable. Literacy assessment criteria are used as a communication tools for teachers, students, parents, and administrators. Table 3.1 is an example of a generic rubric for this purpose.

3-3a Assessment Criteria

In Figure 3.3, we focus on four criteria of effective assessment (authentic instruction, continuous over time, focused on strengths, and varied selection):

- To be authentic, assessment is embedded in the teaching and learning process.
- Continuous and ongoing assessment guides instruction and provides evaluative information for the teacher, child, and parents.
- Focusing on the strengths of each child accelerates literacy development and reading/writing motivation.
- Multilayered assessments that are performance based and developmentally appropriate provide a holistic view of the child's literacy progress.

Teachers need to develop individualized assessment plans based on these four criteria.

Assessment works best when the children collaborate with the teacher and peers. Effective assessment techniques empower children in their own learning and motivate them to become better readers and writers. Monitoring student progress through various assessments improves instruction and assists teachers when making adaptations for a child's success (see Photo 3.6). Teachers design instruction based upon standards, benchmarks, and learning goals. Preplanning what children should know (cognition and conceptual understanding) and how their knowledge will be demonstrated (physical and performance based) is the first step in authentic assessment. Focusing on children's strengths encourages learning and motivation. Assessment should support the emotional development of children and model how to identify success to promote future self-assessment and acquisition of deeper comprehension. Self-reflection and assessment are key components of authentic assessment. Children involved in the assessment process become responsible for their own learning and are motivated by their accomplishments.

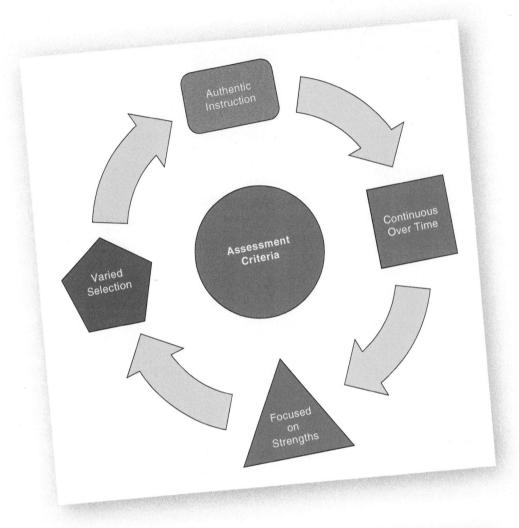

Figure 3.3
Criteria of Effective Assessment

Authentic Instruction

Continuous Over Time

Assessment Criteria

Varied Selection

Focused on Strengths

Photo 3.6
Informal assessment of reading

TEACHER MODELING DURING READING PRACTICE

Frey and Fisher (2010) discuss the importance of teacher modeling based on neuroscience research. The mirror neuron systems of a child are designed to imitate through listening and observing others. Their research focused on repetition that leads to automaticity, which is an important factor in reading fluency.

Think about It

How can you effectively model assessment practices to help children develop skills in self-assessment? For example, when a teacher explains her thought processes during a read-aloud, the children learn to model this reading behavior.

Frequent assessment throughout the year ensures that instruction is aligned with the literacy needs of students. Reading levels and abilities of young children may change drastically over a short period of time. Reading strengths and needs should be evaluated often through assessment tools such as reading running records, miscue analysis, informal reading inventories, and assessment of reading fluency.

3-3b Reading Running Records and Miscue Analysis

Running records offer a quick assessment of a child's oral reading (Clay, 1979). Marie Clay designed the running record to be administered frequently and quickly "on the run." A set of conventions is used to mark a reader's miscues on a form or blank sheet of paper. *Miscues* are responses that are different from what is in the text. Some miscues are significant (change the meaning) and others are not. The purpose of running records is to determine a reader's strategies, strengths, and needs, to confirm that the child is reading an appropriate text.

There are many different types of miscues: substitutions, insertions, omissions, mispronunciations, repetitions, self-corrections, pauses, and reversals. Substitutions, insertions, omissions, mispronunciations, and reversals are reading errors. Repetitions, self-corrections, and pauses are reading behaviors. During miscue analysis, substitution miscues are used to analyze a child's pattern of miscues. The word a child substitutes can be compared to the word in the text. The miscues are analyzed in terms of language cueing systems (MSV): M = meaning (semantic cueing system), S = structure (syntactic cueing system), and V = visual (graphophonic cueing system) (Clay, 1979). When a child makes a substitution miscue, does the word make sense (M), does it sound like English (S), or does it look similar to the word in the text (V)? Figure 3.4 shows a sample reading running record. The teacher read the first line and the child read the rest of the story. The young reader made two substitution miscues ("bug" for "tree" and "blue" for "black"). The first one makes sense and sounds like English so "M" and "S" are listed under the "error column" beside the line that contains the miscue. The second miscue makes sense, sounds like English, and is visually similar (beginning sound), so "M," "S," and "V" are listed. The word *yellow* is omitted in line 12, but cannot be analyzed so the error column is left blank. There are no self-corrections (SC column). Because there are three miscues and a total of 36 words in the passage, the accuracy rate is 92 percent (instructional level). It should also be noted that this running record was completed in September, during the beginning of the child's kindergarten year.

Level 2: I Can See

Name _____ Date 9/05 Gr. K Age 5

School Greenville Elem. Recorder Smith

Introduction:
Read the title and then say: *This story is about things you can see by a pond. Each is
a different color. I'll read the first page. Then you can read the rest.*

Word Count: 36

Circle Accuracy Rate:

%	100	99	98	97	96	95	94	93	92	91	90	89	88
Miscues	0			1			2		③			4	

Page	Level 2: I Can See	E E MSV	SC SC MSV
2	Teacher reads: I can see a blue pond.		
4	✓ ✓ ✓ ✓ I can see a green frog.		
6	✓ ✓ ✓ ✓ I can see a red flower.	l MS	
8	✓ ✓ ✓ ✓ bug I can see a brown tree.	l MSV	
10	✓ ✓ ✓ blue ✓ I can see a black bird.	l	
12	✓ ✓ ✓ (yellow) ✓ I can see a yellow sun...		
14	✓ ✓ ✓ ✓ And I can see a rainbow.		

3-3c Informal Reading Inventories

Another assessment to determine a student's reading level, strategies, strengths, and
needs is an informal reading inventory (IRI). The main difference between informal
reading inventories and running records is the purpose. IRIs are used for assessment
(several times a year), and running records are used during instruction (weekly or
monthly). Running records use previously read text while IRIs use unfamiliar text. IRIs
require teacher and student copies of the text; running records may be recorded quickly
on a blank sheet of paper ("on the run") (Clay, 1979).

An IRI is a collection of reading passages, from pre-primer through grade 8 or 12,
with word lists and comprehension questions. Examples of IRIs are the *Basic Reading
Inventory* by Johns (2012) and the *Qualitative Reading Inventory 5* (Leslie & Caldwell, 2010). Reading levels (independent, instructional, and frustration) are determined
through accuracy in word recognition and comprehension according to the percentages
shown in Table 3.2.

This process requires teacher judgment, so there are gray areas in the percentages required for accuracy in word recognition and comprehension. There are many
IRI forms because the same grade-level passage may be needed throughout the year
for assessing oral reading, silent reading, and listening comprehension. First a child
reads words from specific word lists that are progressively higher in reading level,
until he or she reaches frustration (7+ errors on a list of 20 words). Results of the
word list assessment determine the level in which the child will start orally reading

SELF-ASSESSMENT OF READING STRATEGIES FOR PRESERVICE TEACHERS TO DO WITH CHILDREN

Purpose: Identify language cues that the child uses when decoding unknown words.

Procedure: Teacher selects a book on the child's instructional reading level assessed through reading running records, such as *Kitten's First Full Moon* by Kevin Henkes (2004). The teacher and the child have their own copies of the book. A recording is made (video or audio) while the child reads to the teacher. The teacher uses sticky notes on the book pages to identify the child's significant miscues (where meaning is changed). The miscues are discussed with the child using the audio or video recording to analyze whether visual, meaning, or structure strategies were used. Good readers use all three types of cues to support decoding and word recognition.

Teaching Analysis: Reflective practices are a necessary part of the *literacy assessment cycle* and are key components in preservice preparation and certification, such as edTPA. Analyze the strengths and areas of improvement in this lesson idea. Answer the following:

- What is successful?
- What would you change to improve the lesson?
- What did you learn about teaching literacy?

Links: Making connections to technology and developmentally appropriate practices (DAP) supports lesson planning and literacy instruction. Adaptations of this lesson idea are provided through the following:

- **Technology Link:** Children record themselves reading a passage aloud on a tablet or other recording device.

Video recording the child during the reading session is another option. Children can also use e-books or interactive reading programs. Children can retell stories in their native languages using translation software such as Google Translate.

- **DAP Link:** Matching readers with appropriate text (independent and instructional levels) is a developmentally important practice.
- **Executive Function Link:** Creative play and active engagement during an interactive read-aloud develop children's self-regulation skills in social settings as reflected in the holistic model of literacy (cognitive, socioemotional, and physical).
- **Classroom Link:** Children (0 to 3) can listen to a caring adult reading *Kitten's First Full Moon*. The reading may be videotaped or audiotaped for listening enjoyment in the future. Sound effects, such as a kitten's meow, can be added to the recording.
- **Classroom Link:** Children (3 to 6) can choral read or echo read this story (or another story about cats or kittens) with a sibling, parent, teacher, or other caring adult. Practicing their oral reading will build fluency and knowledge of sight words.
- **Classroom Link:** Children (6 to 9) can listen to the recordings (videos) for fluency (rate and expression). These recordings over time create a portfolio to measure reading improvement. Reading materials (fiction or nonfiction) on a variety of topics can be used.

the IRI passage. Next, oral reading begins on a reading grade level that was determined to be easy for the student based on the word lists (or two grade levels below the child's current grade level for a struggling reader). As the child reads the passage, the teacher marks the child's miscues on a form. Afterward, the teacher asks questions to assess the child's reading comprehension. The questions vary in difficulty, from literal or factual to inferential and critical levels. The process is repeated until the child reaches frustration level (see Figure 3.5) in either word recognition (below 90 percent accuracy) or comprehension (50 percent or below).

Next, the student reads a passage on his or her instructional level silently using a different form (A, B, C, D . . .). There is a variety of passages for each grade level (forms), including narrative and expository text. This process confirms a reader's comprehension level. Finally, a passage on the reader's current grade level or above is read to the child to assess his or her listening comprehension (70 percent or above). The teacher asks questions following the reading. Again, the process continues until the child reaches frustration level (inability to answer comprehension questions about the text). Listening comprehension determines the child's capacity level or potential to read written selections. Analyzing the data includes identifying the child's instructional reading level (for both word recognition and comprehension), patterns of miscues, errors in vocabulary, and comprehension.

> ### Apply & Reflect
>
> Choose an appropriate passage from an informal reading inventory (IRI) based upon a child's instructional reading level. Allow the child to read the passage silently. Ask the comprehension questions to validate whether or not the correct instructional reading level for the child was selected.

Table 3.2 *Reading Levels*

Reading Level	Word Recognition	Comprehension
Independent	98 to 99%	90%
Instructional	90 to 95%	70%
Frustration	Below 90%	50%

3-3d Portfolio Assessment

Portfolios of student work are often used in informal and formal assessments and can document a child's learning over time for a variety of tasks. Portfolio assessment is a collection of artifacts documenting a child's progress in literacy development throughout the year. This interactive process is often informal in nature and includes work that features children's strengths, interests, and areas for improvement. Work samples in a portfolio may include drawings, writing samples, artwork, photographs of projects and children at work, checklists, graphic organizers, book reports, and audio recordings of the child's oral readings and discussion groups. For example, children collect several writing samples during the month and select their best work to be published in a class book. The portfolio assessment process includes critical analysis of work through teacher/student conferences to select representative samples of the child's growth and development. Children can use specific rubrics or guidelines to self-assess their portfolio samples. Teachers can use the portfolio process for diagnostic and formal assessment to determine whether a child has met certain benchmarks or expectations of learning.

Thomas Armstrong's (2009) five components of portfolio development guide the assessment process and provide a rationale and purpose for this approach. Armstrong describes the five components of portfolio development as follows:

- Celebration—to acknowledge and value a child's accomplishments
- Cognition—to encourage self-reflection and self-assessment
- Communication—to inform parents, teachers, and administrators of a child's growth and development

Figure 3.5
Sample Procedure for Administering an IRI

1. **Word Lists—Form A** Begin two grade levels below the child's current grade level. If the child is a beginning reader, start with the pre-primer list. Use the word lists until the child misses five or more words on a word list (instructional/frustration level).
2. **Oral Reading Passages—Form A** Begin on the grade level passage that was independent for the child on the word lists. Ask the child to read the passage orally as you record the miscues on the teacher's copy. Then ask the comprehension questions. Continue to the next grade level in Form A until the child reaches the instructional/frustration level in either word recognition or comprehension. Then determine the child's instructional reading level.
3. **Silent Reading Passages—Form B** Begin on the grade-level passage that was instructional for oral reading. Ask the child to read the passage silently and then ask the comprehension questions. This step is to validate the level of the child's comprehension.
4. **Listening Comprehension Passages—Form C** Begin one grade level above the child's instructional reading level in Form B. You will only need the teacher's copy. Read the passage to the child, telling him or her to listen carefully. Then ask the comprehension questions. The goal is to determine whether the passage is at the child's instructional level (70 percent or above) (Johns, 2012).

ASSESSING EARLY LITERACY BEHAVIORS THROUGH OBSERVATION

Each child's literacy journey is unique. Keeping individual records of every child's reading and writing development over time is important. An observational checklist can be used during guided reading groups to focus on specific skills for individual children. Reading groups change frequently as a result of continual assessment.

Record appropriate dates when the behavior is observed in the classroom. These behaviors may be observed during independent reading or guided reading groups.

Student: _____   Grade: _____

Teacher: _____   Date: _____

+ = Behavior Observed   **X** = Behavior Improving

0 = Behavior Not Observed

Assessment Guide for Observational Checklist of Early Literacy Behaviors

Directions: Observe individual children's literacy behaviors often to determine their progress, strengths, and needs.

Behaviors	Dates
1. Enjoys reading during free time	
2. Self-corrects miscues	
3. Knows many sight words	
4. Satisfactory fluency rate	
5. Uses invented spelling	
6. Finger points frequently when reading orally	
7. Uses phonics when decoding unknown words	
8. Uses all three cueing systems (MSV)	
9. Can retell a story with beginning, middle, and end	
10. Writes independently	

Adapted from DeVries (2011).

Think about It

When assessing young children, how can you assess frequently to represent growth? For example, an audio/video recording of the child retelling a familiar story could be completed several times over the course of the year.

⌄ Professional Resource Download

- Cooperation—to organize and promote understanding of collective group work
- Competency—to compare a child's performance with others based upon a rubric or other set of criteria or benchmark

Portfolio assessment is meaningful to children as an individualized active assessment process, empowering them to participate in their own learning. Children can celebrate their accomplishments and communicate their success during parent/teacher/student conferences. The portfolio process encourages self-reflection, communication, cooperation, and self-evaluation.

Table 3.3   *Self-Assessment Checklist for Narrative Writing*

Check for	Yes, I did this correctly!	No, I need to correct this in my writing
Each sentence begins with capitalization.		
Each sentence ends with punctuation.		
Spelling is correct.		
Handwriting is neat and easily read.		
Organization of writing includes a beginning, middle, and end.		
The writing sample includes a character(s), place, event, problem, and solution.		
Interesting and descriptive words are used.		

❯❯ Professional Resource Download

Writing assessments, a part of the writing workshop, are an important part of children's portfolios. The writing workshop (approximately 45 minutes per day) is a method of teaching writing using a workshop structure that includes reading aloud by the teacher, mini-lessons on writing strategies, independent writing with teacher-student conferences, guided writing sessions, and sharing sessions in small groups and with whole class. During the writing workshop, children are taught to read their writing aloud during the revision stage, listening for correct sentence structure, appropriate word choice, subject-verb agreement, and grammatical errors. Editing checklists are provided to help children edit their own work and the work of other children. Children can assess for grammar, punctuation, and handwriting as well as content and organization. Table 3.3 guides children (ages 6 to 9) through the revision process of narrative writing.

The ability to self-reflect and make decisions of what best represents learning is a valuable lifelong skill for students. The development of a classroom community supports meaningful learning and literacy development for all children.

In addition to checklists, rubrics and learning progressions are useful for assessing children's progress in their writing skills and development. Rubrics may be based on benchmarks according to grade levels or writing traits, such as word choice, voice, sentence fluency, organization, ideas, and conventions. A learning progression is a standards-based pathway that learners travel as they progress toward mastery of skills needed for college and career readiness (Calkins, Hohne, & Robb, 2015). For example, student writing samples can be compared to a selection of writing samples that meet expectations for each grade level at several points throughout the year. Learning progressions for writing skills, as well as checklists, rubrics, and performance assessments, can be found in *Writing Pathways: Performance Assessments and Learning Progressions* (Calkins, Hohne, & Robb, 2015). Performance assessments are "on demand" (timed writing) prompts used for collecting writing samples at specific times throughout the year. These assessments ensure consistency and validity of the writing

learning progression A standards-based pathway that learners travel as they progress toward mastery of skills.

performance assessment Timed writing prompts used for collecting writing samples at specific times throughout the year.

samples across classrooms and grade levels, which is necessary for application of the learning progressions. Assessments are included for narrative, informational, and persuasive (opinion) writing.

 CONSIDER THIS...

> Consider the many ways to assess children's progress in reading and writing through portfolio assessment. For example, children may select one item each month for a showcase portfolio that best represents their learning. Other work samples may include writing assignments, artwork, running records, or research reports. These work samples may be compared to the previous semester to show progression of learning. What informal assessments would you include in a portfolio for a second-grade student in the first semester of school?

3-4 Readability and Matching Readers to Text

Reading levels are determined according to the readability of the text. Readability depends upon the number of syllables in the words and the length or number of words in the sentences. Readability also depends on other factors such as the readers' interest in and knowledge of the topic and the content and format of the actual book. Rather than being labeled according to grade levels, some texts such as those on Scholastic's Reading Counts website, are categorized by lexile levels (reading levels). Lexile measures are based on two fairly reliable predictors of text difficulty, frequency of words and sentence length, and are determined from a reading test or program. Lexile levels are a good starting point, but all of the previously mentioned factors should be considered when selecting books for children.

The level of support provided during reading and a reader's motivation definitely affect the reading experience. Lexile levels are included for reader measures (students' reading levels) and text measures. Matching readers to appropriate texts is very important to their success, especially for struggling readers. It is essential to preview books and other reading materials before recommending them to students. The text must be age appropriate as well as grade-level appropriate. A reader's word recognition and comprehension skills help to determine the correct lexile level for instruction. Excellent readers may be able to read text that is above their maturity level, but teachers must consider the content of text to guide the selection process. On the other hand, older struggling readers should not be reading text that could be deemed *babyish* by their peers; instead these students should be reading high-interest, low-vocabulary text. Teachers utilize a variety of sources to create customized reading lists for students based on their interests and reading levels.

Fountas and Pinnell (2009) use a letter system for leveling books used in guided reading that corresponds to these lexile levels based on characteristics of the text (that is, genre, readability, vocabulary, concepts, figurative language, illustrations, and text features). In Table 3.4, this system is aligned with grade levels and lexile levels.

Teachers should assess reading fluency often to assure that students are reading on their instructional levels (lexile or guided reading).

In their *Continuum of Literacy Learning for Grades PreK–8*, Pinnell and Fountas (2011) have provided goals and benchmarks for each grade level in the following areas: interactive read-aloud and literature discussion; shared and performance reading; writing about reading; writing, oral, visual, and technological communication; phonics, spelling, and word study; and guided reading (Levels PreA-Z). This book is an invaluable resource for beginning teachers. The seven continua are based on the following principles:

- *Students learn by talking.*
- *Students need to process a large amount of written language.*

lexile levels Lexile measures (reading levels) are based on two fairly reliable predictors of text difficulty, frequency of words, and sentence length.

Table 3.4 — Readability Levels of Text

Grade	Lexile	Guided Reading
K	Beginning Reader	A, B, and C
K–1	100–400	D and E
1	100–400	F and G
1–2	100–400	H and I
2	300–600	J and K
2–3	300–600	L and M
3	500–600	N
3–4	500–600	O and P

Adapted from Fountas and Pinnell (2009).

GRADE CWPM

1. 60–90
2. 85–120
3. 115–140

Figure 3.6
Average Reading Rates

letter identification task One of the emergent literacy assessments in Marie Clay's *Observation Survey* (1993) that tests recognition of capitals and lowercase letters.

writing vocabulary task One of the assessments on Clay's *Observation Survey* (1993) when students are asked to write as many words as they can during a 10-minute period.

- *The ability to read and comprehend texts is expanded through talking and writing.*
- *Learning deepens when students engage in reading, talking, and writing about texts across many different instructional contexts.* (Pinnell & Fountas, 2011, p. 2)

3-4a Reading Fluency

Fluency is assessed through observation of the student's oral reading and timing his or her reading rate. Three factors in assessing fluency are accuracy (vocabulary), prosody (or expression), and reading rate. Reading rate is determined by the number of correct words per minute (CWPM). Time the reader for one minute; count the number of words in the passage, subtracting the number of miscues to determine the reading rate. Reading rate varies according to the reading level of the passage and whether the text is familiar or unfamiliar to the reader. Fluency rates should be assessed using passages on the student's instructional reading level. Reading rates for younger children are usually assessed using oral reading passages, whereas reading rates for older children are commonly assessed using silent reading passages. Figure 3.6 indicates the average reading rates (Harris & Sipay, 1990) as found in Allington (2006).

Reading rates vary according to type or genre of text, purpose for reading, and whether or not the text is familiar or unfamiliar to the reader. The average reading rates guide the teacher to match appropriate text to readers. Before children learn to read, teachers assess their emergent literacy skills, such as knowledge of letters and sounds, sight words, and print awareness.

Teachers assess children's strengths and needs to provide instruction, which supports foundational literacy skills.

 CONSIDER THIS...

Consider how you can incorporate nonfiction text (high-interest/low-vocabulary) with beginning readers. For example, how could you use the book *Wild Babies* by Seymour Simon (1998) to introduce text features?

3-5 Assessment of Early Literacy Skills

Marie Clay's *An Observation Survey of Early Literacy Achievement* (1993) is an effective tool for assessing beginning readers in the early stages of literacy (see Photo 3.7). Clay's subtests of observation tasks include running records, letter identification, writing vocabulary and word tests, hearing and recording sounds in words (dictation task), and concepts about print.

- *Running Records*: As explained earlier, a running record is literally an observation of a child's oral reading that is done "on the run" using a blank sheet of paper. Correct words are recorded as "ticks" or check marks, with miscues recorded using a series of conventions. The purpose is to determine if the child is reading on his or her instructional level. Strategies a child uses to read and decode unknown words are also noted. Typically, a teacher will complete a running record on each child during a guided reading group session, approximately once a week. Passages for the completion of the running record used for the observation survey are very short, usually at the pre-primer and primer levels.
- *Letter Identification*: The letter identification task tests both capital and lowercase letters. Children can respond with the name of the letter, the sound, or a word that begins with the letter.
- *Writing Vocabulary Task and Word Test*: During the writing vocabulary task, students are asked to write as many words as they can during a 10-minute period. Proper names also count. Each word counts as one point. Teachers must carefully observe to prevent students from copying words in the classroom. The word test is a list of 15 sight words (List A, List B, or List C).
- *Hearing and Recording Sounds in Words* (dictation task): The teacher reads a sentence for a child to write during the hearing and recording sounds in words task. As illustrated in Figure 3.7, each phoneme counts as one point (Clay, 1993).
- *Concepts about Print*: There is a script for the concepts about print test (CAP) that corresponds to one of Marie Clay's texts: *Sand, Stones,* or *Follow Me, Moon*. The books test a child's concepts about print or print awareness. The questions progress from easy to more difficult, including the concept that a book is read from front to back, left to right, and top to bottom. Other concepts in the 24 items are related to punctuation, sequence of letters in a word, sequence of words in a sentence, and a concept of a letter and words. Some of the pages of text and illustrations are upside-down.

In addition to the subtests on the *Observation Survey*, another important skill for emergent readers is *listening comprehension*. This skill can be tested individually using an *informal reading inventory*. The teacher should begin with the easiest passages

Photo 3.7
Searching for the perfect book

```
I  have  a  big  dog  at  home
1  234   5  678   9 10 11  12 13  14 15 16

T o d a y  I a m   g o i n g   to t a k e   h i m
17 18 19 20     21 22    23 24 25 26 27        28 29 30      31 32 33

t o      s c h oo l.
       34  35   36  37
```

Figure 3.7
Dictation Task as Adapted from Clay (1993)
Courtesy of the authors

(pre-primer), reading the passage to the child and asking comprehension questions afterward. The session should be continued until the child reaches frustration level to determine his or her instructional level (75 percent accuracy).

3-5a Creative Drawings in Early Literacy

For young children, drawing comes more naturally and at an earlier stage than formal writing. Therefore, it is important to validate and assess young children's drawings, because visually representing is one of the six language arts. Lowenfeld and Brittain (1987) carefully studied children's drawings and devised a general assessment guideline of specific drawing traits associated with age groups:

Figure 3.8
3-Year-Old Child's Self-Portrait

A 3-year-old child's self-portrait with dictated sentence ("Head, green, yes, go!")
Courtesy of the authors

- *Scribbling* begins once a child is able to pick up a drawing instrument (crayon, brush, marker, and so on) and makes marks on paper. Children ages 2 through 4 usually make random drawing of marks that are verbally described by the child as specific events and people. As children near age 4, they may depict people often with a group of scribbles that develop into a circle with marks for facial features (see Figure 3.8).
- The *preschematic* stage begins once a child begins to conceptualize forms into their drawings. Drawings look more realistic, but still hold a number of random scribbles that the child can easily explain (see Figure 3.9). Usually between ages 4 and 7, children begin formal schooling, and by working with other children with a range of drawing abilities, children begin to form schemas to represent their ideas. At this age, children are ready for formal writing, but still enjoy drawing the story and verbally explaining it to adults.
- The *schematic* stage ranges from age 7 to 9 and is often referred to as the "golden age" of children's art. At this age, children have developed a wide range of schemas that represent and communicate clearly to others the intent of their artwork. Children want to expressively demonstrate their ideas through the art and often still use imaginative colors and designs.

The creative process includes inventive methods or imaginative ideas that are placed together in novel ways to produce a new entity, or learning experience. A three-step process guides teachers to stimulate creativity in children: (1) *analyze* (organization of pieces or concepts), (2) *synthesize* (putting the pieces together in a new way), and (3) *criticize* (evaluate the effectiveness). Age-appropriate practices (ages 0 to 3, 3 to 6, and 6 to 9) are applied when listening to read-alouds, writing book reports, illustrating stories, or other written and oral assignments. The criticism process of description, analysis, interpretation, and evaluation holds true for creative endeavors of writing and art (Feldman, 1987).

✔ CONSIDER THIS...

Consider how children can visually represent their learning in assessment through drawing. For example, toddlers enjoy making random marks on paper (scribbling stage). How could you help a toddler learn to write his name?

Sticks and leaves...and the sky.
I saw this on the nature walk.
I Kinda like sticks and nature.
Blue in the sky.

Figure 3.9
4-Year-Old Child's Nature Journal Drawing

A 4-year-old child's nature journal drawing with dictated sentence using LEA ("Sticks and leaves . . . and the sky. I saw this on the nature walk. I kinda like sticks and nature. Blue in the sky.")
Courtesy of the authors

3-6 Literacy Assessment Strategies and Practices

Maria Montessori (1914) observed children and researched the assessment process in three age categories:

1. From 0 to 3 (interest in small objects, shapes, and placing them in order);
2. From 3 to 6 (social behavior and sensitivity to stimuli); and,
3. From 6 to 12 (working in groups, intellectual independence, and organization).

We have used similar age groups in this text for suggesting literacy strategies and practices (0 to 3, 3 to 6, and 6 to 9).

The literacy process involves intuition, imagination, problem solving, and critical thinking skills. Teachers should establish stimulating learning environments so that children can expand their imaginations and creativity. Integrating music, drama, interactive movement, and visual arts into literacy assessment allows children to demonstrate multiple ways of knowing, as illustrated in Table 3.5.

Apply & Reflect

Using the 3-year-old child's self-portrait (Figure 3.8) and the 4-year-old child's nature journal drawing (Figure 3.9), list the similarities and differences of each drawing and the dictated sentence. Next, analyze how each drawing compares to Lowenfeld's scribbling stage and preschematic stage of artistic development. Design a literacy activity to encourage each child's strengths using your assessment conclusions.

Table 3.5 *Literacy Assessment Strategies and Practices*

Age Groups	Cognitive	Socioemotional
0 to 3	Use a checklist to assess knowledge of shapes, colors, letters, and numbers. Take observational notes that identify concept of print (open the book, turn the page, point to an illustration). Video assessment of receptive and expressive language development during read-alouds (babbling, use of words and sentences).	Keep anecdotal records of child's play, both alone and with others. Note child's emotional expression during interactive play and read-alouds to assess engagement. Record observation notes that document book choices to support reading behaviors.
3 to 6	Sequence sentences in a story, words in a sentence, and letters into words. Use phonemic awareness assessment to analyze recognition of sounds in spoken words (blending, segmenting, rhyming). Assess using a rubrics with illustrations of beginning, middle, and end of a story. Use audio recording to assess main ideas and details in a retelling of text.	Record role-playing characters using facial expression, masks, or costumes and photographic documentation. Use attitude and interests surveys to assess child's reading interests and attitudes toward reading and writing. Read positive stories about learning to read, and assess child's attitude toward reading.
6 to 9	Document on a graphic organizer results of a debate on two sides of an issue. Assess persuasive writing using a rubric. Complete a self-assessment checklist of a personal narrative. Assess oral reading strategies with running records and miscue analysis. Administer an informal reading inventory to determine reading level and strengths in decoding and comprehension. Research a topic in science or social studies; write a summary of findings for assessment of informational writing.	Use Open Mind Portraits to assess knowledge of character development (draw a portrait of the main character and write about feelings and actions). Use reading logs to assess changes in reading interests and motivation over time. Use interest inventories to select novels for literature circles. Experience visual read-alouds describing the five senses to assess emotional response to illustrations.

❯❯ Professional Resource Download

End-of-Chapter Study Aids

Summary

Assessment is tied to instruction, based on state and/or national standards, in the early literacy classroom. Teachers assess frequently to adapt their literacy instruction and most effectively meet the needs of each child. In this chapter, we include a variety of informal and

Physical	Children's Books	Family Involvement
Use developmental checklist to document concepts about print.	*One Big Pair of Underwear* (counting book) by Laura Gehl and Tom Lichtenheld	Identify triggers for when the child exhibits the four major emotions: happy, sad, anger, and fearful, using a daily checklist.
Make observational notes to assess how children write letters with a variety of materials (crayons, pencils, markers, and chalk).	*Alphabet Book of Animals* by Deborah Bradley	Document concerns for cognitive, emotional, and physical needs through parental interviews and conferences.
Use observational checklist to assess receptive vocabulary (pointing to objects in picture books).	*In My World* by Lois Ehlert *Time for Bed* by Mem Fox *Gossie* by Olivier Dunrea *Max's Breakfast* by Rosemary Wells	Complete a parental survey to assess how often family members read aloud to babies and toddlers.
Use a pocket chart to assess sentence structure (cutting apart words in sentences; placing them in correct order with punctuation).	*How Rocket Learned to Read* by Tad Hills	Read with children daily (fiction/nonfiction text); ask questions before, during, and after reading to assess their comprehension.
Create an interactive Venn diagram using hula hoops and cards to compare two characters or stories.	*Funny Machines for George the Sheep: A Children's Book Inspired by Leonardo da Vinci* by Geraldine Elschner	Create word banks for unknown words; assess mastery.
Collect short poems to use as pocket poems; keep in a pocket or small envelope; pull out and read throughout the day to assess reading fluency.	*You Read to Me, I'll Read to You: Very Short Fairy Tales to Read Together* by Mary Ann Hoberman	Go to a public library at least once a week to check out books; read and discuss one story a week to assess child's oral language.
Draw and write on a full body tracing to explain character traits and actions.	*Won Ton: A Cat Tale Told in Haiku* by Lee Wardlaw	Establish a daily reading time for the family (turn off the TV); talk about what you are reading (books, magazines, newspapers).
Photographic documentation of a tableau that re-creates a scene.	*Sam and Dave Dig a Hole* by Mac Barnett	Play family word games such as Scrabble to assess vocabulary skills.
Video record and portfolio reader's theatre over time to assess reading fluency.	*Viva Frida* by Yuyi Morales	Make a scrapbook with photographs and captions for vacations or special events to assess sequencing and writing composition skills.
Align portfolio writing samples in a continuum to assess child's improvement in six writing traits using a rubric.	*The Noisy Paint Box: The Colors and Sounds of Kandinsky's Abstract Art* by Barb Rosenstock	Cook a favorite family recipe together; assess the child's ability to follow directions.
Write a letter to a friend or relative to assess spelling and sentence structure; address the envelope and mail the letter.	*Nana in the City* by Lauren Castillo	

formal assessments to evaluate children's knowledge and skills in reading and language arts. Informal assessments are introduced for analyzing children's literacy progress through cognitive, socioemotional, and physical contexts, which aligns with our holistic model of literacy (HML).

Our interactive assessment cycle incorporates formal, informal, and self-assessment with interaction and observation. Both formal and informal assessment tools are necessary to fully measure students' growth in literacy and progress over time. Ongoing, informal assessment and daily observations with feedback are key factors to obtain an authentic view of children's skills and abilities. Four criteria of effective assessment were identified (authentic instruction, continuous over time, focused on strengths, and varied selection). Lexile levels are used for reader measures (students' reading levels) and text measures. Matching readers to appropriate texts is key to literacy success. As assessment tools, observation tasks include running records, letter identification, writing vocabulary, hearing and recording sounds in words (dictation task), word tests, and concepts about print. Portfolio assessment (a collection of artifacts to document a child's learning progress over time) is useful in all subject areas.

A risk-free environment within a structured framework is important for the release of creativity and imagination during the assessment process to reinforce children's self-esteem, motivation, and confidence. A collaborative learning environment where each child's contributions are valued and measured is essential. Children prosper in a caring, literacy-rich learning environment. Allowing children the opportunity to respond to assessment tasks in multimodal ways, using their strengths and multiple intelligences (Gardner, 1991), provides authenticity and validation of the learning process.

Chapter Exercises

1. Observe a teacher administering a reading running record or watch a video online. Write a reflection of your experience and share your thoughts with a classmate.
2. Observe a preschool child "pretend" reading a book. Notice behaviors related to the child's concept of print (understanding that print goes from left to right, top to bottom, and front to back). Discuss your observations in class with a small group of peers.
3. Create a checklist for informational writing using the example for narrative writing in Table 3.3.
4. Arrange a set of four picture books (fiction or nonfiction) according to approximate reading levels from easy to most difficult. Confirm your rating by checking the lexile levels of the books online or using an app such as "Book Wizard." Notice the amount of print on a page, types of sentence structure, length and difficulty of vocabulary words, and text features when making your decisions.
5. Analyze a child's writing sample (provided by the instructor or found online) for strengths and needs according to an appropriate writing rubric.

Teacher Toolbox

ASSESSING THE WRITING TRAIT OF ORGANIZATION

Appropriate for Ages 6 to 7

Teaching the concept of sequencing informational text may be integrated into a literacy lesson on the writing trait of organization using the book, *Red-eyed Tree Frog* by Joy Cowley (1999). Children can find answers about the red-eyed tree frog's life in the rain forest through the question format of this book. Using the photographs in the book, the children select and research different rain forest creatures. They list interesting information or facts about the rain forest creatures. In pairs, the children organize the facts in a logical sequence using the book as a model (question/answer format). To check their work, the children use the following Organization Self-Assessment Guide, which helps them revise their writing. The children write questions and answers about the nighttime activities of the rain forest creatures. Each pair selects a photograph of the featured rain forest creature from online resources to illustrate their writing. Each pair shares their work with the whole class.

Organization Self-Assessment Guide

Text Sequence	Think about It	Revise It
Beginning	Did I grab the reader's attention? Does the setting make my writing come alive?	
Middle	Did I use interesting details? Are the details in the right order?	
End	Does my ending make sense? Did I finish my thoughts?	

Adapted from Culham (2008).

Key Terms and Concepts

assessment
authentic assessment
author's chair
criterion-referenced test
formal assessments
formative assessments
informal assessments
kid watching
letter identification task
learning progression
lexile levels
miscues
norm-referenced test
performance assessment
portfolio assessment
reading behaviors
return sweep
rubrics
specific academic praise
standardized test
summative assessment
systematic assessment
writing vocabulary task

Christopher Futcher/E+/Getty Images

STANDARDS ADDRESSED IN THIS CHAPTER

The standards from the following organizations will be used throughout the chapter: Common Core State Standards for English Language Arts, the National Association for the Education of Young Children (NAEYC), and National Core Arts Standards. These standards are discussed further in the chapter as appropriate.

COMMON CORE
STATE STANDARDS

Common Core State Standards for English Language Arts

Anchor Standards for Reading

Reading Standards for Literature and for Informational Text (K–5)

- Range of Reading and Level of Text Complexity

Reading Standards: Foundational Skills (K–5)

- Phonological Awareness
- Phonics and Word Recognition

Anchor Standards for Speaking and Listening

- Comprehension and Collaboration
- Presentation of Knowledge and Ideas

Anchor Standards for Language

- Vocabulary Acquisition and Use

naeyc

2010 NAEYC Standards for Initial and Advanced Early Childhood Professional Preparation Programs

- **Standard 1:** Promoting Child Development and Learning
- **Standard 5:** Using Content Knowledge to Build Meaningful Curriculum

NAEYC Early Childhood Program Standards and Accreditation Criteria

- **Standard 2:** Curriculum
- **Standard 3:** Teaching

NCA

National Core Arts Standards (Dance, Media Arts, Music, Theater, Visual Arts)

Creating

- **Anchor Standard 1:** Generate and conceptualize artistic ideas and work.

Presenting

- **Anchor Standard 4:** Select, analyze, and interpret artistic work for presentation.

Responding

- **Anchor Standard 7:** Perceive and analyze artistic work.

Connecting

- **Anchor Standard 10:** Synthesize and relate knowledge and personal experiences to make art.

Phonics and Word Identification

4

The limits of my language mean the limits of my world. — Ludwig Wittgenstein

Utilizing sound recognition to construct words and meaning is important in early literacy. Phonics is an awareness of letters and sounds in written words, skills that are useful because they help children decode unknown words. Phonics builds a foundation for young children to understand the rules of the English language by allowing them to use decoding strategies and increase their reading fluency. The development of language for young children begins at birth with sound recognition, environmental awareness, and social interaction. This chapter introduces different models for reading and writing instruction, such as top-down (meaning-based), bottom-up (code-based), and the comprehensive or interactive model.

Phonology is a branch of linguistics that encompasses the systematic organization of sounds. **Phonological awareness** is the ability to recognize and use units of sound in spoken words including syllables, onsets and rimes (DeVries, 2011). *Phonemic awareness* is an awareness of letters and sounds in spoken words, and a **phoneme** is the smallest unit of sound in a word. A **grapheme** is the visual representation of a sound (letter or letters).

Phonemic awareness is a precursor to phonics and an indicator of later success in reading (Adams, 1990). Children who do not understand the concept of rhyming, blending, and segmenting sounds in spoken words have difficulty comprehending phonics skills, such as consonant and vowel patterns. The phonemic awareness process begins with parents talking to infants and reading aloud. Once children recognize letters, sight words, and environmental print, their literacy skills progress rapidly. Children who have mastered letter recognition begin building words and creating meaningful sentences (Flint, 2008). The goal of phonics and word identification is to learn patterns of sounds in meaningful contexts (children's literature), practice decoding skills (games and activities), and apply these strategies in continuous text (new reading passages).

LEARNING OBJECTIVES

After you have read this chapter, you should be able to:

- **4-1** Compare reading models for literacy development.
- **4-2** Explain language development and word identification.
- **4-3** Describe effective environments for early literacy instruction.
- **4-4** Summarize foundational skills of early literacy.
- **4-5** Analyze phonics skills and instruction for beginning readers.
- **4-6** Apply literacy strategies and practices for phonics and word identification.

STANDARDS CONNECTION TO THE VIGNETTE

NAEYC Early Childhood Program Standards and Accreditation Criteria

Standard 2: Curriculum

2.E.06 Children are regularly provided multiple and varied opportunities to develop phonological awareness: a. children are encouraged to play with sounds of language, including syllables, word families, and phonemes, using rhymes, poems, songs, and finger plays; b. children are helped to identify letters and the sounds they represent; c. children are helped to recognize and produce words that have same beginning or ending sounds; and d. children's self-initiated efforts to write letters that represent the sounds of words are supported.

Common Core State Standards for English Language Arts

Foundational Skills

Second Grade

3. Know and apply grade-level phonics and word analysis in decoding words.

Teaching phonics and phonetic awareness is enhanced through songs and music. Children remember phonics patterns when playing games or through interactive play (see Photo 4.1). Focused phonics instruction should be systematic and explicit.

phonics An awareness of letters and sounds in written words.

phonology A branch of linguistics that encompasses the systematic organization of sounds.

phonological awareness Ability to recognize and use units of sound in spoken words including syllables, onsets, and rimes.

phoneme The smallest unit of sound in a word.

grapheme The visual representation of a sound (letter or letters).

Ms. Blake is a reading teacher specializing in teaching phonics and word identification to children in the first, second, and third grades. Most of the children in her class understand phonics rules and patterns, although a few children forget to apply them when reading continuous text. Ms. Blake reminds the children that when a word ends with the letter "e," the first vowel is usually long and the "e" is silent. The children brainstorm a list of words with a silent "e" and Ms. Blake writes them on the whiteboard: game, bone, plane, line, home, *and* cake. To practice the silent "e" words in context, Ms. Blake reads predictable books such as *If You Give a Cat a Cupcake* (2008) or *If You Give a Pig a Pancake* by Felicia Bond (1998), and asks the children to clap when they see or hear the words with silent "e." After reading, the children identify some of the silent "e" words in the text for Ms. Blake to write on the word wall.

Ms. Blake introduces a simple jingle to help the children remember the silent "e" rule. She begins to sing: "Twinkle, Twinkle silent "e," we see you but don't say /e/." The children repeat after her to memorize the phonics rule. Ms. Blake also uses flash cards for visual learners, highlighting the silent "e" in a different color from the rest of the letters. Once the children understand the rule, they are able to apply it later, during their guided reading groups.

Teaching skills in context (reading continuous text), as well as in isolation, promotes learning mastery through active engagement. Storytelling or using whiteboards with various colors to identify different phonic rules also help students apply their understanding. Young children enjoy participating in read-alouds, creating silly stories, playing games, drawing, singing, and other engaging activities.

Developmentally appropriate practice (DAP) is featured in the vignette and can be adapted for younger children (birth to age 6) and older children to age 9. Suggested adaptations include:

- *Ages 0 to 3:* Reading books to infants and toddlers and singing songs (for example, "Old McDonald," "Twinkle, Twinkle Little Star," and "The Wheels on the Bus") with rhyme, rhythm, and repetition will help to develop their phonemic awareness skills, an important precursor to phonics.
- *Ages 3 to 6:* Using books such as the ones in the vignette, focus on short vowel patterns (for example, *cat* and *pig*), rather than on the silent "e" rule. The generalization states that when there is one vowel

Photo 4.1 *Playing letter games*

in the middle of two consonants, it usually makes the short vowel sound: "a" as in *apple,* "e" as in *elephant,* "i" as in *insect,* "o" as in *octopus,* and "u" as in *umbrella.*

■ **Ages 6 to 9:** Older children can learn more difficult phonics rules such as, *r*-controlled vowels. The generalization states that when "r" follows a vowel, it usually changes its sound: "ar" as in *car,* "ur" as in *fur,* "or" as in *corn,* "ir" as in *girl,* and "er" as in *mother.* This rule can be practiced in context using informational books or magazine articles in *Sports Illustrated Kids* or *National Geographic Kids.*

Classroom Connection

Games are interactive and entertaining for young children. How can you teach a phonics lesson (on short vowels, for example) using a book appropriate for beginning readers?

4-1 Reading Models for Literacy Development

There are a variety of approaches for teaching children how to read, such as top-down and bottom-up reading models. Top-down reading models are meaning based, and bottom-up reading models are code based. According to Stahl (1992), exemplary phonics instruction includes concepts of print instruction as well as relating the written word to the spoken word. Children should have reading and writing experiences that include parts to whole (bottom-up reading model) and whole to parts (top-down reading model) instruction. The top-down reading model was sometimes called the whole-parts/whole-reading model (Goodman, Goodman, & Hood, 1988; Weaver, 2002). The emphasis

r-controlled vowel When the letter "r" follows a vowel, it changes the vowel sound.

top-down reading model A meaning-based approach to reading instruction.

bottom-up reading model A code-based approach to reading instruction.

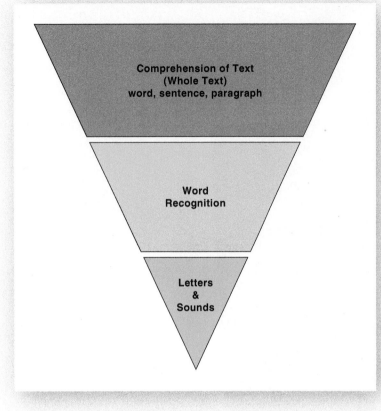

Figure 4.1
Top-Down Reading Model

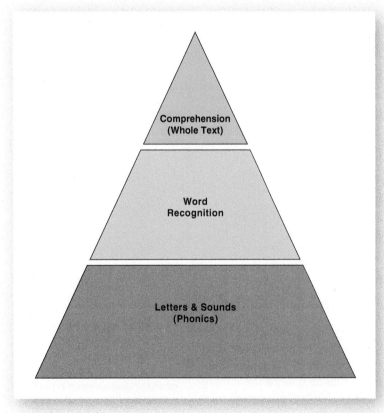

Figure 4.2
Bottom-Up Reading Model

was on using authentic text (children's literature) for reading instruction rather than basal readers (books that featured fiction and nonfiction passages on specific grade levels, based on a scope and sequence of skills). The focus was on comprehension rather than on explicit, systematic phonics instruction. Children were encouraged to learn to read by reading.

4-1a Top-Down Reading Model

Meaning is the foundation of the top-down reading model of literacy development, which comes from a constructivist perspective (Vygotsky, 1978). The teacher begins with the whole (story or passage) before specific skills instruction (vocabulary and phonics). The language experience approach (LEA) is one example of this theoretical model (Allen, 1964; Stauffer, 1970). LEA, which consists of dictated stories and word banks, originated in the 1950s when Sylvia Ashton-Warner used it to teach Maori children in New Zealand to read English (Ashton-Warner, 1963). Some researchers have shown that students are motivated and learn to read more easily if they are using their own words/language. The basic concepts that guide LEA are:

- I think about important things.
- I say important things about what I am thinking.
- I can write about what I say or a friend can write it for me.
- I can read what I write (or what has been written for me). (Allen, 1964)

Using this process of language experience, children are able to create meaningful sentences that weave into creative stories. The top-down reading model is illustrated in Figure 4.1.

4-1b Bottom-Up Reading Model

This parts-to-whole model begins with the parts (letters and sounds) and ends with comprehension of the whole text (story or passage), as shown in Figure 4.2. Letters are combined to make words, and words become sentences. Phonics skills and patterns are taught systematically and explicitly through direct instruction and scripted materials. The premise is that phonics should be taught early and kept simple, from kindergarten through second grade. There are two types of systematic phonics instruction, analytic phonics and synthetic phonics. Beginning with sight words, teachers guide children to identify patterns in words and apply phonics generalizations during analytic phonics instruction. In contrast, children learn how to blend sounds together to form words during synthetic phonics instruction (Devries, 2011).

The main issues with the bottom-up reading model are (1) the inconsistency of the phonics rules in the English language, and (2) that students recognize words and sound patterns from a list, but this knowledge is not always transferred when reading connected text. Comprehension is the goal of reading, and phonics is a necessary tool that children need to successfully read and decode unknown words.

One example of teaching letter identification and letter sounds (including meaning) to young children is to use students' names. Using children's names to explore and practice phonetics or phonics skills can enhance the identification of letters and their sounds. Learning how to write their names helps children identify sounds with letters because they know how to pronounce their names. A variety of names in the class provide many examples of letter sounds. Multicultural names possess uncommon phonemes that can assist young students in understanding sound differences and changes or exceptions to the rules. Many of the 44 phonemes in the English language (see Figure 4.3) can be taught through the spellings of students' names.

English language learners (ELLs) may have difficulty learning these phonemes because they are different from sounds in their native languages. For example, the short /i/ and short /u/ English vowel sounds are not found in Spanish. To make matters more difficult, Spanish vowels consist of /i/ = *keep*; /e/ = *make, vet*; /a/ = *cot*; /u/ = *you*; and /o/ = *sew* (Goldstein, 2011). Teachers must be aware of language differences when planning phonics lessons to meet the needs of ELLs in their classrooms.

4-1c Comprehensive Reading Model

The comprehensive or interactive reading model combines literature-based reading and process-writing instruction (Rasinski & Padak, 2001; Routman, 2002). There is an emphasis on meaning through the use of authentic text (narrative and informational), purposeful writing experiences, and systematic skills instruction that meets the needs of all children.

The comprehensive reading model integrates literacy throughout the curriculum, into content areas such as math, music, science, and visual arts, typically through the use of thematic units. This balanced literacy approach, featuring an equal importance on reading and writing (see Figure 4.4), incorporates a variety of strategies: reading workshop and writing workshop, guided reading and writing, shared reading, independent reading, journal writing, shared or interactive writing, partner reading, and read-alouds by the teacher.

 CONSIDER THIS...

Consider which reading model aligns with your teaching philosophy. Do you think the top-down reading model or the bottom-up reading model will work in your future classroom? Or would a blend of the two reading models (comprehensive reading model) work more effectively?

4-2 Language Development and Word Identification

Language development starts at birth and continues throughout one's lifetime; however, initial phonological and phonemic awareness (auditory awareness of sounds) starts with toddlers who are learning usage of their symbolic language with phonemes (smallest unit of sound in a word). Early words (*ma-ma* and *da-da*) consist of phonemes that

basal readers Textbooks that teach children how to read using controlled vocabulary and leveled passages to learn specific skills.

analytic phonics Beginning with sight words, teachers guide children to identify patterns in words and phonics generalizations.

synthetic phonics Children blend letters and sounds to form words.

Figure 4.3

The 44 Phonemes in the English Language

Consonant Phonemes:

PHONEME	EXAMPLES				
/b/	ball				
/d/	dog				
/f/	fall	graph			
/g/	goat				
/h/	hat				
/j/	joy	fudge	gym	large	
/k/	cake	quiet	pick	fix	Chris
/l/	lion				
/m/	man	lamb			
/n/	nice	knife	gnome		
/p/	pie				
/r/	rabbit	write			
/s/	see	house	rice		
/t/	toe				
/v/	van				
/w/	water				
/wh/	why (regional)				
/y/	you				
/z/	zoo	cheese	his		
/th/	the				
/th/	thick				
/ch/	chin	patch			
/sh/	she	miss	chef		
/zh/	pleasure				
/ng/	sing	think			

Vowel Phonemes:

/a/	cat	
/e/	egg	dead
/i/	dig	wanted
/o/	dog	want
/u/	slug	love
/ae/	rain	say
/ee/	sweet	seat
/ie/	tied	bright
/oe/	toad	low
/ue/	soon	blue
/oo/	book	should
/ar/	car	
/ur/	turn	girl
/or/	born	floor
/au/	caught	claw
/er/	mother	circle
/ow/	cow	mouth
/oi/	join	boy
/air/	fair	bear	care
/ear/	gear	cheer	here

The red letters represent the different sounds of the phonemes.

are blended together to form syllables. Children recognize that words have individual sounds that can be manipulated to create new words like *bat* or *mat*. Phonemic awareness skills include rhyming, blending, segmenting, and manipulating sounds in spoken words, which are essential components of learning how to read (see Photo 4.2).

Children learning to read utilize this decoding process to learn how to sound the full word after it is broken up into smaller sounds or syllables. They blend the sounds together to form words and then these words become sentences. Literacy in early childhood is dependent on the child's ability to sound out a word into its smallest denomination (phonemes) and then putting individual sounds together to form words. Literacy-rich home environments, where children experience listening and reading activities with their parents or caretakers, build a strong foundation of emergent literacy skills.

As children are learning new words, they process and encode them, putting them into long-term memory. The information comes through the senses. Often it takes multiple times of seeing a new word before a child can easily retrieve it from long-term memory. Children learn better when they relate unfamiliar words with known words. These unfamiliar words can then be retrieved later when they read the words again. As readers practice decoding words, the reading process becomes more fluent. Children are able to read with expression, which indicates comprehension. Human connection and social interaction facilitate this process (see Photo 4.3).

This association process is a basis for learning new concepts and new skills. This approach is called <u>teaching by analogy</u>; for example, if a child knows the word *dog*, she can learn the word *frog* through onset and rime and spelling patterns. There are 37 common rimes that are sometimes called <u>phonograms or word families.</u> (The onset is the part of the word before the vowel and the rime is the part of the word from the vowel onward.) More than 500 words can be made from these 37 rimes listed in Figure 4.5 (Adams, 1990).

To practice these words in context, children can write poems with the rhyming words or sentences in their writing notebooks. The words may be written on small index

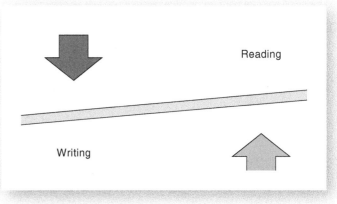

Figure 4.4
Comprehensive Reading Model

onset The beginning part of the word before the first vowel.

rime The part of the word that comes after the vowel (also called a phonogram).

Photo 4.2 *Family reading together*
Josh Weinberger

Photo 4.3 *Teacher and child reading together*

BRAIN BRIDGES

Currently it is believed that two major areas of the brain play a part in speech and language: (1) Wernicke's area (naming objects or syntax and word meaning or recognition), and (2) Broca's area (grammatical processing and picture of words or appropriate usage) (Woolfolk, 2011). The bridge connecting the two major parts of the brain is called the corpus callosum, which is constantly sending impulses back and forth especially when learning to read and write. The motor part of the cortex helps create muscle coordination for speech, eye muscles for word recognition, and handwriting muscles (Woolfolk, 2011).

Think about It

How can teachers help children build their vocabulary and oral language? When children are learning to read, effective learning activities involve rhyme, rhythm, and repetition. For example, singing songs, storytelling, and reciting poetry reinforce word identification and recognition skills in engaging ways.

-ack	-ail	-ain	-ake
-ale	-ame	-an	-ank
-ap	-ash	-at	-ate
-aw	-ay	-eat	-ell
-est	-ice	-ick	-ide
-ight	-ill	-in	-ine
-ing	-ink	-ip	-it
-ir	-ock	-oke	-op
-or	-ore	-uck	-ug
-ump			

Figure 4.5
37 Common Rimes

Apply & Reflect

Collaborate with a group of peers to design a phonics game based upon a selected skill (blends, diphthongs, digraphs, rimes, silent "e," or *r*-controlled vowels). Share your group's game with the whole class.

cards and attached with a curtain ring (flash cards) for reading practice with a partner. Teachers may wish to begin with short vowel patterns and then introduce long vowel patterns, depending on the individual needs of their students. Children can also manipulate letter tiles or magnetic letters to create new words by substituting one initial consonant for another (changing the "b" in *back* to an "s" to make *sack*).

Word study (phonics, spelling, and vocabulary instruction) supports children's understanding of the concept of word and alphabetical identification (Cunningham, 2012; Cunningham & Allington, 2015). Children practice word study to enhance what they know about the written word, letter formation, sound segments within words (word within a word), meaning, and letter sounds. This approach uses the child's ability to compare and contrast words by meaning and sound.

Reading and rereading familiar books helps children improve their word recognition, fluency, and phonics skills. Children become comfortable with the word/sound relationships as they encounter specific words in continuous text. Reading predictable text (or patterned text) like *Brown Bear, Brown Bear* by Bill Martin Jr. (1992) helps children learn sight words (high-frequency words) because of the rhyme, rhythm, and repetition.

 CONSIDER THIS...

Consider how you can teach different rimes (phonograms or word families) (see Figure 4.5) using beginning readers (books with repetition and predictable text). Read a rhyming book such as *The Cat in the Hat* by Dr. Seuss (1957), and ask the children to list words that end with rimes on sticky notes to post on the class word wall.

4-3 Effective Environments for Early Literacy Instruction

Setting up a print-rich environment for literacy instruction is essential for young learners. A classroom for active engagement has a library overflowing with all kinds of books (multiple genres and reading levels), reflecting the interests and cultures of the children.

	Table 4.1	Adaptation of Cambourne's Conditions of Learning

Conditions of Learning	Holistic Model of Literacy Connection
Immersion	Print-rich environments consist of classroom libraries that contain literature such as books, magazines, and comics on a variety of genres, topics, and reading levels based upon children's interests. Read-alouds and literature circles inspire a passion and motivation for reading.
Demonstration	Children observe while teachers model skills, strategies, and behaviors. Next, the students practice while the teacher observes and facilitates their learning. Knowledge is demonstrated through the arts (for example, dance, drama, and singing).
Engagement	Discussion groups, class conversations, creating artwork, performing plays, and dances with music, and guided or shared reading and writing experiences are examples of active engagement.
Expectation	Teachers believe that all children can learn, and have high expectations to promote self-confidence and self-esteem, while providing a safe, risk-free learning environment.
Responsibility	Children use creative problem-solving and decision-making strategies throughout the learning process. Children learn how to be responsible and caring citizens in school, at home, and in the community.
Use	Children practice new learning in meaningful ways with real-world applications, taking action to initiate change in the learning environment.
Approximation	Children must be free to take risks and express new ideas for learning to occur, such as journal writing and creative illustrations.
Response	Children are given relevant and appropriate feedback when demonstrating their learning. For example, children respond using multimodal forms of expression (the visual and performing arts).

The walls are covered with colorful pictures and print related to current units of study or samples of student work. There is usually a rug area where children congregate for stories or mini-lessons, and desks or small tables that allow for flexible grouping. Learning stations with activities for independent practice in language arts and the content areas may line the walls. Brian Cambourne (1988) developed principles for establishing effective learning environments while observing the language development of young children (Rushton, Eitelgeorge, & Zickafoose, 2003), which resulted in eight conditions of learning. Cambourne theorized that young children learn and comprehend by interacting with the world around them. John Dewey (1938) and Lev Vygotsky (1978) influenced Cambourne's research, which is based on the work of early constructivists. Cambourne's conditions of learning are adapted to reflect cognitive, socioemotional, and physical aspects of learning from our holistic model of literacy (HML).

When these eight conditions are present, the teacher creates an open and safe environment for children to express their ideas, creativity, imagination, and increase their motivation to learn. Five examples of Cambourne's conditions of learning follow: immersion, responsibility, use, engagement, and approximation.

4-3a Environmental Print Immersion

Immersion in print-rich environments supports early literacy learning and promotes real-world connections (see Table 4.1). Throughout the day, children are encouraged to notice print in their everyday lives. Children can collect and cut out words from labels, packaging, mail, newspapers, and magazines. Individual or group collages can be created using these cut-outs and displayed in the classroom. Children walk around the classroom and "read the room" (oral language development). During this activity, they write favorite words, adding to the class word wall.

ar	or	ir
car	for	girl
large	short	bird
garden	cord	shirt

Figure 4.6
Sample Word Sort

4-3b Responsibility: Taking Care of the Earth

Children must learn to be responsible citizens of society, in charge of their own learning. For example, after reading _The Earth Book_ by Todd Parr (2010), the teacher and students create a list of ideas for protecting the environment. _Responsibility_ is taught through taking action, problem solving, and critical thinking. _Use_ is practiced when children apply a plan of action based upon the "10 Ways I Can Help the Earth" from Todd Parr's book. For example, the class can recycle, plant a tree, or grow a garden at home or school. Children may add to the list, explaining their own recycling ideas, such as making sculpture using reusable materials.

Key words from the book can be used for a word sort activity (Bear, Invernizzi, Templeton, & Johnston, 2015). First, the children list words such as _bath_, _trash_, _fish_, _bus_, _glass_, _green_, _ocean_, _trees_, _bike_, and _teeth_. Sorting these words into two categories, such as long and short vowels, is a phonics connection. Multiple consonant and vowel patterns can be taught using word sorts (see Figure 4.6).

Photo 4.4
Emergent writing

4-3c Engagement and Approximation with Writing

Engagement means that students are active participants in the learning process (see Photo 4.4). Engagement is an important component of literacy instruction because of its connection to reading achievement (Ivey & Johnston, 2013). One example is engagement in discussion groups and class conversations about a story such as _A Ball for Daisy_ by Chris Raschka (2011), a wordless picture book that helps children to verbalize the story line using illustrations. A picture walk through the book encourages questions and comments about characters and events. "Reading" the illustrations in wordless picture books through visual storytelling engages English language learners, and enhances their language development (Louie & Sierschynski, 2015).

Approximation occurs when children write their own versions of the story using invented or phonetic spelling. They create illustrations to complement their writing. Children can participate in sitting in an "author's chair," when they share their work with the class. Family letter writing is another outlet for authentic writing (see Figure 4.7). This is a meaningful and motivating opportunity for practicing emerging phonics skills. Kathyrn Pole (2015) designed a letter-writing project between her kindergarten students and extended family members to enhance the children's literacy development and strengthen intergenerational bonds. She began by reading picture books about characters who write letters, like *Dear Mrs. LaRue: Letters from Obedience School* by Mark Teague (2002) and *Dear Mr. Blueberry* by Simon James (1991). By the end of the yearlong project, Pole discovered that her students' writing demonstrated improved spelling and handwriting. Their letters contained multiple themes and longer thought patterns. Best of all, family connections between the children and their out-of-town relatives, as well as between the home and school, were strengthened through frequent communication and real-life experiences. Process writing (prewriting, writing, revising, editing, and publishing) is a vital component of the early literacy curriculum (Reutzel, 2015).

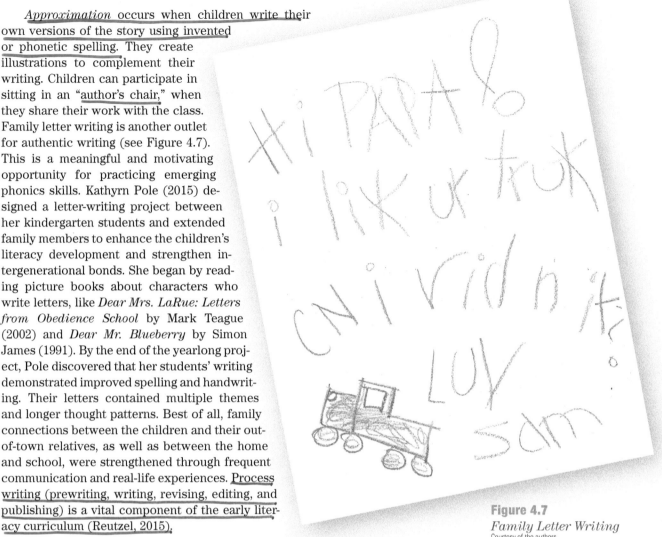

Figure 4.7
Family Letter Writing
Courtesy of the authors

✔ **CONSIDER THIS...**

Consider how you can incorporate role-playing to demonstrate decision-making or problem-solving strategies in the classroom. For example, when reading a chapter in a novel or short story, children can role-play solutions to a conflict in the story. What other activities support independent thinking in the classroom?

4-4 Foundational Skills of Early Literacy

Letter knowledge, sight words, print awareness, and phonemic awareness are building blocks of early literacy. Letter knowledge includes both letter and sound recognition. Sight words are high-frequency words that must be recognized instantly, rather than sounded out. The memorization and recognition of sight words aids in reading development. Sight words are clearly an important key to reading and comprehension success. Concepts about print depict knowledge of print awareness and an understanding of how print works. For example, an English book is read from left to right, top to bottom, and front to back. Phonemic awareness is an awareness of letters and sounds in spoken words, while phonics is an awareness of the written word. Figure 4.8 summarizes these building blocks of early literacy.

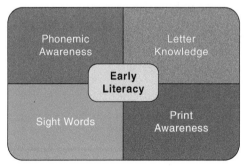

Phonemic Awareness	Letter Knowledge
	Early Literacy
Sight Words	Print Awareness

Figure 4.8
Building Blocks of Early Literacy

MAKING WORDS ACTIVITY FOR PRESERVICE TEACHERS TO DO WITH CHILDREN

Purpose: Practice phonics skills by making words with different consonant and vowel sounds.

Procedure: Children discuss the cover illustration of *Hattie and the Fox* by Mem Fox (1986) and predict what the story is about. The teacher writes a list of words shared by the children, such as *chicken* and *hen*. The teacher reads the story aloud using a big book (large format version). The names of the animal characters in the story are identified and added to the word list. Children or small groups are assigned specific characters for a dramatization of the story (reader's theater). The children read each character's part, while the teacher narrates the story. For example, the child performing the character of the goose expressively says, "Good grief!" After the performance, the teacher uses the making words strategy to teach phonics patterns. For example, the children write the word *pig* and change the first letter "p" to a "d" to make *dig*. Next, they change the vowel to "o" to make *dog*. Then the children change the last letter from "g" to "t" and create *dot*.

Teaching Analysis: Reflective practices are a necessary part of the *literacy assessment cycle,* and are key components in preservice preparation and certification such as edTPA. Analyze the strengths and areas of improvement in this lesson idea. Answer the following:

- What is successful?
- What would you change to improve the lesson?
- What did you learn about teaching literacy?

Links: Making connections to technology and developmentally appropriate practices (DAP) supports lesson planning and literacy instruction. Adaptations of this lesson idea are provided through the following:

- **Technology Link:** Children video-record themselves during the reader's theater for the classroom listening library.
- **DAP Link:** Age-appropriate arts integration strategies are used in the dramatization of the story. Children can create masks of each character to use in the performance.
- **Executive Function Link:** Creative play and active engagement during an interactive read-aloud develop children's self-regulation skills in social settings as reflected in the holistic model of literacy (cognitive, socioemotional, and physical).
- **Classroom Link:** Children (0 to 3) are attracted to colorful illustrations during the teacher read-aloud. Toddlers can repeat words from the story, such as *pig, cow,* and *hen*. They can make animal noises to extend the text.
- **Classroom Link:** Children (3 to 6) can match the words to pictures. Older children can write new words by changing the initial, middle, or final letters of a word.
- **Classroom Link:** Children (6 to 9) can make new words from the letters in a single word. For example, the letters of the word *chicken* are written separately on cards and given to children in random order. Children arrange the letter cards to make as many new words as they can during a 10-minute time period. The children try to guess the original "mystery" word (Cunningham & Hall, 1994).

This cyclical process, where each concept works individually and collaboratively, develops early literacy. As children gain expertise in sight words, letter knowledge, print awareness, and phonemic awareness, their literacy skills improve dramatically. This occurs quickly in young children, and the adults in the children's lives are the facilitators for this process.

4-4a Letter Knowledge

Young children need to understand the alphabetic principle, that letters represent sounds. They must learn to recognize the 26 letters in the English alphabet, both capitals and lowercase, as well as the individual consonant and vowel sounds. Children can learn a key word for each sound, using short sounds for the vowels. When learning to read, children learn letters in their name and how to write them correctly. Alphabet books inspire children of all ages to visualize images related to a variety of topics and

Photo 4.5
Fishing for phonics

themes, which connect to letter knowledge and word identification. Some examples of alphabet books for children include:

- *Once Upon an Alphabet: Short Stories for All the Letters* by Oliver Jeffers (2014);
- *The Turn-Around, Upside-Down Alphabet Book* by Lisa Campbell Ernst (2004);
- *Alphabet Adventure* by Audrey Wood and Bruce Wood (2001); and
- *An A to Z Walk in the Park* by R. M. Smith (2008).

Teaching phonics skills sequentially in order of difficulty, such as consonant sounds, blends, and short/long vowel patterns is an important process (see Photo 4.5).

4-4b Sight Words

Sight words, or words that appear frequently in beginning reading books, are also called high-frequency or instant words (Flint, 2008). These words must be memorized because they cannot usually be decoded. There are 220 high-frequency words (also known as Dolch words) that are important for students to learn by the end of third grade. These utility words typically have no meaning of their own, such as *a, and*, and *the* (the most frequent word in the English language). Playing games and reading predictable books help children build their sight vocabularies.

For example, children create sight word cards using different textures, such as fabric, sandpaper, clay, sticks, colored liquid glue (dried on cards), paint (finger paint or with brush), and sidewalk chalk (to create a sensory experience). Texture cards can be bound with yarn, curtain rings, or placed in a small container, creating individual word banks. Sight words are practiced independently or with a partner by tracing letters through the sense of touch. Children need to see these sight words over and

PICTURE SORTS AND WORD SORTS FOR ENGLISH LANGUAGE LEARNERS (ELLs)

Young children enjoy games that involve phonics and basic reading skills. Teacher-made or predesigned materials, such as flash cards and vocabulary cards with illustrations, work well with young children. Children sort pictures according to initial sounds, naming the objects featured on the cards. Next, children sort word cards into different categories based on specific consonant and vowel patterns.

Think about It

How can picture sorts and word sorts be used to encourage ELLs? For example, children can share cultural books, objects, or photographs and name these items in English.

over again to remember and apply when reading. Being able to recognize these words instantly develops a young reader's fluency and automaticity.

Finger Spelling and Making Words

Finger spelling is a kinesthetic-tactile method for spelling words using hand movements and is based on the manual alphabet. American Sign Language is used by children with hearing disabilities and children with normal hearing to improve spelling skills and learn sight words. The manual alphabet is beautifully illustrated in Laura Rankin's *The Handmade Alphabet* (1991). For example, a hand immersed in fog is the illustration for the "F" page. The diverse learning needs of young children are met through the visual kinesthetic spelling process. These multisensory exercises facilitate teaching diverse students. As an introductory activity, children can learn how to finger spell their names.

In addition to sign language, children can play word games to build vocabulary and phonics skills. Children can learn basic phonics patterns through a word-making activity that is similar to Scrabble. Patricia Cunningham and Dorothy Hall (1994, 2001) have a series of books with lesson plans for primary, intermediate, and middle school students called *Making Words*, *Making Big Words*, and *Making Bigger Words*. In the making words activity, children change letters in existing words to make new words. It is easier for young children to begin by making two-letter words, three-letter words, and so forth. The teacher should model several words with the class before allowing them to work on their own or with a partner. For example, the following words can be made from the letters in *scratch: at, ah, as, cat, rat, hat, sat*, and *chat*. The "mystery" word is the word that contains all of the letters. Longer words with more vowels are appropriate for older students. Children can practice letters and sounds independently in listening and writing centers (see Photo 4.6).

Photo 4.6 *Listening and writing center*

Cut-Up Sentences

Cut-up sentences is a writing strategy based upon Marie Clay's Reading Recovery intervention program for first-grade students (Clay, 1979, 1987). Cut-up sentences is an interactive process that occurs at the end of a half-hour intensive reading session. The child writes a sentence about the lesson in a writing notebook. The teacher helps the child if necessary to edit the sentence by correcting punctuation and spelling on a practice page. The teacher writes the sentence again on card stock paper, cutting apart the words and punctuation. The child is asked to put the cut-up sentence together in the same way, like pieces of a puzzle. For example, a child may dictate the following sentence after reading *The Cat in the Hat* by Dr. Seuss (1957):

> The/Cat /in /the /Hat /made /a/funny/machine/to/clean/up/the/house/.

This cut-up sentence strategy helps children to understand the concepts of phonics, sights words, and sentence structure. Using a manipulative such as cut-up sentences promotes interaction and motivates young children to learn phonic skills. This process promotes self-confidence and helps children remember words and patterns. Children can take the cut-up sentence home to practice connecting words together in meaningful ways, which supports family literacy. Children's own language is valued in this process.

4-4c Print Awareness

When a child understands the way print works—for example, that a book is read from front to back—that child has grasped the concept of print. Reading becomes easier for young children when they understand the concepts of letters, words, and punctuation in sentences. The *Concepts about Print Test* (CAP), developed by Marie Clay (1979), is used to assess beginning readers. *Sand*, *Stones*, and *Follow Me, Moon* are titles of Clay's test booklets, in which many letters and words are scrambled and several pictures are inverted throughout the text. Generic versions of Clay's CAP test are available that can be used with any picture book.

4-4d Phonemic Awareness

Phonemic awareness is an understanding of sounds in spoken words. Children who have phonemic awareness understand the rhythmic nature of language and the concept of rhyme. They are able to blend and segment individual sounds or phonemes in words. Children with phonemic awareness manipulate sounds in words, such as changing the beginning, middle, or ending sounds. This understanding of the sounds of language is learned naturally, through listening to stories or songs from a young age. Phonemic awareness sets the stage for phonics. *Blending* is putting sounds together (for example, $b + a + t = bat$), and *segmenting* is breaking sounds apart (for example, $bat = b + a + t$). Examples of phonemic awareness skills are rhyming, blending, segmenting, and changing sounds in words. For example, some words that rhyme with *cap* are *map*, *rap*, *tap*, and *sap*. Putting phonemes together to make a word is called blending. A phoneme is the smallest unit of sound in a word. The letter within the slashes indicates the letter sound. Blending the phonemes or letter sounds in *cap* would look like this:

> /c/ /a/ /p/ = cap

Segmenting sounds requires separating the individual phonemes in words:

> log = /l/ /o/ /g/

cut-up sentences A decoding strategy where a sentence is written on a strip of paper, cut into words, and put back together.

ASSESSING PRINT AWARENESS SKILLS THROUGH CONCEPTS ABOUT PRINT (CAP)

Any book that has appropriate text with illustrations and includes multiple lines of text on at least one page can be used for this assessment. For this example, we selected *Where Is the Green Sheep?* by Mem Fox (2004). Begin by telling the child, "I am going to read this story and I want you to help me. It is called, *Where Is the Green Sheep?* by Mem Fox." Use the right column for anecdotal notes during the reading session.

Assessment Guide

Skill/Prompt	Anecdotal Notes
Orientation—Front of the book Hand the book to the child vertically with the spine facing the child and ask, "Where is the front of the book?"	
Orientation—Back of the book Ask the child, "Where is the back of the book?"	
Orientation—Layout of text Ask the child, "Where does the story begin?"	
Pictures and print Open the book to page 1 and ask the child, "Show me the pictures." Ask the child to describe the illustration. Next ask the child, "Show me the words."	
Direction of print On page 1, ask the child, "Where do I begin to read the story? Point with your finger." Read the first word and ask the child, "Point to where I read next."	
Page sequencing Point to the last word on the left page and ask the child, "Where do I read next?"	
Punctuation Ask the child to point to a punctuation mark and explain what it means.	
Difference between letter and word Give the child a strip of paper or an index card. Ask the child to use the paper to cover over the words. ■ Ask the child to show only one letter. ■ Ask the child to show one word. ■ Ask the child to show the first letter of a word. ■ Ask the child to show the last letter of a word.	
Return sweep On a page with at least two lines of text, read the first sentence to the child and hold your finger on the last word of the first line. Ask the child, "Where do I read next?"	

Think about It

This assessment is designed for children in kindergarten through first grade. Frequent assessment reflects and documents a child's growth in literacy skills. Teachers use anecdotal notes to adjust their literacy instruction. For example, if you notice the child skips punctuation in the text, you could work on fluency strategies, such as using sentence strips with different punctuation marks.

Adapted from Clay (1979).

Photo 4.7 *Interactive dialogue*

Changing sounds within words is the most difficult phonemic awareness skill. For example, the teacher says *log* and asks the children to change the "l" to a "b" so the word becomes *bog*. Then the "b" could change to an "f" to make fog. The vowel could be changed to an "i" to make fig. You can also start with ending letters in words such as beg. The teacher could tell the students to change the "g" from beg to a "t" to make bet. This process facilitates learning phonemic awareness.

The easiest way to teach concepts about print, sight words, phonemic awareness, and alphabet knowledge is through reading to children (see Photo 4.7), especially books that have predictable patterns or easy decodable text such as *Brown Bear, Brown Bear, What Do You See?* by Bill Martin Jr. (1992), *Where Is the Green Sheep?* by Mem Fox (2004), *Are You My Mother?* by P. D. Eastman (1960), or *Goodnight Moon* by Margaret Wise Brown (1947). Wordless picture books are also highly recommended for beginning readers. Children can look at the pictures and tell their own stories, which helps to develop reading comprehension and oral language skills. *Tuesday* by David Wiesner (1980) and *The Lion & the Mouse* by Jerry Pinkney (2009) are excellent examples of wordless picture books for young readers. Older readers may enjoy reading and discussing wordless books with more complicated story lines (Louie & Sierschynski, 2015), such as *Journey* by Aaron Becker (2013), *Unspoken* by Henry Cole (2012), or *Flotsam* by David Wiesner (2006).

Songs are another fun and effective way to teach early literacy skills. Reading to children daily, from the time they are born, will most likely lead to their later success in reading. This is, by far, the best thing parents can do to help their children become lifelong readers according to Jim Trelease, author of *The Read-Aloud Handbook* (2013).

✔ **CONSIDER THIS...**

Consider how you can teach phonemic awareness through poetry. Children can perform favorite poems (poetry slam) for an audience to reinforce rhyme, rhythm, and repetition.

Apply & Reflect

Select an age-appropriate alphabet book such as *Dr. Seuss's ABC* (1996) or *Alphabet Adventure* by Audrey Wood and Bruce Wood (2001). Read the book with a child and practice phonics skills (letters and sounds). Reflect on your experience with your peers in class.

Phonics is closely related to spelling. Children learn to spell in English through spelling words, letter by letter from left to right (alphabetic), or by learning patterns (CVC, CVVC, CV, CVCV). They must also understand that there are different spellings for the different meanings of the same root word (DeVries, 2011). Children learn phonics and spelling through reading (decoding), writing (encoding), and teacher modeling. DeVries (2011, p. 107–108) lists four key principles of effective phonics instruction:

1. *Base instruction on what students know;*
2. *Provide systematic phonics instruction;*
3. *Use appropriate texts*; and
4. *Embed instruction in meaningful contexts.*

Teachers should observe children during guided reading groups to informally assess their strengths and needs in phonics. Appropriate texts match the students' instructional reading level (90 percent word recognition). Assessing spelling errors in writing samples provides useful information about students' phonics skills. Teachers can also analyze miscues during running record assessments for the readers' decoding strategies (visual, meaning, and structure). Students can be grouped for differentiated instruction according to the results of these informal assessments. An analysis of the children's stage of spelling development using the Primary Spelling Inventory (Bear et al., 2015) is useful for designing appropriate phonics lessons that meet the needs of individual students. The stages of spelling development consist of emergent (PreK through first grade), letter name-alphabetic (K through mid-second grade), within word pattern (first through fourth grade), syllables and affixes (third through eighth grade), and derivational relations (fifth through twelfth grade). There is some overlap in these spelling stages because children progress through the sequence at different rates.

Phonics is an understanding of sounds in written words. Phonological awareness includes (1) a knowledge of consonant digraphs and blends, (2) short and long vowels, (3) *r*-controlled vowels, and (4) vowel digraphs and diphthongs, as well as vowel generalizations: CVC, CVVC, CV, and CVCE. Each of these phonics skills will be described separately:

- **Consonant digraphs and blends:** Single consonant sounds are usually taught first because they are the easiest for children to learn. Next, consonants with more than one sound are introduced, such as "c" and "s." Consonant digraphs and consonant blends are taught after single consonant sounds. Examples of consonant digraphs (two letters that make one sound) are *th, ch, sh,* and *wh*. There are three basic groups of consonant blends (each phoneme is represented): the "r" blends, which are combinations of consonants that end with "r" (*br, cr, dr, gr, pr, tr*), the "l" blends, which end with /l/ (*bl, cl, fl, gl, sl, pl*), and the "s" blends that begin with /s/ (*sc, sh, sk, sl, sm, sn, sp, st*).
- **Short and long vowels:** Short vowels are generally taught before long vowels because they are easier for children to learn. Short vowels are represented by the following sounds: /a/ as in *apple*, /e/ as in *elephant*, /i/ as in *inchworm*, /o/ as in *octopus*, and /u/ as in *umbrella*. Long vowels say their names: /a/ as in *game*, /e/ as in *sheep*, /i/ as in *ice*, /o/ as in *rope*, and /u/ as in *music*. Short vowel sounds are represented with a phonetic symbol called a breve; long vowel sounds are represented with a macron (see Figure 4.9).
- Long vowel sounds can be problematic, especially for children whose native language is not English, because there are many different spellings in English for each of the long vowel sounds.

consonant digraphs Two consonants that make one sound (i.e., *ch, th, sh, wh*).

consonant blends Letter combinations that retain their original sounds (two or three letters); sometimes called a consonant cluster.

short vowels Vowel sounds that are found in words like *apple, elephant, inchworm, octopus,* and *umbrella.*

long vowel A vowel that is pronounced the same as the name of the letter.

breve A phonetic symbol for a short vowel sound.

macron A phonetic symbol for a long vowel sound.

Figure 4.9
Phonetic Symbols

Breve

Macron

- **"R-controlled" vowels:** When the letter "r" follows a vowel, it changes its sound: /ar/ in *car*, /or/ in *door*, /er/ in *her*, /ir/ in *girl*, and /ur/ in *fur*. Children can remember this phonics rule by naming "r" a "bossy r." Children should realize that the sounds for /er/, /ir/, and /ur/ are the same.

- **Vowel digraphs and diphthongs:** Vowel digraphs are two vowels that only make one sound: /oa/ in *boat* or /ea/ in *meat*. The first vowel sound is long and the second is silent. Vowel diphthongs are neither short nor long vowel sounds: /oi/ in *oil*, /oy/ in *boy*, /ou/ in *house*, and /ow/ as in *cow*. Diphthongs are gliding sounds that roll from the front of the tongue to the back. The mouth changes as the sounds are produced so it is helpful to have children look in a mirror as they are making these sounds.

- **Vowel generalizations:** Vowel generalizations are patterns of vowels and consonants that work more than 50 percent of the time. For example, the rule for CVC is that if there is one vowel in the middle of the word, it is usually short. The CVVC pattern has a vowel digraph in the middle. The rule states that if there are two vowels together in the middle of a word, the first one is usually long and the second one is silent. The CVCE pattern has a silent "e" on the end, and the first vowel is silent. The rule for CV indicates that if there is one vowel at the end of a word, it is usually long. However, there are always exceptions to every rule. These exceptions are sometimes called "outlaw" or "elephant" words.

Teachers must know these phonics skills to teach them to children. Children must know these skills to successfully decode unknown words; however, they may not use the same terminology. For example, diphthongs may be called "vowel teams." Phonics is a tool that leads to comprehension, the goal of reading. Pronouncing words without understanding the meaning is not reading.

 CONSIDER THIS...

Consider how you can teach the phonics rules and vowel generalizations through children's literature. For example, you can use *Sheep in a Jeep* by Nancy E. Shaw (1997) to teach the CVVC pattern.

4-6 Literacy Strategies and Practices for Phonics and Word Identification

Phonics instruction should be kept short and simple during literacy activities (see Table 4.2). The sequence of phonic skills (from simple to complex) is usually taught by the end of second grade. Phonics is a tool for decoding unknown words. Phonics skills should be taught and practiced in context (reading text) and in isolation (flash cards, manipulatives, games).

vowel digraphs Two vowels that only make one sound: "oa" in *boat* or "ea" in *meat*; the first vowel sound is long and the second is silent.

diphthongs Vowel combinations like *ou, ow, oi, oy* (two vowels make a new sound).

vowel generalizations Patterns of vowels and consonants that work approximately 50 percent of the time, such as CV, CVC, CVCV, and CVVC.

Age Groups	Cognitive	Socioemotional
0 to 3	Use fabric letters and soft word/picture puzzles Create a play center with variety of objects to build speaking vocabulary Make letters using a variety of materials (crayons, shaving cream, sand, water)	Play using props, toys, and stuffed animals for word association Use simple sign language to express emotion Use mirrors to visualize facial expressions while making certain sounds
3 to 6	Sing along with picture song books Use interactive e-books that read aloud while highlighting words Have children label objects in the learning environment	Make "all about me" books with illustrations and key words (dictate) Identify environmental print during field trips, nature walks, and family outings to build confidence in young readers
6 to 9	Use informational alphabet class books based on a selected topic or theme Use educational computer programs focusing on phonics	Use interactive pocket charts and word walls with partner support to build confidence Read aloud poems using voice inflection to portray emotions

⌄ Professional Resource Download

End-of-Chapter Study Aids

Summary

Emergent literacy develops through authentic and varied reading and writing experiences that are a part of every child's daily life. Teachers plan guided, shared, interactive, and independent reading and writing activities based on reading models. The top-down (meaning-based), bottom-up (phonics-based), and comprehensive reading models are used in balanced literacy classrooms. In addition to language development, the foundational skills of early literacy, including letter knowledge, sight words, print awareness, and phonemic awareness, lead to success in reading and writing. Words and sentences with rhythm and rhyme help beginning readers quickly grasp the meaning of print. Teachers should create a print-rich environment that encourages active engagement, responsibility, and real-world connections (Cambourne, 1988). Phonics rules aid children in recognizing words and patterns when learning to read and write.

  Phonics instruction should be systematic and explicit, taught daily using an appropriate sequence of skills, and based on the needs of individual students. Lessons must connect new information to what students already know. Reading materials should be meaningful and appropriate (on the students' instructional reading level) for best results (DeVries, 2011). Strong phonics and decoding skills build fluent, confident readers. Engaged students are active participants in the learning process. Literacy tasks that engage students invite collaboration and

Physical	Children's Books	Family Involvement
Use alphabet and number texture cards for grasping and tactile exploration Sing chants and rhymes with repetition focusing on movement of hands/fingers, feet/toes, arms, and legs	*Joseph had a Little Overcoat* by Simms Taback *Where is the Green Sheep?* by Mem Fox	Match initial consonant with pictures Use number symbols on finger puppets to sing counting rhymes Label objects in the home
Use picture word cards and touch box with matching word cards Use modeling clay and texture collage of letters and words Use musical instruments and other sound props to create sounds that relate to letters or words	*Bling Blang* by Woodie Guthrie *What a Wonderful World* illustrated by Ashley Bryan; written by George David Weiss and Bob Thiele	Use finger puppets with number words on each finger Read counting books and identify the number words Recognize words associated with routines by reading books that include daily activities
Shadow play with shapes, letters, and words Create a short movement sequence that describes adjectives and verbs	*O Beautiful for Spacious Skies,* a poem written by Katharine Lee Bates; illustrated by Wayne Thiebaud *Cowboys*, a book of poems by David L. Harrison	Play games that identify vocabulary (I spy, guess what is in the box) Use vocabulary cards and sort in categories, synonyms, antonyms, or compound words Create a picture dictionary or scrapbook collage and identify new vocabulary

student interest (Parsons, Malloy, Parsons, & Burrowbridge, 2015). The purpose of phonics and word identification is to learn patterns of sounds in meaningful contexts, practice decoding skills, and apply these skills and strategies to new contexts.

Chapter Exercises

1. To practice phonemic awareness skills, create a list of multisyllable words based upon a theme, topic, or story. Design a syllable segmenting game such as clapping syllables in words. Use kinesthetic movements like snapping, stomping, jumping, and skipping. Play the game with a small group of classmates.
2. To focus on student engagement (one of Cambourne's conditions of learning), select a nonfiction text, such as *Magic School Bus and the Climate Challenge* (series) by Joanna Cole (2010). Develop a series of discussion questions to promote student dialogue.
3. Select a familiar fairy tale such as, "Jack and the Beanstalk" or "Sleeping Beauty." Make a list of five to ten key words. Teach how to sign the key words in American Sign Language to a small group of peers. While retelling the story, the group signs the key words. Reflect on the experience as a class.
4. Choose one of the following phonics skills: consonant digraphs or blends, short or long vowels, *r*-controlled vowels, and vowel digraphs or diphthongs. Write a poem with a partner using one of the phonics skills. Perform the poem for the class.

TEACHING PHONICS THROUGH CHILDREN'S LITERATURE

Appropriate for Ages 6 to 9

Phonics skills should be taught in a meaningful context (children's literature) as well as in isolation (games and activities). For example, *The Peace Book* by Todd Parr (2009) can be used to teach the long "e" sound. First, the teacher talks about the concept of peace and what this word means to the children. This book, using bright colors and simple text, describes different meanings of peace from a child's perspective. After listening and discussing the story, the children can draw their own pictures about peace, including what the story meant to them. Then they share their drawings with the class. The emphasis is on ideas and meaning rather than artistic skills. This type of drawing, called a "sketch to stretch" (see Figure 4.10) is ideal for beginning readers and writers or English language learners who may have limited writing skills (Yopp & Yopp, 2010). Afterward, the teacher can use *The Peace Book* during a phonics lesson to teach different spellings of the long "e" sound using a word sort (*ea, ee*). The children can add other words of their own that match these long vowel patterns.

Word Sort for Long "E" Sound

ea	ee

Word List (words from the text): *peace, keeping, reading, needs, tree, meal, streets, free*

Figure 4.10
Sample Sketch to Stretch
Courtesy of the authors

Key Terms and Concepts

analytic phonics

basal readers

bottom-up reading model

breve

consonant blends

consonant digraphs

cut-up sentences

diphthongs

grapheme

long vowel

macron

onset

phoneme

phonological awareness

phonics

phonology

r-controlled vowels

rime

short vowels

synthetic phonics

top-down reading model

vowel digraphs

vowel generalizations

Ellen B. Senisi/The Image Works

STANDARDS ADDRESSED IN THIS CHAPTER

The standards from the following organizations will be used throughout the chapter: Common Core State Standards for English Language Arts, the National Association for the Education of Young Children (NAEYC), and National Core Arts Standards. These standards are discussed further in the chapter as appropriate.

 COMMON CORE STATE STANDARDS

Common Core State Standards for English Language Arts

Anchor Standards for Reading

Reading Standards: Foundational Skills (K–5)
- Phonological Awareness
- Phonics and Word Recognition

Anchor Standards for Language
- Vocabulary Acquisition and Use

2010 NAEYC Standards for Initial and Advanced Early Childhood Professional Preparation Programs
- *Standard 1:* Promoting Child Development and Learning
- *Standard 5:* Using Content Knowledge to Build Meaningful Curriculum

NAEYC Early Childhood Program Standards and Accreditation Criteria
- *Standard 2:* Curriculum
- *Standard 3:* Teaching

NCA

National Core Arts Standards (Dance, Media Arts, Music, Theater, Visual Arts)

Creating
- *Anchor Standard 1:* Generate and conceptualize artistic ideas and work.
- *Anchor Standard 2:* Organize and develop artistic ideas and work.

Presenting
- *Anchor Standard 4:* Select, analyze, and interpret artistic work for presentation.

Responding
- *Anchor Standard 7:* Perceive and analyze artistic work.

Connecting
- *Anchor Standard 10:* Synthesize and relate knowledge and personal experiences to make art.
- *Anchor Standard 11:* Relate artistic ideas and works with societal, cultural, and historical context to deepen understanding.

Vocabulary Development and Instruction

5

Let us remember: One book, one pen, one child, and one teacher can change the world. — Malala Yousafzai

Early literacy is enhanced when vocabulary develops naturally, through social interactions, and as children experience their daily routines. Vocabulary is a collective sum of words and phrases arranged in the English language to communicate meaning. Children's vocabularies are based on who they are and their relationships in the world. Children develop their unique sense of self through the words they know and use when interacting with others and the environment. Reading, singing, and talking to babies from the time they are born are important experiences for literacy development (Greene, 2014).

There are four categories of vocabulary development: listening, reading, writing, and speaking. Children's listening vocabularies are more extensive than their writing vocabularies. Children understand and use more words when listening or speaking than when reading or writing. Vocabulary involves memory (storing and retrieving words) and comprehension (understanding words) utilizing stored experiences. Children learn vocabulary by adding new words into their current schema (prior knowledge) and conceptual framework. It is important for teachers to introduce new vocabulary in meaningful categories or classifications and encourage children to dialogue and engage in discussions. Children, who have a diverse and rich vocabulary, read and write with confidence. Self-esteem (emotional self), self-concept (mental perception of self), and self-efficacy (belief in mastery of tasks) are characteristics of successful readers and writers.

Children's vocabularies increase when reading widely in a variety of genres. Children's literacy development depends upon interaction (speaking, listening, reading, and writing) with caring adults. Researchers estimate that middle-income American children may hear 30 million more words in their first three years of life than children from lower-income homes (Greene, 2014, p. 90). To close this gap in word knowledge (meaning and application), literacy programs such as the Parent-Child Home Program (PCHP) are providing training programs where literacy specialists visit homes to teach parents with young children essential literacy skills. Vocabulary instruction for young children involves learning new words in different subjects throughout the day. A strong vocabulary is essential for reading comprehension.

LEARNING OBJECTIVES

After you have read this chapter, you should be able to:

5-1 Analyze concepts of vocabulary development.

5-2 Compare sight and meaning vocabulary in the early literacy curriculum.

5-3 Explain vocabulary strategies for young children.

5-4 Adapt vocabulary instruction for English language learners.

5-5 Describe types of vocabulary assessment.

5-6 Apply literacy strategies and practices for vocabulary development.

STANDARDS CONNECTION TO THE VIGNETTE

NAEYC Early Childhood Program Standards and Accreditation Criteria

Standard 2: Curriculum

2.E.04 Children have varied opportunities to engage in conversations that help them understand the content of the book.

Common Core State Standards for English Language Arts

Foundational Skills

Second Grade

2. Demonstrate understanding of spoken words, syllables, and sounds (phonemes).

3. Know and apply grade-level phonics and word analysis in decoding words.

Young children enjoy activities that build their vocabulary in a creative way. List-group-label strategies help children to improve their vocabulary by organizing, categorizing, grouping, and labeling new concepts as related to prior knowledge. By linking culture and children's literature, teachers have an opportunity to develop English vocabulary and relate words in different languages to English words. English language learners should be allowed to read bilingual books in their native languages whenever possible to support their acquisition of English (see Photo 5.1).

Mr. Wills, a second-grade teacher introduces the children's book, *What Can You Do with a Paleta?* by Carmen Tafolla (2009). The children brainstorm about the cover of the book and list words that they think go with the main topic of the title. Because there are children who speak Spanish in class, they share what a *paleta* is and help to list words that are associated with this type of popsicle. A rainbow of colors is also listed to illustrate a variety of flavors. Mr. Wills records all the words on a chart as the children brainstorm on the topic.

Next, the children divide into small groups to organize the word list into meaningful categories. The children explain why they grouped certain words together and discarded others. The word grouping process is negotiated among the children in the small work group. Some of the words are in Spanish, so the children are instructed to identify an English word corresponding with the Spanish word. Each word list or category is labeled with a heading or main topic.

Mr. Wills then reads the book aloud to the class, and the children raise their hands when they hear words from their list. Finally, the children independently read the story and highlight the words they recognize from their list.

Group recognition of new vocabulary words builds confidence in using these words in future reading and writing activities. Children enjoy reading books in their native languages, and dual-language books promote vocabulary development. Developing an extensive vocabulary starts at birth for young emergent readers. Stories that use vibrant descriptive language with colorful illustrations should be frequently read to children.

Developmentally appropriate practice (DAP) is featured in the vignette and can be adapted for younger children (birth to age 6) and older children to age 9. Suggested adaptations include:

- *Ages 0 to 3:* Reading simple alphabet books to babies and toddlers teaches letters and sounds. Bilingual alphabet books are available in many languages such as Spanish, French, Chinese, Japanese, and Russian. Preschoolers enjoy picture alphabet books, such as *Mi Dia de la A a la Z* by F. Isabel Campoy (2009). Children benefit from learning words (colors, numbers, days of the week, and so on) in other languages.
- *Ages 3 to 6:* Before reading *Abuela* by Arthur Dorros (1997), children are introduced to key words in Spanish and English, such as *abuela* (grandmother), *buenos dias* (good day), *me gusta* (I like), and *mira* (look). Word meanings are reviewed in context during the teacher read-aloud.

vocabulary A collective sum of words and phrases arranged in the English language to communicate meaning.

Photo 5.1 *Boy reading in his native language*

- ***Ages 6 to 9:*** Children listen to a familiar fairy tale read in two languages, such as *Caperucita Roja* by Eva Sykorova-Pekarkova (1996) in English and Spanish. With a partner, children retell the familiar fairy tale ("Little Red Riding Hood") in their native languages using the illustrations. Then the teacher reads the story in English. Children compare their retellings of the English version.

Classroom Connection

What bilingual activities can you integrate into this literacy lesson? For example, children can label objects in the classroom in two languages.

5-1 Concepts of Vocabulary Development

Vocabulary is an important component of an effective literacy program, which also includes phonemic awareness, phonics, comprehension, fluency, and writing. Vocabulary knowledge is directly linked to reading comprehension and conceptual knowledge (Anderson & Freebody, 1985). There are several layers of reading comprehension: word level, sentence level, and passage level. As illustrated in Figure 5.1, children need a strong foundation in print knowledge (letters and sounds) and word knowledge (sight and meaning vocabulary) to understand text (meaning). Children should be self-confident, active, and independent learners to become successful readers and writers. An environment that supports children's cognitive, socioemotional, and physical development is important for early literacy success.

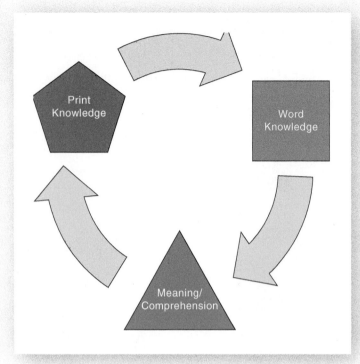

Figure 5.1
Components of Vocabulary Development

Children increase vocabulary through word immersion. Words are everywhere and children's awareness in a print-rich environment contributes to vocabulary development (see Photo 5.2). Reading aloud to children and independent reading are effective strategies for expanding vocabulary. Word knowledge is directly related to reading achievement (Nagy, 1988; Stahl, 1999). Strong and avid readers increase their reading ability through exposure to more complex text and higher-level vocabulary.

Children who are confident readers have self-efficacy, which means they believe in themselves as readers and writers. Using their abilities to learn new skills through self-motivation allows children to be successful. When using the natural social tendencies and behaviors of children, teachers who allow independent learning encourage children to be self-motivated and self-regulated (see Photo 5.3). Children who become self-regulated learners master the personal skills and necessary strategies for controlling their own behaviors (Bandura, 1986).

When infants are exposed to language by listening, they learn to form their own particular sounds, which eventually become words, phrases, and sentences. Parents who interact and read to their children enhance their children's oral language development. This oral language development process forms the foundation for reading and writing.

By their first year, children use simple words such as *Daddy*, or *Mama*, *bye, bye*, and sounds of animals like *meow, moo*, or *bow-wow*. However, by the second year they might say, "More milk," "My catched the ball," or "Where did Nana go?" Phrasing is well established with simple sentences. Children use the present tense and active voice and do not use the passive voice until early elementary school, when they start to use complex grammar sentences. By age 6, children's vocabularies increase dramatically, to approximately 844,000 words (Woolfolk, 2011).

Photo 5.2 *Print immersion*

Photo 5.3 *Toddler exploring a picture book*
Janet Towell

This language base is necessary when children learn new concepts, which they interpret based on their prior knowledge and experience. Teachers can provide support by activating and building children's background knowledge before introducing unfamiliar topics. Children learn through frequent exposure to new words (repetition). More difficult words require application and meaningful connections to children's lives. Words used in context are more meaningful than in isolation. Children's literature engages and brings vocabulary alive through the story. For example, in the book *Henry's Freedom Box* by Ellen Levine (2007), a young boy mails himself to gain freedom from slavery. Key vocabulary from this book can be introduced to children to help them understand concepts about this time in history such as *slave, Underground Railroad, master,* and *freedom.*

Words are meaningful when they are related to children's daily routines, such as waking up, playtime, nap time, eating, and bedtime. Having a solid vocabulary base will enable children to understand and enjoy reading in various genres of children's literature. The more they read, the stronger readers they will become. Wide reading will also help to improve children's writing skills, through exposure to new words and sentence structures. Language learning progresses as children engage in speaking, listening, reading, and writing experiences in the early literacy curriculum.

The three main paths to vocabulary growth are life experiences, vicarious experiences, and explicit instruction (DeVries, 2011; Yopp & Yopp, 2007). Life experiences include everyday routines like going to the beach or grocery store, shopping in department stores, attending birthday parties, listening during story time at the library, or eating at a restaurant (see Photo 5.4).

Because of the rich language, poems are an easy and entertaining way to learn new words. Some popular children's poets are Shel Silverstein, Jack Prelutsky, Brod Bagert, Judith Viorst, Lee Bennett Hopkins, and Eloise Greenfield. Children may enjoy participating in a poetry slam, when they memorize and perform special poems for an audience of parents and friends. Children increase their reading fluency when practicing poems using strategies like choral reading (reading together as a group), echo reading (repeating lines after the teacher), or reading poems in two voices (alternating lines or stanzas). Internet websites and educational videos also introduce children to a vast range of vocabulary words, although adult supervision may be required. Reading Rockets is one educational website that has many articles and ideas for parents and teachers. Viewing educational videos or television shows and reading various texts are examples of vicarious experiences.

Although vocabulary words are learned best through natural experiences, sometimes explicit or direct instruction is necessary to introduce specific types of vocabulary words that may be unfamiliar to students, such as academic vocabulary (specific to the content areas of science, social studies, or math) or words with multiple meanings. Similar to the response to intervention model or RTI (a method of differentiating instruction to meet the requirements of inclusion for children in Exceptional Student Education), there are three tiers of vocabulary instruction (Beck, McKeown, & Kucan, 2002).

Photo 5.4 *Exploring the beach with baby*
Josh Weinberger

genres Different types of children's literature: picture books, traditional literature, poetry, realistic fiction, historical fiction, fantasy, and informational books.

response to intervention (RTI) A method of differentiating instruction to meet the requirements of inclusion as defined in the Disabilities Education Improvement Act.

Tier One consists of words acquired naturally through everyday language. Tier Two words appear frequently in a variety of texts, and Tier Three words are associated with academic language or reading in the content areas. Selecting appropriate words for explicit instruction (Tier Two and Tier Three) is an essential part of effective vocabulary instruction. Teachers should consider the importance or utility of the word, how it relates to other familiar words or ideas, and if the students have the conceptual understanding necessary to learn the word.

Some children will need additional scaffolding and modeling when learning new words. To help struggling readers, motivate them through word play (silly poems, joke books, or children's books with humor). Words should be introduced in meaningful contexts, based on interesting and familiar topics (Fisher & Blachowicz, 2005). Children can be encouraged to collect new words in personal picture dictionaries or writing journals for frequent review. Discussing books (nonfiction and fiction) in book clubs, literature circles, or in guided reading groups encourages vocabulary learning in a risk-free environment through social interaction.

✔ CONSIDER THIS...

Consider how teachers can help parents learn to stimulate their children's vocabulary growth in the early years. For example, parents could record bedtime stories so their children can listen to them over and over again. What strategies or activities would you recommend?

5-2 Sight and Meaning Vocabulary in the Early Literacy Curriculum

There are two main types of vocabulary that children must learn to be fluent readers: sight vocabulary and meaning or content vocabulary. Children memorize 220 to 300 sight vocabulary words in the early years—words such as *a, I, and, the, was,* and *by* (also known as Dolch words, after Edward Dolch who created these word lists in 1948). *Sight words* are words that appear frequently in beginning reading texts. These words usually have no meaning individually and can rarely be decoded. Sight words, the foundation of literacy, facilitate the connection process of words to meaning. Exposure to sight words through repetition in reading and writing assists children to establish neural connections. These cognitive connections help children remember the sight words in a different context (Woolfolk, 2011).

In a text selection, whether fiction or nonfiction, certain words are critical to the meaning of the passage. To read fluently, children need to comprehend the text. Word knowledge is the foundation for comprehension. Identifying meaning vocabulary in text is an important skill for beginning readers. Meaning vocabulary consists of key words that are important for comprehending the text. Meaning vocabulary is especially important in nonfiction text because of the specialized terminology. Readers must be taught how to use text features including the table of contents, index, graphs or tables, and glossaries.

Semantic or word maps are helpful to show related concepts and enhance meaning as illustrated in Figure 5.2. To really understand a word, children must be able to define it, use it in a sentence, draw a picture of it, and/or provide appropriate synonyms and antonyms. Synonyms are words that have similar meanings, such as *pretty* and *beautiful*; antonyms are words that have opposite meanings, such as *wide* and *narrow*. Homophones are words that sound similar but have different meanings and spellings, like *two* and *too, knight* and *night,* or *hi* and *high*.

Define the word:	Use the word in a sentence:
Draw a sketch:	List synonyms or antonyms:

❯❯ Professional Resource Download

Figure 5.2
Elements of a Word Map

meaning vocabulary Key words that are important for comprehending the text.

synonyms Words that have similar meanings, such as *pretty* and *beautiful*.

antonyms Words that have opposite meanings, such as *wide* and *narrow*.

homophones Words that sound similar but have different meanings and spellings, like *two* and *too, knight* and *night,* or *hi* and *high*.

Words can have multiple meanings, depending on the context and grammatical usage. It is important for children to recognize the correct meaning of a word, depending on the context of the sentence. Playing word games like Scrabble or reading joke books and riddles are engaging ways to help children learn new words. Other suggestions for developing vocabulary are as follows:

1. Categorize or classify words when stories are read, such as animals or flowers (or parts of speech, such as nouns, verbs, and adjectives).
2. Sing songs, and perform dramatic readings or reader's theater.
3. Use a picture dictionary or thesaurus to improve word choice (one of the six writing traits) during writing workshop.
4. Read and discuss stories with idioms and multiple-meaning words, like *Amelia Bedelia* books by Peggy Parish (book series begun in 1963), where the main characters comically misunderstand the meaning of words, or *Maestro Stu Saves the Zoo* by Denise Brennan-Nelson (2012), about a boy who convinces city officials to keep the local zoo open, featuring a glossary of the idioms in the back of the book.
5. Use synonyms or antonyms in word games such as Concentration, where the word cards are placed face down and the child recalls from memory where the matching cards were placed.

These learning strategies work well with diverse learners including Exceptional Student Education (ESE), English language learners (ELLs) and other children who are at risk. Using these strategies helps all children, especially struggling readers, improve their vocabulary knowledge and reading skills. Reading aloud and using manipulatives, games, interactive technology, and educational videos build sight and meaning vocabulary.

5-2a Teaching Vocabulary Skills through Children's Literature

A print-rich classroom environment motivates young children to read what they love and love what they read. The classroom is filled with children's literature including a classroom library, displays of favorite books with children's illustrations, and writing samples displayed along with the books, along with containers of all colors, shapes, and sizes of books from a variety of genres. A writing and reading center is a part of every classroom and contains resources such as pens, pencils, crayons, an assortment of paper, picture dictionaries, collage materials, and computers.

When reading a book to the whole class, the teacher can use a sense of dramatic play to bring books to life for young children. One example of a vocabulary building book is *Big Words for Little People*, by Jamie Lee Curtis (2008), which celebrates the power of words and how language is used to connect young children with the adults in their world. The story explains words like *intelligence*, *privacy*, and *impossible* in a way that children can understand. Shared reading experiences, when the teacher and children read the same book (usually in circle time with the teacher reading aloud), promote vocabulary development through children's literature. During the first shared reading experience, the teacher typically uses a big book on an easel and a pointer (a wand used to indicate specific areas of the book). The teacher and children identify unknown words in the text during the read-aloud. The teacher writes the unknown words on sticky notes, which are attached beside each word in the text or on a word wall. A word wall is a necessary tool and is often displayed on a bulletin board in the classroom. Throughout daily instruction, teachers and children add unknown words to the word wall in the classroom (usually teachers have a list of words to begin each school year).

Shared reading experiences continue by reading the same book for a period time to promote fluency and comprehension for each child. At first, the teacher reads alone, but

Apply & Reflect

Design an interactive vocabulary game, dance, or song for young children in a selected age group (0 to 3, 3 to 6, or 6 to 9). Share your idea and ways to adapt this strategy for different age groups with a peer.

pointer A wand used to indicate specific areas of the big book during shared reading.

POETRY ACTIVITY FOR PRESERVICE TEACHERS TO DO WITH CHILDREN

Purpose: To teach vocabulary words through writing poetry

Procedure: Read examples of different types of poems in *A Kick in the Head* by Paul Janeczko (2005). Children can choose one of the poetic forms, such as a concrete, five senses, or color poem, to create a poem of their own (see Photo 5.5). These poems could be written individually, with a partner or in small groups.

Teaching Analysis: Reflective practices are a necessary part of the *literacy assessment cycle* and are key components in preservice preparation and certification, such as edTPA. Analyze the strengths and areas of improvement in this lesson idea. Answer the following:

- What is successful?
- What would you change to improve the lesson?
- What did you learn about teaching literacy?

Links: Making connections to technology and developmentally appropriate practices (DAP) supports lesson planning and literacy instruction. Adaptations of this lesson idea are provided through the following:

- **Technology Link:** Children can view more examples of poems online and watch videos of poets reading their work.
- **DAP Link:** The difficulty of the poem will depend on the ages and abilities of children in the class. For example, the formula for a bio-poem could be shortened to require fewer lines and examples.
- **Executive Function Link:** Creative play and active engagement during an interactive read-aloud develop children's self-regulation skills in social settings as reflected in the holistic model of literacy (cognitive, socioemotional, and physical).

- **Classroom Link:** Children (0 to 3) can explore real objects (stuffed animals, feathers, and fabric) that relate to poetry read aloud by caring adults.
- **Classroom Link:** Children (3 to 6) can draw a shape with crayons and dictate the words for a concrete poem.
- **Classroom Link:** Children (6 to 9) can write and illustrate their own poems. The poems are based on their interests. For example, a love of basketball inspired the concrete poem: "Basketballs are orange. You can bounce them and you shoot with them."

Photo 5.5 *Concrete poem*
Courtesy of the authors

quickly children join in by reading aloud memorized sections of the book. Participation in read-aloud sessions for all children is encouraged.

Once unknown words are identified in the book, teachers use different strategies to promote vocabulary development. One strategy involves placing a blank card or sticky note over the word in the book. Children use context clues from the surrounding words or sentences to "guess" the hidden word. The teacher lists all potential word choices to further promote vocabulary development.

5-2b Vocabulary Knowledge Charts

Children acquire vocabulary skills by learning words and developing meaning through context and visualization. Using words in meaningful ways through context, imagery, and verbal or written application develops vocabulary skills. There are many types of

Table 5.1 *Vocabulary Knowledge Chart*

Meaning of Word in Context	Word Parts (Root, Prefix, or Suffix)	Predicted Meaning	Dictionary Definition	Illustration	Antonyms or/ and Synonyms
Art class was over, but Vashti sat glued to her chair.	Glu(e)-ed	Stay down	To make stick as with glue		Stand up Sit down
Vashti grabbed the marker and gave the paper a good, strong jab.	Jab	Point	To poke as with a sharp instrument		Delicate mark Poke
Vashti thought for a moment.	Moment	A second or two of waiting time	A brief period of time		A second A century
Vashti kept experimenting.	Experiment -ing	To try out something new	A test or trial undertaken to discover something		Same Invent
She discovered that she could make a green dot.	Discover-ed	To find something new	To be the first to find out or see		Found Lost

word concept maps or charts to help children comprehend new vocabulary. A Vocabulary Knowledge Chart, such as the one shown in Table 5.1, is one example that provides an analysis of word meanings in context and related words.

For instance, children identify unfamiliar words in *The Dot* by Peter H. Reynolds (2003). In this story, Vashti is inspired by her art teacher to create dot-shaped designs, which resulted in a successful school art exhibition. Using the Vocabulary Knowledge Chart, children organize thoughts and ideas to learn new vocabulary.

Technology tools can be used to create word clouds or word shapes on any topic. Words are typed into the program (for example, in the text box on websites such as Wordle or Tagxedo) and when the "create button" is selected, the words are randomly organized into a colorful and artistic arrangement (see Figure 5.3). This strategy works well with English language learners because words are related in a meaningful context through a visual image.

CONSIDER THIS...

Consider how to introduce sight vocabulary through children's literature. Which words will you focus on during the lesson, and how can children learn these words through activities in learning centers?

Figure 5.3
Sample Word Cloud
Courtesy of the authors

5-3 Vocabulary Strategies for Young Children

Vocabulary is the key to improving reading and writing skills according to Melissa Forney, author of *Razzle Dazzle Writing* (2001) and *Writing Superstars* (2007). The six components of effective vocabulary instruction identified by Forney in *Razzle Dazzle Writing* (2001) are:

1. Respect
2. Humor, novelty, and innovation
3. Touch
4. Movement
5. Eye anchors
6. Validation

These components, explained below, build children's schemata through cultural literacy experiences, creating a strong foundation of comprehension.

5-3a Respect

Respect needs no explanation. In a successful learning environment, teachers must respect learners, learners must respect teachers, and learners must respect each other. Knowing that others respect you as an individual fosters a safe learning environment and encourages literacy skill development. This character trait can be taught through modeling and role-play.

5-3b Humor, Novelty, and Innovation

Melissa Forney (2001) believes in "gimmicks" to help children remember important information. One example is a creative "Out of this World" hat. She suggests decorating a straw beach hat with items from a discount store such as a propeller, silk flowers, sunglasses, or seashells. The teacher wears this special hat approximately 10 days per year, when he or she wants to tell the class something incredibly important (for example, on the last day of the school year).

Another example Forney (2001) recommends for teaching sentence variety is a "sentence squeezie." She uses green cardstock paper cut in one-inch strips and folded accordion style (about six inches in length). Children can measure lengths of sentences in a piece of literature to see if they are short, medium, or long. They can also use this tool in their own writing, to make sure they are not boring their readers with a series of short sentences.

Forney's (2001) strategy for expanding word knowledge is called a "vocabulator," a large plastic tube that contains objects and word cards suspended in a medium such as colored rice, pasta, or sand. Each vocabulator is based on a particular theme: dinosaurs, the ocean, a state, animals, insects, vegetables, holidays, clothes, seasons, a book series, a country, transportation, community helpers, or pets. Children shake the tube to discover words and objects to add to their word banks for the writing workshop. This manipulative tool is one way to expand children's vocabulary on a variety of themes and topics. Providing a sense of playfulness and caring supports vocabulary development. Children use their imagination and sense of discovery to develop stronger vocabulary, leading to stronger reading and writing skills.

5-3c Touch

The sense of touch encourages a love of word knowledge through direct sensory experiences (Forney, 2001). Stimulating the senses through hands-on learning helps to broaden children's cultural literacy. One example is teaching children about proper nutrition by making and eating healthy snacks. Examples include connecting food to popular stories, such as having a tea party when reading *Alice in Wonderland* or making oatmeal when reading "Goldilocks and the Three Bears." For more suggestions, see Jane Yolen's *Fairy Tale Feasts* (2006), a collection of fairy tales with matching recipes.

Children are introduced to ethnic foods from other countries as a part of this cultural experience. To connect vocabulary to the sense of touch, Forney (2001) suggests that teachers make a texture box with a variety of objects that appeal to the sense of touch, sight, smell, and hearing with a matching set of vocabulary cards. Using this texture box, learners are encouraged to increase their vocabulary by exploring real objects. See Figure 5.4 for a list of possible items to include in your own texture box.

To create a texture box, fill a box with 40 to 60 everyday objects from nature and around the home. Interesting objects for children are those that would be encountered in their lives, and these types of objects provide the best source for vocabulary development. The texture box can be placed in a learning center where children can match objects to words (descriptive adjectives). Some examples of descriptive adjectives inspired from the objects in a texture box are *rough, smooth, shiny, soft, furry, silky, bumpy, velvety, coarse, hairy, smelly, pungent, spicy, crunchy, gritty, sharp, dull, sticky, rubbery, slimy, rusty,* and *glittery.* The texture box motivates learners to use these descriptive words in their everyday writing.

5-3d Movement

Movement adds drama and/or dance to the learning process and makes learning come alive. For example, after reading about Rosa Parks, children can reenact the bus scene, to better comprehend racial injustice and prejudice. When reading The Magic School Bus series by Joanna Cole, the class can act out Mrs. Frizzle's adventures (in the waterworks, under the ocean, inside the Earth, or flying through outer space). Props and costumes enhance learning. Allowing the children to move around in the classroom promotes reading and writing in different places on a regular basis. Children love to go outside on a sunny day for a reading or writing workshop, which adds a new dimension to the learning process.

Kitchen utensils
Grated nutmeg
Cloves and cinnamon
Basil or sage
Vanilla beans
Ginger
Sunflower seeds
Almonds and walnut
Seashells
Sand
Seaweed
A variety of leaves
Violets and pansies
Daisies and orchids
Screwdriver and hammer
Wrench and pliers
Cotton balls, foil, and saran wrap
Different types of fabric
Sandpaper
Costume jewelry
Bubble wrap
Feathers and pine cones

Figure 5.4
Sample Items for a Texture Box

THE ARTS AND BRAIN DEVELOPMENT

Drama, dance, music, and visual art contribute to the formation of neurological connections starting at birth (Carlton, 2000). Developing neurological connections is crucial for young children. For example, the occipital (visual) region of the brain links to the auditory part of the brain to recognize letters and words, and associates these images with the sounds of language, thus creating meaning.

Think about It

How can you incorporate the arts into your vocabulary lessons? For example, children can dance or use dramatic play to define the meaning of new vocabulary words or use whole body movement to create the shapes of letters when spelling new words.

5-3e Eye Anchors

Eye anchors are objects, photos, or cards with written topics that help to keep children engaged and on task (Forney, 2001). Eye anchors can be small for a desktop or large for a classroom wall. Labels on objects in the classroom are a form of eye anchors. These labels may be printed in different languages, depending on the culture and ethnicity of the children. Labels can be displayed in various languages to represent the cultures of the children in the class. Children can wear hats with sight words as eye anchors during writing workshop to encourage using new words.

5-3f Validation

Validation supports the children's decisions and affirms their actions (Forney, 2001). All children need praise. Teachers must tell learners when they are doing something well; perhaps the teacher makes an announcement in front of the class or quietly praises the child. General praise can include ringing a bell or shaking a tambourine for notable achievements. A child who reaches a reading goal (a set number of books) could wear a fancy crown or receive a special bookmark. A photo of the child can be posted on the bulletin board. Forney likes to honor a child by lowering a decorative hula hoop over his or her head to celebrate significant accomplishments. Forney's (2001) mantra to her class is: "I'm preparing you for greatness."

When teaching vocabulary and other literacy skills, the teacher should have these components in mind. Visuals (eye anchors), manipulatives (texture box, vocabulator), and movement are especially important for English language learners. Children from diverse backgrounds must learn to identify and name what they observe in their world. Providing young children with tools for their literacy toolkits (for example, sentence squeezie) makes their work easier and more enjoyable. With lots of praise and positive feedback in a loving, nonthreatening environment, readers blossom like *Leo the Late Bloomer* by Robert Kraus (1994), a story about a tiger whose mother believes that he will learn to read when he is ready.

5-3g Vocabulary Self-Collection Strategy (VSS)

The vocabulary self-collection strategy assists early learners in developing meaning and comprehension through prior knowledge and interests. Nonfiction or fiction books are read as a whole class. A particular theme or topic is selected, such as mammals of the world (science) or family roles in different countries (social studies), and the class creates a list of unknown words that they want to learn more about through the reading selection. Learners write their own sentences using the unknown words

eye anchors Objects, photos, or cards with written topics that help to keep children engaged and on task.

vocabulary self-collection strategy Students self-select their new vocabulary words.

Table 5.2	VSS Word List from Ish	
Target Word (VSS)	**Origin or Reference (where word was found)**	**Meaning/Context**
Vase-ish	"Well it looks *vase-ish!*" she exclaimed.	To be like a vase or container
Energized	Ramon felt light and energized.	To activate the capacity for work
Inspired	His "ish" art inspired "ish" writing.	To stimulate or impel to create

Adapted from Reynolds (2004).

(see Photo 5.6). These sentences are shared with the whole class. The original sentence in the text is used to check the specific usage of the word. During this activity, children choose vocabulary words that are culturally relevant and meaningful. Children explain rationales for their word choices and define meanings of each word.

They act out meanings, draw images that promote vocabulary skills, or tell a story that includes the meaning, origin, derivative, and reason why the word was selected. For example, a game can be played where children guess the meaning of the word derived from their experiences. To establish context of vocabulary usage, children discuss when and where the words were used. Children better understand each other through language development and cultural literacy. Children build self-confidence in their vocabulary skills through individual and group work in a creative way. Table 5.2 is an example of a VSS word list using *Ish* by Peter H. Reynolds (2004), a story about how a young artist realizes his talent and is encouraged by his sister.

5-3h Teaching Meaning Vocabulary through Important Words

To enhance reading comprehension and focus on meaning vocabulary, children select important words in the reading selection. Words are selected individually first while each child reads the text. Children then compare their individual lists of words within a small group. They discuss whether or not they agree on the importance of the word and share rationales for their word selection. The teacher creates a large chart of the word choices for each small group. Differences in word choice for each small group are discussed.

As a whole class, the children decide on the 10 or 5 important words for the text selection. These words help to create the meaning and assist children in comprehending the reading selection. Remember that the relationship between text and illustrations is important. The illustrations can help guide learners who speak other languages. Children create sentences using the 10 words and share them with the class or in small groups. The 10 important words are shown in Figure 5.5, based on a selection from *Tar Beach* by Faith Ringgold (1991). The story is about Cassie Louise Lightfoot, a third-grade girl, and her desire to fly among the stars as a metaphor for a successful life.

Photo 5.6 *Imagining new words before writing*
Courtesy of the authors

Cassie Louise Lightfoot
Bridge
Skyscraper
Possession
Hoisting
Diamond
Fly
Girders
Union
Tar Beach

Possible Summary Sentence: <u>Cassie Louise Light-foot</u> imagined she could <u>fly</u> above the George Washington <u>Bridge</u> and <u>skyscrapers</u>.

Adapted from Ringgold (1991).

Figure 5.5
*Ten Important Words
from* Tar Beach

5-3i Teaching Vocabulary through Meaningful Discussions

Children's literature can stimulate meaningful discussions that represent children with a range of reading abilities or cultural backgrounds. When children make personal connections during independent reading, they develop a positive attitude, understanding that meaning is the goal of reading (Moses, Ogden, & Kelley, 2015). During meaningful discussions, children question the text, build opinions, use text-based evidence, and make personal connections (see Photo 5.7).

To further stimulate meaningful discussions, children can independently read the same book (literature circles) with simple text and opportunities for inferring ideas, such as *Sam & Dave Dig a Hole* by Mac Barnett (2014), *I Want My Hat Back* by Jon Klassen (2011), or *Don't Let the Pigeon Drive the Bus* by Mo Willems (2003). While independently reading, the children can mark the book with sticky notes to identify their favorite text or illustrations. Small groups can form to discuss these choices and describe the illustrations through visual elements (line, shape, form, color, value, texture, space, and pattern). To focus on literal comprehension, children may use the story High Five strategy, which includes the basic parts of a narrative: characters (who), setting (when and where), beginning, middle, and end. Finally, the children can retell the story using this strategy to help remember sequence and details (see Figure 5.6).

During the discussion, the teacher instructs how to draw inferences from text and illustrations. In small groups, children further discuss the connections between the text and their lives. This deeper level of comprehension (inferring) enhances children's vocabulary knowledge through social interactions. Children may read other books by

Photo 5.7 *Sharing language*
Josh Weinberger

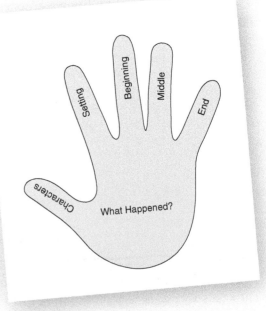

Figure 5.6
Story High Five

the same author (author study) to discuss their thinking and inferences. Natural dialogue is promoted through reading and discussing a text set (a collection of books on a central theme, topic, or by the same author).

CONSIDER THIS...

Consider how you might create a vocabulator based on an ocean theme. For example, select a book, such as *The Rainbow Fish* by Marcus Pfister (1999). With a partner, take turns interacting with the book. What key words and related objects would you include in your vocabulator?

5-4 Vocabulary Instruction for English Learners

Learning new vocabulary and a new language presents a challenge for young children, especially for English language learners (ELLs). All young children benefit from repeated exposure to new vocabulary. Labeling items in the classroom with clearly printed cards is a simple technique to help young children, including ELLs, recognize new vocabulary words. Repeatedly reviewing the words associated with objects in the classroom builds a vocabulary foundation. The cards may be removed so the children can label objects on their own. This allows teachers to informally assess word recognition of environmental print. If children practice "reading the room" on a daily basis, these words soon become a part of their daily lives. Writing and illustrating acrostic poems using the letters in their first names is another meaningful activity for English language learners (see Figure 5.7). Children think of words (adjectives) or phrases that reflect their personalities.

Routines for building vocabulary skills are effective in the ELL classroom. It is important to set up structured time each day to introduce new words and practice the new vocabulary in different situations and contexts. For example, each morning the children and teacher identify the day of the week, the date, the weather, and important events. The teacher writes the information about the day on a whiteboard, anchor chart, or on sentence strips in a pocket chart. Afterward, the children and teacher read the sentences together, which reinforces and builds their knowledge of sight words.

Today is Wednesday, April 18, 2012. The weather is rainy and windy outside. We will have a police officer visit our class for career day. Today is Brittney's birthday.

Writing and drawing in a journal on a daily basis create effective writing habits and develop vocabulary use. Children can draw an image and then write sentences, either with the teacher's assistance or independently. Vocabulary instruction for English language learners is facilitated by using environmental print such as pictures, stories, posters,

Figure 5.7
Sample Name Poem
Courtesy of the authors

text set A collection of books in different genres on the same theme or topic.

MAKING ACCORDION BOOKS: STRATEGIES FOR ENGLISH LANGUAGE LEARNERS (ELLs)

English language learners can make simple accordion books using folded art paper and cardboard covers (see Photo 5.8).

Choose a topic you are studying in science or social studies, such as the rain forest. The children illustrate each page and label the insect or animal. They will be proud of their handmade books!

Directions: Cut a large piece of art paper or other sturdy paper into strips. Fold the strip into four or five equal parts. Cut two pieces of cardboard the same size for the front and back cover. Glue the paper onto each end piece of cardboard. Tie the book together with a ribbon. (The strips of paper may be illustrated on both sides.)

Think about It

How can you validate the diverse cultures of your students through allowing them to create books about family traditions? Perhaps they could include a few words in their native language with a glossary to explain the meanings.

Photo 5.8 *Accordion rain forest book*
Courtesy of the authors

charts, books, games, bulletin boards, and other items displayed in the classroom. The link to illustrations and understanding new vocabulary words guides children to comprehension (Ray & Smith, 2010).

5-4a Vocabulary Flash Cards

Children who are reading aloud often mispronounce or substitute known words for unknown words. While listening to a child read aloud a text selection, record his or her miscues on a running record form or blank sheet of paper (substitutions only). Teachers record the sentence and note location of the sentence in the reading selection to return to this word when checking context clues. From the list of miscues, teachers select five words to focus on during an individual reading session. The goal is to increase sight or meaning vocabulary and reading fluency through individualized instruction. The teacher pronounces the words and asks the child to write the words on index cards. The teacher and child check for accurate spelling. The teacher demonstrates how to chunk long words into meaningful sections (for example, prefix, root, and suffix). Teaching words through analogy helps children transfer understanding from the known to the unknown. For example, knowing the word *moon* will help them recognize the word *soon*. While reviewing the text, the child uses context clues and illustrations to understand the meaning and usage of the word.

Horned toads	Fascinated	Refrigerators	Dough
Decorated	Barbeque	Treatment	Incense
Communicate	Imagination	Pilgrimage	Chaperoning

Figure 5.8
Sample Words for Vocabulary Flash Cards

Children illustrate word meanings or write definitions to understand new vocabulary. Children are taught how to use a dictionary as a resource (to learn guide words, multiple meanings, and alphabetical order). Picture dictionaries are a great addition to a classroom library and can help young children visualize the meanings of unfamiliar words. Vocabulary flash cards increase word recognition and reading fluency. This strategy can be repeated with new reading selections until children understand the process. Sample vocabulary words in Figure 5.8 are from *In My Family* by Carmen Lomas Garza (1996). In this book, the author describes her childhood memories of a traditional Mexican American lifestyle.

5-4b Connecting Visuals with Text

Visuals and *realia* (real-world objects) are especially important for English language learners to promote early literacy development. Children's schemata are activated through cultural literacy experiences. Vocabulary relationships are created through interactive activities that link new words with real objects. For example, when learning the word *apple*, teachers provide an array of apples for children to explore with the senses. Young children can use different literacy strategies to increase vocabulary development through cognitive, socioemotional, and physical learning experiences.

Understanding relationships between words in a reading selection based upon a topic can be accomplished through the list-group-label strategy (Johns & Lenski, 2010; Taba, 1967). First, children list words after brainstorming about a certain topic. The class reads a selection on the same topic and list words found in the passage. Next, children group the words into categories with labels. The process of list-group-label helps them to recognize new words and comprehend the meaning of these words. Collages of their words or abstract art can be created to enhance understanding.

For example, *A is for Art: An Abstract Alphabet* by Stephen T. Johnson (2008) helps children to create lists of words for each letter of the alphabet. The abstract artwork featured for each letter may inspire children to make their own artwork. The "C" artwork is made up of colorful pieces of candy. Hidden within the pattern is a blue letter "C," which also exemplifies camouflage. "Countless colorful candies consciously collected, crammed, crushed, and confined crowd a clear circular container filled to capacity" (Johnson, 2008, p. 3). A possible label or category for some "C" words could be action-oriented vocabulary: *collected, crammed, crushed,* and *confined. Animalia* by Graeme Base (1993), with rich language and detailed illustrations, is another option for the list-group-label strategy that works with children of all ages.

5-4c Using Wordless Picture Books with English Language Learners

Learning through meaningful contexts is critical for children who are learning English. This notion that ELLs must understand what they are listening to and reading in the classroom was first promoted by Steve Krashen (1982) and labeled "comprehensible input." English language learners should participate in meaningful activities (reading, writing, listening, and speaking), to enhance their English language skills. For example,

realia Real-world objects that are used as a visual strategy during reading instruction with English language learners.

comprehensible input ELLs acquire language by listening and comprehending verbal communication at a higher level than their current speaking/reading/writing English language level.

reading wordless picture books enhances the language development, oral reading skills, and close reading strategies of English language learners (Louie & Sierschynski, 2015). Children with different English proficiency levels and diverse linguistic backgrounds can successfully participate in literature discussion groups.

Wordless picture books "allow ELs to engage with complex content as they discuss meaning and work toward oral language proficiency" (Louie & Sierschynski, 2015, p. 106). Children learn how to observe and analyze details and visual elements (color, line, texture) in illustrations through visual storytelling, which improves their close reading skills, an important skill in the Common Core State Standards for English Language Arts. Language instruction can be differentiated using wordless picture books. Beginning ELLs can label images in the pictures; emerging ELLs are able to write sentences; more proficient ELLs can participate in oral or written retellings using story maps. When working with English language learners, teachers should first select simple wordless books that have singular levels of meaning, a simple structure (text features), and familiar concepts. Some examples are *A Ball for Daisy* by Chris Raschka (2011) or *The Girl and the Bicycle* by Mark Pett (2014). Complex wordless picture books have unconventional text structures, multiple layers of meaning, and may require a deeper level of conceptual knowledge or inference skills (Louie & Sierschynski, 2015). Books such as *Journey* by Aaron Becker (2013), *Unspoken: A Story from the Underground Railroad* by Henry Cole (2012), and *Flotsam* by David Wiesner (2006), are appropriate for children with a higher level of English proficiency.

When teachers select activities for English language learners, they should adapt literacy instruction to the needs of their students: interests, prior knowledge, linguistic diversity, English language proficiency, reading levels, and cultural relevance. Meaningful activities (differentiated instruction and cooperative learning) provide motivation for ELLs to learn new concepts and vocabulary in a safe and nurturing environment.

 CONSIDER THIS...

Consider how you will teach a vocabulary lesson on the rain forest in a diverse first-grade classroom. How can you assess and build children's background knowledge on this topic before reading a book about the rain forest, such as *The Great Kapok Tree* by Lynne Cherry (1990)?

5-5 Types of Vocabulary Assessment

There are many ways to assess a child's knowledge of vocabulary in context (reading passages or writing samples) and in isolation (word lists). Teachers should use a variety of assessments to measure the complex layers of children's vocabulary knowledge. One of the most common word lists is the *San Diego Quick Assessment of Reading Ability* (La Pray & Ross, 1969), which tests word recognition using isolated word lists grouped in categories according to grade levels. For example, the first-grade list consists of the following words: *road, live, thank, when, bigger, how, always, night, spring,* and *today.* A word list with one error is considered *independent level,* and two errors place a child at *instructional level.* Children read the 10 words in each list until they reach *frustration level* (3 or more errors). This test measures a child's decoding and vocabulary skills; therefore, the level of accuracy is not the same as a child's reading level, which involves comprehension of text. Informal reading inventories (IRIs) also have word lists grouped by grade levels to match the selected reading passages. Although there is no assessment of comprehension (as in the *San Diego Quick Assessment),* these word lists can be used to estimate a child's vocabulary knowledge and decoding skills.

To assess vocabulary knowledge of emergent readers, teachers ask children to write familiar words during a 10-minute period (Clay, 1993). They may write words like *Mama* and *Daddy,* which are acceptable. Words with letter reversals count as long as

ASSESSING VOCABULARY KNOWLEDGE SKILLS THROUGH WRITING CONFERENCES

Vocabulary knowledge can be assessed through writing samples, analyzing the child's use of one of six writing traits: word choice. The other five writing traits are voice, sentence fluency, organization, ideas or content, and conventions (Sulzby & Teale, 1985).

Directions: During a writing conference, the teacher asks the child to underline all of the nouns, verbs, or adjectives in his or her own writing piece. Substitutions are suggested for the words that could be more vivid or descriptive. The teacher uses the assessment guide to record responses.

Assessment Guide:

Teacher Reflection Prompts	Word Choice Overall	Nouns	Verbs	Adjectives
Strengths of the child to guide future instruction				
Areas of improvement based upon child's needs				
Strategies and practices to support child's development				

Think about It

How can you use children's literature as models for teaching word choice? One good example is *Martin's Big Words* by Doreen Rappaport (2007), a biography of Martin Luther King Jr.

⌄ Professional Resource Download

the words can be recognized. When the time is up, the teacher counts the total number of words and records this information in the child's portfolio. This assessment is given frequently to determine the child's progress in word knowledge. Sight word lists are also used to assess word knowledge of beginning readers. To administer this assessment, the teacher checks off words on a master list as the child reads the words on flash cards (25 at a time). The next group of words is assessed after the child has mastered the initial set of sight words. These words must be read instantly, rather than sounded out. Some sight word lists are grouped according to the first 100 words for first graders, the second 100 for second graders, and the third 100 for third graders. The Dolch list of 220 sight words is not divided by grade level. These high-frequency words should be mastered by the end of second grade.

During oral reading, vocabulary assessment in context involves analyzing a child's use of the language cueing systems (graphophonic, syntactic, and semantic). This assessment is called miscue analysis. *Miscues* are responses that are different from the actual words in the texts, such as *substitutions* (replacing a word with a different word), *omissions* (omitting a word or phrase), *reversals* (reversing letters in a word or words in a sentence), and *insertions* (adding a word). Assessing a child's patterns of miscues will determine his or her reading strengths and needs. (More information on this process can be found in Chapter 3 on assessment.) Good readers use the following language cueing systems automatically as they are reading and decoding unfamiliar words:

- Graphophonic, or visual
- Syntactic, or structure
- Semantic, or meaning

miscue analysis Analyzing miscues (substitutions) during oral reading to understand the reader's use of strategies (that is, language cueing systems) during the reading process.

Age Groups	Cognitive	Socioemotional
0 to 3	Make word banks from key vocabulary words in favorite stories and match cards to words in the text. Read counting books and ABC books; ask the child to find the matching magnetic letter or number; place on a cookie sheet or magnetic board.	Show color cards and say color names; talk about how different colors portray a variety of emotions. Match colors and words in a pocket chart while singing a rhyming song. Make facial gestures to represent different emotions.
3 to 6	Collect objects that emphasize shape, texture, or color, and label. Use environmental print to create signs (stop, go, left, right). Photograph objects and post with word labels. Pretend or reenact everyday jobs and list all words associated with tasks on index cards (flash cards).	Predict emotions related to new words based upon illustrations and pantomime. Read fairy tales and associate characters with new words. Celebrate mastery of sight words with food, balloons, party games.
6 to 9	Observe nature and record field notes. Compare and contrast synonyms and antonyms of new words. Invent new uses for everyday objects using descriptive vocabulary. Read articles about current events and retell in sequence with a partner.	Read different historical perspectives about an event and write an opinion or persuasive essay. Use new words to write a commercial to convince someone to purchase a product. Learn a new dance taught by classmates and perform to music.

⌄ Professional Resource Download

When learning new vocabulary, young children associate unknown words with known words in the context of the sentence to gain a better understanding. This process of using context clues embeds the new vocabulary word in children's prior knowledge and helps them build new knowledge. Children use cueing systems that work for them when decoding unknown words. Often the first step is "sounding out" or decoding the new word.

The *graphophonic* or visual cueing system uses the knowledge of written sounds. Children try out different pronunciations and practice what the new word sounds like on others. The teacher is usually the first to respond when reading in a group, but often other children recognize a word and help children self-correct. Self-correcting is an important process, and repeating the word aloud several times in different situations or reading another text selection helps to cement the new word in a child's working vocabulary. The teacher starts with familiar words that sound the same and have the same spelling (teaching by analogy). Parts of a known word help children verbally express the unknown word. For example, *excited* (unfamiliar word) can be linked to *extra* (known word), because both words start with the same sound and letters. This process leads children to recognize other words with similar spellings and sounds, such as *exit, exclaim,* or *excel.* Often dictionaries, even picture dictionaries, can help children figure out new words and lead to other words with a similar spelling and perhaps a similar pronunciation.

Physical	Children's Books	Family Involvement
Print the child's first name on big cards; trace letters with fingers.	*First the Egg* by Laura Vaccaro Seeger	Take photos during a trip to the mall, a park, or a zoo.
Using felt/textured fabric, make letters of the child's name and trace with fingers.	*Pete the Cat: I Love My White Shoes* by Eric Litwin	Make a scrapbook of photos and label them.
Using letter cards, ask child to order letters in the proper sequence.	*Hello Ocean* by Pam Muñoz Ryan	Put board books in every room in the house for easy access.
		Find objects related to stories and discuss.
Create a nature/found-object collage, and describe textures.	*Museum ABC* by the Metropolitan Museum of Art	Make books based on child's interests.
Draw a path on a map and verbalize directions.	*Max's Words* by Kate Banks	Create a word bank, using index cards on curtain rings; label cards with child's favorite words with heart symbol.
Move like animals and dictate sentences using new vocabulary.	*Behold the Bold Umbrellaphant and Other Poems* by Jack Prelutsky	Illustrate new words to create a picture dictionary.
Act out the meanings of words in content areas: transportation, weather, or other topics.	*A River of Words* by Jen Bryant	Establish a family reading time several days a week.
Video record children dancing and replay adding descriptive text.	*America: A Patriotic Primer* by Lynne Cheney	Watch *Jeopardy* and create your own version at home.
Arrange related objects in categories according to descriptive words.	*The Z was Zapped* by Chris Van Allsburg	Go to the library once a week to check out books based on your child's interests.
Play music, dance, and sing new words in text.		Read a chapter book together and discuss (your own book club).
		Read books about environmental issues; discuss and create an action plan.

Reading the entire sentence with the new word again helps children to recognize new words through the *syntactic cueing system*. The grammar and word use leads children to identify whether the new word could be a noun, verb, adjective, or adverb. Identifying the parts of speech in a sentence through diagramming or labeling is part of the process of learning new vocabulary and being able to use the new word in future situations. For example, *The dog has fuzzy fur* would not be written as *The dog has fur fuzzy*.

Making sense of the word meaning in the sentence involves the *semantic cueing system*. Communication of ideas through the spoken and written word is important. Often the words surrounding the unfamiliar word help children to identify the meaning of the new word and thus the meaning of the sentence and text selection as a whole. A child may not recognize the written word *stop* in the following sentence: *I will st__ the car at the end of the street.* He or she can figure out what makes sense based upon prior experiences using context clues. Understanding the context or culture for the text selection leads children to understand the new word. When assessing children's understanding of new vocabulary, parents and teachers need to interact and ask questions when they notice children hesitating or pondering.

One way to determine a reader's use of the cueing systems is through a simple cloze activity (Johns & Lenski, 2014). The cloze procedure is an informal tool for assessing reading comprehension. To create a cloze test, teachers select an excerpt

cloze A reading comprehension assessment using passages with deleted words.

from an informational text, deleting approximately every fifth word. The deleted words are replaced with blanks. Children then read the passage and supply the missing words using context clues. A passage with 40 percent accuracy is considered to be on the child's instructional reading level. To make the cloze test easier for beginning readers, adapt it by adding three word choices in the blanks (converting the cloze into a maze test). For example, the following text includes both cloze and maze test applications:

A severe storm with _____ rain, and a funnel-shaped cloud is called a _____ (hurricane, tornado, cyclone).

Children would use their vocabulary knowledge to fill in the first word, *wind* (cloze test), and select from the word choices provided (maze test) for the word *tornado*. Assessing vocabulary knowledge using a variety of strategies helps teachers meet the needs of individual children.

The Vocabulary Knowledge Scale (VKS) is a self-report assessment based on stages of word learning (Dale, 1965). Students assess their knowledge of teacher-selected words from content area texts according to the following categories:

1. I have never seen this word. (1 point)
2. I have seen this word before, but I can't tell you the meaning. (2 points)
3. I have seen this word and I believe it means _____ (synonym). (3 points)
4. I know this word and it means _____ (synonym). (4 points)
5. I know how to use this word in a sentence: _____. (5 points)

A score of 5 means the child used the key word correctly in terms of meaning and grammar. The VKS is usually given as a pretest before teaching a chapter or unit and as a posttest to measure growth.

 CONSIDER THIS...

Consider how children learn new vocabulary words through reading and writing. How will you assess their vocabulary knowledge throughout the year?

5-6 Literacy Strategies and Practices for Vocabulary Development

Supportive and nurturing learning environments promote vocabulary development. Effective strategies and practices involve a variety of texts (books, magazines, newspapers) in different genres (fiction, nonfiction) for multiple purposes (informative, persuasive, enjoyment). Building a child's vocabulary supports fluency and comprehension (see Table 5.3).

maze A reading comprehension assessment using text with deleted words that includes word choices.

End-of-Chapter Study Aids

Summary

Knowledge of vocabulary development concepts assists teachers in planning effective instruction. Children utilize metacognitive strategies to learn what words mean and how to read fluently based on their own experiences. Print-rich learning environments facilitate this process.

The early literacy environment supports learning to read through the use of words with rhyme, rhythm, and repetition found in stories, songs, and poetry. Vocabulary increases as parents and children interact through everyday experiences: eating dinner, playing in the park, watching movies, and entertaining guests. Teachers expand children's word knowledge through modeling, demonstration, practice, and evaluation or assessment. Playing with words through reading, writing, poetry, and games leads to laughter and joy in learning.

Vocabulary instruction involves sight and meaning vocabulary. Sight vocabulary (high-frequency words) builds a foundation for reading. Meaning vocabulary assists readers in understanding content. Cueing systems help children understand the syntax, semantics, and pragmatic applications of language. Meaning (comprehension) is the goal of reading. Vocabulary and word recognition are also important in a child's literacy toolbox. Learning words through association (list-group-label, 10 important words, vocabulary self-collection [VSS], and word clouds) enhances children's vocabulary acquisition. Effective strategies for vocabulary instruction for English language learners include vocabulary flash cards, wordless picture books, and connecting visuals with text (realia). Word lists, observation checklists, miscue analysis, and the Vocabulary Knowledge Scale (VKS) are examples of assessment practices. Children gain confidence, self-efficacy (belief in doing tasks well), and higher self-esteem as they accomplish goals in literacy. Vocabulary development and instruction play important roles in a child's journey to become a successful reader and writer.

Chapter Exercises

1. Select a children's picture book on a science or social studies theme. In a small group, choose five words for each tier of vocabulary instruction (Tier One, Tier Two, and Tier Three). Share word lists with the class and discuss selections.
2. Choose a children's picture book (fiction or nonfiction). Identify five to 10 key vocabulary words from the text. Read the book aloud to a small group of peers. Randomly assign one word per group member. Each member completes a word map (see Figure 5.2) for the key word and shares with the whole group.
3. Create a texture box with 10 to 12 items and matching descriptive adjectives written on index cards (for example, *rough, shiny, smooth,* and *bumpy*). With a partner, match objects with word cards and discuss.
4. Take a picture walk using a wordless picture book and discuss illustrations in a small group. Write new vocabulary words on sticky notes related to images in the book. Collaboratively decide where to place sticky notes on the pages as a group.
5. Analyze a child's writing sample using the assessment guide for vocabulary knowledge found in Section 5-5. Complete one column individually and discuss results with a peer.

Teacher Toolbox

LEARNING NEW VOCABULARY THROUGH MOVEMENT: TEACHING WORD CHOICE

Appropriate for Ages 4 to 7

A variety of genres inspires children to fall in love with words. Historical and realistic fiction, traditional literature, informational books, and poetry create a passion for reading and learning new words. Children listen for interesting words (nouns and verbs), while the teacher reads aloud stories with rich vocabulary, such as from *The Grand Old Tree* by Mary Newell DePalma (2005). After the book is read, children identify words and phrases that are interesting to them. The teacher writes the words and divides these into parts of speech columns (nouns and verbs) on a chart (Interesting Words Anchor Chart). The teacher models examples on the anchor chart, while the children write their word choices in their writing journals. The teacher explains that a noun is a person, place, or thing. Most verbs are action words. Phrases are written on sentence strips for children to read together. The teacher and children decide on creative movements that are associated with the selected words and phrases. For example, when reading aloud, "The grand old tree flowered," children spread their arms wide to symbolize a flower blooming.

Interesting Words Anchor Chart

Nouns	Verbs
Tree	Sank
Earth	Reached
Sky	Nested

Key Terms and Concepts

antonyms	maze	synonyms
cloze	meaning vocabulary	text set
comprehensible input	miscue analysis	vocabulary
eye anchors	pointer	vocabulary self-collection
genres	realia	strategy
homophones	response to intervention (RTI)	

Monkey Business Images/Shutterstock.com

STANDARDS ADDRESSED IN THIS CHAPTER

The standards from the following organizations will be used throughout the chapter: Common Core State Standards for English Language Arts, the National Association for the Education of Young Children (NAEYC), and National Core Arts Standards. These standards are discussed further in the chapter as appropriate.

Common Core State Standards for English Language Arts

Anchor Standards for Reading

Reading Standards for Literature/Informational Text K–5
- Key Ideas and Details
- Craft and Structure
- Integration of Knowledge and Ideas

Anchor Standards for Writing
- Text Types and Purposes

Anchor Standards for Speaking and Listening
- Comprehension and Collaboration

Anchor Standards for Language
- Knowledge of Language
- Vocabulary Acquisition and Use

2010 NAEYC Standards for Initial and Advanced Early Childhood Professional Preparation Programs
- *Standard 4:* Using Developmentally Effective Approaches
- *Standard 5:* Using Content Knowledge to Build Meaningful Curriculum

NAEYC Early Childhood Program Standards and Accreditation Criteria
- *Standard 2:* Curriculum
- *Standard 3:* Teaching

NCA

National Core Arts Standards (Dance, Media Arts, Music, Theater, Visual Arts)

Connecting
- *Anchor Standard 10:* Synthesize and relate knowledge and personal experiences to make art.

There is no such thing as a child who hates to read; there are only children who have not found the right book. — Frank Serafini

The goal of early childhood literacy is comprehension and meaning. **Comprehension** is the act of understanding knowledge and the power to seize ideas. Teachers create an environment that is conducive to learning, where children are immersed in the world of literacy. Children interact with text to create their own interpretations, based on their experiences and interests. In our holistic model of literacy, children connect their cognitive abilities, socioemotional well-being, and physical capabilities to create their understanding of the world. Sensory experiences awaken cognition and a passion to learn. Active interaction in a print-rich environment sparks motivation for reading and writing (Tompkins, 2013).

Comprehension is defined as "the process of constructing meaning using both the author's text and the reader's background knowledge for a specific purpose" (Tompkins, 2013, p. 374). Some children are better at comprehending text, and others are stronger in their decoding (sight words and phonics) skills. Children who are **word callers** are just pronouncing words (without meaning), and are not really reading (Cartwright & Duke, 2010). Word callers have a bottom-up or skills-based concept of reading. Children who have a top-down or meaning-based concept of reading understand that reading must make sense. Good readers have **metacognition**, which means they are able to understand their own thinking during the reading process. If they realize that something is not making sense, good readers usually go back and reread the text to see if they can figure out the problem. Good readers have a repertoire of comprehension strategies that can be used as needed, such as predicting, summarizing, inferring, visualizing, questioning, and making connections. As teachers, our goal is to help our students become independent, strategic readers. Our students must be able to comprehend a variety of genres, including fiction and nonfiction. The emphasis of the national Common Core State Standards (2010) is on **close** reading in informational text. Children, even in the primary grades, must be able to think critically, actively engaging with the text while reading or listening. Each child will comprehend the same text differently, because each person has a unique *schema* or knowledge of the world.

LEARNING OBJECTIVES

After you have read this chapter, you should be able to:

6-1 Explain reading comprehension concepts.

6-2 Determine factors that impact comprehension instruction.

6-3 Describe motivation for literacy engagement.

6-4 Analyze comprehension instruction in the Common Core State Standards (CCSS).

6-5 Apply comprehension strategies for children's literature.

6-6 Demonstrate literacy strategies and practices for reading comprehension.

STANDARDS CONNECTION TO VIGNETTE

NAEYC Early Childhood Program Standards and Accreditation Criteria

Standard 2: Curriculum

2.B.07 Children have varied opportunities to learn to understand, empathize with, and take into account other people's perspectives.

Common Core State Standards for English Language Arts

Key Ideas and Details

Grade 3

1. Ask and answer questions to demonstrate understanding of a text, referring explicitly to the text as the basis for the answers.
2. Recount stories, including fables, folktales, and myths from diverse cultures; determine the central message, lesson, or moral; and explain how it is conveyed through key details in the text.
3. Describe characters in a story (for example, their traits, motivations, or feelings), and explain how their actions contribute to the sequence of events.

One of the most effective ways to teach comprehension strategies is through interactive read-alouds with accountable talk (Ramirez, 2006), a powerful teaching tool in balanced literacy classrooms (see Photo 6.1). The read-aloud is usually separate from a reading workshop (mini-lesson and independent reading), although it often relates to the same theme or concept. For the read-aloud, it is important for teachers to choose an appropriate book that relates to a current unit of study in the classroom. The teacher should write questions for higher-level thinking and comments for think-alouds ahead of time on sticky notes for the children to answer. Children should be asked to provide text evidence when discussing the questions in small groups, which is accountable talk. As the teacher, you verbalize your thoughts as you read the text aloud to the students (think-alouds), making connections or demonstrating strategies used by good readers. Stop several times during the reading to have children talk to a partner about what they are thinking and feeling (Keene & Zimmerman, 2007).

comprehension The process of constructing meaning for a specific purpose that involves the reader's understanding of the author's text and his or her prior knowledge.

word callers Readers who can pronounce the words but do not understand the meaning.

metacognition Understanding one's own thinking during the reading process.

close reading An instructional strategy that requires students to read and critically examine the same text multiple times for different purposes.

informational text A type of nonfiction or expository text that contains information on one or more topics.

accountable talk Discourse within a learning community that involves accurate and appropriate knowledge to promote critical thinking skills.

think-alouds Teachers verbalize their own thinking while reading orally in order to demonstrate how skilled readers construct meaning.

text evidence Examples from the text to support the reader's interpretation.

Photo 6.1 *Accountable talk*

Photo 6.2 Crow Call *by Lois Lowry, illustrated by Bagram Ibatoulline*

Source: Lowry, L. (2009). *Crow Call*. New York: Scholastic Press. (This book is illustrated by Bagram Ibatoulline.)

Mrs. Taylor chose *Crow Call* by Lois Lowry, illustrated by Bagram Ibatoulline (Scholastic, 2009), as her read-aloud during a unit on writing memoirs. The story is about the day the author went hunting with her father. Mrs. Taylor begins by asking her third graders to predict what the story will be about, based on the cover illustration and title. The children predict that the story will be about a little girl looking for crows, but they don't know why she would be doing this. The teacher also asks the children to notice the landscape (bare tree and brown grass) and the girl's clothing to guess the time of year (see Photo 6.2). They're not sure about the setting (place) and time period, so Mrs. Taylor tells the class that the time period is in the 1940s, just after World War II. She has on a plaid flannel shirt like the one the little girl is wearing on the cover, as a prop to provide interest and excitement before reading.

Mrs. Taylor begins reading the text, stopping frequently to ask questions that encourage higher-level thinking, such as:

- Let's think for a minute about the relationship Lizzie has with her Dad at this point in the story. Turn and talk to your partner about what you are thinking.
- Why would Lizzie's Dad be hunting for crows? Stop and jot your thoughts on a sticky note.
- Do you think that Lizzie's Dad will use his rifle to kill the crows? Why or why not?

(Ask students to provide evidence from the text.)

The teacher ends with a think-aloud strategy: "When I finish a book, I like to think about big themes and deeper meanings I got from it. Turn and talk to your partner about what Lois Lowry is trying to tell us." She asks one or two children to share their responses. They understood that the real message was love and family relationships, not about hunting crows.

During this interactive read-aloud, the teacher demonstrated many different comprehension strategies that she wants her students to use in the future. One example is visualizing. On the page where Lizzie and her Dad are in a diner ordering breakfast, Mrs. Taylor asks the class to close their eyes, pretending they are in the restaurant. She asks: "What do you smell? Hear? Taste? Touch? See?" Using their five senses will help readers make personal connections to the text. Mrs. Taylor will continue to model these strategies in many different genres and subject areas throughout the year in the hopes that her students will begin using one or more of these strategies during their independent reading.

Developmentally appropriate practice (DAP) is featured in the vignette and can be adapted for younger children (birth to age 5) and older children to age 9. Suggested adaptations include:

- *Ages 0 to 3:* Infants and toddlers can be exposed to interactive books that feature the senses, such as "touch and feel" books with multiple textures or books that have flaps to open and close. Books with bright colors and interesting shapes are also appealing to this age group. One example for this age group is *Dog* by Matthew Van Fleet (2007).
- *Ages 3 to 6:* Interactive read-alouds can be used with children as young as the preschool level to support vocabulary, oral language development, and listening comprehension. Choose a book based on the same theme (family relationships), perhaps about the love between a father and a child. Asking questions during the reading and explaining key vocabulary words will help children in this age group better understand the story. Another option is to read another book in this genre (memoir), because this story is autobiographical. One example for young children is *Memoirs of a Goldfish* by Devin Scillian (2010).
- *Ages 6 to 9:* Children can read other popular books by Lois Lowry, such as the Anastasia Krupnik series (1979), the Sam Krupnik series (1988), and the Gooney Bird books (2002).

Classroom Connection

How can you use comprehension questions to make personal connections during read-alouds?

6-1 Reading Comprehension Concepts

Comprehension is the "ability to read or listen and understand text" (Morrow, 2009, p. 191). Comprehending text is an active process. Readers or listeners construct meaning based on their prior knowledge, connecting new knowledge to what they already know. This concept is called schema theory (Anderson & Pearson, 1984; Vygotsky, 1978). Think of our schemata or background knowledge as a giant file cabinet in our brain with categories of knowledge. New knowledge that connects to what we already know is filed away for future reference. Comprehension is enhanced by knowledge that is meaningful and relevant to our students' lives. As teachers, we must activate and build our students' prior knowledge on a variety of topics across the curriculum. Schema is based upon the child's real-world experiences including cognitive, socioemotional, and physical growth. In Chapter 1 (Figure 1.2), we first introduced our holistic model of literacy (HML) consisting of the cognitive (yellow/mind), socioemotional (red/heart), and physical (blue/arms and legs) parts of self to promote creative thought and passion for literacy. We revisited the HML illustration in Chapter 3 (Figure 3.1), where we added a lightbulb to represent creative thought during the learning process. We are again building on the HML in Figure 6.1 by placing a book in the model's hand, which implies a passion for reading and writing through critical thinking.

schema theory The concept that readers or listeners construct meaning based on their background knowledge, connecting the unfamiliar to the familiar.

Reading changes how we view the world. The more we read, the more we learn about ourselves and others. Fluent readers make predictions, reread when they are confused, visualize what the author is describing, and use context or picture clues to figure out the meaning of unfamiliar words. To help struggling readers improve their comprehension and decoding skills, Yetta Goodman, Dorothy Watson, and Carolyn Burke (2005) developed a process called *miscue analysis* that is based on Kenneth Goodman's early work on the language cueing systems and the reading process (1982). A *miscue* is a response that a reader makes when reading orally that is different from the word in the text. The teacher analyzes the reader's use of the three language cueing systems in the context of a passage when decoding an unknown word. Sample miscues are: substitutions, insertions, omissions, and reversals. According to Goodman (1982), good readers use all three language cueing systems—syntactic (structure), semantic (meaning), and graphophonic (visual)—automatically as they read and comprehend text.

Reflective readers use metacognitive strategies as they are reading and comprehending text. Self-regulation, metacognition, and knowledge about a person's individual way of thinking include understanding how one interprets information and makes meaning. Metacognition develops as children become stronger cognitively and achieve success in completing tasks while gaining awareness of their unique learning process (Bandura, 1986). Early childhood educators need to help children develop their sense of metacognition by exposing them to a series of activities where they develop their own awareness, motivation, skills, and cognitive abilities. When children come to an unknown word while reading independently, encourage them to read to the end of the sentence, skipping the unknown word (omission). Then ask them to

Figure 6.1
The Holistic Model of Literacy (HML) with Creative Thought and Passion

think of a word that would make sense in that space, while paying attention to the beginning sound of the unknown word (substitution). Extra words added verbally that are not in the text (insertions) or reversing the order of the words or letters within the words (reversals) may confuse readers. Miscue analysis during oral reading assists teachers in identifying types of cueing systems students use—semantic, phonological, syntactic, or pragmatic (Goodman, 1982)—and guides future instruction (Leslie & Caldwell, 2010). For example, a child may read the following sentence aloud:

The boy rode a bicycle down the sidewalk.

If the child does not recognize the word *bicycle* when reading aloud, he may skip or omit the unknown word and read to the end of the sentence. The teacher may prompt the child to think about what the boy can ride down a sidewalk (skateboard, wagon, or bike) and make personal connections about prior experience through questioning (activate schema). When substituting during a read-aloud, the child predicts the unknown word by verbalizing a meaningful word that begins with the /b/ sound, such as *bike*. The teacher considers whether the substitution changes the meaning or intent of the text. Comprehension questions assist in confirming whether or not the child understood the text. Teachers use reading comprehension strategies to guide young readers to make connections to text: text-to-text, text-to-self, and text-to-world (Keene & Zimmerman, 2007).

Reading comprehension is supported by applying literacy strategies with non–text examples (images). Analyzing images prior to reading text allows children to use multiple modalities when creatively expressing their understandings. Reading comprehension can be challenging for young children. Teaching first through illustration allows for practice and application of comprehension skills that can be used when reading text. Children scaffold their experiences with images to the text environment. After reading text, children can create their own artwork demonstrating comprehension (Keene & Zimmerman, 2007; Klein & Stuart, 2012).

 CONSIDER THIS…

Consider reading strategies that activate prior knowledge (schema) before, during, and after reading text aloud. How can children utilize illustrations to make predictions before and during reading? Explain how children dramatize a retelling of the story.

6-2 Factors That Impact Comprehension Instruction

Effective comprehension instruction involves breaking up complex concepts into key ideas. For example, before teaching a lesson on any topic, teachers must make sure their students are familiar with the content and concepts. By introducing new vocabulary prior to the lesson, children prepare to connect meaning to context during reading. Key words can be translated into multiple languages, depending on individual needs. For example, when reading *Fox* by Margaret Wild (2006), the children may be told that the Spanish word for fox is *zorro*. This practice recognizes children's language and culture.

During comprehension instruction, teachers can initiate questions and activities that engage children's thinking about text. Many factors affect a child's comprehension of text, including the following key ideas:

- Level of interest
- Prior knowledge
- Text complexity (readability)
- Genre
- Type of text (narrative or expository)
- Vocabulary
- Pictures or other text features
- Sociocultural context
- Reading fluency
- Decoding skills
- English language proficiency

These factors influence how children understand what they are reading. Children comprehend from different perspectives depending upon their culture, language, and prior knowledge. Teachers assess their students' oral reading and decoding skills through running records (informal assessment and observation) and retellings to make sure they are matched to appropriate texts. Decoding is "using word-identification strategies to pronounce and attach meaning to an unfamiliar word" (Tompkins, 2013, p. 374). Reading levels tend to change often in the early years, so flexible grouping is essential during guided reading. The informal reading inventory (IRI) assists teachers in determining a child's oral, silent, and listening comprehension levels (Johns, 2012). Children should be reading on their *instructional reading level*, which means they can decode 90 to 95 percent of the words accurately and they understand approximately 70 percent of the text concepts. For independent reading, the word accuracy should be 98 to 99 percent with 90 percent comprehension. Children reading on their *frustration level* have a word accuracy rate below 90 percent with a comprehension level of 50 percent or less, which indicates an easier text is needed.

6-2a Strategies for Reading Comprehension

Specific teaching and learning strategies are recommended to meet the needs of diverse learners and assure practical application of new concepts. Comprehension strategies

Apply & Reflect

Select a picture book of your choice to read with a child. Identify and write an explanation of three factors that appear to affect the child's comprehension of text.

COMPREHENSION STRATEGIES FOR ENGLISH LANGUAGE LEARNERS (ELs)

ELLs benefit from explicit instruction of comprehension skills. Texts or key words that are translated into multiple languages assist ELLs in comprehending what is read. Teachers should model comprehension strategies by explaining step-by-step the process of utilizing skills such as think-alouds and fix-up strategies. For example, the teacher can reread a confusing part of the text aloud or children can quietly read ahead in the text before going back to reread the confusing selection. It is important for the teacher to "think aloud," making the reading comprehension process transparent for ELLs (Keene & Zimmerman, 2007).

Think about It

How can you teach figurative language, such as idioms (for example, "break a leg") through children's literature? For example, the book *Maestro Stu Saves the Zoo* by Denise Brennan-Nelson (2012) includes a variety of idioms. Children can use context clues and illustrations to determine the meanings. Their interpretations can be dramatized through facial expressions, gestures, and exaggerated movement.

can and should be taught to improve reading comprehension (Duke & Pearson, 2002). Previewing before reading and predicting before and during reading help readers make better connections with both fiction and nonfiction text. For example, picture walks during guided reading help children preview the story to get a gist of the overall meaning as well as an understanding of difficult words and concepts. Picture walks in an informational text will help children better understand text features and content area vocabulary. There are six basic comprehension strategies that readers need as a foundation for understanding text:

1. Making connections
2. Predicting and inferring
3. Questioning
4. Monitoring and clarifying
5. Summarizing and synthesizing
6. Evaluating (Oczkus, 2012)

Lori Oczkus (2012) refers to these research-based strategies as the "super six" (Keene & Zimmerman, 2007). She has developed props and gestures to match each strategy, which helps young children remember to use them in their reading workshop and during independent reading. Using the physical cues from Oczkus (2012), we have adapted each concept and added literacy strategies to support young readers.

1. Connect

Gesture = interlocking fingers; prop = paper chain

Children comprehend better if they make personal connections (text-to-self) as they are reading, identify with the characters, and compare similarities between events in the text with their personal lives. They can also connect to other books (text-to-text), comparing characters in similar situations. A third connection is called "text-to-world," when children compare the text they are reading to their everyday lives (Keene & Zimmerman, 2007).

Paper Chain Symbolizes Connect Strategy

Magnifying Glass Symbolizes Predict/Infer Strategy

2. Predict/Infer

Gesture = form fingers into a crystal ball; prop = magnifying glass

Children enjoy predicting what a story will be about, based on the title and cover illustration. When readers make predictions, they use evidence from the text and/or illustrations to prove their answers. If predictions are recorded on a chart, they can be confirmed, deleted, or expanded throughout reading the story. Sticky notes can be used to record predictions while reading independently. Inferring is similar to predicting. Children use what they know from the text and their background knowledge to figure out what is happening or to understand what the characters are thinking and feeling.

Microphone Symbolizes Question Strategy

3. Question

Gesture = form fists (one on top of the other) into a pretend microphone; prop = toy microphone

Fluent readers question the author's craft (style of writing, character development, and text features) and ask questions before, during, and after reading. Factual or literal questions have answers that are found within the text ("reading on the lines"). Inferential questions are harder because the answer is found both in the text and in the reader's head ("reading between the lines"). Critical questions are hardest, when the answer is found in the reader's head, based almost entirely on prior knowledge or schema ("reading beyond the lines"). Children in the primary grades can learn to ask and answer higher-level thinking questions. The children can pretend to interview characters as if they are a talk show host, using a microphone as a prop.

Silly Glasses Symbolize Monitor/Clarify Strategy

4. Monitor/Clarify

Gesture = Use fingers to form pretend glasses; prop = big silly glasses

Effective readers stop periodically to monitor their own reading, to ensure that the text makes sense. Sometimes even good readers start daydreaming, losing track of what they are reading. When readers' thoughts stray, they use fix-up strategies, looking back to see what they missed, visualizing or rereading a few pages if necessary. The glasses signify that the readers are looking more closely at the text, to determine if they are on the right track.

5. Summarize/Synthesize

Gesture = Make a circle like a lasso above your head; prop = a small rope with a loop on the end

Summarizing is a difficult strategy, especially for young children. They must learn how to distinguish between the main ideas and the details, and to sequence the events in the right order. Children can supplement their summaries with drawings or drama. Story maps help with narrative text, and graphic organizers—such as semantic webs or concept maps—support comprehension of informational text. Synthesizing goes beyond summarizing and includes creative thinking. Readers think about what they have learned and how their thinking has changed.

Rope Lasso Symbolizes Summarize/Synthesize Strategy

fix-up strategies Strategies that are used when readers lose track of their reading, looking back to see what they missed or rereading a few pages if necessary.

6. Evaluate

Gesture = Make a fist and hit it on your open palm; prop = a toy gavel

Evaluating is a high-level comprehension strategy that involves analysis and making judgments. The gavel represents a decision made by a judge in a courtroom. Readers evaluate what they thought about the story, character's decisions and actions, or the author's craft (see Photo 6.3). They should practice using evidence from the text to justify their answers and opinions.

According to Fountas and Pinnell (2011), there are 12 systems of strategic actions for teaching reading comprehension when thinking within the text, beyond the text, and about the text. Thinking within the text consists of the following strategies: word solving, monitoring, and correcting for accuracy and meaning; searching for and using information (meaning, structure, visual); summarizing key information; maintaining fluency; and adjusting reading rate for purpose and genre. Thinking beyond the text involves inferring, synthesizing, making connections, and predicting. Critiquing and analyzing the writer's craft and text structure are important strategies for thinking about the text. In their literacy curriculum for prekindergarten through eighth grade (2010), Irene Fountas and Gay Su Pinnell provide seven continua with assessments and benchmark systems for each area of the language arts curriculum. Each continuum describes behaviors and understandings that are required at each level for students to demonstrate thinking within, beyond, and about the text.

Gavel Symbolizes Evaluate Strategy

 CONSIDER THIS...

Consider how you can use one of the "super six" reading comprehension strategies in your future classroom. For example, when reading *The Three Questions* by Jon Muth (2002), children can use a magnifying glass to make inferences based on the text and illustration details.

6-3 Motivation for Literacy Engagement

As teachers, our goal is to create real readers who love to read. Enjoyment must be a central part of teaching reading (Murphy, 2012). Children who enjoy the act of reading will become lifelong readers. Reading will become a habit in their everyday lives. As teachers and parents of young children, we can be role models at home and school, demonstrating how much we read for pleasure and information every day. Reading all kinds of materials: books, magazines, e-readers, newspapers, or surfing the Web is important, as we are mentors in this process. The power of reading cannot be underestimated. During reading instruction, we must get to know our children individually—their dreams, interests, needs, and desires. Then we can teach them to read (Calkins, 1994).

6-3a Literacy Strategies for Motivation

There are many ways to motivate students. In *The Power of Reading* (1993), Steven Krashen promotes the value of free voluntary reading as a necessary component of the reading/language arts curriculum. Children should be allowed to read for at least 30 minutes daily, just for the pleasure of reading in a book of their choice. They should have time afterward to talk about their reading with peers, just as adults share favorite books with their friends. Krashen (1993), an educational leader from California, describes how school and public libraries in high socioeconomic areas are well stocked, while the books and resources of libraries in disadvantaged areas tend to be very limited. Krashen (1993) advocates that children in low-income households must have equal access to books.

Photo 6.3 *Child evaluating text features*

Effective teachers of reading need a vast knowledge of quality children's literature in multiple genres: picture books, historical and realistic fiction, fantasy, nonfiction, poetry, informational books, and traditional tales. They must also understand the visual elements of art to help their students "read" the illustrations in picture books, which are

| Table 6.1 | *The Elements of Visual Art* |

Element of Visual Art	Definition	Illustration
Line	A path of a moving point	
Shape	A two-dimensional (length and width) area surrounded by a line that ends where it begins (Examples: geometric circle, triangle, square or organic and amorphous)	
Form	A three-dimensional (length, width and depth) area such as, a sphere, cube, cylinder, pyramid	
Color	The reflection of light involving hue (color name), value (dark/light), and intensity (bright/dull); primary colors = red, yellow, and blue; secondary colors = orange, purple, green	
Value	Dark and light elements of color and various shades of white/black/gray	
Space	The area around an object (positive/negative) that illustrates depth and perspective/distance (foreground, middle ground, and background) through overlapping objects	
Texture	The sense of touch that can be actual texture or implied texture	

just as important as the text for young readers. The basic elements of visual art (Dow, 1899) are defined and illustrated in Table 6.1.

When analyzing illustrations using the elements of art, children are explaining their comprehension, which is associated with the text. Multimodal literacy connects visual formats to written text and is defined as "the practice of moving from one sign system to another (for example, transmediation from verbal-visual, visual-verbal, visual-spatial)" (Martinez & Nolte-Yupari, 2015, p. 12). Expressing knowledge and understanding through different media supports children's literacy development.

Donalyn Miller, a sixth-grade teacher and author of *The Book Whisperer* (2009), knows how to motivate her students to read. To create a classroom where readers flourish, Miller recommends the following:

1. Reading volume matters (Her sixth graders read 40-plus books a year.).
2. Read for pleasure at least 30 minutes a day.
3. Encourage students to read whenever they have free time during the school day.
4. Provide reading choice.
5. Use read-alouds to introduce books and authors.

Teachers should model their love of reading to their students. Parents who are readers can transfer their love of reading to their children. Miller (2009) believes that reading volume matters because students who read lots of books develop a habit of reading for enjoyment. Teachers can help beginning readers select appropriate books by using the "Goldilocks" method or the five-finger rule:

> Make a fist on one hand. Begin reading one page of the book. Put down one finger for each word you miss. If you still have a fist or just 1 finger showing, the book is *too easy*. If you have 2–3 fingers showing, the book is *just right* and if you have 4–5 *fingers* showing, the book is *too hard*. (Miller, 2009)

Motivation strategies are important to instill the desire to pursue literacy goals. Children become self-motivated (intrinsic) when they practice reading, writing, speaking, and listening skills in a nurturing, supportive, and print-rich learning environment.

 CONSIDER THIS...

Consider what types of genres you enjoy reading and how you can share your interests with children. For example, if you enjoy cooking magazines, what recipes could you share with the class?

6-4 Comprehension Instruction in the Common Core State Standards

Literacy instruction has changed significantly since the creation of the Common Core State Standards (CCSS) (Calkins, Ehrenworth, & Lehman, 2012). These new standards are designed to prepare K–12 students for college and careers. The CCSS are much more rigorous than previous standards, requiring much higher-level comprehension skills that require critical thinking in all areas of the curriculum. Lucy Calkins and her co-authors state:

> Even young children are asked to analyze multiple accounts of an event, noting similarities and differences in the points of view presented, assessing the warrant behind people's ideas. Readers of today are asked to integrate information from several texts, to explain the relationships between ideas and author's craft. (Calkins, Ehrenworth, & Lehman, 2012, p. 9)

Writing is just as important as reading. In the No Child Left Behind initiative (U.S. Department of Education, 2002), the key components of literacy instruction consisted of the five pillars: phonics, phonemic awareness, vocabulary, comprehension, and fluency with no mention of writing. Each of the reading skills was given equal weight, although comprehension is the goal of reading. Today's students must be able to read and understand complex texts in multiple genres across the curriculum. In the CCSS, the emphasis on writing standards is equal to the emphasis on reading standards. Reading and writing are integrated across the curriculum (see Photo 6.4). Close reading and text complexity in fiction and nonfiction text are two critical components of the CCSS (Calkins, Ehrenworth, & Lehman, 2012).

Photo 6.4 *Child writing in response to reading*

6-4a Close Reading

Reading comprehension includes the ability to read text, process it, and understand the meaning. Beginning readers interpret text on a literal level, only comprehending the words in the sentence. Comprehension is a creative, interactive process that depends on language skills. The notion of close reading is critical for the implementation of the CCSS, beginning at the kindergarten level. "Close reading is an instructional routine in which students critically examine a text, especially through repeated readings" (Fisher & Frey, 2012, p. 179).

According to Douglas Fisher and Nancy Frey (2012), the two primary objectives of a close reading are:

1. To give students opportunities to integrate new textual information with their existing background knowledge or schema; and
2. To expand the essential strategies of readers as they comprehend a complex piece of text.

Through *close reading*, children become familiar with text through repeated reading and critical analysis, which promotes comfortable and self-confident readers. Independent readers must learn: how to identify their purpose for reading, the author's purpose for writing the piece using different text structures, how to develop their own schema, and how to make personal connections to the text. Close reading is an instructional practice that should be infused into other essential and effective instructional practices: shared reading, guided reading, interactive read-alouds, mini-lessons, reading and writing workshops, teacher modeling, collaborative reading, and small group discussions.

Fisher and Frey (2012) describe five key features of close reading:

- *Short passages* (three paragraphs to two pages)
- *Complex texts* (narrative text with complex characters or points of view, expository texts with multiple text features)
- *Limited preteaching* or frontloading of information
- *Repeated readings* (with a new purpose or question for each reading)
- *Text-dependent* or *explicit questions* (so that students are able to provide text evidence for their responses)

These five key features of close reading are used consistently throughout the lesson to assure comprehension of text. Students can begin practicing close reading with either narrative or expository text. Teachers select short passages and have children read the piece with a specific purpose or question in mind. Children record their thoughts and ideas on sticky notes or underline key words or ideas. Students share their responses afterward with a partner or in small groups.

Another way to teach close reading, especially with young students, is through an interactive read-aloud. Often teachers focus on text-dependent or explicit questions to promote comprehension of text. There are five main types of text-dependent questions that are interrelated to consistently assure comprehension (see Figure 6.2).

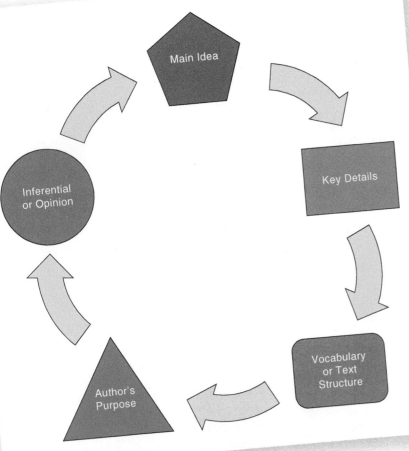

Figure 6.2
Types of Text-Dependent Questions

	Sample Text-Dependent Questions for Fox
Table 6.2	*(Wild, 2006)*

Main Idea or General Understandings	Character and Setting Descriptions
Key Details	How did dog and magpie escape from the fire?
Vocabulary and Text Structure	What did Fox mean when he said that Dog looked extraordinary?
Author's Purpose	Who tells the story?
Inferences	Why did Fox leave Magpie alone in the desert?
Opinions or Intertextual Connections	Do you think this is a happy story or a sad one? Why?

Teachers should consciously include all five types of text-dependent questions when discussing text with children. For example, some questions based on *Fox* by Margaret Wild (2006) are shown in Table 6.2 and focus on the different type of text-dependent questions. *Fox* (Wild, 2006) is a story about the friendship between a blind dog and a magpie with a broken wing. A fox tries in vain to destroy their friendship in this tale.

Children are directed to key ideas and concepts in this story through a variety of questions. By varying text-dependent questions, teachers assure a deeper comprehension of text and model comprehension strategies that children can practice independently.

6.4b Text Complexity and Struggling Readers

Text complexity is a term that appears frequently in the Common Core State Standards (Common Core State Standards Initiative, 2010). This term goes beyond readability (based on sentence length and syllables in words) to include quantitative and qualitative factors such as, text structures, text features (index, table of contents, maps, charts, or captions), graphics, illustrations, concepts, and key vocabulary. Students in today's world must be able to read and analyze complex text in all subject areas in preparation for college and careers. Struggling readers may have difficulty comprehending any type of text, especially on the inferential or critical level. One strategy that will help students understand complex text is teaching text structures in both narrative and informational or expository text.

Narrative text structure is easier because *story grammar* is familiar to most children. Story grammar consists of the basic parts of a story: characters, setting, events, problem, solution, and ending. Text complexity with narrative text involves multiple plots featuring characters with diverse perspectives that change over time. Expository or informational text is much harder because of the variety of text structures and scientific terminology in the content areas (science, social studies, and math). Types of text structures in informational text are: (1) problem and solution, (2) cause and effect, (3) sequence, (4) description, and (5) comparison and contrast (Tompkins, 2013).

One example of teaching comparison and contrast with narrative text is to have students analyze two different versions of the same fairy tale such as "Cinderella" or "Little Red Riding Hood." Character maps with specific character traits and examples from the text (called *text evidence*) will help learners understand character development. Teaching struggling readers how to create semantic webs or concept maps helps them to understand and remember key concepts and important ideas. An example of teaching cause and effect can include Laura Numeroff's book, *If You Give a Mouse a Cookie* (1985). Teachers can introduce text features (table of contents, title page, maps, and illustrations) during read-alouds with mentor texts (texts that illustrate concepts), while teaching the concept of cause and effect (chain reaction). For example, in this

text complexity This term refers to characteristics of informational text, which are critical for reading comprehension including text structures (cause and effect, question and answer, main idea and details), text features (table of contents, index, maps, and charts), as well as illustrations, concepts, and key vocabulary.

character maps Graphic organizers with specific character traits and examples from the text to help readers understand character development.

semantic webs Graphic organizers that represent the meaning of text.

concept maps Graphic organizers that represent the relationships between concepts or ideas in text.

mentor texts High-quality texts that illustrate specific skills or concepts for reading and/or writing instruction.

VISUALIZATION STRATEGY: ACTIVITY FOR PRESERVICE TEACHERS TO DO WITH CHILDREN

Purpose: Using mental imagery and the five senses as a visualization strategy enhances comprehension of text. Debbie Miller (2013) teaches retelling with thinking strips (drawing mental images on paper) using a book such as, *Make Way for Ducklings* (McCloskey, 1966).

Procedure: The teacher reads the story and uses the "think-aloud" strategy to help children create mental images of key events. Children focus on the five senses through questioning (for example, What sound do the ducklings make? How do feathers feel?). After discussion, the teacher rereads the story, asking children to draw their mental images on thinking strips. Finally, the children sequence their thinking strips. They retell *Make Way for Ducklings* with a partner, using their sketches on the thinking strips as prompts.

Teaching Analysis: Reflective practices are a necessary part of the *literacy assessment cycle* and are key components in preservice preparation and certification such as edTPA. Analyze the strengths and areas of improvement in this lesson idea. Answer the following:

- What is successful?
- What would you change to improve the lesson?
- What did you learn about teaching literacy?

Links: Making connections to technology and developmentally appropriate practices (DAP) supports lesson planning and literacy instruction. Adaptations of this lesson idea are provided through the following:

- **Technology Link:** Small groups work together to research online facts about ducks. Interesting facts are shared with the whole class.
- **DAP Link:** Children participate in an interactive read-aloud of the story with a dramatic interpretation of the text.
- **Executive Function Link:** Creative play and active engagement during an interactive read-aloud develop children's self-regulation skills in social settings as reflected in the holistic model of literacy (cognitive, socioemotional, and physical).
- **Classroom Link:** For children (0 to 3), use feathers to create a texture collage.
- **Classroom Link:** Children (3 to 6) can visit a nearby park to feed ducks and write a class story about the event.
- **Classroom Link:** Children (6 to 9) can write a research report with a partner about ducks and present to the class.

---

humorous children's story, the mouse consistently requests another item to illustrate the *effect* of giving a mouse a cookie.

In addition to text structure, other factors that affect complexity in narrative or informational text are: (1) language conventions (vocabulary load), (2) background knowledge requirements, (3) levels of meaning (literal, inferential, and critical) in text, and (4) purpose for reading in text (Weaver, 2002). Text complexity also depends on the reading skills and abilities of the children as well as the difficulty of the comprehension tasks (for example, tasks such as sequencing story events and summarizing the main idea and key details). Teachers can differentiate learning by adapting the comprehension tasks to the reading skills of each child.

 CONSIDER THIS...

Consider which reading comprehension strategies can be used in your classroom. For example, you can write text-dependent questions on sticky notes to use during a read-aloud.

6-5 Comprehension Strategies for Children's Literature

Comprehension strategies involve interactive activities to engage children cognitively, socioemotionally, and physically (holistic model of literacy). Through collaborative interaction, teachers observe and assess children's comprehension of text (fiction and nonfiction). Children's literature should connect and be relevant to their daily lives. This process allows

children to identify with story characters, encouraging their imagination and cooperative learning skills (see Photo 6.5). Reading informational text helps build a knowledge foundation for the construction of new knowledge. Literacy learning occurs through association and real-world experiences. Comprehension is the goal of reading.

6-5a Book Talks

Teachers can create book talks on a selected theme, topic, or genre to entice students to read the books (Johns & Lenski, 2010). A book talk can be a poster, musical jingle, commercial sound byte, flyer, or short presentation by the teacher or students promoting different types of text in various subject areas. Book talks with reading partners motivate children to read and write (see Photo 6.6).

book talks Short previews of a book to provide interest or motivation.

VISUALIZATION AND THE BRAIN

The loop between the occipital lobe, Broca's area in the left frontal lobe (language processing), and Wernicke's area in the left temporal lobe (language comprehension) must coordinate efficiently for reading comprehension to occur (Perfetti, 1985). Visualizing during read-alouds can assist reading comprehension. Soundy and Lee (2013) focus on children's visual thinking as related to meaning and comprehension through drawing processes within literacy activities. Interaction with peers and teachers is necessary during the drawing activity to support children's verbal, visual, spatial, and other forms of representation as they are developed.

Think about It

How can teachers help children to visualize text? For example, children can draw events that were read aloud by the teacher. Details can be added to their drawings when prompted by comprehension questions asked by their teacher or during small group work.

What are your thoughts and feelings about the story?

What if:
What will the story be about?
What happens next?
How does the story end?
Did you like the story?

Draw your prediction:

⌄ Professional Resource Download

Figure 6.3
What If? Chart

To make the book talk interesting, include a variety of components: reading an excerpt or quotation, developing an interview with the main character, using props when appropriate, making personal connections, creating a monologue based on the main character, or asking children to participate in a role play based on a particular "scene" in the story. After the book talk, ask the children to fill out a prediction chart, writing what they think will happen in the story, based on the book talk. Then they can compare their predictions to what really happens in the text.

A "What If? chart" (see Figure 6.3) is another comprehension strategy that allows children to use their curiosity and imagination to predict the story plot. This practice is especially valuable for young children to depict meaning, both cognitively and socioemotionally. Children can use the "What If?" chart at the beginning, the middle, and just before the end of the story to enhance imagination and creativity.

6-5b Jackdaws

Jackdaws are collections of artifacts or "realia" (concrete objects) that relate to a specific book topic or theme (Rasinski, Padak, & Fawcett, 2010). The term comes from a British name for a relative of the crow that scavenges for bright objects to take to its nest (Kiefer & Tyson, 2009). Jackdaws build background knowledge (foundation for comprehension), stimulate predictions, and create interest in a story. For example, children may collect photographs or pictures, newspaper articles, maps, recipes, or time lines that relate to important characters, settings, or events in the story. The class or teacher can create a mystery box with objects placed inside and have other children predict the story. Jackdaws for the story *Petite Rouge—A Cajun Red Riding Hood* by M. Artell (2001) could be Cajun music, a stuffed alligator, a map of the United States with a star on Louisiana, and a recipe for gumbo or jambalaya. This version of the well-known folk tale ("Little Red Riding Hood") is about a young duck named Petite Rouge who goes to her sick grandmother's house with a basket of gumbo and boudin sausage.

jackdaws Collections of artifacts (concrete objects) that relate to a specific book, topic, or theme for the purpose of providing interest or background knowledge.

ASSESSING COMPREHENSION SKILLS THROUGH SELF-EVALUATION

Children should self-monitor during independent reading. Using a comprehension checklist, they learn to recognize strategies that are effective before, during, and after reading. This checklist may be used with either narrative or informational text. Children complete the checklist independently and the teacher reviews their responses during reading conferences.

Comprehension Checklist

Directions: When you are reading, you may come to a part in the text that is confusing or doesn't make sense for some reason. If that happens, place a check beside each of the following comprehension strategies that you used before, during, or after reading.

Before Reading

Did you . . .

_____ Set a purpose for reading?

_____ Make predictions about the story or passage?

_____ Do a picture walk to determine what is going to happen based on the illustrations?

_____ Do a text walk to read the table of contents, summaries, graphs, tables, or bold words in informational text?

During Reading

Did you . . .

_____ Make mental images in your head to imagine what is happening?

_____ Reread a section of the text that is confusing or doesn't make sense?

_____ Use a graphic organizer to help you determine the main ideas and details?

After Reading

Did you . . .

_____ Summarize key ideas in the story or passage?

_____ Check your predictions to confirm if they were correct or not and why?

_____ Draw a sketch to show what the text selection meant to you, illustrating the main idea or important details in the piece?

_____ Decide if this text was too easy, too hard, or just right?

Think about It

This assessment is designed for children to self-evaluate their comprehension strategies. During the reading conference, how can you encourage children to use varied comprehension strategies? For example, you can provide art supplies to remind children to draw main ideas or key points after they finish reading.

Source: Adapted from Johns & Lenski (2010).

Professional Resource Download

6-5c Open Mind Portrait

To understand character development, we recommend open mind portraits. This strategy can be used to stimulate students to think inferentially about a character's thoughts, feelings, or actions (Johns & Lenski, 2010). Open mind portrait is a drawing of the characters' facial features depending upon textual clues and the child's creative interpretation of the physical qualities (drawing), emotions (child's socioemotional connection), and cognition (thought process and actions) of the character. Children use the text (quotes from the book) to provide evidence for their open mind portrait. Choose a chapter in a novel that has several well-defined characters. Ask children to read the chapter, stopping periodically to visualize what each of the characters may be thinking or feeling. Show the class how to draw a portrait of a character's head and neck only, making it look as realistic as possible. Children build their comprehension skills by analyzing the characters' thoughts, feelings, and actions throughout the story.

6-5d Quick Write or Quick Draw

In quick write or quick draw, readers reflect on what they know about a topic, or they make personal connections to the text during interactive read-alouds. Children may write freely or draw for several minutes before sharing their writing/drawing with a partner or small group. Peter Elbow (1973) introduced the freewriting strategy as a way to focus on content rather than on format (spelling and mechanics). For example, quick writes can be used in

open mind portrait A drawing (facial portrait) of a character using textual clues for authenticity; the character's thoughts and/or feelings based on text evidence are included to support the reader's understanding of character development.

quick write A brief piece of writing that children create and share to demonstrate what they know about a topic, theme, character, or plot during interactive read-louds using fiction or nonfiction text.

quick draw A simple sketch a child creates and shares to show his or her understanding of a character, theme, plot, or topic during interactive read-alouds using fiction or nonfiction text.

freewriting Writing freely to focus on content (ideas) rather than format (mechanics).

Table 6.3 Literacy Strategies and Practices Supporting Reading Comprehension

Age Groups	Cognitive	Socioemotional
0 to 3	Lap reading and listening Receptive vocabulary Real objects connected to the written word (labels) Vocabulary repetition	Storybook reading with puppets, stuffed animals Music, rhythm, and rhyme Color designs Facial expressions during read-alouds
3 to 6	Concepts about print Fairy tales ABC books Mother Goose rhymes Reading and listening centers Word walls	Storytelling with costumes, masks, and props Wordless books/picture books Nurturing animals and plants
6 to 9	Aesop's Fables Mythology Biography Historical fiction Informational books Story maps Story predictions and alternative endings	Environmental issues debates Community work Picture carousels Nature walks Reader's theatre Celebrating literacy success through awards and recognition

⋎ Professional Resource Download

many different ways: (1) to activate background knowledge; (2) to describe a favorite character; (3) to discuss and compare favorite books and characters; (4) to learn vocabulary through real-world connections; and, (5) to question author's craft (Tompkins, 2013).

Apply & Reflect

Choose one of the comprehension strategies (book talk, jackdaws, open mind portrait, or quick write or draw) to practice in a small group of peers. Afterward, share your experiences and opinions about this strategy with the group. Brainstorm adaptations for classroom applications.

 CONSIDER THIS...

Consider different formats for presenting book talks. For example, your students can create paper bag book reports. The outside of the paper bag is decorated to match the theme of the book. Information related to the author, characters, story events, and related topics are glued to the outside of the bag. Inside the bag, children place items that connect to the text.

6-6 Literacy Strategies and Practices for Reading Comprehension

Active participation when applying comprehension strategies and practices is necessary to promote literacy development. Making personal connections with others through inquiry and discussion enhances learning and understanding of text. Utilizing

Physical	Children's Books	Family Involvement
Books with textures Cloth books Flannel boards Board books Baby sign language Clapping and finger play	*Pete the Cat—I Love My White Shoes* by Eric Litwin *Happy Hippo, Angry Duck: A Book of Moods* by Sandra Boynton *First the Egg* by Laura V. Seeger *The Earth Book* by Todd Parr	Family trips to zoos, farms, or parks, followed by reading books to reinforce vocabulary through repetition in different contexts Creating a collage of magazine pictures to explain concepts in a book
Puzzles Geometric forms/blocks Dioramas Paper folding and cutting Found-object sculpture	*Joseph Had a Little Overcoat* by Simms Taback *Art and Max* by David Wiesner *What Do You Do with a Tail Like This?* by Steve Jenkins and Robin Page	Naming and labeling household items Writing words and sentences for each letter of the alphabet on dry erase or chalkboards
Acting out poetry and plays Role-playing characters Drawing character webs Clay modeling of imaginative characters Writing and singing songs	*Henry's Freedom Box* by Ellen Levine *Wild Babies* by Seymour Simon *The Brand New Kid* by Katie Couric *Diary of a Worm* by Doreen Cronin	Family book clubs to read and discuss books in a variety of genres Discussing current events during family dinners

comprehension strategies with children's literature builds background knowledge and provides a stimulus for discussion and debate. Children respond to text through the cognitive, socioemotional, and physical parts of self (holistic model of literacy). It is important to select text that is meaningful and interesting for the children in your classroom. In Table 6.3, we provide examples of text and activities that can enhance reading comprehension for infants and children (birth to age 9).

End-of-Chapter Study Aids

Summary

Children construct meaning based upon prior knowledge and personal experiences both at home and in school. In this chapter, we focused on reading comprehension for emergent and early readers. Our learning objectives, which correspond to the main heading topics, facilitate understanding the reading comprehension factors present in today's classrooms. Theoretical perspectives on reading comprehension emphasize schema theory, the holistic model of literacy (HML), and metacognition. Utilizing the theoretical perspectives, we explained how the holistic model of literacy promotes passion and motivation for reading. We listed multiple factors in this chapter that impact a child's comprehension of text, such as interests, prior knowledge, text complexity, genre, and linguistic backgrounds. Motivation is important for literacy engagement. We described the role of motivation when making connections: (1) text-to-self; (2) text-to-text; and, (3) text-to-world. Comprehension strategies should be aligned with the Common Core State Standards (CCSS) to promote critical thinking in literacy. Teachers analyze instructional strategies and connect teaching and learning to the CCSS.

This chapter identifies comprehension strategies, such as book talks, jackdaws, open mind portraits, and quick writes or quick draws. Through comprehension strategies that promote active engagement, children are motivated to understand inferred meanings of the selected literature (fiction and nonfiction). Our vision of comprehension integrates literacy, psychology, and the arts. Comprehension is the goal of reading. Literacy development is supported when children respond to text through creative expression and active participation. Selecting text that is relevant and meaningful to each child promotes self-esteem and reading motivation.

Chapter Exercises

1. Create a semantic web that illustrates your understanding of reading comprehension using at least four main ideas with corresponding details.
2. Select a favorite picture book from your childhood, and discuss with a partner your childhood memories about reading this book.
3. Draw a sketch to stretch (a quick drawing of your understanding of reading motivation), and explain your ideas to a partner.
4. Choose a short informational passage from a newspaper or magazine, and design a close reading activity.
5. Find objects related to a book of your choice (jackdaws), and explain your selections to the class.

Teacher Toolbox

METACOGNITIVE STRATEGIES

Appropriate for Ages 5 to 9

To practice metacognition strategies with children, choose a wordless picture book, such as *The Red Book* by Barbara Lehman (2004). Create an anchor chart with thinking stems (prompts). Instruct the children to work with a partner and to "read" the illustrations using the thinking stems to guide their discussion. Each pair will interpret the narrative and share their ideas with the whole class. Write the interpretations from each pair on a comparison chart for whole class discussion.

THINKING STEMS FOR METACOGNITION

I'm thinking . . .
I'm noticing . . .
I'm wondering . . .
I'm seeing . . .
I'm feeling . . .
_____

Adapted from McGregor (2007).

Key Terms and Concepts

accountable talk	freewriting	quick write
book talks	informational text	schema theory
character maps	jackdaws	semantic webs
close reading	mentor texts	text complexity
comprehension	metacognition	text evidence
concept maps	open mind portrait	think-alouds
fix-up strategies	quick draw	word callers

Len44ik/Shutterstock.com

STANDARDS ADDRESSED IN THIS CHAPTER

The standards from the following organizations will be used throughout the chapter: Common Core State Standards for English Language Arts, the National Association for the Education of Young Children (NAEYC), and National Core Arts Standards. These standards are discussed further in the chapter as appropriate.

Common Core State Standards for English Language Arts

Anchor Standards for Reading

Reading Standards for Literature K–5
- Key Ideas and Details

Reading Standards: Foundational Skills K–5
- Print Concepts
- Phonological Awareness
- Phonics and Word Recognition

Anchor Standards for Writing
- Text Types and Purposes
- Production and Distribution of Writing
- Range of Writing

Anchor Standards for Speaking and Listening
- Comprehension and Collaboration
- Presentation of Knowledge and Ideas

Anchor Standards for Language
- Conventions of Standard English
- Knowledge of Language
- Vocabulary Acquisition and Use

2010 NAEYC Standards for Initial and Advanced Early Childhood Professional Preparation Programs
- *Standard 1:* Promoting Child Development and Learning

NAEYC Early Childhood Program Standards and Accreditation Criteria
- *Standard 2:* Curriculum
- *Standard 3:* Teaching

National Core Arts Standards (Dance, Media Arts, Music, Theater, Visual Arts)

Connecting
- *Anchor Standard 10:* Synthesize and relate knowledge and personal experiences to make art.
- *Anchor Standard 11:* Relate artistic ideas and works with societal, cultural, and historical context to deepen understanding.

Writing and Spelling Development 7

It is not often that someone comes along who is a true friend and a good writer. — E. B. White

Writing is a process where words are used to express coherent language. This involves composing text in a specific style or voice expressing one's ideas, thoughts, and feelings. Preschool children (ages 2 to 5) demonstrate stages of writing depending on the ability of each child (Clay, 1987). Children begin their writing stages with drawing and scribbling. As they start to discern writing from drawing, letters soon take shape and children start writing their names or using environmental print (Schickendanz, 1999). Writing and spelling development for young children involves cooperating with other children and teachers by expressing creative ideas to fully engage the whole child. Children are eager to explore their ideas when supported in a safe environment. Reading and writing develop together so both are equally important. Writing involves the cognitive, socioemotional, and physical aspects of self, as we describe in the holistic model of literacy (HML). Children's background experiences, represented in their schemata, create connections between reading, writing, and their knowledge of the world.

Metacognitive awareness (knowing why you think the way you do) and comprehension are enhanced by active engagement in literacy, which is the focus of the HML. Teachers can incorporate activities so that children read and write daily. Avid readers are good writers, and writing strengthens reading abilities. Teachers and parents need to encourage children to practice writing tasks such as, writing thank-you notes, grocery lists, or to-do lists, and engaging them in the practical efforts of writing. Writing about a range of topics for various audiences and purposes supports children's literacy skills. Through literacy exposure, children learn quickly that reading and writing go together. All types of writing (that is, narrative, informational, and persuasive) are necessary in a balanced literacy curriculum.

LEARNING OBJECTIVES

After you have read this chapter, you should be able to:

7-1 Compare writing and spelling concepts.

7-2 Interpret connections between reading and writing.

7-3 Explain stages of spelling development.

7-4 Describe stages of the writing process.

7-5 Analyze components of writing workshop with arts integration.

7-6 Apply literacy strategies and practices for writing and spelling development.

STANDARDS CONNECTION TO THE VIGNETTE

NAEYC Early Childhood Program Standards and Accreditation Criteria

Standard 2: Curriculum

2.A.12 The curriculum guides teachers to plan for children's engagement in play (including dramatic play and blocks) that is integrated into classroom topics of study.

Common Core State Standards for English Language Arts

Key Ideas and Details

First Grade

2. Retell stories, including key details, and demonstrate understanding of their central message or lesson.

Writing involves word choice, which leads to a focus on parts of speech that convey meaning, such as nouns, verbs, adjectives, and adverbs. Knowing how to select words to create fluent sentences encourages children to develop a curiosity about language. The following vignette depicts effective word choice and creative expression.

A first-grade teacher, Mr. Ortiz, reads *Where the Wild Things Are* by Maurice Sendak (1988) to begin the creative writing unit plan. Mr. Ortiz and her students discuss how word choice affects presentation while she reads the story aloud using a big book. Children repeat words and phrases aloud that spark their imaginations, such as "gnashed their terrible teeth."

Max, the main character in the story, gains confidence as he explores unknown territory and experiences different relationships with imaginary creatures. During the read-aloud session, the children write down emotions identified in the book. For example, the children may identify fear when Max arrives at the island and sees the monsters showing "their terrible claws." Children write their favorite words on sticky notes and post them on the class word wall (display of words) for use during writing workshop.

Next, the class and teacher pretend to be "wild things" and move to express the story line about the "wild rumpus." Mr. Ortiz plays a short selection of Rimsky-Korsakov's "Flight of the Bumblebee" (1900), while the children create movement that expresses the rhythm and beat of the music. The frenzy of movement and sound ends abruptly and everyone sits immediately on the floor, just like in the story when the characters stop at Max's command. The children write new words on sticky notes that describe their movements and add these words to the word wall.

Group play develops cooperative learning skills and supports active engagement. Brainstorming sessions that include dramatic group play can expand children's vocabulary (word choice) and motivate creative thinking to enhance writing development (see Photo 7.1). Dramatic play while pretending to be imaginary creatures leads children to develop empathy for others and increases imagination.

Developmentally appropriate practice (DAP) is featured in the vignette and can be adapted for younger children (birth to age 5) and older children to age 9. Suggested adaptations include:

- ***Ages 0 to 3:*** Reading aloud to infants and toddlers develops word recognition and leads to expressive word choice when speaking. Dramatic play with soft stuffed toy animals and exaggerated facial expressions during read-aloud sessions support language development. Toddlers can explore mark making by painting to music for expression.

- ***Ages 3 to 6:*** Children can dramatically reenact the story line using costumes and masks that they created. Painting or drawing to music enhances the mark-making abilities of young children. Identification of letters and words in text during teacher read-aloud sessions leads children to write their own words when retelling a narrative. Teachers can write on chart paper while children explain key details and main ideas (dictation).

metacognitive awareness Knowing or realizing why you think the way you do.

Photo 7.1 *Interactive read-aloud*

■ **Ages 6 to 9:** Children can write alternative endings or extensions to the narrative and illustrate what happens next. Children can create illustrations of their own imaginary creature, decide upon a name for their new species, design a habitat, and write an acrostic poem (using each letter in the name) that explains the creature's characteristics.

Classroom Connection

How can you creatively promote better word choice in children's writing?

7-1 Writing and Spelling Concepts

When children are immersed in a print-rich environment, they have opportunities to interact with words, which facilitate literacy success. Understanding the alphabetic principle (that letters represent sounds) helps children realize that marks they make have meaning, such as learning the letters in their names. The application of spelling concepts, including syllables within a word, compound words, contractions, and inflectional endings (-s, -es, -ed, -ing), are important for children to progress in their spelling development (Bear et al., 2015; Tompkins, 2013). "Becoming fully literate is absolutely dependent on fast, accurate recognition of words and their meanings in text . . ." (Bear et al., 2015, p. 3). Children begin writing using invented spelling (phonetic spelling). Using children's invented spellings, the teacher designs effective instruction in phonics, spelling, and vocabulary, known as word study.

Our holistic model of literacy (HML) includes the cognitive, socioemotional, and physical parts of self. These domains are developed simultaneously through a child's interactions with others and with the environment. For example, children's interests can guide the selection of literature that inspires their passion for reading. Exploring words through letters and sounds encourages spelling development and builds confidence. During the writing process, a strong sense of self (cognitive, socioemotional, and physical) promotes successful written expression. Children need to have passion, curiosity, and inspiration

alphabetic principle Knowledge that letters represent sounds.

invented spelling Phonetic spelling.

word study Effective instruction in phonics, spelling, and vocabulary focusing on specific words usually selected from text.

Photo 7.2 *Creative group interaction*

when learning to read and write. The knowledge of self becomes the foundation for early literacy learning (HML). When children read and expand their sensory abilities, by visiting places such as a zoo (petting animals), farm (picking apples), or beach (flying a kite), they become more motivated to write. Children must construct new knowledge based upon their prior understanding. This concept of *constructivism* includes ideas that all learning should flow from the students' desires and connections to the real world (Piaget, 1964).

Writing is built upon experiences. Collaborative reading and writing activities encourage children to communicate and discuss their own ideas (see Photo 7.2). Vygotsky's (1978) theory includes social interaction in a supportive environment. When children interact and collaborate with others in a learning environment, developmental processes are internalized and eventually become a part of their independent learning achievement. Therefore, interaction with peers in a learning environment is a crucial part of children's development. For example:

- Working with peers can involve choreography in creating a dance that explains a topic of study such as the phases of the moon. Each child can represent the moon phase through a series of combined movements after reading *Kitten's First Full Moon* (Henkes, 2004). Children can write words that describe the various moon phases.

- Children can collaborate on painting a group mural in class that illustrates a rain forest habitat, including plants and animals, after reading *The Great Kapok Tree: A Tale of the Amazon Rain Forest* (Cherry, 1990). Children can write the names of animals on sticky notes and label the mural once displayed.

- A collaborative musical performance can result in a new composition of sound to understand how sound travels through waves and the different instruments in an orchestra. Sections from *Story of the Orchestra: Listen While You Learn about the Instruments, the Music, and the Composers Who Wrote the Music!* (Levine, 2000) can be shared with children. While the children listen to the musical selections, they can write a list of descriptive words to add to their personal dictionaries.

COGNITIVE FUNCTIONS OF THE BRAIN

The frontal lobes of the brain are involved in cognitive functions such as language, reasoning, problem solving, and judgment (D'Esposito & Chen, 2006). In a study by Li, Cao, Cai, and Li (2011), researchers found that hypothesis testing activates the frontal cortex and parietal lobes in 9-year-old children, which stimulates the function of logical operation.

Think about It

How can you activate children's prediction and hypothesis testing before reading or writing? For example, children can predict what the text is about by the title or illustrations (narrative and informational) or write a new title based upon their predictions.

All of these experiential and creative starting points lead to writing in the classroom. Children can learn effectively through assisted and supportive learning strategies while working with teachers and peers.

> ### ✔ CONSIDER THIS...
>
> Consider how collaborative literacy activities can affect children's learning. For example, students can participate in literature circles or book clubs and discuss main ideas, characters, and themes.

7-2 Connections between Reading and Writing

Writing is encoding (expressing thoughts) while reading is decoding (interpreting thoughts). The more you read, the better you write and read. Children read to learn information about writing topics, to review and revise writing, and to share writing ideas with others. Writing improves reading comprehension and promotes critical thinking. Both reading and writing are thinking and meaning-making processes (Gipe, 2014). When students are writing, they use metacognitive strategies to develop from factual to inferential and critical thinking. Factual thinking involves basic information gathering and knowledge. Inferential thinking includes "reading between the lines," predicting outcomes, applying information from the story to real-world situations, and writing continuation of the story line. All children write, but to write reflectively and at a higher order, *metacognition*, the ability to think about your thinking is needed. Higher levels of thinking involve analysis, evaluation, and synthesis of ideas. Children often begin the metacognitive process by analyzing illustrations when reading. They can create artwork that expresses the concepts in the text, such as characters, events, and settings. Drawings about specific scenes depicted in text can be organized into a story sequence. Verbal discussion of their illustrations helps children to consider how text is organized, which can serve as a model for their own writing. Children search for meaning in their writing and artwork. Artwork by children is a part of the writing process.

A 4-year-old in a preschool classroom drew a picture (see Figure 7.1) after listening to his reading buddy (a sixth grader) read *Go, Dog. Go!* by P. D. Eastman (1966). The young boy laughed as he described his drawing about a dog party in a tree.

Figure 7.1
Drawing of Dog Party
Courtesy of the authors

encoding Writing to express thoughts.

decoding Reading or interpreting thoughts; pronouncing words in text.

Figure 7.2
Artwork with Dictation
Courtesy of the authors

"I like the books that they bring. The first one was very long and interesting."

The child's drawing in his writing journal helps him remember this story. Dictation can be added to the drawings in a writing journal (see Figure 7.2).

Through the process of describing their artwork, children form sentences using descriptive words that add definition to the story line they are developing. By analyzing their artwork, they discover relationships and recognize patterns that evolve through the story line. By listening to others interpret artwork (art criticism), children can imagine and understand different perspectives. As children develop writing skills, this critique process evolves from an initial discussion to purposeful writing. As metacognition develops, children become more aware of their choices, and this influences their writing.

Metacognition implies a complex cognitive process that includes comprehension and thinking about thinking, including monitoring and controlling how one processes information, or takes action. Monitoring and controlling one's own thought process is a key goal in education. For example, children can write in their daily journals, expressing their feelings for the day, and then paint using colors to express their feelings. This leads to self-awareness and then self-analysis of their feelings. This creative process allows children to consider how their feelings affect their daily work. Once the feelings are managed, children are able to control their emotions and expand their cognitive abilities (HML).

As illustrated in Figure 7.3, the levels of thinking include: (1) factual thinking (dates, names, character, events); (2) inferential thinking (emotions, personalities, decision making); (3) metacognition (analyzing, understanding, reflecting); and (4) higher-order thinking (evaluating, comparing, critical analysis).

Metacognition involves children analyzing their thinking when reading and writing. The levels of thinking lead to improved comprehension of text, which improves vocabulary when writing. When they are reading and writing, children need to make personal connections, and this inspires confidence in their higher-level thinking. Children develop their thinking, reading, and writing skills through observing others at these tasks. To be better writers, children need to read a variety of genres and establish a routine for reading and writing each day. Proficient readers and writers need models in literature

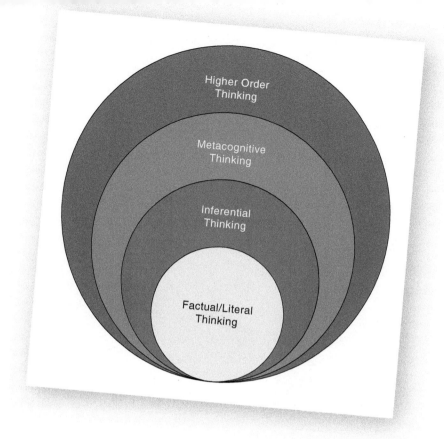

Figure 7.3
Levels of Thinking

and peer or adult role models in their lives. Teachers should emphasize the reading and writing connection as an important part of the literacy process.

 CONSIDER THIS...

Consider how children express their thoughts and ideas through writing and drawing. For example, young children can draw their favorite part of a story and then dictate a sentence describing their illustration.

7-3 Stages of Spelling Development

Researchers agree that there is a strong connection between reading and writing (Gipe, 2014). Children learn to read by reading, and they learn to write by reading. The more exposure young children have to books, the better writers they will become. Children who have parents who have read to them from a very young age have a great advantage in terms of literacy skills such as oral language development, vocabulary knowledge, phonemic awareness, and concepts about print (Trelease, 2013). Imagination is inspired through reading, and it is fostered by reading aloud to children. Their reading abilities increase through this reading model, which also supports their writing. Children benefit from spelling instruction that includes picture and word sorts, which are games to learn spelling patterns. Children sort words or pictures into categories according to vowel and consonant sounds. Spelling activities are organized in picture sorts, letter sorts, word sorts, and concept sorts.

Children typically progress through five stages of spelling development: emergent spelling, letter-name spelling, within-word pattern spelling, syllables and affixes spelling, and derivational relations (Bear et al., 2015) (see Photo 7.3). Each child progresses through the stages at his or her own rate; however, instruction in spelling conventions, phonics, and word study can help children progress from one stage to the

picture and word sorts Games to learn spelling patterns where children sort words or pictures into categories according to vowel and consonant sounds.

Photo 7.3
Emergent writing
Janet Towell

other in a shorter period of time. We will only focus on the first three stages of spelling development in this early childhood text.

7-3a Stage 1: Emergent Spelling

During this stage, which is usually between the ages of 3 to 5, children string scribbles and letters together randomly without an understanding that letters represent sounds. The letters may be written upside-down or sideways, in the midst of shapes, lines, circles, dots, and squiggles. Sometimes emergent spellers represent letters in their names or sight words such as *stop*, *Mom*, *Dad*, or *love*. They may draw a picture that represents people, objects, and places rather than use letters for writing. During this stage, they gradually learn how to form letters, begin to understand the differences in drawing and writing, focus the direction of print on a page, and recognize some letter-sound matches. Children in this stage tend to prefer using capital letters rather than a mixture of capitals and lowercase. Figure 7.4 shows an example of emergent spelling.

Figure 7.4
Emergent Spelling
Courtesy of the authors

7-3b Stage 2: Letter-Name Spelling

Children in this semiphonetic stage of spelling development are usually between 5 and 7 years of age. They begin to understand how to write phonemes in words with letters, although many of the phonemes may be omitted. Because of their consistency of sounds, consonants are more prevalent than vowels. They learn how to spell many words with consonant blends, digraphs, and short vowel patterns such as, the *cvc* (consonant-vowel-consonant) pattern in words like *cat* or *dog*, so common in beginning reading texts. Children learn the *alphabetic principle*, which is the relationship between letters and sounds. This is the beginning stage of reading and writing development. By the middle of the letter-name stage, children can recognize most beginning and ending consonant sounds, but they still have trouble with medial vowel sounds. Their concept of a word is fully developed. In the late stage of letter-name spelling, young writers may be confused about silent letters such as the silent *e* pattern (*cvce*), nasals, and some long vowel patterns (*cvvc*). This process of experimentation with writing letters and sounds assists students in their spelling development.

Figure 7.5 *Letter-Name Spelling*
Courtesy of the authors

More sight words may appear in their writing, such as *a*, *and*, or *the*. For example, children may write the word *team* as "TM" or *people* as "PL" or "PPL" or "PEPL." The word *sick* may look like "S," "SC," "SK," or "SEK" (Bear, Invernizzi, Templeton, & Johnston, 2008). Directionality will become apparent, and children will begin leaving spaces between words. They will also begin to use a capital letter at the beginning of the sentence and a period at the end. Letter-name spelling is sometimes referred to as "temporary" spelling or "invented" spelling (Tompkins, 2013). Figure 7.5 shows an example of letter-name spelling.

7-3c Stage 3: Within-Word Pattern Spelling

Within-word spellers are usually aged from 7 to 9 years old. This is the phonetic stage of reading, but the emphasis is still on one-syllable rather than multisyllable words. Although the words may be spelled phonetically, using invented spelling, they are easily decoded because most, if not all, of the sounds in the word are represented. Children in this stage experiment with long vowel patterns and other vowel combinations like *diphthongs* (*ou*, *ow*, *oi*, *oy*) or vowel *digraphs* (*oa*, *ea*, *ee*, *ai*). GROUND may appear as GROWND, or NAIL as NALE. Although these spellers are still considered to be beginning readers and writers, they are close to becoming fluent. Children learn most sight words, long vowel patterns, and *r*-controlled vowels, but they may confuse spelling patterns for homophones such as DEAR for DEER or MEET for MEAT. They may occasionally reverse the order of letters, such as SAW for WAS, GRIL for GIRL, or CHEKE for CHEEK (Bear et al., 2015). In the late stage of within-word pattern spelling, children may still be confused about some spelling conventions such as silent letters, the "e" drop, changing *y* to *i*, or consonant doubling when adding suffixes to a root word. For example, they may write BATTING as BATING, BUDGE as BUGE, or DIVING as DIVEING. Figure 7.6 is an example of within-word spelling (a child's letter to author/illustrator Eric Carle).

Figure 7.6 *Within-Word Pattern Spelling*
Courtesy of the authors

Consider strategies that support teaching children how to write their names. For example, an acrostic poem using the letters of their first names helps children associate words with these letters. Young children can draw images to match the letters of their names.

7-4 Stages of the Writing Process

The writing process has five stages: prewriting, drafting, revising, editing, and publishing (Graves, 1983). However, the stages of writing are cyclical rather than sequential. Writers may get to the revision stage and decide to start over. Editing and publishing may only be used for select pieces of writing. This concept may be especially difficult for children in the primary grades (Tompkins, 2013).

7-4a Stage 1: Prewriting

Prewriting is the most important—and perhaps the most difficult—stage of the writing process. Young children may need prompts to help them generate ideas. They must write about what they know or have experienced, such as stories about their families, pets, favorite foods, or outings. Another option is to have students write something related to a story that has just been read to the class. Brainstorming ideas with classmates can be helpful for children in the primary grades. Often children can make a word web on a topic they are interested in or other type of graphic organizer that organizes their ideas in a visual format. Additional options are creating time lines for informational writing and story mountains for narrative writing (see Figure 7.7). Children enjoy drawing and painting their ideas in a creative way. Artwork can be a stimulus for writing. When viewing artwork by others, children are often inspired to write down their own interpretations of the piece. Verbalizing the story behind the artwork is a step toward planned writing. Even young children who scribble lines on paper have stories to tell about their images. Storytelling by young children is a bridge toward their written stories.

Sometimes teachers provide an opening sentence and allow students to continue the story. Story prompts can be written or visual. Children enjoy imagining what a character in an image might say, or predict what might happen next. Story sequence models help young children imagine the story line. For example, a comic strip with blank speech bubbles can inspire descriptive writing. Modeling the prewriting phase of the writing process is critical for young writers. Establishing a purpose and audience for the writing is a first step. Children's literature can provide an effective stimulus, such as:

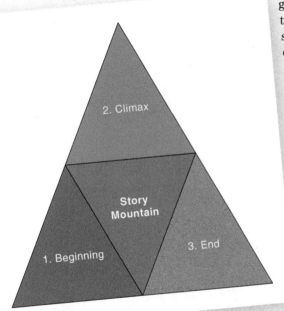

Figure 7.7
Story Mountain

1. Narrative or descriptive writing: After reading or listening to *There's a Nightmare in My Closet* by Mercer Mayer (1992), students can draw and write about their own imaginary monsters.
2. Informational writing: After reading or listening to *Diary of a Worm* by Doreen Cronin (2003), students can research and write about earthworms.
3. Letter writing: After reading or listening to *Amber on the Mountain* by Tony Johnston (1994) or *The Jolly Postman* by Janet and Allan Ahlberg (2001), students can write their own letters to friends or family members.
4. Essay writing: After reading or listening to *The Great Kapok Tree: A Tale of the Amazon Rain Forest* by Lynne Cherry (1990), students can write a persuasive essay about the importance of taking care of the rain forest.

During the prewriting stage, graphic organizers are used to plan and sequence main ideas (see Figure 7.8). Prewriting strategies should be varied and promote motivation to write for young children.

Writing brief responses to topics using the first, next, and last paragraph approach can also motivate young students to sequence their ideas (see Figure 7.9). This approach provides a structure for organizing thoughts and details about a topic.

Georgia Heard (1998) uses heart maps as a tool to inspire writing about special people, places, or events. Heart maps are a visual representation of a child's interests and passions (see Figure 7.10). A color-coded key or legend is used to categorize ideas about favorite memories or loved ones. Words and pictures are used to label different segments of the heart map. Details are written in the sections to spark the imagination. Some prompts include people who are important and why, unforgettable events, secrets, favorite stuffed animals, family celebrations, and memories.

Autobiographies and biographies are examples of informational writing. For example, children write about a selected category in the heart map, which becomes the main idea of the piece. Three facts about this category are listed to support the main

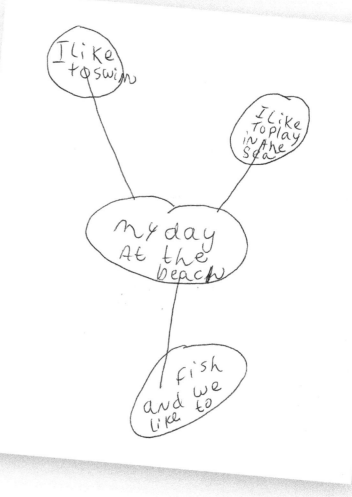

Figure 7.8
Prewriting Web
Courtesy of the authors

Figure 7.9 *First, Next, and Last Paragraph Writing Based upon a Prewriting Web*
Courtesy of the authors

concept. Finally, the child writes a summary sentence. Teachers need to frequently model the informational writing process in different subject areas, such as science and social studies (Tompkins, 2013).

Lucy Calkins (1994) emphasizes rehearsal and partner work in her writing workshop model during the prewriting phase. Each child is asked to think of three small moments or possible ideas for writing based on their personal experiences. They discuss each idea with a partner to see which one seems to be the best choice (at least temporarily). Partners are encouraged to ask each other questions during this process to flesh out the main idea and details. During the rehearsal stage, writers practice telling stories from different perspectives.

Writing ideas can be collected from a variety of sources, including environmental print, such as signs around the school or community, which can provide fuel for writing prompts. Children can write questions about what they are thinking and place these into a "What's on Your Mind?" box (Flint, 2008). The teacher can select one question for a daily group discussion. For example, a sign in the library that prohibits food or drink can be a starting point for planning a persuasive essay (see Figure 7.11). In small writing groups, the children record the supporting and contradicting arguments, which become paragraphs in their essays (Flint, 2008).

The children select which side of the argument they will write about. Working with a writing partner helps young children develop their ideas and revise their writing. Persuasive writing allows children to express their opinions about current issues or events. Modeling this type of writing with the whole class and in small groups guides young writers in this process (see Figure 7.12).

The steps of the writing cycle are depicted in Figure 7.13, as adapted from Calkins (1994).

Figure 7.10
Child's Heart Map
Courtesy of the authors

Figure 7.11
What's on Your Mind Prompt
Courtesy of the authors

Why can't we eat or drink in the library?

Austin

7-4b Stage 2: Drafting

During the drafting stage of the writing process, students write down their thoughts and ideas freely, without worrying too much about the mechanics of writing. Teachers should encourage the use of invented (temporary) spelling for unknown words. Picture dictionaries should also be available for children. Writers may enjoy typing their rough drafts ("sloppy copies") on the computer, or they may be given special pens and paper to make the process more enjoyable. Young children can be taught the basics of word processing on the computer, and some find the process exciting through the integration of technology. They should be encouraged to write several rough drafts before proceeding to the revising stage. All drafts should be saved in a writing folder. Partner work continues during the drafting stage of the writing process. Children need to listen to each other while reading aloud their writing drafts.

1. Select a controversial topic.
2. Debate both sides of the issue (pros/cons).
3. Record the arguments, and select a point of view.
4. Plan the essay to include a topic sentence (main idea), three supporting details, and a concluding statement.
5. Write a draft of the essay and share with writing partner.
6. Revise and edit for final draft.

❯❯ Professional Resource Download

Figure 7.12
Persuasive Writing Guide

7-4c Stage 3: Revising

The revising stage can be challenging for young children. They can improve their writing techniques and skills with teacher scaffolding and modeling. In narrative writing, children should check their drafts to determine if they used complete sentences and if their stories have a beginning, middle, and end. The purpose of writing is communication, so it is essential that the content makes sense to readers. Reading their work aloud helps young writers recognize their own mistakes. Writing buddies may also be a good idea, so that strong writers can assist peers who are struggling with the writing process. Remind children to continuously reread what they write. Verbal discussions in larger groups about selecting the "right" word can help children during the revision process.

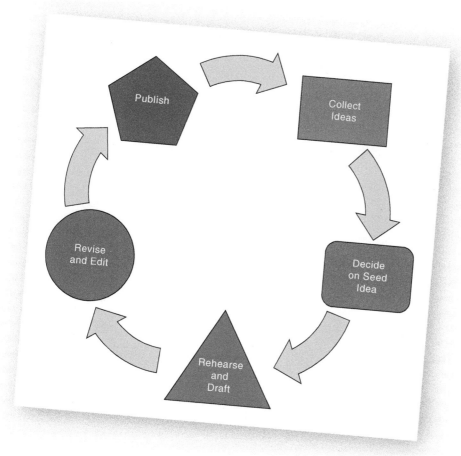

Figure 7.13
The Writing Cycle

7-4d Stage 4: Editing

Mechanics are the focus of the editing phase of the writing process, which includes grammar, spelling, and punctuation. The editing process should be completed in three steps for the primary grades:

1. Children should proofread their own compositions.
2. Children should share their work with their writing buddies. Mechanical errors should be identified and corrected.
3. Children should submit their work to the teacher for a final editing.

Children should be allowed to choose their best draft for editing if they intend to publish their piece. A writing portfolio may contain different types of writing, such as informational, narrative, argument, and poetry.

Lessons that specifically focus on grammar and punctuation help young children to understand and edit for language conventions in their writing. For example, children can complete a "print search," which identifies specific punctuation marks and their meanings in text (Flint, 2008). First, children select a passage from a familiar book that they are reading as a class. Next, each child draws a line down the center of a sheet of paper to create two columns. In the left column, the child writes sentences from the text, making sure to copy punctuation exactly. Each punctuation mark is circled. In the right column, the child writes the rule or convention with an arrow drawn to connect left and right sections (see Figure 7.14). Children write the rule in their own words to

Figure 7.14
Print Search
Courtesy of the authors

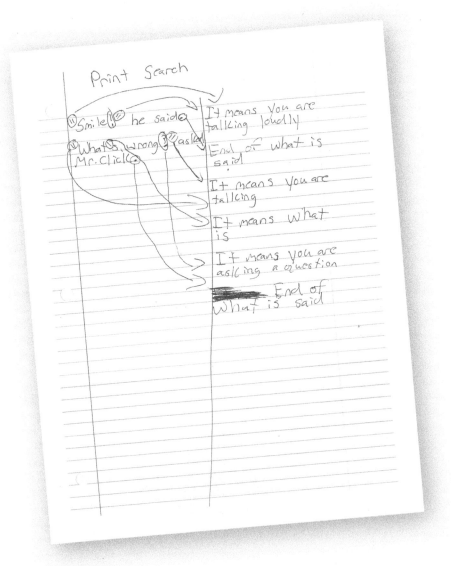

Figure 7.15
My Dog Champ
Courtesy of the authors

explain why the author chose that particular convention of language (Flint, 2008). Using *The Best Class Picture Ever!* by Denis Roche (2003), children can focus on the conventions of language and word choice. The story describes a group of young children brainstorming words that make you smile for a class picture.

7-4e Stage 5: Publishing

Once the editing stage has been completed, children will be ready to share their work with their classmates. Even if the children do not publish their writing in an individual or class bookmaking project, they should share their writing with peers. Sometimes this sharing time is called "author's chair." The author sits in a special chair to read his or her work. The audience makes comments and asks questions about the piece. It is a time of celebration for the children. Author's chair gives them a sense of accomplishment and pride. The teacher may decide to allow children to publish one piece a month in a book format for the classroom library (Calkins,1994). The resulting book can also be a class project and created in a big book format for all to enjoy. Simply using cardboard and paper bound with string can provide the structure for the big book. The novelty of group writing and illustration in the big book format excites children and inspires individual book writing and design (see Figure 7.15).

> ✔ **CONSIDER THIS...**
>
> Consider how you could assess vocabulary use and sentence structure through journal writing. For example, prompts (for example, "Yesterday I saw . . .") can support the use of different sentence structures (sentence fluency). Checklists of vocabulary can guide children to vary their word selections (word choice).

7-5 Components of Writing Workshops with Arts Integration

The writing process takes place in most primary classrooms in the form of a writing workshop, a block of time for writing instruction and practice typically provided on a daily basis, or approximately 60 to 90 minutes three to five times a week

writing workshop A block of time for writing instruction and practice, approximately 60 to 90 minutes three to five times a week.

(Ray & Laminack, 2001). Students work at an individual pace, so the class will be at many different stages of the writing process. The three major components of writing workshops are:

1. Mini-lessons: A brief lesson when the teacher demonstrates an appropriate writing skill
2. Writing practice: Time to write without interruptions and time for students to talk to each other about their writing
3. Writing conferences: Time for the teacher to meet with students at different stages of the writing process when necessary

Teachers must be well organized to manage writing workshops on a regular basis without chaos and confusion. The goals should consist of helping students develop their own writing identities, so that they think of themselves as writers with a sense of purpose as members of a vibrant, literate community (Ray & Laminack, 2001).

7-5a Mini-Lessons

According to Calkins and Harwayne (1987), mini-lessons have four basic components. These brief lessons (5 to 10 minutes) focus on one important concept that will improve children's writing. Mentor texts (exemplary models of writing traits) and student writing samples can be used during explicit instruction (direct, focused, and purposeful). Children discuss their writing with a partner to clarify their ideas. The four components are:

- *Connection*: Teacher links prior learning to the lesson.
- *Teach:* Teacher models the strategy or technique.
- *Active engagement:* Teacher facilitates or monitors student-guided practice of strategy or technique.
- *Link:* Teacher provides a hook (mnemonic device) to remind children to use this strategy or technique in future work.

The children are encouraged to practice the new strategy or technique in their own writing practice.

7-5b Writing Practice

During this part of the writing workshop, children write independently or with partners (see Photo 7.4). They will apply skills they learned in the mini-lesson to their writing. Classroom organization and management are essential. The teacher moves from group to group, talking with various children about their work.

Children may choose to work with a small group of students on a common area of need. Writing workshops provide a block of uninterrupted time when students can write and think about their writing every day.

7-5c Writing Conferences

Carl Anderson (2000) and Ralph Fletcher (1999) have written about the topic of *conferring*, considered to be the architecture of writing. Conferring is the most difficult and the most important part of a writing workshop. Like everything else, conferring gets easier with practice. According to Carl Anderson (2000), there are four basic steps in an effective writing conference:

1. *Research a child* (to understand what the child is thinking and feeling). Review a child's piece of writing quickly and ask, "How's it going? What are you working on as a writer? How can I help?"
2. *Feedback* (give the writer a compliment). Name something specific the child is doing in the writing.

Photo 7.4
*Descriptive writing
using the five senses*

3. *Teaching* (decide on a target skill or writing trait based on the writer's draft). Demonstrate the skill through your own writing or use a *mentor text* (exemplary models of children's literature). You may also coach by prompting children to expand their writing using different traits.

4. *Try it* (give children a link or trigger phrase to use the skill or trait in the current piece as well as future writing). Help students set two or three realistic writing goals based on their individual needs (for example, focus, detail, voice, or conventions). The goals may be written on a sticky note, writing journal, or in an assignment box.

A writing conference guide can be used while conversing with children to record anecdotal notes (see Table 7. 1). Sharing a child's writing strengths is a great way to begin a conference.

A relaxed classroom environment with adequate materials and supplies is essential for a successful writing workshop. Each student has a writer's notebook, a folder or portfolio for writing drafts, and a toolkit (notebook) with information of the qualities and characteristics of good writing (see Photo 7.5).

The toolkit may include a list of strong verbs, juicy color words, specific emotion and sensory words, personal narrative writing prompts, or revising questions (Forney, 2001). Anchor charts are posted all over the room, in every nook and cranny. Student work hangs from the ceiling on old-fashioned clotheslines. A bookcase in the classroom library holds picture dictionaries and published work by student authors next to a class set of laptop computers. Curtains on the windows with soft lighting, pillows, rugs, a sofa, and beanbag chairs complete the cozy atmosphere. Fletcher (1999) describes the perfect toolkit for young writers as including words, imagination, creativity, passion for reading, knowledge of story elements, and ideas that make writing come to life.

Table 7.1 *Writing Conference Guide*

Child's Name: Date:	Research about the Child/ What I Noticed/Feedback	Teaching Strategy	Next Steps/Goal Setting
Anecdotal Notes	What do I know about the child's strengths and needs? What writing strategies does the child use on his or her own?	Today's conference focused on what writing strategy? How can I connect to children's literature to support this strategy?	What writing strategies could be taught in future lessons that will support this child's needs?

❯❯ Professional Resource Download

Photo 7.5
Journal writing

7-5d Writing Process and Art

The writing process is similar to the arts process in that artists develop fluency in their work. Artists and writers both use their chosen media to communicate ideas to others and have extensive experience with media (words and art materials) itself. Therefore, both artists and writers allow the media to guide them while they guide the media themselves in a push-and-pull fashion. Just as writers aspire to make meaningful connections through text-to-text, text-to-self, and text-to-world, artists strive to have their art forms communicate the same connections. Creativity, imagination, and inspiration fuel the writing and artistic process equally.

Looking at and discussing artworks involves the art criticism process. The art criticism model (Anderson, 1995; Feldman, 1973), where one has an initial reaction to the work and then describes, analyzes, interprets, and evaluates the arts form, directly relates to the writing process.

Description

To understand the message, one must look carefully and notice the details to fully describe what is seen, heard, or read. Being able to communicate through this descriptive process and explain your point of view is an important part of comprehension. Questions to consider include the children's initial reactions to and descriptions of artwork:

- What are your first thoughts?
- What do you notice about the space, room, or area?
- What do you see?
- What lines do you see (shapes, colors, and textures)?
- What objects, people, and places, do you see?

art criticism model To comprehend and interpret the meaning of artistic expression through four basic steps: description, analysis, interpretation, and evaluation.

Analysis

Next, one analyzes and explains how the elements of form relate to one another. Does an author repeat specific words or sentence patterns to create a dramatic effect? Does an artist use specific colors or shapes to create unity or balance? Does a musician use specific sounds to create rhythm? How does an artist/author put the

IDEAS THAT INSPIRE WRITING: ACTIVITY FOR PRESERVICE TEACHERS TO DO WITH CHILDREN

Purpose: In this lesson, students will brainstorm ideas to inspire their writing based upon *Tulip Sees America* by Cynthia Rylant (1998).

Procedure: The teacher shows the cover illustration of a mentor text, *Tulip Sees America* (Rylant, 1998), while the children describe the illustration and predict what they think the story will be about. After the teacher reads the story aloud, the children will brainstorm a list of places they have been or would like to visit. Using magazines and newspapers, the children create a collage that depicts a place (or state) of their choice. Children add captions and labels to the collage. The teacher uses the mentor text to "dig deeper" in the details of specific places (states). The children use their imaginations and knowledge of the five senses to describe what might be seen, heard, touched, smelled, and tasted during a visit to their selected place. The children write their ideas down and share with a small group of peers.

Teaching Analysis: Reflective practices are a necessary part of the *literacy assessment cycle* and are key components in preservice preparation and certification such as edTPA. Analyze the strengths and areas of improvement in this lesson idea. Answer the following:

- What is successful?
- What would you change to improve the lesson?
- What did you learn about teaching literacy?

Links: Making connections to technology and developmentally appropriate practices (DAP) supports lesson planning and literacy instruction. Adaptations of this lesson idea are provided through the following:

- **Technology Link:** Children can watch videos of their recent family vacations. Travel websites or state information brochures can be shared.
- **DAP Link:** Children use images to help them organize their ideas as a prewriting activity. Analyzing images promotes critical thinking skills for young children.
- **Executive Function Link:** Creative play and active engagement during an interactive read-aloud develop children's self-regulation skills in social settings as reflected in the holistic model of literacy (cognitive, socioemotional, and physical).
- **Classroom Link:** For children (0 to 3) a large laminated map of the United States can be used to draw on with water-based markers to locate where their families have visited.
- **Classroom Link:** For children (3 to 6), puzzles of the different states or the United States can reinforce the details learned while reading the story.
- **Classroom Link:** Children (6 to 9) can create a poster in the outline of the selected state and create a map of the details they learned.

Adapted from Culham (2008).

---

elements together to create the whole? Some questions to ask children to support analysis include:

- How does the artist put these things (lines, shapes, and colors) together to make the artwork have balance?
- Is it the same on both sides (symmetrical) or not (asymmetrical)?
- If you were a tiny person and could walk through the artwork, where would you go and what would you see (movement)?
- What do you see first (emphasis)?

Interpretation

During the criticism process, students and teachers ask questions to interpret artwork or writing. The responses from children will be simplistic at first. By developing higher-order thinking skills through continued questioning and modeling of responses, however, children will develop more advanced rationales for their thoughts and reactions to works of art and various genres. Children interpret artwork and writing from different perspectives based upon their prior knowledge. Older children have more detailed responses due to vocabulary growth and cognitive development. The older children can write more detailed paragraphs that illustrate and explain their understanding of the

USING MENTOR TEXTS AS WRITING MODELS

Mentor texts that authentically feature children with disabilities can nurture social acceptance and positive attitudes in the classroom (Rieger & McGrail, 2015). Teachers should know how to discuss sensitive topics with children and how to select high-quality children's literature. Authentic representation of children with disabilities should promote empathy, depict acceptance, include positive images, demonstrate respect, understand various disabilities, stress person-first language, and represent realistic characters, settings, and events. Role-play and dramatic activities assist children in understanding and expressing their feelings about varying disabilities (Rieger & McGrail, 2015).

Think about It

How can you teach social acceptance of children with learning disabilities through mentor texts? For example, *Ian's Walk: A Story about Autism* (Lears, 1998) describes siblings' experiences and reactions during a walk to the park. Ian, who has autism, reacts differently than his sisters to specific situations in the story. After reading this book, children can write a dialogue based on their own feelings to a selected scene. After writing, the children partner to role-play their written dialogues.

topic with reference to real-world experiences. Some questions to prompt children during interpretation include:

- What does it mean?
- What is the artist or author trying to tell you?
- Tell us a story about the artwork (make-believe stories by children using what was seen in the work as described by previous answers to earlier questions)? Note: Always direct children back to the artwork or text for evidence to support their ideas.

Evaluation

Finally, children decide if they value the artwork or not using the rationales they discussed earlier in the process. Children explain their opinions with supporting details shown in the artwork or text. The acceptance of different perspectives is key in this open-ended discussion. All answers are valid and accepted to promote confidence and motivate dialogue using the following questions:

- Was the artwork or writing good/bad, beautiful/ugly or happy/sad,?
- Do you think the artist was successful/unsuccessful in telling the story about the artwork (clear communication of meaning)?
- Did you learn anything by thinking and talking about this artwork/text?
- What did you learn?

Practice in comprehending visual images can happen through a variety of classroom activities, such as discussions while sharing a student's own work and the work of others (either other classmates or artists beyond the classroom), and by engaging in creative art-making activities.

This process of description, analysis, interpretation, and evaluation is a standard process in art criticism (Feldman, 1973) and supports emergent literacy. Visual literacy, using images to interpret and communicate meaning, is essential for emergent readers and writers. Nonverbal and verbal symbols are interpreted during the literacy process.

visual literacy Using images to interpret and communicate meaning.

Through active engagement in visual literacy strategies, children become more sensitive to the images in their lives and thus able to comprehend these images in a variety of contexts. It is important in today's society to develop visual literacy skills because so much of the information in our culture is passed through images on television, billboards, online, websites, and movies. Picture books, with and without text, are important to enable young children to develop their interpretive skills through imagination. Contextual clues are used in visual literacy just as in literacy. Interpretation of the visual symbols relies on your perspective and past experiences, background knowledge, and schema. Pictures often help young readers to comprehend the text. Both the written word and images are important for interpretation.

Teachers can design activities that focus on interpreting images and creating new images as a part of the literacy curriculum. One approach to teaching visual literacy is to develop visual thinking skills (VTS). Visual thinking skills focus on guiding students through the process of becoming visually literate and developing creative and critical thinking skills. The VTS approach targets the primary grades to develop early visual literacy. In this process, it is important to view a variety of images from different cultures and to develop personal connections to these images. Young children are encouraged to talk about what they think by describing and interpreting images. Children also take different viewpoints about the images they study in VTS activities. Consequently, they come up with new questions for themselves based upon the image and everyday life, while trying to discover as much information as possible about the images (Housen, 2000).

7-5e Writing Traits

Lessons typically focus on the six common writing traits that can be easily and effectively taught in primary classrooms (Culham, 2004). The six traits involve content and format, the organization of ideas, the writer's style and voice, word choice, sentence fluency, and conventions (for example, spelling, punctuation, grammar, and capitalization). After learning and practicing the six traits, children present their work to the class. Presentation includes how the writing is formatted in the final work: handwriting, visuals, fonts used for word processing, spacing, and layout of the text with images. Culham (2004) explains this concept as $6 + 1$, which represents the six traits plus presentation. These traits give teachers a common focus for teaching writing through mini-lessons as well as a plan for assessment. *Word walls* (class display of key words) can help children with their word choice and vocabulary skills. Modeling good writing through read-alouds using quality children's literature will provide writers with ideas for style and voice. When children get into the habit of writing on a daily basis, they will increase their sentence fluency naturally. The environment of the classroom builds self-confidence and a motivation for writing. Young writers need an extraordinary amount of encouragement, support, and guidance to become proficient at the writing process.

Learning how to write using the six traits is not easy. As noted previously, we learn to read through reading, and we also learn to write through reading. If you want to be a good writer, you need to read a lot. Good writing takes years of practice, just like playing the piano or becoming a good basketball player or ballerina. As any competent author will tell you, the craft of writing is a lifelong learning process. Writing is hard work! It requires many drafts and much revision and editing. Good writing takes time and motivation.

One of the best ways to teach writing effectively for all ages is through the use of picture books. Ruth Culham (2004) uses picture books to demonstrate the common traits of writing with her middle school students, and it works. Books in her classroom library are organized according to their strongest writing trait. The following choices are suggested children's books, categorized by traits.

A. Inspiring Ideas
- *Lilly's Purple Plastic Purse* by Kevin Henkes (Greenwillow, 1996)
- *Thank you, Mr. Falker* by Patricia Polacco (Philomel, 1998)

Apply & Reflect

Design a writing center for your classroom. Create a list of writing tools and materials for children, including supplies that encourage expression in visual art, music, dance, and dramatic play.

visual thinking skills (VTS) Focus on guiding students through the process of becoming visually literate and developing creative and critical thinking skills by viewing a variety of images from different cultures and discussing personal connections to these images.

ASSESSING WRITING SKILLS AND TRAITS THROUGH A WRITING CHECKLIST

This self-evaluation checklist can be used to improve children's writing skills and focus on the six writing traits (Culham, 2004). The child selects a writing sample (informational, persuasive, or narrative) to evaluate. If appropriate, the teacher can read each question to the child and record the answers. Teachers should model this self-evaluation process prior to the children using the assessment guide on their own.

A Self-Evaluation of the Six Writing Traits Guide

Directions: Using your writing sample, answer the following questions. This will help you to remember the six writing traits.

1. **Voice:** Does my personality show in my writing style?
2. **Ideas:** Did I come up with interesting ideas about my topic? Do I have lots of details? Is anything missing?
3. **Word Choice:** Do I have a variety of nouns, verbs, and adjectives?

4. **Organization:** Are my ideas in sequence? Is there a clear beginning, middle, and end?
5. **Sentence Fluency:** Have I used different kinds of sentences in my writing? Do they all make sense?
6. **Conventions:** Are my words spelled correctly? Do I have capital letters at the beginning of my sentences and punctuation at the end? Did I used quotation marks and commas when needed?

Think about It

This guide is designed for children to assess the quality of their writing through the six writing traits (Culham, 2004). Mentor texts can be used to introduce and practice these qualities of good writing. For example, how can you use *When Sophie Gets Angry—Really, Really Angry* by Molly Bang (2004) to help first graders develop their personal writing styles (voice)?

⌄ Professional Resource Download

B. Shaping Organization
- ■ *Click, Clack, Moo, Cows that Type* by Doreen Cronin (Simon & Schuster, 2000)
- ■ *Dear Mrs. LaRue: Letters from Obedience School* by Mark Teague (Scholastic, 2002)

C. Sparking Voice
- ■ *Diary of a Worm* by Doreen Cronin (Joanna Cotler Books, 2003)
- ■ *Hooray for Diffendoofer Day!* by Dr. Seuss, Jack Prelutsky, and Lane Smith (Alfred A. Knopf, 1998)

D. Expanding Word Choice
- ■ *Dog Breath* by Dav Pilkey (Scholastic, 1994)
- ■ *Flossie and the Fox* by Patricia McKissack (Dial Books, 1986)

E. Developing Sentence Fluency
- ■ *Gathering the Sun* by Alma Flor Ada (Rayo of HarperCollins, 2001)
- ■ *Oh, the Places You'll Go!* by Dr. Seuss (Random House, 1990)
- ■ *Possum Come a-Knockin'* by Nancy Van Laan (Dragonfly Books, 1990)

F. Strengthening Conventions
- ■ *A Cache of Jewels and Other Collective Nouns* by Ruth Heller (Putnam & Grosset Group, 2008)
- ■ *Kites Sail High: A Book about Verbs* by Ruth Heller (Putnam & Grosset Group, 1991)

G. Spotlighting Presentation
- ■ *A Bad Case of Stripes* by David Shannon (Scholastic, 1998)
- ■ *Charlie Parker Played Be Bop* by Chris Raschka (Scholastic, 1992)

Table 7.2 *Comparison of Writing and Art Criticism*

Stages of the Writing Process	Writing Traits	Arts Criticism Stages
Brainstorming or Prewriting Activities	Ideas and organization (initial), rehearsal	Initial reaction, description (initial)
Drafting	Organization, voice (initial), word choice (initial)	Description, analysis, interpretation
Revising	Organization, word choice, sentence fluency (initial), conventions (initial)	Description, analysis, interpretation
Editing	Voice, word choice, sentence fluency, conventions	Description, analysis, interpretation
Publishing	Presentation	Evaluation

The connections between the writing process, writing traits, and the art criticism stages can guide curriculum planning (see Table 7.2). By understanding the relationship between arts, child development, and writing process, teachers are able to create lesson plans that are interdisciplinary.

As Table 7.2 illustrates, throughout the drafting, revising, and editing process, authors/artists rework areas of organization, voice, word choice, sentence fluency, and conventions prior to presentation of the work. In art criticism, the writing process of the description, analysis, and interpretation is also revised and edited prior to final evaluation, which is the presentation format in art criticism. This process is cyclical in nature as one can constantly revise and edit. Under a teacher's guidance, children must move past this point and present their final work.

 CONSIDER THIS...

Consider how collaborative writing activities such as writing a shared poem with the teacher or a classmate can motivate children to write. Besides using word walls, what techniques or strategies can be implemented to help children improve their spelling skills?

7-6 Literacy Strategies and Practices for Writing and Spelling Development

A key point when incorporating literacy strategies in lesson plans is to ensure that children at all levels of learning are actively engaged in the reading and writing process. Part of this process is teaching the rules of writing and spelling. Another part of this process is teacher and peer modeling of the reading and writing process at all age and ability levels. Active engagement often involves the interdisciplinary process of including the arts in your lessons. Providing a wide variety of children's literature is necessary. As illustrated in Table 7.3, learning to write is an interactive process that requires working with others for success.

Age Groups	Cognitive	Emotional
0 to 3	Sing alphabet songs and associate sounds with letters and words. Read aloud favorite stories while toddlers draw/write their ideas. Have toddlers create artwork and verbalize story while teacher writes. Use lines, shapes, and textures to illustrate letters (sandbox writing, water play, bubbles/soap writing).	Dramatize an emotion using facial expression and actions Have toddlers illustrate the emotion. Use artwork to identify emotions and dictate children's ideas. Taste a food item and describe likes or dislikes while teacher writes the food *word*. Listen to music while drawing, emphasizing specific emotions.
3 to 6	Brainstorm strategies that focus on words and sentence structure. Create sentence strip stories with class. Use prewriting scribbles and have children "read" their stories. Use magnetic letters to write words and sentences. Collect and describe items for a favorite recipe and write/illustrate the steps to make the food dish.	Use color to associate words and sentences with emotions. Discuss emotions when brainstorming group stories. Use props and masks to dramatize a story, with teacher writing the story for the group. Illustrate a picture of themselves and families depicting different emotions. Describe emotions during a food tasting experience and dictate likes and dislikes.
6 to 9	Write collaborative stories about familiar topics (vacation, celebrations, family). Write recipes for favorite foods (ice cream sundaes, vegetable soup). Journal write with and without prompts. Use dictionary (picture or word) and thesaurus for word choice when editing.	Draw storyboard with written captions emphasizing characters. Write informative text that focuses on a particular viewpoint (research and debate). Write a news heading or short article that focuses on emotional issue. Write poems, similes, metaphors, or shaped prose that express emotions.

End-of-Chapter Study Aids

Summary

Emergent literacy for young children is not only a physical (using writing instruments) and mental exercise (imagination and ideas), but also an emotional experience because writing stems from feelings of expression. Children need to practice writing before it becomes part of their daily habit. They need to understand spelling and grammar rules. The writing stages progress from doodling, writing numbers, pictures, and to structuring words in sentences. The writing process involves prewriting, drafting, revising, editing, and publishing to develop a final composition (Tompkins, 2013).

Physical	Children's Books	Family Involvement
Use clay, paint, crayons, and other art materials to strengthen motor skills.	*Frederick* by Leo Lionni *The Important Book* by Margaret Wise Brown	Find household objects; label and discuss their use.
Manipulate board books featuring letters and words.		Draw pictures and dictate stories.
Use textured letters to stimulate tactile senses.		Parents model writing the alphabet while child sings song.
Finger painting letters and short words.		Parents create a chart with the child explaining likes or dislikes.
Move fingers, hands, and feet to trace letter shapes.		Trace letters and numbers on paper.
Explore real objects and repeat name of object.		
Practice writing sheets that guide hand motion and develop fine motor skills.	*Epossumondas* by Coleen Salley *Dumpy LaRue* by Elizabeth Winthrop	Parents and children draw pictures together, either writing or telling a related story.
Dramatize story line and write collaboratively.		Create books on topics of interest.
Form letter shapes and word shapes with their body individually or in groups.		Write poetry about emotions.
Create stage sets for story play.		Write using a prompt and expand.
Create labels or signs for classroom physical environment.		Create treasure maps with a legend.
Practice writing on individual dry erase board.	*Gathering the Sun* by Alma Flor Ada *The Polar Express* by Chris Van Allsburg	Write menus for special family occasions.
Draw an imaginary creature and write a description of its appearance, habitat, and life cycle.		Create recipes for favorite dishes (cooking and eating).
Create a pop-up or moveable book.		Write shopping lists.
Write a secret message with a white crayon and paint over with watercolor paint to read.		Do a writing workshop at home.
		Expand stories through imagination (fiction or nonfiction).
		Write letters to family members and friends.

We reviewed the five stages of spelling that give children basic tools for writing. Understanding syllables and rules of spelling usually starts with children in first grade or pre-K, depending on their development. The writing process has five stages. Initially, children begin to write about their ideas and what they know. As they progress in learning grammar rules, they are able to revise what they wrote and make choices to pick words that accurately express their thoughts and feelings. This is a holistic process and takes into account the cognitive, socioemotional, and physical aspects of children. We need playful classroom environments that allow freedom of expression as children become more comfortable learning grammar rules. When children understand the process, including revisions, they can relax and let their ideas flow freely. Children can associate learning to write as a comfortable and familiar process in a supportive environment. In a caring and supportive learning environment, children can become motivated writers who want to write about their thoughts, opinions, and feelings.

Chapter Exercises

1. List potential field trip locations in your community that spark interest and writing motivation for young children. Design writing prompts for each field trip experience.
2. Select a familiar children's book, and write metacognitive questions on sticky notes that could be used during a think-aloud activity. (Attach notes to appropriate pages of the book.) Practice reading and discussing the book with a partner.
3. Research and locate a word sort example online, print it out, and demonstrate the strategy with a peer.
4. As a whole class, brainstorm a list of different publishing formats for children's writing (for example, class big book, folded accordion book, and computer-based programs for classroom publishing).
5. Design a mini-lesson that focuses on one of the writing traits, and share your idea with a partner.

Teacher Toolbox

TEACHING SENTENCE FLUENCY

Appropriate for Ages 5 to 9

To practice the writing trait of sentence fluency with children, choose a children's book, such as *Dizzy* by Jonah Winter (2006). Create an anchor chart that features strategies, such as how to begin sentences in different ways, varying lengths of sentences, and sentences flow. Divide the class in half and begin by showing the first illustration in the book. Ask the children in the left half of the class to share sentences that describe the illustration. Turn the page to the next illustration and ask the right half of the class to add a sentence that describes the illustration, using a different word to begin the sentence. Play a selection of music that relates to the book (for *Dizzy*, play any jazz song on the album *Bird and Diz* by Mercury Records in 1952).

The children brainstorm words that describe the music. The teacher reads the book aloud and emphasizes the sound words (onomatopoeia) in the text, such as "diddly diddly bop de biddly wah wah de bleep." The children create sentences of varying lengths that use sound words. Finally, the children, with guidance from the teacher, write a class story to describe their interpretation of the book.

Adapted from Culham (2008).

Sentence Fluency Questions

Do I start with different words?
Do I use words to begin a sentence other than the subject?
If I decide to repeat words in sentences, is it a rhyme or pattern?
Are my sentences different lengths?
When I read my sentences aloud, do the words sound smooth?
Does the dialogue sound real?

Key Terms and Concepts

alphabetic principle	invented spelling	visual thinking skills
art criticism model	metacognitive awareness	word study
decoding	picture and word sorts	writing workshop
encoding	visual literacy	

Tania Kolinko/Shutterstock.com

STANDARDS ADDRESSED IN THIS CHAPTER

The standards from the following organizations will be used throughout the chapter: Common Core State Standards for English Language Arts, the National Association for the Education of Young Children (NAEYC), and National Core Arts Standards. These standards are discussed further in the chapter as appropriate.

COMMON CORE
STATE STANDARDS

Common Core State Standards for English Language Arts

Anchor Standards for Reading

Reading Standards for Literature/Informational Text K–5
- Craft and Structure
- Integration of Knowledge and Ideas

Anchor Standards for Writing
- Production and Distribution of Writing

Anchor Standards for Speaking and Listening
- Comprehension and Collaboration

Anchor Standards for Language
- Vocabulary Acquisition and Use

2010 NAEYC Standards for Initial and Advanced Early Childhood Professional Preparation Programs
- *Standard 2:* Building Family and Community Relationships

NAEYC Early Childhood Program Standards and Accreditation Criteria
- *Standard 7:* Families
- *Standard 8:* Community Relationships

NCA

National Core Arts Standards (Dance, Media Arts, Music, Theater, Visual Arts)

Creating
- *Anchor Standard 1:* Generate and conceptualize artistic ideas and work.
- *Anchor Standard 2:* Organize and develop artistic ideas and work.
- *Anchor Standard 3:* Refine and complete artistic work.

The single most important thing a parent can do to help a child learn to read is to transmit a love of reading. — Phyllis Hunter

Family members play an important role in the daily life of the child by participating in school/classroom events and through reading and writing experiences. Teachers should build family and school partnerships to empower young children in their literacy development. Young children learn best when having fun, laughing, playing, and experiencing social connections. For example the popular British TV show, *Peppa Pig* (produced by Phil Davies), depicts family life engaged in ordinary daily activities such as going on picnics, boat trips, or hanging pictures. The show has simple shapes and colors (to facilitate comprehension) that represent a house on a hill, a car, and a garden. Peppa's family of four (parents and young brother George) also includes grandparents, and fun activities with friends. Nurturing the love of reading through family bonding experiences (cuddling and lap reading) and through family-school partnerships establishes a foundation for literacy development.

Young children need meaningful activities at both home and school with cognitive, socioemotional, and physical connections, including play, expressing their feelings, and using real-world experiences (holistic model of literacy [HML]). Building a classroom environment that is conducive to creative literacy is a worthy goal for all teachers. Learning to read and write involves motivation, passion, and creativity by allowing all children to achieve their full potential. In the book, *Teach Your Child to Read in 100 Easy Lessons* (Engelmann, Haddox, & Bruner, 1983), children are engaged with parental interaction that promotes positive reinforcement after learning words and concepts. Parent/child relationships and teacher/child relationships require trust, honesty, connection, communication, and commitment. Classroom interaction encourages all children to participate and engage in learning, thereby becoming confident readers and writers.

Classroom interaction requires an active and engaged learning environment for young children. When children are learning to read, teachers can utilize repetitive sound and rhyming patterns, such as "*Sam sat,*" and then, "*Mat sat,*" followed by "*Mat sat on Sam,*" using pictures to associate sounds with events). This process encourages active engagement in a supportive learning environment. A variety of experiences during literacy instruction (whole group, small group, and individual) also inspires learning. Classrooms should include structured and unstructured activities that are guided and facilitated by the teacher.

Continued on page 176

LEARNING OBJECTIVES

After you have read this chapter, you should be able to:

8-1 Describe family involvement in the literacy curriculum.

8-2 Discuss home and school partnerships to build creativity.

8-3 Analyze strategies for collaboration and differentiated literacy instruction.

8-4 Explain ideas for documenting literacy learning.

8-5 Design libraries and literacy centers for creative exploration.

8-6 Apply literacy strategies and practices for family literacy and classroom connections.

STANDARDS CONNECTION TO THE VIGNETTE

NAEYC Early Childhood Program Standards and Accreditation Criteria

Standard 8: Community Relationships

8.B.04 Program staff invite members of the performing and visual arts community, such as musical performers, coordinators of traveling museum exhibits, local artists, and community residents, to share their interests and talents with the children.

Common Core State Standards for English Language Arts

Craft and Structure

Second Grade

4. Describe how words and phrases (for example, regular beats, alliteration, rhymes, repeated lines) supply rhythm and meaning in a story, poem, or song.

Interactive read-alouds using quality children's literature (fiction and nonfiction) engage children in meaningful ways, while building vocabulary and comprehension skills (see Photo 8.1). In this vignette, children work collaboratively to write stories or poems, which they share with the class.

Mr. Fischer introduces the award-winning picture book, *Locomotive* by Brian Floca (2013) to his second graders by wearing a train engineer's cap and blowing a whistle. The children share what they know about trains, and predict what this story will be about, based on the cover illustration (see Photo 8.2). The teacher points out the two awards on the cover. The gold sticker is the 2014 Caldecott Medal for the illustrations, and the silver sticker is the Robert Sibert Medal for informational text. The children notice the smoke coming out of the engine and wonder where the train is going. Mr. Fischer introduces key words, such as *locomotive, engineer, transcontinental,*

Photo 8.1 *Imagining during story time*

Photo 8.2 Locomotive *by Brian Floca*

Source: Floca, B. (2013). *Locomotive.* New York: Atheneum Books for Young Readers.

crew, and *steam engine,* and writes them on the board or on an anchor chart. Together the children describe the detailed illustrations in this story about America's first transcontinental railroad journey in 1869. They participate during the read-aloud by reading the sound words with the teacher such as, *"Huff, huff, huff"* and *"Whoo, whoo."* Afterward, Mr. Fischer divides the class into small groups for writing stories and/or poems based on the book. He encourages the children to use the new vocabulary words and sound words in their writing. At the end of this literacy activity, the small groups come together to share their stories or poems. The children have opportunities to hear how the new vocabulary words are used in a variety of contexts. As an extension activity, a child's grandfather, who was a train engineer, visits the class to discuss his experiences working the railroad. Additional follow-up activities may include drawing and labeling a map of the train's journey or drawing and labeling the parts of a train.

Building classroom relationships enhances a trusting and safe environment that is supportive of self-development. If children learn to self-monitor during the literacy experience, they will become active participants in their own learning.

Developmentally appropriate practice (DAP) is featured in the vignette and can be adapted for younger children (birth to age 5) and older children to age 9. Suggested adaptations include:

- Ages 0 to 3: Parents or teachers can read simple train books to infants and toddlers (such as the Thomas the Tank Engine series by Reverend W. Awdry), emphasizing the sounds of the trains. They can also sing songs about trains like "I've Been Working on the Railroad" from the album by Pete Seeger called *American Favorite Ballads* (available on iTunes).

- Ages 3 to 6: The children can learn simple facts about trains by listening to informational picture books, such as *The Train Book: A Kids Book about Trains* by William Martin (2014). Five- and six-year-olds may also enjoy drawing and labeling the parts of a train.
- Ages 6 to 9: In addition to the ideas in the vignette, children can research the first transcontinental railroad, and create a PowerPoint presentation or poster to share their information with the class. Modern trains can be compared to the steam-powered trains used in the 1800s.

Classroom Connection

How can you integrate community resources into your literacy curriculum?

Children learn best through a combination of individual and group activities in a flexible and creative classroom. Imaginative ideas based upon individual strengths and talents can then flourish. Effective classroom organization and classroom management provides safety, security, and structure to promote risk taking and the self-confidence required for personalized learning (Maslow, 1954). Family literacy experiences and the home/school partnership provide positive role models for all children to become independent, lifelong readers and writers.

8-1 Family Involvement in the Literacy Curriculum

Family literacy involves family members (immediate and extended) participating in literacy experiences at home and in their communities. Examples of family literacy activities are writing notes or letters, making grocery lists, exploring children's museums, reading favorite books, cooking with a recipe, and drawing or writing to share ideas (see Photo 8.3). Culture and ethnic heritage are reflected in these experiences. The home/school connection is built through family participation in school events such as parent-teacher conferences, back-to-school night, and volunteering in the classroom. Teachers can also visit students' homes to learn more about their cultural backgrounds, interests, hobbies, career goals for students, and family dynamics, including social histories and family stories (Moll, 2015).

Teachers and families should work together to promote children's growth and literacy development. The reasons for collaboration are trifold: (1) children's attitudes and motivations are affected by parents and family members; (2) informing families about behavior and achievement helps in comprehending a child's strengths and areas of need; and (3) as valuable resources, families can provide support both in school and outside of school. Families have a positive influence on the behavior and achievement of their children when they hold high expectations, assist with school/homework, and support their children's efforts and perseverance in the learning process (Hoover-Dempsey et al., 2005). Early communication to parents and family members through phone calls, emails, text messages, and school newsletters facilitates the home-school partnership. Teachers should send personal notes or letters to children and their families before the first day of school to introduce themselves and welcome children to the class (see Figure 8.1).

effective classroom organization The arrangement of the physical environment to promote children's learning potential.

classroom management A set of techniques and skills that allow a teacher to maintain a positive learning environment for all students.

family literacy Involves family members (immediate and extended) participating in literacy experiences at home and in their communities.

Building a relationship with families requires respect and a welcoming environment during home visits or volunteer opportunities (see Photo 8.4). Most schools have open houses or parent workshops early in the academic year to introduce families to the school and individual teachers. A parent information letter should explain the teacher's interest in developing positive teacher-family relationships, general classroom expectations, and opportunities for volunteering at the school. The letter should be sent a few days prior to the beginning of school. Polite phone calls to parents during the first week of school initiate open communication throughout the school year. If parents speak languages other than English, both the letter and the phone call would need to be translated.

To build a positive relationship with children and families, teachers should research children's strengths and needs through surveys and interviews. Parent surveys help the teacher to gain information about the child's interests, attitudes, and personalities. Through surveys and other forms of communication, teachers can learn about family activities, places where they have lived, experiences, home language, and cultural traditions. Teachers empower families through their active role in addressing children's needs in the classroom based upon information from these surveys (see Figure 8.2).

In class, children can complete reading and writing attitude and interest surveys with the guidance of a teacher. Information from these surveys helps teachers understand their students' reading preferences and attitudes toward reading and writing. McKenna and Kear (1990) developed a

[Date]

Dear (*Child's Name*) and Family,

Welcome to _____ grade! My name is _____ and I will be your teacher this year. I can't wait to meet you next week, so you can tell me all about your summer vacation. We are going to have an exciting year together.

See you on Monday!

Teacher's Name

⌄ **Professional Resource Download**

Figure 8.1
Sample Child/Family Letter

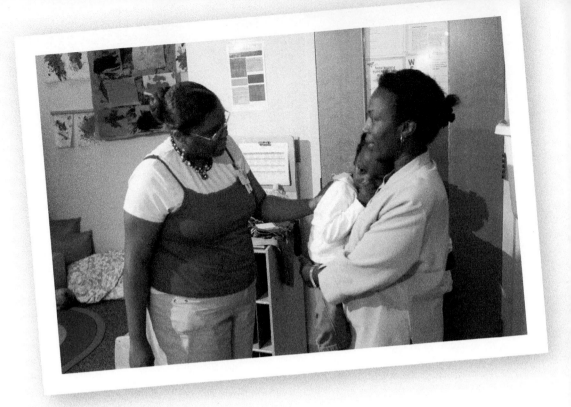

Photo 8.4 *Family connections*

Family Survey

Directions: Please answer the following questions. This information helps me to get to know your child.

1. Child's name and birth date:
2. Father's name and mother's name:
3. Names and ages of siblings:
4. What language is used in the home?
5. Where else has your child lived and at what age?
6. Who else spends time with your child at home (for example, sisters, brothers, grandparents, and friends)?
7. List your child's favorite foods.
8. How often do you read to your child?
9. What are your child's favorite books?
10. Is there any other information you wish to add about your child?

Adapted from Tabors (1997).

⌄ Professional Resource Download

Figure 8.2
Sample Family Survey

dialogue journal Written conversation shared in a journal format.

literature circles A discussion group that reads the same book; the members usually reflect their thoughts in writing prior to each discussion.

reading attitude survey for children using the cartoon character Garfield to depict emotional expression (very happy, a little happy, a little upset, and very upset). After reading the statement (either aloud by the teacher or silently by the child), the illustration of Garfield that best represents the child's feelings is circled. Teachers use the child's answers to interpret attitudes toward reading in school and at home. For example, on the McKenna and Kear (1990) survey, the question, "How do you feel about reading for fun at home?" (p. 1) balances the question, "How do you feel about reading in school?" (p. 4).

Interest surveys can also be used in the classroom to help teachers better understand the interests of children in class. For example, children can create an illustrated "All about Me" book with drawings or photographs focusing on topics about school, family, friends, favorite books, and future dreams (see Figure 8.3).

Family support has a significant impact on children's success and literacy development. When communicating with families, teachers must be clear about the curriculum, instructional/learning goals, and classroom behavioral management. Early and frequent communication builds a positive relationship with parents. A dialogue journal (written conversation shared in a journal format) can be used to encourage communication between the teacher and parents about school concerns. Teachers and students can also communicate using dialogue journals. Some children prefer to express their feelings in writing using a journal. After reading in class, dialogue journals can support peer discussion and comprehension of text.

Literacy Assessment

ASSESSING MY CHILD'S LITERACY DEVELOPMENT THROUGH OBSERVATION

This observation checklist can be used by parents to assess their children's progress in literacy. Parents reflect upon their children's literacy behaviors and use the responses to guide children's reading and writing experiences. Information from observations is shared with the teacher during parent-teacher conferences. Tracking reading and writing behaviors over time (repeated use of the observation checklist) documents a child's progress in literacy.

My Child's Literacy Development Guide
Directions: Check the appropriate response for each prompt.

Think about It

When observing young children, what other reading and writing behaviors can you discuss during a parent-teacher conference? For example, a child could use phonics, picture clues, or context clues to figure out an unfamiliar word. *Someday* by Alison McGhee (2007), a book about parental love and the potential of children, can be used during parent-child reading times to build positive attitudes about reading.

Child's Name Date:	Always	Sometimes	Never
1. My child likes to be read to.			
2. My child enjoys reading books independently.			
3. My child understands what he/she is reading.			
4. My child knows how to hold a book and turn the pages.			
5. My child pretends to read.			
6. My child likes to write.			
7. My child talks about his/her writing.			
8. My child reads signs and labels.			
Comments:			

❯❯ Professional Resource Download

Interaction with families and classmates allows older children to engage in "deep reading" strategies that include group discussion to demonstrate comprehension of text and writing exercises to synthesize or compare text. Literature circles, a discussion group that reads the same book, encourage conversations about books and support comprehension. At first, the teacher leads the discussion groups and models the different roles to be assigned (which can be rotated). Some teachers may prefer open-ended discussions rather than assigning roles in each group. Afterward, small groups of children independently (without the teacher) guide a discussion based upon their assigned group roles, such as discussion director (group leader), word finder (key vocabulary words in context), illustrator (artist),

All about Me!

ME!

Name:

Age:

Favorite Color:

Favorite Animal:

Favorite Holiday:

Favorite Clothes:

Favorite Food:

Favorite Sport:

MY FAMILY AND FRIENDS!

Names of Parents:

Names of Brothers and Sisters:

Names of Friends:

Names of Pets:

Favorite Family Trip:

MY SCHOOL!

Name of School:

Favorite Subject:

Favorite Part of the School Day

MY DREAMS!

What do I want to be when I grow up and why?

❯❯ Professional Resource Download

Figure 8.3 All about Me Book Ideas

creative connector (text-to-self, text-to-text, text-to-world), and summarizer (brief overview) (Daniels, 2002). Children write questions, key details, and personal connections on sticky notes to mark passages for discussion in literature circles.

Book clubs, a similar concept to literature circles, encourage enjoyment of reading and discussing ideas in a group. The beauty of book clubs and literature circles is the rich dialogue representing many different perspectives. Parents and guardians can also benefit from book clubs facilitated by the teacher. Some great books for sharing in a book club with parents are *The Read-Aloud Handbook* by Jim Trelease (2013) and *Reading Magic: Why Reading Aloud to Our Children Will Change Their Lives Forever* by Mem Fox (2008). Another option is to organize parent and child groups, such as mother/daughter and father/son book clubs. Fathers and sons may enjoy reading *Cam Jansen: The Mystery of the Dinosaur Bones* (series) by David Adler (1997). Mothers and daughters can begin their book club by reading *Because of Winn-Dixie* by Kate DiCamillo (2009) and then watch the movie together. For younger children, teachers and parents can use picture books or beginning chapter books. Parents and teachers can ask questions to encourage problem-solving skills, which increases comprehension of text and illustrations. Young children and parents can express emotional connections to picture books to promote a deeper understanding of characters.

Teachers can suggest *cuddle read* (when a child snuggles in an adult reader's arms during read-aloud sessions) as a strategy to build a love for reading. Many titles are available as e-books (electronic books), which can be read on electronic devices such as tablets and smartphones (see Photo 8.5).

Photo 8.5
Sharing new literacies
Janet Towell

✔ **CONSIDER THIS...**

Consider different children's literature (narrative and informational text) that could be used in a classroom literature circle. What are some titles and authors that you could recommend? Include the appropriate grade level when sharing with peers.

8-2 Home and School Partnerships to Build Creativity

Literacy development that actively engages each child is essential for reading and writing success. Creating a safe learning environment requires the commitment of teachers, children, and parents. A sense of pride, accomplishment, and responsibility promote a child's self-esteem and self-efficacy.

Creative classrooms engage children and allow opportunities for innovative problem solving. Teachers must consider their own values and beliefs carefully when creating a successful classroom that integrates professional development and current research while focusing on the children's strengths and needs, developmental learning levels, and cultural values. Working together, teachers and parents develop successful young readers and writers. The gears of a successful learning environment both at home and school (see Figure 8.4) depend upon motivation to promote effective literacy practices.

Families can use dialogue journals to introduce children to teachers in the beginning of the school year. Communication through the family dialogue journals (interactive writing notebooks) supports the partnership between home and school. Children need to be stimulated and motivated to learn through sharing family stories in their journals.

creative classrooms Classrooms that engage students and allow opportunities for innovative problem solving.

family dialogue journals Interactive writing notebooks that support the partnership between home and school.

NEUROLOGICALLY TYPICAL BRAINS

The ability to verbalize, think and learn abstractly, and understand logical patterns is guided by the wiring of the neurologically typical brain and the complexity of the learning environment. Most educational instruction is presented for verbal and auditory learners in a sequential and logical spatial pattern. Difficulty arises for children who are not *neurotypically* wired and do not perceive the world in a logical sequential way, such as children with autism and other learning disabilities who have difficulty in analyzing, comprehending, and interpreting verbal/auditory instruction (Levine, 2002).

Think about It

How can teachers help children express their ideas in diverse ways? What modes of expression are available beyond verbal and auditory? For example, children can express their understanding of a narrative through dramatic play or dance.

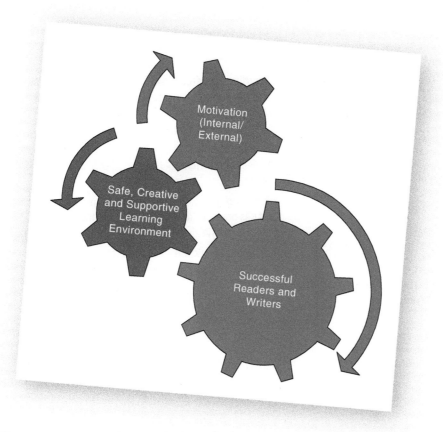

Figure 8.4
The Creative Literacy Environment

8-2a The Start of the School Year

The first day of school is important for children, parents, and teachers around the world. Each country has different traditions. In Israel, this day is celebrated by pouring honey in letter shapes onto pieces of slate for the children to taste, symbolizing that "learning is sweet" (Dallabrida, 2015, p. 36). In Austria and Germany, children bring large, decorated paper cones full of school supplies, candy, and other treats. The entire community in Kenya helps celebrate the first day of school through special church services, praying for the well-being of the children and their parents. Children in Russia bring flowers to their teachers, and Indian children receive a bright new umbrella on the first day of

FAMILY POETRY: ACTIVITY FOR PRESERVICE TEACHERS TO DO WITH CHILDREN AND THEIR FAMILIES

Purpose: Children can learn about their family background when parents, grandparents, and other relatives tell stories about family history. Using the book *I Am America and America Is Me!* by Charles R. Smith Jr. (2003) as a model, children can write a poem with family members' help to describe the children's feelings, physical characteristics, favorite foods, and cultural/ethnic/religious connections.

Procedure: The child writes a poem using rhyme modeled after *I Am America and America Is Me!* by Charles R. Smith Jr. (2003). Children can use the following steps to create the poem:

- The parents and children discuss family history, physical characteristics that are common or inherited, and cultural/ethnic/religious connections.
- A list of words and phrases are written with the parent's assistance to be used in the poem.
- Using the following poem structure, the parent and child write a poem about themselves and their families.

  "I am America. I am (feeling)."

  "I am (feeling). I am (feeling that rhymes with line above)."

  "I am (descriptive adjective) hair. I am (descriptive adjective) skin."

  "I am (family member and descriptive adjective) grin."

  "I am (favorite food)."

  "I am (favorite food). I am (favorite food that rhymes with above line)."

  "I am (cultural/ethnic/religious connection)."

  "I am a new branch sprouting in my majestic family tree."

  "I am America, and America is me."

Teaching Analysis: Reflective practices are a necessary part of the *literacy assessment cycle* and are key components in preservice preparation and certification such as edTPA. Analyze the strengths and areas of improvement in this lesson idea. Answer the following:

- What is successful?
- What would you change to improve the lesson?
- What did you learn about teaching literacy?

Links: Making connections to technology and developmentally appropriate practices (DAP) supports lesson planning and literacy instruction. Adaptations of this lesson idea are provided through the following:

- **Technology Link:** Children search online with family members' help about their genealogy. Children can interview and record (video/audio) a family member's memories.
- **DAP Link:** Children develop oral language through storytelling and family discussion to answer questions about family heritage.
- **Executive Function Link:** Creative play and active engagement during an interactive read-aloud develop children's self-regulation skills in social settings as reflected in the holistic model of literacy (cognitive, socioemotional, and physical).
- **Classroom Link:** For children (0 to 3), use photographs of familiar family members and tell the child a story about that person.
- **Classroom Link:** Children (3 to 6) can draw a family tree that has branches for immediate family members including photographs. Children can share their family tree with the class.
- **Classroom Link:** Children (6 to 9) can interview grandparents or other family member and ask about their childhood, or they can write an article about an event in the selected family member's life to share with the class.

Adapted from *I Am America and America Is Me!* by Charles R. Smith Jr. (2003).

school. In Japan, students carry origami paper and slippers in their backpacks, because outdoor shoes are not allowed inside the school. They also bring tools for weeding if the school has a garden. Their school year, which begins on April 1 and lasts 250 days, is one of the longest in the world (Dallabrida, 2015).

In the United States, the first day of school is also one of the most important days of the year because the tone for teaching and learning is set, and the rules of engagement and behavior for the classroom are introduced. Scheduling and daily routines are an important part of a child's day, and becoming accustomed to the classroom organization is a key part of learning success. Part of the first day involves setting rules of behavior in specific learning situations. Involving children in the rule-setting process promotes a sense of ownership and belonging.

Most teachers use the first week to repeat the rules each day (as needed) and start the classroom communication process and expectations. These classroom rules are verbalized and posted in the classroom, as a contract between teachers, children, and parents. Motivation is an important aspect of creative classrooms, and children must learn the participatory process of classroom organization. Everyone must play a part in the classroom management script as this process develops the best in each and every child. Children and teacher dynamics are occurring both individually and as a group. These classroom connections with optimal benefits for each child support clear communication. Motivation can be increased with activities that promote confidence, active engagement, and participation in collaborative projects. Circle time is often a daily occurrence in early childhood classrooms. This is the type of classroom organization that promotes connections between children and the teacher.

Building a creative classroom community requires an understanding of how children are motivated to learn. Albert Bandura's (1986) theory aligns motivation with self-regulation. Because self-motivation is internal or intrinsic and not dependent on external influences, the child's interest and perseverance is maintained, and success is more likely to be achieved (see Photo 8.6). Bandura's *observational learning theory* states that behavior is imitated and learning occurs through observation of role models. Children learn literacy behaviors through observations of role models (parents, teachers, and other children) engaging in effective reading and writing activities (see Photo 8.7).

When open to the many aspects of creativity, the cognitive, physical, and socioemotional aspects of a person becomes aligned or centered to ignite the creative self. Many activities develop the creative self, such as journal writing about personal experiences or reactions to experiences, contemplation, reflection, and self-assessment.

Photo 8.6 *Creatively exploring the outdoor environment*
Josh Weinberger

8-2b Creative Learning Spaces

Creative learning spaces provide support and active engagement for early literacy development (see Photo 8.8). Clear learning objectives and goals are part of this creative classroom community. Classroom space and design clarifies what is important and valued in learning.

We recommend that teachers provide classroom space for children to explore and create new environments both individually and collaboratively. For example, families can visit a local football stadium to attend a sporting event. Afterward, families can use a large cardboard box to create an interactive center replicating the stadium. Working together, children and families can paint the sides and interior of the box. The children draw pictures of people (spectators, players, coaches, photographers, and daily news reporters), write signs (environmental print), and create numbered gates that are glued to the appropriate stadium areas. Families can talk about their experiences and discuss their own model of the stadium, which promotes oral language development.

Children benefit from activities that expand their creative talents. Allowing children to construct creative spaces at home and school that encourage experimentation

creative learning spaces Provide support and active engagement for early literacy development.

and playful learning is an important part of emergent literacy. For example, children can build cities from boxes, models from papier-maché, and found-object sculptures. Oral language develops through dramatic play and interaction with others in these creative spaces.

Children enjoy looking at and discussing their work with others. Time to reflect on their creative work promotes further creative exploration and conversations that lead to new learning. Teachers can use children's discussion about creative work that is displayed in the classroom to help guide future study based on children's interests.

Interactive spaces where children learn new vocabulary are an important part of the literacy learning at home and in school. *Word walls* (displays of words in the classroom or home) that allow children to select and display their own definitions and illustrations of the new vocabulary promote literacy development. A word wall can take many forms, from a simple pocket chart with blank cards and markers for student use, or a more creative display area, such as a giant palette painted on the wall using chalkboard paint where children illustrate and write using chalk or magnetic letters on the refrigerator. The key is to provide an interactive space where children can demonstrate their understanding of vocabulary.

Labeling objects, pictures, and furniture in different languages throughout the learning

Photo 8.7
Motivated listening
Josh Weinberger

Photo 8.8
Display of children's creative work

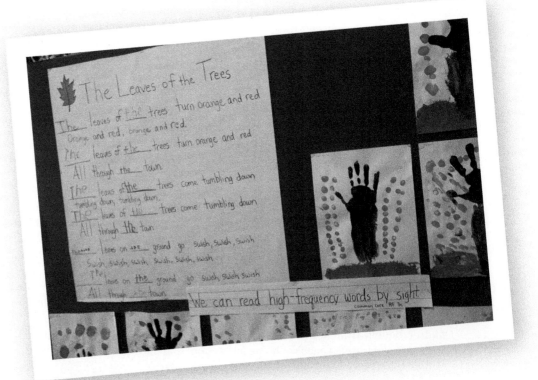

USING ASSISTIVE TECHNOLOGY IN THE CLASSROOM

All children should participate in learning activities. Fisher, Frey, and Kroener (2013) discuss three dimensions for successful learning in an inclusive classroom (class for all students including students with diverse needs). Personal supports, instruction and assistive technology, and accommodations and modifications form the basis of learning for children with diverse needs. For example, a child with visual impairment may use word-processing software that creates larger text or a specialized text reading device/software. A child with a physical limitation that makes writing difficult can use voice recording or dictation software. A child with a hearing impairment can watch videos related to the lesson that incorporate sign language and closed captioning (Coleman & Cramer, 2015).

Think about It

What assistive technology can be used for children with varying disabilities? For example, a child with physical limitations may use computer software that automatically types text while the child speaks or tells the story into a microphone. Teachers can read books that depict children with varying disabilities as positive roles models. *Granny Torrelli Makes Soup* by Sharon Creech (2003) can be read to the class to share how a special friendship is formed between a young girl, her grandmother, and a boy with a visual impairment.

environment at home and at school promotes letter and word recognition as well as print awareness. Language development is supported through the use of real objects associated with the written and spoken word. Through repetition and practice, young children comprehend new vocabulary.

 CONSIDER THIS...

Consider designing creative spaces at home or at school that encourage reading, writing, and expression of ideas. How can you design an interactive word wall for teaching literacy lessons?

8-3 Strategies for Collaboration and Differentiated Literacy Instruction

Cooperative learning or group participation in completing projects has been accepted as an important process for expanding knowledge. Developing optimal groups of students that blend and work well together are key assets to this process. Individual participation is part of the process, but even more important is building teams to accomplish projects where children learn both individually and as part of a group. Personality, skills, and knowledge levels must be complementary for teams to work at an advantage and be successful in their endeavors. Being clear with classroom literacy goals and having children participate in designing the learning goals keep children engaged and creative. Vygotsky's (1978) theory of social interaction, culture, and collaboration is the basis of social constructivism in a classroom that fosters optimal learning. The organization of the classroom is the framework for teaching, learning, and children's literacy achievements.

8-3a Literacy and Collaboration

Teaching creatively and collaboratively in the classroom or at home to motivate children to learn is an important challenge for all teachers and parents. Understanding group dynamics and relationships, as well as individual strengths, can help teachers develop motivation to achieve goals, whether individually or in groups. The process of creative literacy development involves supporting children in the classroom and valuing their thoughts, personalities, emotions, intelligence, and imagination. Part of creative literacy development involves establishing communication standards and methods clearly by example (modeling) and by verbalizing expectations. Observing nonverbal behavior and communication techniques such as body language and facial expressions helps teachers evaluate children and determine how well the classroom is functioning as a whole. Creative literacy activities to build confidence and cognitive awareness may be practiced via two major methods: (1) personal activity focusing on individual experience, and (2) group or interactive activity.

8-3b Differentiated Reading Model

Children develop behavioral and social skills while working in groups and independent work. The differentiated reading model, based upon Marie Clay's (1987) Reading Recovery research (early intervention model), focuses on specific skills for varied groups of children. Early readers progress through five stages—emergent, beginning, fledgling, transitional, and independent (Tyner, 2004). Children with similar reading and writing needs are grouped to teach short lessons focusing on specific literacy skills. Some instructional strategies that are implemented in small groups are rereading, word study, and writing (shared, dictated, and independent). For example, children can retell a familiar fairy tale or classroom event while the teacher writes on a large chart to model shared writing. Sentences are constructed as a group to create a quality draft that the children reread and edit with teacher guidance. Children can focus on composing while the teacher transcribes the concepts during shared writing (Routman, 1994). Social interaction plays an important role in developing higher-order thinking skills for children. This organization of group work allows the teacher to have high-quality interaction with children while focusing on the small group's needs. Teachers can provide more direct feedback, listen to more questions from children, and assess children's reactions and interactions in a quick and effective manner.

Beverly Tyner's (2004) small group differentiated reading model focuses on instructional strategies that specifically target the needs of early readers for each of the five stages. As children progress through the five stages of reading, they are able to work on more complex activities for each instructional strategy. The instructional strategies to provide focus for readers are rereading, word bank, word study, writing, and new read (Tyner, 2004, p. 6).

Tyner indicates expectations in each instructional strategy for the different stages of reading. For example, during a rereading activity, emergent readers should be able to practice tracking print (for example, following along as the teacher reads aloud with a finger or pointer). During word bank instruction, emergent readers should be able to identify at least 10 sight words before moving on to the next stage of reading (beginning reader). While using word study strategies, emergent readers demonstrate alphabet recognition, while beginning readers identify consonant sounds in words. Writing activities for emergent readers include shared writing (the teacher and children write together), concepts of print activities, alphabet identification, and cut-up sentences (sentences written on paper strips and words cut apart for children to reassemble). Tyner's new read strategy emphasizes that children should read a new book daily. Emergent readers can echo read or repeat the words after the teacher. Another new read strategy is using illustrations in a text for a picture walk and discussing main ideas with children.

Using the differentiated reading model, teachers can focus on the specific needs of each child and tailor small group reading instruction to meet these needs. Small group work is an instructional strategy that promotes creative literacy development.

creative literacy development Supporting children in the classroom by valuing their thoughts, personalities, emotions, intelligence, and imagination.

differentiated reading model A model of early literacy instruction that focuses on specific skills for different groups of children, according to their individual strengths and needs.

To address the different strengths and needs of each child, collaborative and differentiated literacy strategies should involve creativity and imagination, allowing for personal expression.

8-3c Creativity and Imagination in Literacy Groups

Everyone has the ability to be open, confident, and artistic, which involves having a creative vision, being inspired, and discovering skills or parts of the creative self that may be buried in one's personality, intelligence, or emotional life. Self-expression is a tool for children to interpret knowledge and develops skills or understanding through painting, sculpting, acting, dancing, writing, or other artistic endeavors. Creativity involves individual self-realization in a specific situation or environment, using one's intelligence, imagination, illumination, intuition, and inspiration to invent something new from within (Csikszentmihalyi, 1997).

Imagination involves the ability to think in pictures or abstract thought and to develop images that do not exist. Personal characteristics that support imagination include mindfulness, commitment, unity, truthfulness, courageousness, communication, perseverance, and openness. Some strategies that teachers use to guide children's imagination include:

1. Calming the mind and using concentration techniques such as repeated statements that focus on tranquility or affirmation;
2. Daydreaming or visualizing, which encourages imagination by placing oneself in new situations that one would like to experience; and
3. Reading, listening to music, or fantasizing what can happen to characters in a book if situations, settings, or characters were different.

Journaling or creative writing to express emotions helps to manage thoughts that flood one's mind and allow the mind to invent new ideas. Some literacy strategies that allow teachers and children to build a creative literacy community include creating bio-poems (formula poetry describing personal characteristics), sharing written autobiographies, discussing autophotographies (using photographs and captions to create personal stories), and developing personal time lines (graphic design of life events).

 CONSIDER THIS...

Consider which differentiated reading model strategies you could implement in the classroom. For example, children can reread a selected passage to identify text-based evidence explaining an opinion.

8-4 Ideas for Documenting Literacy Learning

The creative literacy classroom provides space for children to express their learning using a variety of media (artwork, writing, dramatic play). Symbolic recognition and language development are supported through play in these creative spaces and contribute to children's overall cognitive, socioemotional, and physical growth. One approach to documenting and sharing literacy learning is found in the Reggio Emilia–inspired schools.

Within the concept of emergent curriculum, the Reggio Emilia approach focuses on what interests children while designing learning experiences. Teachers listen to children's discussions and guide conversations to motivate individual learning. Learning concepts are expressed and documented through the children's languages, such as puppetry, water play, sand play, light play, art, music, and dance. Documentation of the learning experience through photographs and learning products are displayed throughout the classroom to promote reflection and continued study (Gandini, Etheridge, & Hill, 2008).

creativity The result of an active imagination and the capacity to form mental metaphors, new ideas, and fantasies.

autophotographies Visual autobiographies that incorporate photographs with captions to describe personal stories or memoirs.

Often, culminating projects that reflect children's interests in real-world situations are the result of a series of learning experiences. For example, children can design and plant a class garden. Caring and nurturing for plants promotes interdependence and a deeper understanding of how plants grow. The garden can inspire artistic work, such as poetry that describes the nature experience; artwork inspired by observation of nature (drawings, paintings, sculptures, video, and photography); musical composition from sounds in nature (instrumental and vocal); dances that relate to nature's movement; and dramatic play reenacting the beauty of nature. Children's experiences grow as the garden does, encouraging creative blooming.

The Reggio Emilia approach focuses on interactive activities for young children. For example, flannel boards with shapes and colors support manipulative skill development and visual acuity. Felt shapes of trees, people, houses, and animals promote storytelling and sharing. Felt letters allow children to spell words and create sentences to support print awareness. Through playful and interactive centers, children develop language skills, such as richer and more diverse vocabulary and the ability to adjust language for new situations.

8-4a Project-Based Learning

Another strategy for documenting and sharing literacy learning is through project-based learning (Katz and Chard, 1989). Similar to the Reggio Emilia approach, project-based learning begins with a topic that interests the children. Concept webs are created and displayed to tie learning to the topic of study. Project-based learning includes three phases of learning experiences.

Phase One includes the selection and introduction of the concept or theme that evolved from the children's interests. Teachers or parents can discuss the topic with children and create an initial web of concepts illustrating what the children know and what they are interested in learning. New vocabulary is written on the large poster, which is continually displayed in the classroom.

In *Phase Two*, parents and community members who are experts in the field are invited to speak with the children about the topic. For example, when children began studying the ocean, they explored a touch tank with a sea cucumber and sea urchin brought into the classroom by a parent/expert. New vocabulary words are continually recorded and posted in class. Photographs of the different learning activities and artwork from the children are displayed on a large poster throughout the project.

In *Phase Three* of the project-based approach, children participate in a culminating learning activity. Storybooks are read throughout the project that link to the topic of study. Often special guests read stories as part of culminating activities. Children's responses to the learning experience are recorded and are included as part of documentation and assessment. A final concept web is created to summarize the children's understanding of the topic. The project-based approach encourages children's creativity, interests, inquiry, exploration, and investigation.

Creatively documenting and displaying children's learning experiences furthers imagination. Reflective thinking, journaling, and creation through the arts, such as taking walks in nature, dancing, painting, playing an instrument, reading books, and playing games, develop creativity in children. A supportive learning environment includes teachers, parents, and children that recognize each other's success by sharing and documenting comprehension in the creative literacy classroom (Katz and Chard, 1989).

project-based learning A style of literacy learning (in three phases) that begins with the interests of the children in the classroom (preschool+). Concept webs for the unit of study are created with the guidance of the teacher, based on a specific theme or topic. *Phase One* includes the selection and introduction of the concept or theme that evolved from children's interests. In *Phase Two,* parents and community members who are experts in the field are invited to speak with the children about the topic. In *Phase Three* of the project-based approach, children participate in a culminating learning activity.

✔ CONSIDER THIS...

Consider how you can document children's learning through photographs, graphic organizers, posters, and classroom displays. For example, children can sequence photographs taken during a field trip or family outing, and write captions.

Libraries and Literacy Centers for Creative Exploration

Classroom libraries (designed space for a variety of reading materials) and literacy centers (designed learning spaces targeting specific reading, writing, and listening skills) are an important part of the creative literacy classroom. A classroom library or reading area at home is an interactive and colorful space designed to encourage reading (see Photo 8.9). A wide variety of books for different reading levels should be easily accessible for young children. Books can be organized by themes, reading levels, authors, and genres. Usually bookshelves or bins/baskets are labeled to help guide the children when selecting books to read. Colorful displays attract children to the reading area. Comfortable seating areas (bean bags, small chairs, and couches), a carpet, soft blankets, and pillows encourage children to read immediately after selecting a book. Stuffed animals placed in the reading area provide a friend for modeling cuddle read or just for snuggling comfort.

When selecting books, focus on children's interests and reading levels to start. A quick visit to the school or community library provides a variety of books that usually can be brought into the classroom and rotated frequently to continually spark interest. The local public library is another source of books that can be shared at home or in the classroom. Be sure to explain to children the importance of caring for books properly. Another great source for books is parents and other family members of children in the class. Send home a request that favorite books be brought to school for sharing, or ask for donations of gently used books for classroom use. Over time, your classroom library will grow to include favorite authors and illustrators in all genres and reading levels.

Teach children how to maintain and organize the reading area to promote ownership and respect of books. For toddlers and older children, the process of properly handling a book becomes a game with a bit of imagination. Gather the children around the classroom library and select a book to share by explaining: (1) how to hold the book (oriented for reading), (2) how to turn the pages, and (3) how to return the book where it belongs or to hand it to another child. *One, Two, Three, Read to Me* is a game where children sit in a circle while music is playing (select a slow, relaxing beat) and pass a book to each other. The children must orient the book (one), turn a page (two), and close the book carefully when passing to the next child (three). Once the book has returned to the teacher, the children say, "Read to me."

Libraries instill a passion for reading. Fluent reading requires practice, and to practice reading, children need access to a wide variety of books. The more opportunities children have to enjoy reading, the more children grow to love reading books. When designing the classroom library, include books that you have read aloud in class to allow for independent practice. Books children make are also great additions to the classroom or home library as children are encouraged to see their work published and read by others.

Reading bags or backpacks are another addition to a classroom library that promotes reading outside of school. Children can place selected books in a reading bag to take home, thus encouraging family participation in reading development. Teacher-created reading bags focusing on specific reading levels or topics of study can be

Photo 8.9 *A wide variety of books available in the classroom*

classroom libraries A collection of reading materials that includes a variety of genres for classroom use.

literacy centers Designed learning spaces targeting specific reading, writing, and listening skills, based on different subject areas in the language arts curriculum.

Photo 8.10 *Molly the Monkey with journal at home*
Susannah Brown

Apply & Reflect

Create a children's book list for a specific topic of study or genre. Share your ideas with a colleague and brainstorm four more children's books that can be added to the original list.

manipulatives Small objects that children move around during multisensory lessons to learn mathematical and other concepts.

story pyramid A graphic organizer (type of story map) that consists of a formula for labeling parts of a story.

graphic organizers A visual map of concepts.

taken home on a rotating basis to ensure that each child has the opportunity to read the selected books at home. A class reading journal can be included in the reading bags for children to write about their favorite books and the reading experience. Another idea is to include a stuffed animal mascot in the reading bag as reading buddy (see Photo 8.10).

Children document their reading adventure in the reading journal and share the entry with their class the next day. Parents can include a photograph of the child reading with the stuffed animal mascot to create a visual storyboard of the reading adventure.

8-5a Literacy Centers

Literacy centers are designated creative spaces that include planned hands-on activities that target specific reading, writing, and listening skills. For example, word work activities involve learning experiences designed for children to individually manipulate letters and words, such as letter tiles, magnetic letters, and letter stamps. Literacy centers are designed to promote successful learning and classroom community.

Effective literacy centers focus on how young children think and learn through active engagement, creative problem solving, independent work, and collaborative work. Allowing for decision making and choice, literacy centers are responsive to different levels of learners and their interests.

Literacy centers promote a variety of skills in reading, writing, and listening. For example, children can illustrate their own dictionary, write in a journal, paint on an easel, create illustrations for a story (storyboards), use reading software on the computer, or listen to an audio-recorded book. Literacy centers include manipulatives (hands-on objects for active learning), such as alphabet blocks, precut letters or written words on cards, yarn and modeling clay for forming letters, and found objects and small toys for story prompts. Games and puzzles focusing on literacy

Photo 8.11 *Dress-up story time with mirror*

development can include letter bingo, alphabet flip books, picture/word sorting cards, word searches, crossword puzzles, and dramatic play with puppets, costumes, and props (see Photo 8.11).

Another idea for a literacy center is creating story pyramids using wooden blocks and sticky notes. Similar to a story map, children begin by naming a character (for example, Cinderella) and then include two words that describe the character (*beautiful, dreamer*). Next, they add three words that describe the setting (*majestic, kingdom, castle*). A four-word sentence that describes one problem in the story is inserted in the pyramid ("Cinderella can't attend ball."). Finally, they can add a five-word sentence that describes an event or solution to conclude the story pyramid ("Fairy god mother uses magic."). After creating the story pyramid, children can act out the story using costumes and props in the dramatic play center.

Another idea for a writing center is to develop graphic organizers (visual maps of concepts) that allow children to represent the story sequence in a visual way. A herringbone graphic organizer is sometimes called a fishbone (a horizontal line with vertical angled lines), as illustrated in Figure 8.5. This type of organizer or story map focuses on answering who, what, when, where, why, and how questions. The main idea of the story is written on the horizontal straight line, and the questions about the story are written on the angled lines extending from the horizontal straight line.

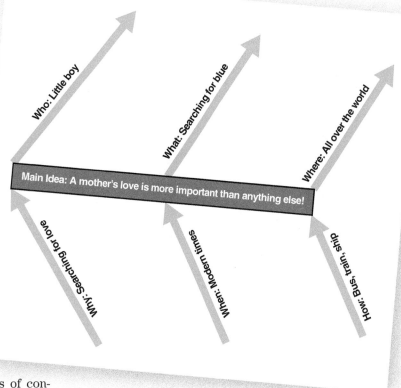

Who: Little boy

What: Searching for blue

Where: All over the world

Main Idea: A mother's love is more important than anything else!

Why: Searching for love

When: Modern times

How: Bus, train, ship

Figure 8.5
Herringbone Graphic Organizer for *A Blue So Blue* by Jean-Francois Dumont (2005)

Table 8.1 — Literacy Strategies and Practices Supporting Family Literacy and Classroom Connections

Age Groups	Cognitive	Socioemotional
0 to 3	Create colorful displays with toys and objects that encourage sensory experiences. Keep a variety of board books, cloth books, sound books, and texture books in reach of infants and toddlers. Create reading areas, circle time, or lap reading time.	Use soft cushioned mats to promote interaction with other infants and toddlers. Use stuffed animals to cuddle when exploring durable books. Have seating areas that allow toddlers to read books together and interact.
3 to 6	Make library organized and accessible. Attractive literacy centers focus on active practice of reading, writing, and listening skills (rotated to spark interest). Use circle time and group interaction for literacy activities.	Display work to celebrate achievement. Display photographs of families, children, and pets at the child's eye level. Play music to promote quiet reflection. Have special events to celebrate literacy development (families invited).
6 to 9	Have a library with a variety of genres with different reading levels and topics (rotated often). Create literacy centers designed to use technology, interactive games, and writing (story pyramids, character/story maps).	Use gardens and natural areas to promote nurturing and caring for living things. Collaborative literacy centers promote diverse perspectives and focusing on multicultural literature.

Professional Resource Download

Character Report Card		
Green Forest Elementary School		
Student: Red Riding Hood		
E-Excellent	**S-Satisfactory**	**N-Needs to Improve**
Area	**Grade**	**Rationale**
Obedience	E	*She went into the forest to deliver food to her sick grandma at her mother's request.*
Adventurous	N	*She did not stray from the trail through the forest.*
Observant	N	*She did not realize the wolf was in grandma's clothes and bed. She thought it was her grandma when she asked questions about the wolf's ears, eyes, and teeth.*

Figure 8.6
Character Report Card for Little Red Riding Hood

Sample questions can be: Who is the character in the story? What is the main idea of the story? Where is the setting of the story? What event or action happened in the story? When did the event or action take place? How did the event or action happen? Graphic organizers work well at literacy centers that check for reading comprehension.

Using "character report cards" is an interactive reading comprehension strategy that focuses group discussion on a story character's actions, statements, and thoughts as evidenced in the text. In small groups, children *grade* the story character on the character report card and discuss rationales in support of the decided grade with the whole class. Figure 8.6 includes a sample character report card for "Little Red Riding Hood," written by the Brothers Grimm in the early 19th century.

The learning tasks in a literacy center can focus on individual work or small group work allowing the teacher to work with other groups of students at the same time. New

Physical	Children's Books	Family Involvement
Use manipulative toys such as rattles, mobiles, and squeaky, soft stuffed animals placed on soft matts both inside the classroom and outside play area. Use kitchen centers, dress-up areas, push carts.	*Llama Llama Red Pajama* by Anna Dewdney *Pete the Cat* (series) by Eric Litwin *Where Is the Green Sheep?* By Mem Fox	Create spaces for art, music, and dance activities.Cuddle read favorite stories. Read plastic waterproof books in the bath. Put labels on storage boxes (for example, toys, etc.) that are accessible for children.
Use child-sized furniture that promotes playful interaction and reading/writing time. Have a library that includes books with dramatic activities and dance.	*Anna Banana: 101 Jump-Rope Rhymes* by Joanna Cole *Diary of a Fly* by Doreen Cronin *Olivia* (series) by Ian Falconer	Use wooden blocks, puzzles, literacy centers that involve physical skills (magnetic letters). Parents and children play board games together. Children design a family library with a variety of reading materials.
Group activities both indoors and outdoors connect reading and comprehension (questions asked while catching a ball). Create art-making centers (for story character sculpture, puppet making, dramatic play with props and costumes).	*Let Me Be the Boss: Poems for Kids to Perform* by Brod Bagert *Wemberly Worried* by Kevin Henkes *Art & Max* by David Wiesner	Create a family travel journal with labels, drawings, and photos. Hold family literacy awards ceremony and display children's work. Organize a reading/writing backpack for car trips.

centers are created and display designs are changed to promote continual interest in the learning tasks. Classroom libraries, family reading areas, and literacy centers promote creative exploration of reading, writing, and listening skills. Designing innovative spaces for active engagement is an important part of the creative literacy classroom. Encouraging a child's successful literacy development supports independent and collaborative learning.

 CONSIDER THIS...

Consider which reading materials to include in a reading area to represent narrative, informational, and persuasive text. For example, research a children's literature website to find examples of each genre.

8-6 Literacy Strategies and Practices for Family Literacy and Classroom Connections

Developmentally appropriate practices, both at home and school, support emergent literacy for young children. Creative learning spaces (literacy centers, reading areas in the home, and classroom libraries) actively engage children in expressing their imaginative learning. Embedding children's literature integrates the cognitive, socioemotional, and physical parts of the creative self. In Table 8.1, we provide examples of children's books and activities that encourage learning in creative literacy environments for infants and children (birth to age 9).

Apply & Reflect

Design a literacy center for a children's book of your choice. Focus the actively engaged activities on specific reading, writing, or listening skills to encourage learning success. Share your center with a small group of peers in the class. Discuss adaptations and extensions to the literacy center for specific students, such as for children who speak different languages and children with physical or cognitive needs.

Summary

Family involvement in the literacy curriculum encourages family members and teachers to work together building upon the strengths and interests of children. Building a safe, supportive, and creative community of learners is an important goal of early literacy. We described family involvement in the literacy curriculum to support a creative classroom community. Clear and open communication with families promotes literacy development in children's lives. We also discussed how to build a creative learning community through effective literacy instruction, motivation of learners, and innovative learning spaces. Strategies for collaboration and differentiated literacy instruction were compared using the differentiated reading model and arts integrated activities. Documentation of literacy learning was explained through the Reggio Emilia approach and project-based approach. Both approaches emphasize displaying various forms of expression. In this chapter, we also shared how to design libraries, reading areas in the home, and literacy centers for creative exploration. The cognitive, socioemotional, and physical parts of self (HML) are supported by literacy strategies that emphasize family involvement and classroom connections.

Chapter Exercises

1. Write a welcome back to school letter for the children and families of your future classroom.
2. Draw a sketch of a creative word wall that promotes children's participation and interaction with new vocabulary. Share with a partner and brainstorm new ideas to create interesting word walls.
3. Complete a shared writing task with four peers that explains strategies such as rereading, word banks, and new reads.
4. Select a theme that could be used in project-based learning, and create a concept web of what you already know about the theme.
5. Create a list of five children's books that are appropriate for babies and toddlers (age 0 to 3) for your future classroom library. Share your reasons for selecting these books with a peer.

Teacher Toolbox

BUILDING POSITIVE FAMILY RELATIONSHIPS

Appropriate for Ages 4 to 9

Reading books that highlight positive family interactions inspires children to write about experiences and choose words that best describe family events. *Mama Zooms* by Jane Cowen-Fletcher (1993) portrays family outings from the child's point of view. In the story, the child and his mother ride in a "zooming machine" (the mother's wheelchair) across different settings, such as the lawn (like a racehorse), down the sidewalk (like a race car), and across bridges (like an airplane). After reading the story aloud to the class, ask the children to discuss words that imitate sounds. Use an anchor chart that lists items, such as a race car, a train, a spaceship, and an airplane. Ask the children to brainstorm words that describe the sounds each item makes. Children illustrate a sound word of their choice. To expand their list, ask children to describe a family outing or event and the sounds that they heard during the experience. For example, children may pop balloons during a birthday party. Then children write (or dictate) descriptive sentences and share with the class. Use a thinking chart featuring questions about word choice to help children edit their writing.

Did I use words that work and sound great together?

Did I use different words?

Do the words make sense?

Do my words paint a picture?

Do my words excite the senses (taste, touch, hearing, sight, smell)?

———————————

Adapted from Culham (2008).

Key Terms and Concepts

autophotographies

classroom libraries

classroom management

creative classroom

creative learning spaces

creative literacy development

creativity

dialogue journal

differentiated reading model

effective classroom
   organization

family dialogue journals

family literacy

graphic organizers

literacy centers

literature circles

manipulatives

project-based learning

story pyramids

Elizabeth Crews/PhotoEdit

STANDARDS ADDRESSED IN THIS CHAPTER

The standards from the following organizations will be used throughout the chapter: Common Core State Standards for English Language Arts, the National Association for the Education of Young Children (NAEYC), and National Core Arts Standards. These standards are discussed further in the chapter as appropriate.

Common Core State Standards for English Language Arts

Anchor Standards for Reading

Reading Standards for Literature/Informational Text K–5

- Key Ideas and Details
- Craft and Structure

Anchor Standards for Speaking and Listening

- Comprehension and Collaboration
- Presentation of Knowledge and Ideas

Anchor Standards for Language

- Conventions of Standard English
- Knowledge of Language
- Vocabulary Acquisition and Use

naeyc

2010 NAEYC Standards for Initial and Advanced Early Childhood Professional Preparation Programs

- *Standard 1:* Promoting Child Development and Learning
- *Standard 4:* Using Developmentally Effective Approaches

NAEYC Early Childhood Program Standards and Accreditation Criteria

- *Standard 1:* Relationships
- *Standard 2:* Curriculum
- *Standard 3:* Teaching

NCA

National Core Arts Standards (Dance, Media Arts, Music, Theater, Visual Arts)

Connecting

- *Anchor Standard 10:* Synthesize and relate knowledge and personal experiences to make art.
- *Anchor Standard 11:* Relate artistic ideas and works with societal, cultural, and historical context to deepen understanding.

Diverse Learners and Literacy

9

It is time for parents to teach young people early on that in diversity there is beauty and there is strength. — Maya Angelou

American schools are becoming more ethnically and culturally diverse. Literacy instruction in early childhood is child centered and must therefore meet the needs of diverse children. Literacy should include a variety of contexts, such as cognitive, cultural, historical, economic, moral, physical, and socioemotional (Gee, 2015). Diverse learners include children who speak languages other than English (ELLs); are gifted and talented; have learning disabilities; have physical disabilities; or live in poverty. Multicultural classrooms include children from different cultures, ethnicities, languages, traditions, religions, communication skills, learning strengths/needs, and physical abilities. Using only one style of teaching precludes the possibility of reaching all types of learners. Because there are different learning styles, the best teaching method involves having a variety of learning approaches connected with Howard Gardner's *multiple intelligences theory* (1983, 1999a).

Diversity in the classroom involves teaching young children with various backgrounds and different learning and physical characteristics. Linguistic diversity and cultural diversity also include children at risk (for example, children with autism, attention deficit/hyperactivity disorder (ADHD), learning disabilities, and struggling readers). Literacy for young children encourages collaboration with children, families, teachers, administrators, and community members (Wardle, 2003). Families of different cultures must learn to live together in a diverse world. Learning about others through dialogue and communication is known as "cultural synthesis" according to Paolo Freire (1993). His theory emphasized sharing knowledge of diverse groups through awareness and discussion. Freire believed that children learn about oppression or prejudice from their home atmosphere and if that environment is free and caring, children will learn to be more tolerant of each other. Critical consciousness (self-knowledge) starts in the home and, with active participation, will be transferred to the classroom.

James Banks (1993) had similar ideas about multicultural diversity in that sharing experiences of different cultures helps children understand

Continued on page 199

LEARNING OBJECTIVES

After you have read this chapter, you should be able to:

9-1 Explain diverse learners and literacy concepts.

9-2 Analyze language and vocabulary development.

9-3 Discuss literacy instruction for diverse classrooms.

9-4 Describe the value of multicultural literature for learning about cultural diversity.

9-5 Examine teaching strategies for children with special needs.

9-6 Apply literacy strategies and practices for diverse learners.

STANDARDS CONNECTION TO THE VIGNETTE

NAEYC Early Childhood Program Standards and Accreditation Criteria

Standard 1: Relationships

1.D.04 Teachers help children talk about their own and others' emotions. They provide opportunities for children to explore a wide range of feelings and the different ways that those feelings can be expressed.

Common Core State Standards for English Language Arts

Speaking and Listening
Second Grade

1. Participate in collaborative conversations with diverse partners about grade 2 topics and texts with peers and adults in small and larger groups.

Teachers should embrace the cultural diversity found in schools. Diverse classrooms encompass different cultural backgrounds all working together in a collaborative environment (see Photo 9.1). Children bring unique perspectives from their homes representing ethnic backgrounds and cultural experiences. Sharing across cultural boundaries helps teachers break through language barriers with young children.

One day, Mrs. Bradford was told by her school principal that a new student named Miguel would be attending her second-grade class. The principal explained to Mrs. Bradford that Miguel had just immigrated to the United States and that he did not speak English. Mrs. Bradford realized the confusion Miguel was grappling with while being immersed in a school with others who spoke a different language.

In class during the literacy lesson, Mrs. Bradford read *Swing, Slither, or Swim: A Book about Animal Movements* by Patricia Stockland (2005). The children, led by Mrs. Bradford, practiced bending their arms and legs to reenact and visualize animal movement. The children laughed while having a fun and interactive time. Mrs. Bradford noticed that after the first 10 minutes, Miguel began to look around and absorb the classroom activity. Next, the children discussed their emotions during the activity with their "turn and talk" partner. After discussion, the children drew different animals. Miguel began to draw animals with the other children. Because this was his first day in class, Mrs. Bradford could not take any credit for teaching Miguel how to draw so well; however, with her support in a caring classroom, his creative passion for learning allows him to express his ideas with confidence.

All children desire to express their ideas in a variety of ways including the arts. Often, children's drawings enlighten us as teachers to a deeper understanding of their lives. With this knowledge, a positive relationship between teacher and child builds the foundation of early literacy.

Developmentally appropriate practice (DAP) is featured in the vignette and can be adapted for younger children (birth to age 5) and older children to age 9. Suggested adaptations include:

- *Ages 0 to 3:* Reading aloud to infants and toddlers helps to develop their listening comprehension. Animal sounds can be included in stories for infants and toddlers. Babies often babble along with songs, nursery rhymes, and poems. Toddlers enjoy sharing their ideas and stories to a caring listening adult or friend.
- *Ages 3 to 6:* Children 3 and 4 years old can share photographs of their pets or favorite animals. Using masks and costumes, children can dramatize the animal movements. Children 5 and 6 years old can create a list of favorite animals with the teacher's help (writing on a chart). Names of animals can be written (with teacher's help) in multiple languages to accompany children's illustrations.

diversity The concept of diversity means accepting, valuing, and respecting the uniqueness of each child; recognizing differences and appreciating similarities.

Photo 9.1
Reading corner

■ ***Ages 6 to 9:*** Children can read informational text about animals and complete research online to create a presentation for the class (groups or individuals). Bilingual books and resources (websites, video) can be shared with the class about animals. Children can compare and contrast the characteristics of animals found in different ecosystems. Endangered animals can be discussed along with children's feelings about the importance of protecting a species.

Classroom Connection

What children's books and other types of text and/or activities can spark the engagement of a child who is bilingual or multilingual?

and accept each other. Banks (1993) devised four approaches to multicultural education reform:

1. *Contribution approach*—Select books and activities that celebrate holidays, heroes, and special events to incorporate in the curriculum. For example, teachers can design activities involving the life of Dr. Martin Luther King and his contributions after sharing *A Picture Book of Martin Luther King, Jr.,* written by David A. Adler (1990).
2. *Additive approach*—Add to your curriculum content, concepts, and items corresponding to literature by and about people from diverse cultures. For example, children can compare folktales from different cultures using books such as *Stories from Around the World* by Heather Amery (2001).
3. *Transformation approach*—Change the structure of the curriculum and encourage children to view concepts, issues, and themes from several ethnic perspectives and points of view. For example, explore current events to increase critical thinking and consideration of diversity. Children can compare informational and opinion articles on a specific event.

4. *The social action approach*—Combine transformation and social approach activities to strive for social change. Children not only understand issues, but also do something to create positive change. For example, children write letters to senators and congress representatives to express their opinions on local concerns, such as safe parks and clean playgrounds.

In addition to the various approaches to multicultural education, sociopolitical influences, such as the economy and structures of society, affect the educational success of diverse students (Banks, 1993; Nieto, 2003). Moving beyond tolerance, teachers must learn about their students, and this includes the sociopolitical realities of their lives. Understanding children's lives leads to respect, caring, and kindness in the classroom. To care for others, children and teachers must first understand themselves (Nieto, 2010).

In summary, the important aspects of diversity in education allow children to:

1. Learn about diverse cultural backgrounds and different abilities;
2. Appreciate and accept differences to promote respect and caring; and
3. Discover how to solve problems or complete tasks using multiple perspectives (critical thinking).

Children express their understanding of diversity in a variety of ways (Gardner, 1983, 1999b). Individual pacing can also help children at risk reach their learning goals. For example, children with ADHD and autism may have cognitive, emotional, social, and physical challenges. Emotional challenges can affect cognitive interpretation, while physical behaviors can affect social interaction (Jacobs & Wendel, 2010). This requires creative classrooms that are consistent with cooperative learning techniques to meet the literacy needs of all children. Teachers should present an assortment of activities and strategies to engage children in literacy learning.

9-1 Diverse Learners and Literacy Concepts

Diverse learners are supported through innovative, activity-based, sensory education models, such as Montessori (1914) and Reggio Emilia (Gandini, Etheridge & Hill, 2008) approaches. Children develop literacy skills and strategies through discovery learning. Montessori's approach focuses on developing creative problem-solving abilities for young children to be independent and self-sufficient. *Manipulatives* and real-world objects are introduced to children during multisensory lessons that evolve from children's needs and interests (emergent curriculum). This approach focuses on the teacher as the facilitator of learning through carefully designed and sequenced lessons. The emphasis is learning through self-determination and self-realization. In the Montessori curriculum, children learn practical life skills, such as buttoning clothes, tying shoelaces, and setting a table. Children learn through the five senses and interpret information about the learning tasks. Using textures from nature, children create tactile alphabet symbols that can be manipulated to create words. The lessons support the natural curiosity and imagination present in all children (Montessori, 1914).

The concept of emergent curriculum is also present in the Reggio Emilia approach, which originated in a region of Italy (Gandini, Etheridge, & Hill, 2008). The teacher as facilitator listens to the child and evaluates what is important to this individual and thus designs learning experiences tailored for the child. Capturing the child's interests motivates literacy learning and communication in a variety of ways (reading, writing, listening, speaking, viewing, and visually representing). Children decide how they want

emergent curriculum Lessons that evolve from children's needs and interests.

to communicate their ideas, through art, music, dance, drama, and play. The different ways of communication are called children's languages. Puppetry, dramatic storytelling, word play, shadow play, water play, sand play, light play, art, music, and dance are just a few of the languages in the Reggio Emilia approach.

The Reggio Emilia and the Montessori curriculum designs involve teachers, parents, students, and other community members. These approaches to curriculum design foster the collaborative connection between home, school, and the community (Gandini, Etheridge, & Hill, 2008; Montessori, 1914; Vecchi, 2010). "Reggio-inspired pedagogy is a way of being in the world—a way of seeing, listening, speaking, a commitment to relationships that honor identity and culture, a commitment to dialogue and action" (Gandini, Etheridge, & Hill, 2008, p. 114). Our holistic model of literacy (HML) connects to these literacy and diverse learning concepts. The cognitive, socioemotional, and physical aspects of self are important for all learners. Every child is unique; therefore, a child-centered approach with differentiated instruction will meet the needs of all children. Teachers should be sensitive to diverse learners by valuing their abilities, cultural heritages, and native languages, while teaching Standard English.

Our classrooms must be prepared to accommodate the needs of our growing multicultural population. Teachers should create a welcoming and safe environment where all children learn from each other by sharing personal stories, cultural celebrations, and traditions. The learning environment is richer from the varied backgrounds of children. For example, word walls or flash cards in multiple languages help all children learn new words. Games or activities, such as having children devise menus in different languages, can help all children in the classroom become aware of new cultures and concepts from various countries.

 CONSIDER THIS...

Consider how active engagement is supported through sensory activities. What kinds of manipulatives and real-world objects can support children's literacy learning?

9-2 Language and Vocabulary Development

Language contains meaningful symbols used to communicate thoughts and feelings. When learning language, children process sounds, letters, words, and sentences to create meaning. Teachers must address the needs of all children considering cultural and linguistic resources they bring to the classroom. Children who recently immigrated to the United States may be beginning English language learners or emergent English readers (Bauer & Arazi, 2011). "Comprehension and vocabulary instruction provided to ELLs is dependent on each child's acquisition of literacy in his or her native language. Children who have well-developed oral and written skills in their native language (L1) are able to proceed with the acquisition of L2 (English) reading much faster" (Bauer & Arazi, 2011, p. 383). It is important for teachers to include learning strategies that support children's diverse language abilities (see Table 9.1). Many children who were born in the United States fluently use words, syntax, and language patterns that are different from Standard English. Dialects of English differ greatly in regions of the United States such as New England, Appalachia, and the South. Teachers who are working with children in the areas of language and vocabulary development must take all of these considerations into account (Fromkin, Rodman, & Hyams, 2010).

Teachers should adapt literacy instruction to meet the diverse needs of children learning English. Some examples of how to make English more understandable for English language learners (ELLs) are previewing, real-world connections, guided reading instruction, and story retelling. When previewing, teachers introduce key vocabulary and makes personal connections. Bilingual and picture dictionaries are helpful tools for children during instruction. Children can also create their own personal illustrated dictionaries and word

children's languages Different ways that children communicate with each other, such as dramatic play, music, dance, art, and puppetry, usually associated with the Reggio Emilia approach.

beginning English language learners Children who have recently immigrated to the United States and are just starting to learn English.

emergent English readers Another term for beginning English language learners.

Table 9.1 | *Examples of Diverse Language Abilities*

1. Children who speak little or no English and are limited in their primary language

2. Children who speak their primary language fluently, but speak limited English

3. Bilingual or multilingual children who speak English and other language(s) fluently

4. Children who speak mainly English but have limited speaking skills in other language(s)

5. Children who only speak English fluently

banks. When children make real-world connections to text, they expand their vocabulary (see Photo 9.2). Meaning is developed through language they already know and increases as they learn new words. Structured guided reading instruction promotes oral and written language development. Examples of guided reading instruction include asking questions before, during, and after reading or using context clues to figure out unknown words. Another example is choral reading (reading together), which supports development of fluency and expression. Children need to interact with text multiple times to increase comprehension and vocabulary development. Story retelling supports conversations about the text between children and the teacher through ongoing scaffolding activities (building language skills from simple to complex) (Bauer & Arazi, 2011, p. 383).

Vocabulary strategies that help children who are at risk (ELLs and children with learning/physical disabilities) include the F.R.I.E.N.D.S. model. This model consists of seven components:

- **F (*Foster conversations*)**—Engage in meaningful conversations, ask questions, and provide specific feedback intentionally using key vocabulary.
- **R (*Robust and motivational instruction*)**—Motivate children's interest, choice, and active use of new vocabulary words through interactive word walls, word sorts, games, and writing.
- **I (*Interactive reading*)**—Inspire children through personal connections (text-to-self) during interactive reading using illustrations and context clues to understand new vocabulary.
- **E (*Engaging and literacy-rich environment*)**—Provide a multimedia learning environment, including vocabulary board games/puzzles, children's magazines, books (varied genres), computer word games, and e-books.
- **N (*Numerous opportunities to practice*)**—Encourage conversations about key vocabulary words throughout the day, allowing for interactive use (bulletin board display, anchor charts, word of the day, journal writing).

Photo 9.2 *Children reading*
Susannah Brown

Brain Briefs

MUSIC, DRAMA, AND THE BRAIN

Music and songs can promote language development for young children. Carlton (2000) emphasizes that important brain connections are made through music and dramatic movement from birth to age 3. Props, costumes, hats, masks, puppets, and stuffed animals should be used daily to encourage dramatic play during singing time. Video record children during the musical dramatic play and allow children (age 2 and older) to view short video clips to reinforce language development at an individual center or as a whole class.

Think about It

How can teachers integrate dance and music to represent the diversity of the classroom? For example, cultural diversity can be shared through music and dance using traditional costumes. Depending upon children's abilities, movement can be adapted to include hand clapping, foot tapping, finger wiggling, and head nodding.

- ■ **D (*Direct and explicit instruction*)**—Select new words important to text comprehension in various content areas (science, math, social studies, arts) and focus on these words during mini-lessons.
- ■ **S (*Sophisticated and rare words*)**—Expand and enrich vocabulary through reading aloud, dialogue, classroom routines, videos, and online resources to connect new words with familiar words. (Dashiell & DeBruin-Parecki, 2014)

Using the F.R.I.E.N.D.S. model helps children who are at risk with "acquisition, sustainment, and acceleration of vocabulary skills" (Dashiell & DeBruin-Parecki, 2014, p. 513). These strategies also support word identification, word recognition, reading fluency, and comprehension of text. Motivating children to be interested in and aware of new vocabulary in their daily lives encourages them to apply these new words in meaningful ways.

Expanding and enriching vocabulary through creative activities allows ELLs to express their understanding of new concepts. Frequent exposure to content-specific vocabulary, such as in the arts, science, math, and social studies, reinforces retention and application of advanced words. According to Craig and Paraiso (2008), children who discuss artwork or illustrations benefit from increased vocabulary use, which supports their proficiency in speaking English. The communication skills developed through art discussion helps ELLs to succeed in all academic areas. Dramatic activities are also positively associated with literacy success by increasing a child's ability to read text accurately and fluently (Keehn, Harmon, & Shoho, 2008).

 CONSIDER THIS…

Consider how you would use vocabulary development strategies in your classroom. How can you foster meaningful dialogue that reinforces key vocabulary words?

9-3 Literacy Instruction for Diverse Classrooms

Diversity involves teaching children of various backgrounds with many different challenges, such as language development, linguistic diversity, cultural diversity, struggling readers, and children with special needs (physical or emotional) or learning disorders

Photo 9.3 *Lap reading*

(such as autism and ADHD). Teachers should know the strengths and needs of all children in their classrooms as well as their hopes and dreams to inspire them to reach their full potential (see Photo 9.3).

9-3a Differentiated Instruction and Response to Intervention (RTI)

Differentiated instruction is essential in a diverse classroom. Differentiated instruction means tailoring teaching to the individual needs of your students, either in small groups, or in one-on-one instruction. For example, when teaching comprehension skills in the Common Core State Standards, use additional support and simpler tasks with the same text, rather than using simpler texts for struggling readers or English language learners. Scaffolding techniques consist of modeling or demonstration, using visuals, providing a rich introduction for unfamiliar stories, monitoring for understanding, and guided practice. Entry points (accessible adaptations of curriculum), content, learning activities (process), and outcomes (products) are adapted to meet a child's needs (Hall, Strangman, & Meyer, 2003). For example, children can explore new concepts by working in a literacy center, researching a new topic online, or collaborating with a partner to discuss text. Application of literacy skills is different for each child. Teachers should consider three aspects of learning before instruction:

- Utilize informal diagnostic assessments for student readiness, such as running records, KWL charts, vocabulary lists, or informal reading inventories.
- Identify student reading motivation and interests through surveys, interviews, and interest inventories.
- Determine student learning styles and preferences through observations, checklists, interviews, anecdotal notes, and questionnaires.

differentiated instruction Tailoring instruction to the individual needs of students, either in small groups, or one-on-one instruction.

entry points Accessible adaptations of curriculum.

Teachers use the information gathered from these three aspects of learning to determine the students' readiness for learning and to plan differentiated instruction.

Differentiation strategies that assist children in developing a range of literacy skills include:

- Tier assignments focus on essential literacy skills by varying levels of complexity depending upon the child's abilities or readiness. Children with limited comprehension skills can answer literal (factual/explicit) questions. Children with advanced comprehension skills can write a sequel to the story or rewrite the story from a different point of view.
- Compacting is a process of varying instruction to allow for previous student mastery of learning objectives. Compacting consists of three steps: (1) Assess the current knowledge level of the topic to determine objectives for instruction; (2) design a lesson to meet the students' current needs; and (3) create extension activities for advanced learning.
- Interest centers or interest groups are organized for children to self-select learning experiences according to their preferences. An interest center can focus on themes of interest such as outer space, famous Americans, sports, photography, and music. Interest groups are similar to literature circles or book clubs where children want to read and discuss a common book.
- Flexible grouping allows for interchangeable work/study groups based upon the content and task. For example, children can create their own groups based upon a specific interest and collaboratively write a book report.
- Learning contracts are agreements between the teacher and student that set learning goals. A child can decide what topic to research and how to present the information to the class.
- Choice boards organize a variety of activities to be selected by individual children to complete. The activities usually represent a range of multiple intelligences, such as visual/spatial, musical, kinesthetic, and naturalistic (Gardner, 1999a).

Response to Intervention

Response to intervention (RTI) is one method of differentiating instruction. The application of the IDEIA (U.S. Department of Education, 2004) in schools involves response to intervention (RTI). Legislation, such as the Individuals with Disabilities Education Improvement Act (IDEIA) (U.S. Department of Education, 2004), ensures that all children are included in classes to the fullest extent possible (inclusion). IDEIA defines the terms of specific disabilities, which guide how states define disabilities and determine who is eligible for appropriate education under the IDEIA legislation. Children with a disability must fully meet the definition to be eligible for special education and services. This includes the concept that a child's educational performance is adversely affected as a result of the specific disability. IDEIA identifies specific disabilities, such as autism, deaf-blindness, deafness, developmental delay, emotional disturbance, hearing impairment, intellectual disability, multiple disabilities, orthopedic impairment, other health impairment, specific learning disability, speech or language impairment, traumatic brain injury, and visual impairment, including blindness (U.S. Department of Education, 2004). Autism is further defined by guidelines from the *Diagnostic and Statistical Manual of Mental Disorders* (American Psychiatric Association, 2013).

The Council for Exceptional Children (2013) publishes research and policy pertaining to children with special needs. The organization has created a *Public Policy Agenda for the 113th United States Congress, 2013–2015* (The Council for Exceptional Children, 2013), which advocates for federal policies that support people with disabilities. The following policy relates specifically to young children:

> Advocate for federal policies that result in the development and implementation of evidence-based, best practices for children and youth with disabilities and/or gifts and talents, including school-wide initiatives such as Response to Intervention (RTI), Universal Design for Learning (UDL), and Positive Behavioral Interventions and Supports (PBIS) and policies that reduce restraint and seclusion practices and support and promote positive school climates. (The Council for Exceptional Children, 2013)

tier assignments Focus on essential literacy skills by varying levels of complexity depending upon the child's abilities or readiness.

compacting A process of varying instruction to allow for previous student mastery of learning objectives.

interest centers or **interest groups** Organized for children to self-select learning experiences according to their preferences.

flexible grouping Allows for interchangeable skills groups based upon the content, purpose, and task.

learning contracts Agreements between the teacher and student that set learning goals.

choice boards A variety of extension activities or projects, based on the multiple intelligences that are related to a specific book, topic, or theme.

inclusion The Individuals with Disabilities Education Improvement Act (IDEIA) (U.S. Department of Education, 2004) ensured that all children were included in classes to the fullest extent possible.

ASSESSING COMPREHENSION SKILLS THROUGH NARRATIVE RETELLING

Retelling guides can be used to assess readers' knowledge of story elements in narrative text. Teachers can ask children a series of questions to encourage retelling strategies. When listening to a child's retelling, the teacher checks that the discussion includes important information and details in sequential order. Specific details that set the stage, setting, or background of the story are included first. Next, children should share events in the story leading to the crisis/problem. Finally the resolution to the problem is presented. If appropriate, children can reread the text (the "look back strategy") to confirm thoughts or add ideas that were missed during the initial retelling. This strategy supports comprehension along with memory development (Leslie & Caldwell, 2010).

Retelling Question Guide

Directions: Ask the following questions:

1. Who are the characters?
2. What is the setting (time and place)?
3. What is the problem?
4. Describe the story events in sequence.
5. How was the problem solved?
6. What is the ending?

Think about It

When children with special needs are having difficulty retelling stories, how can you provide additional support? For example, the teacher could model the story retelling process. Children can use illustrations, story maps, or draw pictures as guides during retelling.

❯❯ **Professional Resource Download**

RTI assesses the effectiveness of research-based interventions to improve academic performance for a child with a specific disability. Eight areas of low achievement provide indicators for identifying specific learning disabilities. Six of these indicators involve literacy development, including oral expression, listening comprehension, written expression, basic reading skills, reading fluency skills, and reading comprehension (International Literacy Association, 2009).

Special remedial reading programs, such as Reading Triumphs, Wordly Wise 3000, Wilson Foundations, and Rewards, are used in schools to fulfill the federal mandate from special education legislation. Response to intervention is a three-tiered approach to meet the needs of at-risk learners in reading, math, behavior, and other areas. The classroom teacher typically provides Tier 1 (standard curriculum) and Tier 2 (scaffolded curriculum) instruction. Struggling students who are not making progress after a sufficient period of time are placed in Tier 3 instruction, usually provided by a reading coach or reading specialist.

Strategies teachers use in Tier 1 are simply best practice, such as stating and restating objectives, explicit instruction, providing feedback, and hands-on instruction. According to research (Stephens, Cox, Downs, et. al., 2012), Tier 2 interventions will be successful if children:

- Understand that reading is meaningful;
- Believe in themselves as readers;
- Think that reading is fun;
- Know how to self-monitor consistently;
- Have the knowledge, skills, and strategies to problem-solve for meaning;
- Use this information flexibly and independently; and
- Are able to use this information in increasingly complex text.

Although implementation models vary, typically Tier 2 instruction consists of 30-minute sessions two to three times per week with small groups of students. Tier 3 instruction is primarily individualized, according to the needs and learning styles of each student.

 CONSIDER THIS...

Consider how the response to intervention approach can improve the academic performance of a child with a specific disability. For example, what strategies are effective to increase oral expression and listening comprehension?

The Value of Multicultural Literature for Learning about Cultural Diversity

We are living in a multicultural society. Multiculturalism is a complex issue, involving race, ethnicity, class, religion, sex, and age (Morrow, 2009). Multicultural children's literature represents one or more cultures from the United States and other countries throughout the world. Teaching tolerance and cultural awareness through self-reflection and self-awareness is an important component of any curriculum. In her multicultural picture book *Whoever You Are*, Mem Fox (2006, pp. 1–3) exemplifies the similarities rather than the differences in children from countries all over the world. Even young children can understand the author's powerful message of tolerance. Fox writes:

> *Little One,*
> *Whoever you are,*
> *Wherever you are,*
> *There are little ones just like you*
> *All over the world.*

After reading this story, children can interview each other to discover and value their similarities and differences. Writing letters to pen pals from other areas or countries can help children understand diverse culture.

Multicultural literature is an effective way to value diversity, and to celebrate the various cultures and backgrounds of the children. In a diverse, culturally responsive classroom, there should be books in classroom and school libraries that represent different cultures. Multicultural literature helps children realize that even though their skin color may be different, there are many ways that they are all the same. Teachers in diverse classrooms must understand children, their families, and their cultural backgrounds to teach them effectively. We need to know children as individuals, realizing that not all members of a cultural or ethnic group are the same. We must acknowledge our cultural biases and stereotypes, so that we can recognize the strengths and needs of all children.

Multicultural literature, such as *The Other Side*, written by Jacqueline Woodson and illustrated by E. B. Lewis (2001), can stimulate constructive conversations about racial issues from a historical perspective. Two young girls in the 1950s, one African American and one Caucasian, live in rural homes that are separated by a long, white fence (symbolizing the cultural barriers of the time period). At first Annie and Clover (the narrator) are prohibited from playing together, but by the end of the story they are jumping rope and sitting together on the fence. Students can discuss racial prejudice and how it still exists in today's world after reading this book.

Children who are immigrants to the United States should be given opportunities to tell or write stories about their homelands, revealing the hardships they endure as they become acclimated to a new country. English language learners may be able to paint or draw their thoughts and feelings when they are not able to put them into words. When immigrant children are allowed to share experiences about their lives through storytelling from the heart (with either pictures or words), they feel accepted and valued in their new surroundings. Children from different countries may feel shy or intimidated when learning new languages.

Multicultural books must be evaluated for their cultural authenticity, represented throughout the text and illustrations. The dialect used in the story must be accurate and authentic to the culture as well. One positive example is *Flossie and the Fox*, written by Patricia McKissack and illustrated by Rachel Isadora (1986). McKissack uses southern African American dialect to tell this story, based on "Little Red Riding Hood." Flossie's mother asks her to take a basket of eggs to a nearby farm, but she warns Flossie to watch out for the fox. Flossie outsmarts the sly creature

multiculturalism A complex issue with the understanding that the various cultures in our society deserve an equal amount of respect.

READING COMPREHENSION STRATEGIES FOR CHILDREN WITH AUTISM

Reading comprehension may be difficult for children with autism because of their limited communication skills (Kluth, 2010). They may not understand the story, or they may know the answer to a question but are unable to verbalize their answer clearly. Teachers can use strategies such as building background knowledge before reading, thinking aloud during reading, and recording thoughts (teacher's or children's) on a whiteboard using a graphic organizer to assist children's comprehension.

Think about It

What are some ways that teachers can build background knowledge about civil rights before reading *Martin's Big Words* by Doreen Rappaport (2007)? For example, they may ask the class to share personal connections, ask questions, brainstorm and write ideas on chart paper, or share other books about civil rights (Kluth, 2010).

---

1. Are the values and beliefs of the people in the book authentic?
2. Are the geographical and social settings authentic?
3. Do the major events that make up the plot of the story seem possible for the time period and culture?
4. Are the major themes consistent with other literature written about the same time period or culture?
5. Is the author a native of the culture represented ("insider" perspective) or a researcher ("outsider" perspective)?

⩔ Professional Resource Download

Figure 9.1
Criteria for Evaluating Multicultural Literature

in this story. When reading multicultural children's literature, emphasize the rich vocabulary and figurative expressions that are part of the represented culture. Certain text, however, may confuse young readers without guidance from the teacher. "Miz Viola over at the McCutchin Place. Seem like they been troubled by a fox. Miz Viola's chickens be so scared, they can't even now lay a stone" (McKissack, 1986, p. 4). Some children may not understand that the chickens are not laying eggs. When reading the text aloud, teachers can use think-aloud strategies to help children understand cultural expressions.

When selecting multicultural children's literature, teachers should consider many different factors. Figure 9.1 lists questions that teachers can use to critique multicultural literature in terms of authenticity of the text and illustrations.

Teachers should have a vast knowledge of quality multicultural literature in multiple genres (picture books, traditional literature, poetry, realistic and historical fiction, science fiction and fantasy, biographies, and informational books) to plan effective lessons that are meaningful and relevant to the lives of their students. Historical fiction and biographies are useful for teaching critical thinking. This can be done effectively for younger students through interactive read-alouds. For example, children can discuss issues and concerns connected with slavery while listening to *Henry's Freedom Box*, written by Ellen Levine and illustrated by Kadir Nelson (2007). This is a true story about the Underground Railroad in which a slave named Henry mails himself to freedom in a wooden box.

Including a wide range of texts that feature diversity in the classroom library encourages children to understand and connect cultural concepts. Teachers should consider how well the books in the class library represent the diversity of ethnic and cultural backgrounds of the children.

Consider how multicultural literature is selected for the classroom. What qualities do you believe are important when selecting multicultural literature for young children?

9-5 Teaching Children with Special Needs

Diversity in literacy includes students who have various challenges, such as struggling to read due to a physical disability (for example, vision impairment). The cause of young children's challenges can be myriad or a combination of disabilities (visual, auditory, emotional, or social). These disabilities may occur together or separate and are sometimes difficult to diagnose. Structured routines, guiding strategies, and using visuals to engage children will help them feel more in control of their learning. Cultural and linguistic diversity are intertwined. Language is the mainstay of culture, and many traditions, such as song and poetry or literature, are based on common customs. Children with special needs may require assisted learning or *scaffolding* through teachers and peers (cooperative learning).

9-5a Gifted and Talented Children

In a diverse classroom, teachers must address the needs of all types of learners, such as children with cognitive disabilities (Down syndrome or dyslexia), emotional disabilities (ADHD, autism spectrum), and physical disabilities (auditory, visual). Gifted and talented children also have special needs. For example, a teacher might develop an enriched curriculum based on the child's personal interests, strengths, and talents. The child and teacher can work together to create individual learning goals using a learning contract.

Children with gifts and talents in areas such as language arts, music, and visual art often have unique needs that are supported through teaching and learning accommodations (Clark, 2002). Research indicates that approximately 3 percent to 5 percent of the population is gifted and talented (Hallahan, Kauffman, & Pullen, 2011). Gifted (intellectual) pertains to children who retain and critically analyze large amounts of information and make cognitively advanced connections between knowledge sets. Talented (creative) children demonstrate abilities often through the arts that usually indicate the following characteristics: awareness of creativity, attraction to complexity, curious, energetic, humorous, independent, intuitiveness, and originality.

According to the Gifted and Talented Children's Education Act, passed in 1978, but later repealed (U.S. Department of Education), creative abilities in the arts are included when identifying children who are gifted and talented. The U.S. Department of Education added a newer definition of gifted and talented children in 1993:

> Children and youth with outstanding talent perform or show the potential for performing at remarkably high levels of accomplishment when compared with others their age, experience, or environment. These children and youth exhibit high performance capability in intellectual, creative, and/or artistic areas, possess an unusual leadership capacity, or excel in specific academic fields. They require services or activities not ordinarily provided in the schools. Outstanding talents are present in children and youth from all cultural groups, across all economic strata, and in all areas of human endeavor. (U.S. Department of Education, 1993, p. 3)

More recently, the No Child Left Behind Act (NCLB) (U.S. Department of Education, 2002) was passed as the reauthorization of the Elementary and Secondary Education Act (U.S. Department of Education, 1965). The NCLB Act defines the concept of

gifted and talented Gifted children are advanced intellectually and talented children excel in their creative skills. These children often have unique needs that require special teaching and learning accommodations.

GIVING VOICE TO DIFFERENT PERSPECTIVES IN LETTER WRITING: ACTIVITY FOR PRESERVICE TEACHERS TO DO WITH CHILDREN

Purpose: Practice letter-writing skills focusing on word choice and voice. Children represent different perspectives in their writing and illustrations. *The Day the Crayons Quit* by Drew Daywalt (2013) provides inspiration for creative letter writing. The class could write letters to friends or family members, mailing them to those who live far away.

Procedure: The teacher shares the cover illustration with children and asks them to describe what they see and predict what the story will be about. Next, the teacher reads the story aloud, stopping to discuss with the class each of the letters written by the crayons. The teacher shares and explains an anchor chart that identifies the parts of a written letter. As a prewriting strategy, the children discuss all the different colors in a box of crayons and select their favorites. Each child shares with a partner how he or she thinks his or her selected colored crayon would feel about being used to draw pictures. The children write a letter written by their selected crayon and illustrate a picture using only that color.

Teaching Analysis: Reflective practices are a necessary part of the *literacy assessment cycle* and are key components in preservice preparation and certification such as edTPA. Analyze the strengths and areas of improvement in this lesson idea. Answer the following:

- What is successful?
- What would you change to improve the lesson?
- What did you learn about teaching literacy?

Links: Making connections to technology and developmentally appropriate practices (DAP) supports lesson planning and literacy instruction. Adaptations of this lesson idea are provided through the following:

- **Technology Link:** Children can watch short videos found online that describe how crayons are made as a starting point for discussion.
- **DAP Link:** Children can dramatize the emotions and voice of their selected crayon and perform a skit or play as a class.
- **Executive Function Link:** Creative play and active engagement during an interactive read-aloud develop children's self-regulation skills in social settings as reflected in the holistic model of literacy (cognitive, socioemotional, and physical).
- **Classroom Link:** Children ages 2 to 3 can color masks with a single color and dramatize emotions associated with that color.
- **Classroom Link:** Children ages 3 to 6 can work in groups and illustrate on a large piece of paper using the same color. Each group can share their ideas verbally with the class while the teacher records/writes the letter for the group.
- **Classroom Link:** Children ages 6 to 9 can create a class book that includes illustrations and letters.

children who are considered gifted and talented, including the concept that these gifts and talents should be fully developed in schools.

Teachers should adapt instructional materials, strategies, practices, and assessments to meet the needs of children who are gifted and talented. For example, a teacher could modify an assignment through acceleration, either by presenting information at a faster pace or introducing complex content earlier in the instruction. Another strategy to meet the needs of children who are gifted and talented is enrichment or presenting content with more depth, breadth, or complexity (see Photo 9.4).

9-5b Planning Curriculum for Children with Special Needs

When planning curriculum for children with special needs, teachers should consider the following concepts: inclusion, age-appropriateness, participation levels, empowerment, children-first language, and values. IDEIA identifies specific disabilities, which include autism, deaf-blindness, deafness, developmental delay, emotional disturbance, hearing impairment, intellectual disability, multiple disabilities, orthopedic impairment, other health impairment, specific learning disability, speech or language impairment, traumatic brain injury, and visual impairment, including blindness (U.S. Department of Education, 2004). Accommodations or modifications are needed to support children in literacy development. Table 9.2 features selected early literacy strategies that can be part of reading and writing mini-lessons (Calkins, 1986). Using the strategies that include connection, demonstration, active involvement, and links to learning, the teacher and children can create an interactive environment that facilitates emergent literacy development.

Teachers should strive to keep topics, media, and materials age-appropriate for children. All children should have an equal opportunity to have a high quality of life, work on developmentally and age-appropriate assignments, and have opportunities to develop their unique abilities through playful creative interactions (see Photo 9.5).

Participation levels may vary among children depending upon cognitive, physical, and socioemotional development. Fostering independent work helps children to develop their own strengths in learning, and empowers them to reach their full potential. Valuing each child for his or her own unique abilities is part of the process of empowerment and encourages self-esteem. See Table 9.3 for roles of teachers and children in diverse literacy classrooms.

9-5c Autism Spectrum

Autism is a spectrum of cognitive, socioemotional, and physical (neurological) disorders manifested when speaking or connecting with others. Children with autistic disorders have trouble with eye-to-eye contact and listening to what others

Photo 9.4 *Engaged in literacy*
Susannah Brown

Photo 9.5 *Creative painting*

autism A spectrum of cognitive, socioemotional, and physical (neurological) disorders that usually occur when speaking or connecting with others.

Table 9.2 — Meeting Children's Needs through Reading/Writing Mini-Lessons

	Students Are English Language Learners (ELLs)	Students Have Difficulty Concentrating and May Be Disruptive during the Lesson
In General (Tips to Remember)	Use lots of visuals and expressive body movements along with exaggerated facial expressions. Demonstrate using the same materials the children will use for the lesson. Use clear, concise language, and repeat key information. Consider preteaching prior to your mini-lesson with the whole class—e.g., when teaching idioms or metaphors (figurative language that might be confusing for ELLs) review the concept with a small of group first.	Keep eye contact. Move closer to the child and arrange seating for focus. Remind children of behavior expectations, and be consistent while praising appropriate behavior. Use shorter mini-lesson focusing more on active engagement and less on teacher talk. Integrate dramatic play, movement, music, and art into the lesson. Have peers/other adults model appropriate behavior nearby. Use gestures to check comprehension often (e.g., thumbs up or down if you understand the strategy).
Connection	Use gestures (pointing) to indicate materials and information on charts. Allow children to verbalize the lesson connection to a partner using key words from the lesson connection.	Be brief and concise to focus time on demonstration and active involvement. Engage children to use nonverbal cues to respond to information. Give specific praise often.
Demonstration (Instruction by Teacher)	Act out or dramatize the steps. Use gestures and point to charts illustrating the steps for using the strategy. Use text with illustrations that help with comprehension.	Use gestures to indicate when children are ready to work ("Thumbs up if you are ready to explain your idea to a partner"). Ask questions at crucial points of the demonstration.
Active Involvement	Have children use gestures during work. Use a familiar text if appropriate with illustrations. Complete one active involvement strategy as a whole class to model, then have independent practice. Create mixed work groups that include children that can mentor others.	Have children use gestures that signal their involvement. Share clear expectations for involvement. Break up the activity into small parts with clear directives prior to action. Have children self-check their involvement at key times for the lesson.
Link	Dramatically act out the link to model behavior and use of strategy. Use "think-aloud" questions to link to learning.	State link clearly and briefly. Ask children to close their eyes and imagine using the strategy on their own and describe to a partner.

Adapted from Teachers College Reading and Writing Project (2009) and Calkins (1986).

Students Are Not Connected to the Lesson	Students Don't Apply What Was Taught Independently
Make and keep eye contact.	Recheck that your content is appropriate for children's reading levels and interests.
Use expressive gestures to convey interest and emotion.	Sometimes children don't need a specific strategy to complete the lesson.
Use a signal or key word to refocus attention (e.g., "This is important" or "Let's write that down").	Remind children of the strategy using an anchor chart with an image or icon that relates to the strategy.
Use children's names periodically throughout the lesson (make sure to randomize and call on as many children as possible during the lesson).	Use key words that target specific strategies.
Focus on children's interests (e.g., child selects a mentor text for the lesson).	Conference with small groups and refocus on using the strategy.
Focus on active involvement to keep up interest.	
Have children partner to share what was learned yesterday or in a previous lesson.	Share examples from past students who applied the strategy successfully.
Use artifacts, charts, visuals to illustrate connection.	Connect to another lesson where the strategy was used in the past.
After explaining, have children use "Talk and Turn" to explain the connection in their own words to a partner.	
Capture children's attention through drama/expression.	Use texts that children are familiar with or are at the same reading level.
Change the level or sound of your voice to emphasize points.	End demonstration with encouraging statements that support use (e.g., "See how that helped me? It can help you too!").
Ask for a volunteer to help during the demonstration.	
Begin with a prompt or teaser question to pique interest.	
Allow children to use strategy at least twice.	Have children write in their own words what they will do.
Engage children to turn and share with a partner what they learned.	Create a plan of action using a graphic organizer.
Use dramatic play or movement to refocus attention.	Use an anchor chart to guide usage (e.g., "When I see this . . . I will do this . . .").
	Use a book of their choice to practice the strategy.
Use "Think Pair Share" to connect link to what children will do next.	Retell the goal of the lesson using a prompt statement (e.g., "Today or any time you get stuck on . . . remember to try using a specific strategy.").
	Talk about how the strategy can help in specific situations.
	Have children indicate or signal when they are using a specific strategy during their work so you can stop by to listen how they used the strategy (e.g., place a brightly colored sticky note on the top of their desk).

Table 9.3	Roles of Teachers and Children in the Diverse Literacy Classroom

Teachers	Children
Accept and recognize children's strengths and needs.	Self-reflect to recognize their own strengths and needs.
Evaluate various strengths and needs of each student.	Self-regulate strengths and needs through active engagement.
Encourage parental involvement.	Work with others (peers, parents, other adults).
Work cooperatively with teacher assistants to meet children's needs.	Know personal skills and abilities and when to ask for help.
Research and select specific teaching and learning strategies to promote growth and development.	Utilize skills and strategies in appropriate settings.
Advocate for accessibility and inclusion.	Demonstrate a caring and empathetic attitude when helping others.
Acquire and utilize technology and specialized devices.	Use assistive devices and technology appropriately.

are saying to them. The highest cognitive level is Asperger's syndrome, with which children can have exceptional IQs and talents in areas such as math, music, or art.

Young children with autism spectrum disorder may find specific situations challenging including: (1) requirements to follow rigid routines and specific directions due to disorientation; (2) engagement in repetitive language or behaviors like shaking hands or heads; (3) stressed or frustrated feelings due to overwhelming learning disabilities; (4) avoiding eye contact or running from social connections because of emotions; and (5) sensory integration problems and avoidance of expression. The following management strategies may assist children with autism:

1. Structure classrooms where activities are routine and occur at the same time each day. Each child has a list of routines and corresponding pictures to follow.
2. Incorporate all styles of learning, especially multiple intelligences (Gardner, 1999a), using visual/spatial, musical, and kinesthetic techniques that engage children comfortably.
3. Have an individual education program (IEP) for each child with challenges that teachers, children, and parents follow.
4. Use technology for individually paced programs, and ensure that parents are involved in all aspects of their child's learning.
5. Accommodate children at risk, and evaluate their reading strategies to ensure progress and effective learning.

Children with disorders in the autism spectrum should feel accepted as valued members of the class. Patience, tolerance, acceptance, and kindness are wonderful virtues we should all practice in the classroom.

Currently the term "autism spectrum" covers the many variations for autism disorders. The diagnosis for autism spectrum is confusing because of the many variations and individual differences. Most disorders are diagnosed by age 3; however, all disorders vary in stages of impairment, social interaction, communication, repetitive behavior, and interests in activities (Marohn, 2002).

In her book on autism, Stephanie Marohn (2002) describes Asperger's syndrome (the mildest form of autism) in children as: (1) having speech delays, such as using only 20 spoken words by age 4 and engaging in speech repetitions; (2) acting without awareness and avoiding eye contact; (3) singing to self and being oblivious of social cues; (4) having motor skills such as fidgeting and short attention span; and (5) using a loud voice and having physically aggressive tendencies. Marohn (2002) describes reeducating children in listening skills by taking children from birth to all developmental stages of listening and using calming influences such as children's songs or soft chanting music to increase their listening ability. There are different approaches, but Marohn (2002) found that after using this listening training, children could speak, read, and write while ultimately learning to participate in social functions. It takes a team effort (teachers, children, and family members) to support children with autism, but the rewards are worth it.

9-5d Attention Deficit/Hyperactivity Disorder

Children with attention deficit/hyperactive disorder (ADHD) can be perceived as having autism early on, and some young children could have both challenges with complicated disorders. Children with ADHD usually demonstrate problems sitting still (hyperactive) or focusing on learning (attention deficit).

A range of disorders are connected with hyperactivity. The most common manifestation of this disorder is restlessness and difficulty concentrating on completing homework or classroom activities (Jacobs & Wendel, 2010).

Young children with ADHD may exhibit the following characteristics:

1. Distractibility where following directions is almost impossible;
2. Struggling with reading that could also be compounded with dyslexia;
3. Learning new facts and organizing them so they can be remembered;
4. Restlessness when expected to concentrate, such as during testing or other tasks; and
5. Problems with assignments and inability to focus or follow instructions.

Young children develop at different stages; however, when not talking coherently or connecting to others by age 3, a developmental disability should be investigated. The earlier a correct diagnosis is made by appropriate professionals, teachers, and parents, the sooner affected children can begin intervention programs. We recommend the following management and teaching strategies for children with ADHD:

1. Prepare curriculum with parents and children.
2. Use appropriate evaluation techniques to give accurate readings of progress.
3. Incorporate cooperative learning techniques.
4. Instruct with appropriate pacing using multimedia aids or computers.
5. Build daily advance organizers or lists of learning goals. (Willems & DeHass, 2006)

Children can be self-reliant and responsible if teachers communicate clear expectations. Graphic organizers are effective for children with autism and ADHD because they can organize their tasks and monitor their progress (Willems & DeHass, 2006). Games and exercises that can increase concentration need to be integral in the classroom. Routine activities that help children focus assist their ability to succeed and therefore build their confidence. Children with reading and literacy challenges can progress and overcome many adversities with the help of teachers, parents, and peers working together as a team. Using visual aids such as picture and word walls helps children feel connected and increases comprehension.

In their guide for parenting children with ADHD, Carole Jacobs and Isadore Wendel (2010) wrote that researchers do not know what exactly causes ADHD. There is much speculation on environmental toxins and food allergies, as well as emotional relations with parents and peers. We believe that whatever the cause, the goal of teachers is to increase self-confidence and produce a safe environment for all children. Jacobs and Wendel (2010) recommend support groups that can help parents manage children with ADHD. Each child's situation is unique, requiring specific adaptations to meet his or her needs. We recommend that teachers work with parents, children, and the

Apply & Reflect

Reflect on the various strategies that can assist children with ADHD presented in this chapter. Select a strategy that you consider important when teaching children with ADHD. Discuss your selected strategy with a classmate, and consider adaptations or other accommodations that support literacy learning for children with ADHD.

attention deficit/hyperactive disorder (ADHD) A child who typically has problems sitting still (hyperactive) or concentrating on learning (attention deficit).

Age Groups	Cognitive	Socioemotional
0 to 3	Label items in the classroom and at home to verbally discuss vocabulary relating to real objects. Interact with natural spaces encouraging exploration, and discuss what is discovered. Read a variety of books (genres), including bilingual and multicultural stories. Provide safe art supplies to explore mark making.	Use cultural masks and puppets to depict emotions during multicultural storytelling. Create a behavioral reward chart to support positive interactions. Allow for lap reading and story time cuddle read to promote quiet reflection. Snuggle with a favorite toy during story time. Share and discuss favorite foods during snack time.
3 to 6	Listen to audio books in different languages spoken by children in the class. Chart text concepts utilizing graphic organizers and visual images. Display interactive word walls. Sing, dance, and dramatize story details and events. Categorize objects using vocabulary and verbal descriptions to verify each object's inclusion.	Share and encourage storytelling through visuals, puppetry, costumes, and through supportive smiles and silent cheers. Recognize literacy success by clapping and other demonstrations of support. Record literacy development milestones and share compliments with the class and parents. Use colors while painting that depict emotions.
6 to 9	Provide bilingual illustrated dictionaries and books. Model reading practices and use of English language through read-alouds and group reading. Encourage the use of technological and assistive devices to promote reading and writing.	Invite guest speakers for cultural sharing events. Pair with a peer and discuss how the selected text is related to emotions. Share ideas about emotions depicted in the text with a partner. Present online research on different countries to the class.

Professional Resource Download

school administrators to plan developmentally appropriate curriculum and individual learning goals.

Young children cannot be expected to sit all day; therefore, instruction should be informal with periodic breaks and a variety of relevant topics to hold their attention. Medical doctors formally diagnose ADHD when impulsivity, hyperactivity, and inattention are extreme, such as when a child cannot focus for any length of time and constant monitoring may be required (Jacobs & Wendel, 2010).

 CONSIDER THIS...

Consider different approaches to meeting the needs of children with varying abilities. How can you arrange the classroom to support a child with ADHD?

Physical	Children's Books	Family Involvement
Use boundaries to emphasize a work space (plastic trays on tables and soft mats or tape on the floor to mark learning centers). Celebrate cultural holidays with storytelling, music, and movement. Explore safe cultural objects such as toys and sculpture. Use sign language for key vocabulary in songs and stories. Draw letters/words in sand, water, or shaving cream in outside play areas.	*More, More, More Said the Baby* by Vera B. Williams *Global Babies* by the Global Fund for Children *The Colors of Us* by Karen Katz *My Big Animal Book* by Roger Priddy	Look at old family photo albums. Share dual-language board books. Read simple multicultural folk and fairy tales. Read animal picture books and make animal sounds. Identify colors in objects in the room. Use finger paints and chalk to draw shapes and lines.
Utilize a touch table or box, flannel boards with various textures, building blocks, and other manipulatives to create visual representation of text. Re-create story events through dramatic play and dance. Use assistive devices to explore the physical world (magnifying glass, microscope, pointers). Write words using a variety of materials (paint, clay, pipe cleaners, markers, crayons, found objects).	*Yoko* by Rosemary Wells *Amazing Grace* by Mary Hoffman *The Name Jar* by Yangsook Choi *Cookies Bite-Size Life Lessons* by Amy Krouse Rosenthal	Celebrate family traditions through food, music, and dance. Create a family tree collage with drawings and photos. Use a large world map to discuss different cultures, and plan family trips. Learn simple phrases in different languages. Play games and sports that are popular in different cultures.
Play games that promote vocabulary and language acquisition. Participate in field trips that provide physical interaction and real-world experiences. Use computers/software to illustrate text concepts and research related text. Attend a shopping field trip to a grocery store or farmer's market to learn about food from other cultures.	*In Jesse's Shoes* by Beverly Lewis *Walking through a World of Aromas* by Ariel Andres Almada *My Special Family* by Paige Snider	Interview grandparents and write these stories in a handmade book along with current family stories. Research online information about a state or country they would like to visit and create a scrapbook or collage.

9-6 Literacy Strategies and Practices for Diverse Learners

In diverse classrooms, teachers use a variety of strategies and activities to engage children in reading and language arts. Learning styles according to Gardner's multiple intelligences theory (1983, 1999a) vary according to children's strengths and needs. Table 9.4 focuses on strategies and practices for English language learners and children with special needs.

Summary

Teaching and learning strategies vary according to children's literacy development and needs. Diverse learners require accommodations in the learning environment and for specific tasks. Multicultural literature helps children from different backgrounds understand similarities and differences between cultures and value their cultural identity. Children's books in bilingual formats are meaningful and relevant to English language learners. All children benefit from hands-on learning through real-world experiences, visual representations, and cooperative learning. Parental involvement in the literacy classroom to promote cultural sharing enhances children's literacy development. Teachers must know their student's strengths, needs, interests, hopes, and dreams to guide them to reach their full literacy potential.

Chapter Exercises

1. Design a multisensory lesson that uses manipulatives (real-world objects) to promote oral language through discussion.
2. Using the F.R.I.E.N.D.S. model, focus on E (*engaging and literacy-rich environment),* and create a game or puzzle to teach new vocabulary. Share with a small group of classmates.
3. Model differentiated instruction by creating a choice board related to a children's book, which includes a variety of activities based upon different learning styles.
4. Select a multicultural children's book for teaching concepts about social justice and civil rights. Design two comprehension questions to share with a partner.
5. Select a book that features a character with special needs, and share a personal connection (text-to-self) with a peer.

Teacher Toolbox

DIVERSE STRATEGIES USING CHILDREN'S LITERATURE

Appropriate for Ages 4 to 9

American Sign Language can be practiced, and children who have hearing disabilities or are deaf may be included in storytelling using the book series *Moses Goes To . . .* (1998–2003) by Isaac Millman. In the book, *Moses Goes to the Circus* (Millman, 2003), the main character, Moses, who is deaf, and his family attend a special circus that features acts for all the senses. Moses teaches his little sister how to sign during their circus adventure. In class, the teacher creates an anchor chart after reading the story by asking the children to list all the different acts and type of performers in the circus. The teacher models the appropriate sign for each word while the class practices American Sign Language. In small groups, children use the signs they learned to discuss the story.

A VISIT TO THE CIRCUS

What did Moses see first?
Which act do you think was Renee's or Moses' favorite?
Which act did you like best?
What performers did you like best?

Key Terms and Concepts

attention deficit/hyperactive disorder (ADHD)
autism
beginning English language learners
children's languages
choice boards

compacting
differentiated instruction
diversity
emergent curriculum
emergent English readers
entry points
flexible grouping

gifted and talented
inclusion
interest centers
interest groups
learning contracts
multiculturalism
tier assignments

Oksana Kuzmina/Shutterstock.com

STANDARDS ADDRESSED IN THIS CHAPTER

The standards from the following organizations will be used throughout the chapter: Common Core State Standards for English Language Arts, the National Association for the Education of Young Children (NAEYC), and National Core Arts Standards. These standards are discussed further in the chapter as appropriate.

Common Core State Standards for English Language Arts

Anchor Standards for Reading

Reading Standards: Literature/Informational Text K–5
- Key Ideas and Details

Reading Standards: Foundational Skills (K–5)
- Print Concepts

Anchor Standards for Writing
- Production and Distribution of Writing

Anchor Standards for Speaking and Listening
- Presentation of Knowledge and Ideas

Anchor Standards for Language
- Vocabulary Acquisition and Use

2010 NAEYC Standards for Initial and Advanced Early Childhood Professional Preparation Programs
- **Standard 4:** Using Developmentally Effective Approaches

NAEYC Early Childhood Program Standards and Accreditation Criteria
- **Standard 2:** Curriculum

National Core Arts Standards (Dance, Media Arts, Music, Theater, Visual Arts)

Creating
- **Anchor Standard 1:** Generate and conceptualize artistic ideas and work.
- **Anchor Standard 3:** Refine and complete artistic work.

Presenting
- **Anchor Standard 4:** Select, analyze, and interpret artistic work for presentation.
- **Anchor Standard 6:** Convey meaning through the presentation of artistic work.

Responding
- **Anchor Standard 8:** Interpret intent and meaning in artistic work.
- **Anchor Standard 9:** Apply criteria to evaluate artistic work.

Connecting
- **Anchor Standard 10:** Synthesize and relate knowledge and personal experiences to make art.
- **Anchor Standard 11:** Relate artistic ideas and works with societal, cultural, and historical context to deepen understanding.

Teaching Literacy Through the Arts

10

We are all creative. Creativity is the hallmark human capacity that has allowed us to survive thus far. Our brains are wired to be creative. ...

— Shelley Carson

LEARNING OBJECTIVES

After you have read this chapter, you should be able to:

10-1 Compare arts and literacy concepts.

10-2 Describe connections between literacy and the arts.

10-3 Explain literacy and arts integration.

10-4 Analyze artistic experiences for early literacy.

10-5 Apply creativity in literacy.

10-6 Demonstrate literacy strategies and practices for arts integration.

Creativity and the arts play important roles in early literacy by involving the cognitive, socioemotional, and physical aspects of self, as we describe in the holistic model of literacy (HML). Children develop and strengthen language, as well as cognitive, socioemotional, and physical skills through opportunities to express creativity (Bodrova & Leong, 2006). We advocate cultivating artistic skills and imagination to connect creativity with reading and writing. For example, we activate and build schemata (linking to prior knowledge) through visual literacy and artistic expression.

The arts (visual arts, music, drama, and dance) help children connect new information with what is already learned. Teachers set the stage for creative learning in environments that entice the senses based on children's interests, and focus on active engagement in the creative process. "As young children move and explore their worlds, they are learning through touch" (Schwartz, 2015, p. 2). Movement and physical activity is essential for young children's intellectual development as they construct their knowledge through interaction (Montessori, 1936; Piaget, 1969). For children, the *process* of creating is more exciting than the end result, as young children learn about themselves and the world through this *process-based approach* (Kohl, 1994). Children are focused on imagination and immersing themselves in the artistic media while learning (Koralek et al., 2015; Lowenfeld, 1968). Children need daily opportunities to creatively express their own ideas and represent how information is processed (Copple & Bredekamp, 2009). During creative experiences, children plan and solve problems, focus their attention, use critical thinking skills, and persevere to find conclusions, which are important skills in literacy and in life (Pitri, 2001). The arts allow children to consider new questions and seek innovative answers (Robinson & Aronica, 2015). According to Robinson and Aronica (2015), flexibility (adapting to change) and creativity when generating new ideas are priorities of education.

The arts are an integral part of the literacy process. Children need an enriched, creative, and supportive learning environment in the early years (birth to age 9), as these years are critical to developing their first graphic symbol system, which occurs when recognizing symbols and interpreting meaning conveyed (Cartwright, 2008). This **graphic symbol system** is created through the arts as a

Continued on page 224

Vignette | Fluency, Expression, and Rhythm

STANDARDS CONNECTION TO THE VIGNETTE

NAEYC Early Childhood Program Standards and Accreditation Criteria

Standard 2: Curriculum

2.J.04 Children are provided varied opportunities to learn new concepts and vocabulary related to art, music, drama, and dance.

Common Core State Standards for English Language Arts

Key Ideas and Details

First Grade

2. Retell stories, including key details, and demonstrate understanding of their central message or lesson.

7. Use illustrations and details in a story to describe the characters, setting, or events.

Effective literacy instruction is integrated with creative expression and activities to actively engage young children (see Photo 10.1). Reading and writing comes alive with color to increase fluency and expression. Children paint their stories with words, emphasizing color and rhythm. This vignette depicts a classroom snapshot of how the arts are integrated within a literacy lesson.

Mrs. Witte, a first-grade teacher, dressed as Vincent van Gogh, is reading *Camille and the Sunflowers* by Laurence Anholt (1994) to the class to increase fluency in their read-aloud activities. In this children's book, the story of van Gogh is told through the eyes of a child, Camille. Adding a sense of drama to the reading, Mrs. Witte exaggerates the facial expressions that relate to the emotions depicted in the story line and in the illustrations throughout the book. The children identify illustrations and details in the story that connect characters and events to the emotions in the story. During the reading, the children and Mrs. Witte discuss van Gogh's paintings featured in the book, such as *Sunflowers* (1888), *Portrait of the Postman Joseph Roulin* (1888), and *Portrait of Camille Roulin* (1888). They discuss:

- How the colors in van Gogh's painting express feeling and emotions;
- How van Gogh's brushstrokes express feeling and emotions; and
- How the subject of the paintings relate to the expression of feeling and emotions.

After reading the story, the children and Mrs. Witte pretend to be "paintbrushes" and move to express the same brushstrokes present in van Gogh's artwork. During this creative movement exercise, Mrs. Witte plays Vivaldi's *Four Seasons,* focusing on the *Summer* selection of this composition while the children create movements that express the rhythm and beat of the music and van Gogh's paintings. Next, the children create their own tempera paintings using expressive brushstrokes inspired by van Gogh's paintings. The teacher and children discuss their artistic literacy experiences. The children dictate a sentence describing how their painting relates to the book and musical selection. Mrs. Witte writes the children's comments on a chart to organize the connections between the arts and literacy that are discussed and that can then be used in future literacy lessons.

arts A term that includes creative work in dance, drama/theater, music, and visual arts.

graphic symbol system Earliest marks made through creative expression in the emergent literacy process that are developed in written language.

Integrating the art forms, such as music, dance, and visual arts, helps children understand the world around them and express their imaginations by utilizing creative skills. Children use illustrations (visual art) and text to guide comprehension during reading. Arts integration allows children to express their understandings in unique ways.

Developmentally appropriate practice (DAP) is featured in the vignette and can be adapted for younger children (birth to age 5) and older children to age 9. Suggested adaptations include:

- ***Ages 0 to 3:*** Reading aloud to infants and toddlers helps to develop their listening comprehension. Toddlers can use paint to make random brushstrokes, emphasizing expression and texture. Infants can

Photo 10.1 *Creative drawing and writing*

explore color and texture with adult interaction by touching fabric, feathers, and other soft materials to the babies' skin while reading the book aloud or listening to music.

- *Ages 3 to 6:* Children 3 to 4 years old enjoy dancing to music with costumes that use colorful fabrics. Children ages 3 through 6 can paint in the air to music while holding colorful scarves. As a class, children can write poems that express emotions, colors, and textures.
- *Ages 6 to 9:* Children can read other books about van Gogh, such as the biography *Vincent van Gogh: Portrait of an Artist* by Jan Greenberg and Sandra Jordan (2009). Children can compare and contrast the information in the biography with the details of the narrative.

Classroom Connection

What dramatic activities for children can you integrate into this literacy lesson?

Photo 10.2 *Young artists painting*

child's earliest marks are made through creative expression in the emergent literacy process. Young children make marks in all areas of their lives, such as scribbles in the sand, designs with food items (pudding to mashed potatoes), lines on a frosted window, sculpture with bubbles in the bathtub, and finger marks on the wall. Graphic marks are visually enticing to young children, and even babies will focus their eyes on bold line designs and simple graphic illustrations. Young children play with materials in their environment while discovering that they have the creative power to change and affect their world by communicating their ideas and emotions. "Just as body movement and involvement can have a huge impact on learning, so too can the spaces where we learn" (Schwartz, 2015, p. 3). All aspects of cognitive, socioemotional, and physical development are connected through the creative manipulations and actions of young children (HML). The arts are an important part of our lives, and artistic learning activities for young children support their growth and literacy development (Eisner, 2002; Koralek et al., 2015) (see Photo 10.2).

10-1 Arts and Literacy Concepts

Literacy involves reading, writing, listening, speaking, viewing, and visually representing, including artistic expression such as visual art, music, dance, and drama to represent meaningful thoughts and ideas. Because the arts are a natural part of our culture, it is important to help our children become artistically literate. "The arts are the child's first language" (Koster, 2009, p. 8). Drawing lines and squiggles is the first expression of writing. Children can use artistic materials and tools from their environment to share their view of the world and creatively express their perceptions (see Photo 10.3).

Photo 10.3 *Creative writing with illustrations*

imagination Involves creating an idea or perception that has not yet been formed, such as a dream, story, or image that can be shared with others.

In Chapter 1 (Figure 1.2), we first introduced our holistic model of literacy (HML) consisting of the cognitive (yellow/mind), socioemotional (red/heart), and physical (blue/arms and legs) parts of self to promote creative thought and passion for literacy. We revisited the HML illustration in Chapter 3 (Figure 3.1), where we added a lightbulb to represent creative thought during the learning process. Then in Chapter 6 (Figure 6.1), we updated the figure so that the model is holding a book, representing a passion for reading and writing through critical thinking. In this chapter, we are focusing on the arts as a path to creative action that connects these aspects of self. The addition of the paintbrush in the HML illustration (see Figure 10.1) implies creative action through the arts. The HML recognizes the arts as a form of communication and expression for young children.

Creativity is the result of an active imagination and the capacity to form mental metaphors, new ideas, and fantasies. Acknowledging the five senses (sight, hearing, taste, touch, and smell) and using them in the learning process enhances imagination. Imagination involves creating an idea or perception that has not yet been formed, such as a dream, story, or image that can be shared with others (Lowenfeld, 1968). Reading and writing are two skills that require imagination to be fully engaged. Young children use their five senses to explore their world, allowing them to become creative, self-aware, and confident. Imagination and creativity are at the core of arts integration in early literacy. Through the arts, young children make sense of their world and communicate their understanding to others. Culture and personal experience are reflected in children's artistic expressions.

Viktor Lowenfeld (1968) describes creative intelligence as being subjective in nature. Lowenfeld believes that children must find the arts media that best express their ideas. The creative act is associated with self-identification and complete involvement in what children create. The child is immersed in creative work, and the result becomes an extension of the self. Teacher guidance during this expressive process is necessary for success. Teachers can dance, sing, play an instrument, act in a play while wearing costumes, paint, sculpt, and draw to become fully engaged in educating young children. Through creative participation, teachers design lessons that are more sensitive to the emerging potential of each child.

Figure 10.1
The Holistic Model of Literacy (HML) with Creative Thought and Action

Because children express ideas in multiple ways, Howard Gardner's (1999a) multiple intelligences theory can guide curriculum development. Imagine a prekindergarten teacher who is reading Dr. Seuss's *ABCs* (1963) to the class. To incorporate Gardner's multiple intelligences theory, the teacher designs the lesson to include movement, visual art, and interpersonal, intrapersonal, and linguistic strategies. The children and teacher start by drawing a variety of lines and shapes with crayons on paper. Then children are given flexible materials (modeling clay, fabric, string) to make lines or shapes to translate into three-dimensional experience and stimulate tactile senses. Any flexible material, such as, yarn, string, clay, or fabric strips, can be used for this activity. The flexible material allows for self-correction and teacher correction. The teacher instructs children to create specific lines and shapes to form letters. While sculpting the letters, children verbally repeat the letter and its sound. Next, the teacher leads children through creative movement exercises in which they form letters using their bodies individually and in small groups. The teacher photographs the activity and posts these photographs in the classroom as a learning resource for children. This lesson connects Gardner's multiple intelligences theory with an arts-integrated literacy lesson and promotes active engagement for cognitive, socioemotional, and physical development.

Children who experience the arts with integrity, sensitivity, and perceptiveness create a deeper understanding of the world around them, and develop insightful abilities to interact with others throughout their everyday lives. Children express their sense of awe and beauty through the arts and discover confidence in their abilities through interaction with caring adults and peers.

 CONSIDER THIS...

Consider how children can express their knowledge in multiple forms. How can you design literacy lessons that integrate dance, dramatic play, music, and visual art as forms of expression?

10-2 Connections between Literacy and the Arts

In early literacy and artistic development, mark making is an important discovery for young children. Once they recognize that their marks symbolize meaning, this empowering realization creates avenues of communication to develop language and writing skills. In literacy development, the prewriting stage is part of this mark making experience. Young children scribble marks with their fingers (finger painting, drawing in the sand) and by holding a writing/drawing implement (crayon, marker, paintbrush). The development of eye–hand motor skills is part of the child's literacy and artistic development. Providing the opportunity for children to engage in mark making with a wide variety of materials is necessary in early literacy (The Department for Children, Schools and Families, 2008).

As children develop their mark making skills, they begin to recognize the marks as a symbol system and alphabetic recognition occurs. As part of the writing and spelling process, children begin to make words by connecting letters (symbols). Often young children think of the alphabet with each letter as a symbol or picture of a particular sound. The relationship between visual symbol making and alphabetic writing is strengthened by allowing children to write and illustrate their ideas, such as creating an illustrated journal entry (Bromley, 2006).

10-2a Emergent Graphic Symbol System

A child's graphic symbol system is born through the visual arts (see Photo 10.4). As young children develop their symbol making system, engaging and responsive activities promote literacy development (for example, drawing a picture about a visit to the park with family and friends). Remember that children are not realistically representing the events, but expressively and artistically representing the events. Concepts of color and space (size and

mark making Scribble marks made with fingers (finger painting, drawing in the sand) and by holding a writing/drawing implement (crayon, marker, paint brush) to encourage the development of eye–hand motor skills and communication meaning.

Photo 10.4 *Visual artist at work*
Susannah Brown

distance relationships) are not the focus for young children, which explains why children may use purple to color grass or draw themselves as the largest person in a family illustration (see Photo 10.5). Children share their thoughts and inspiration for their artistic work nonverbally (smiles, body movements, random sounds, laughter, and exclamations) and verbally (detailed explanations and stories). Caring adults that are receptive to children's expressions understand the importance of this communication process in language development. Teachers and parents should sensitively interact with children during the mark making process and allow time for children to share their thoughts, ideas, and feelings through a variety of expressive forms (Koralek et al., 2015).

10-2b Vocabulary Development in the Arts

Experiences in the arts (visual arts, music, dance, and drama) allow children to communicate their ideas through a broad range of activities. The arts incorporate a variety of elements for children to use when expressing their creativity. The selected elements of dance, drama, music, and visual arts shared in this chapter represent concepts that link to literacy development. The following list includes specific elements that relate to how children learn and use language:

- Visual art allows children to conceptualize and compare perceptions of line, space, value, form, color, texture, and shape (Dow, 1899). These visual elements form the foundation of all artistic visual representations for young children. Understanding the visual art elements and how to combine these elements to emphasize meaning is an important part of a child's artistic and language development.
- Some of the basic elements of music include melody (pitch and timbre), rhythm (basic beat), repetition, and contrast (Andress, 1973). Children explore music by experimenting with these elements to communicate meaning and intent.
- Dance involves the elements of movement, space, time, and energy (National Dance Association, 1990). Because all dance is based upon movement, children enjoy discovering how their bodies can move in space to convey their own thoughts and emotions.

Photo 10.5 *Family and friends at the park on a sunny day, age 4*
Courtesy of the authors

Photo 10.6 *Me and my dog, Champ, age 5*
Courtesy of the authors

■ The elements of drama include space, rhythm, movement, lighting, time, and character (Koster, 2009). Through collaboration, children create and use costumes, scenery, and props during dramatic activities.

There are many different ways of integrating the arts in the literacy curriculum. A wide variety of creative experiences should be a part of every child's life. Children are often inspired by creative learning experiences when they speak, listen, read, and write.

The richness of the literacy experience allows us to express our thoughts through language (written and oral). In language development, the *receptive language* involves listening and reading, and the *expressive language* involves speaking and writing (Devries, 2011). Teachers set the foundation by providing opportunities for young children to draw shapes and lines, and lead children to successful reading and writing through the recognition of the written/drawn symbol. Gentry's *Raising Confident Readers* (2010) emphasizes the importance of learning to draw as part of the process of learning to read and write. From early random scribbles to the correctly formed alphabet, children build upon each experience in their literacy development. According to Durkin (1966), early readers learn to write/draw before they learn to read. Children depend upon prior knowledge and real-world experiences to build their literacy foundation and graphic symbol system (see Photo 10.6).

Photo 10.7 *Young sidewalk chalk artist*

Being artistically literate in our society involves the interpretation of many forms of communication. The four original language arts (reading, writing, speaking, and listening) now include the concepts of viewing and visually representing because of the expansive nature of literacy demands in the 21st century (Kasten, Kristo, & McClure, 2005). Beyond the traditional viewing of regular printed materials such as books, newspapers, and magazines, viewing encompasses meaningful interaction with many forms of media, such as film, computer websites, and blogs, as well as using smartphones, tablets, computers, and other electronic devices. Visually representing involves producing something other than typical written or spoken language as a meaningful response to literature, such as in the visual arts, technology (movies, web page animation), drama, dance, music, or other nonprint media (see Photo 10.7). Reading, listening, and viewing are examples of receptive written language, whereas writing and visually representing are examples of productive written language (Gentry, 2010).

Some ideas to encourage arts integration in the classroom stem from children's interests. For example, young children are often curious about different jobs in their community, such as firefighter, doctor, nurse, or police officer. Inviting community visitors to the classroom (for example, a parent who is a firefighter) can inspire creative work for young children and help them to better understand life skills (see Photo 10.8).

Infusing reading/language arts and the arts through personal and culturally significant issues celebrates the relationship between children and their cultural backgrounds (see Photo 10.9). A deeper and more meaningful understanding of the topic of study is a result of focusing on the issues that evolve from young children's lives.

An overarching theme selected from the children's interests can provide inspiration for creative activity. For example, in a prekindergarten class, children were interested in the theme of kindness and how to show others that you care about them. In class,

Photo 10.8 *A child's response to a visit from a fireman*
Courtesy of the authors

INCLUSION: CHILDREN WITH SPECIAL NEEDS

"The arts are important in learning for all children" (Very Special Arts, 2012, p. 17). Children with special needs bring a variety of learning styles to the classroom, and the arts can support their learning needs (Riccio, Rollins, & Morton, 2003). When planning literacy lessons integrated with the arts for children with special needs, the following questions serve as a guide:

- Can I vary the outcomes of the activity to meet all learning needs?
- What modifications or adaptations are needed in areas such as pacing, group size, physical space, and arts materials?
- Can I include modified arts and literacy activities for parents to allow their child to practice at home?

Think about It

How can you create a lesson that incorporates creative movement for children of varying abilities? For example, children with limited physical movement can use fingers to express rhythm.

Photo 10.9 Child's drawing of a home with dictated sentence (I made bedrooms and lots of people who live inside. The red dots are balls.)

Courtesy of the authors

children created drawings on a long piece of paper illustrating what kindness means to them, and this drawing became a scroll book with teacher guidance. Group projects provide important opportunities for children to interact creatively.

 CONSIDER THIS...

Consider how children can express ideas through the arts, written word, and oral language. For example, children can sing new vocabulary words and spell these words using creative movement (full-body movements to form letters).

10-3 Integration with the Arts

Integrating the arts with literacy opens new avenues of communication for children. To better understand the arts-integrated approach to literacy, it is important to understand teaching and learning perspectives. Arts integration is an integral part of teaching reading and writing for young children. Arts integration is not a sampling of knowledge from different content areas; rather, it is meaningful connection that emphasizes the enduring knowledge inherent in each content or discipline. The study of the arts disciplines contributes to a rich, complex diversity of learning that cannot be matched fully by another discipline. Each arts form has different knowledge domains and expressions of understandings that are unique. There are many different views of arts integration. The various forms of arts integration often overlap, and different terms are used. Some of the arts integration terms are *insertion, multidisciplinary,* and *interdisciplinary.* To better understand and plan arts-integrated curriculum, examples of these three different levels in the continuum of arts integration are included, linking the arts, sciences, and language arts (Anderson, 1995; Bresler, 1995; Krug & Cohen-Evron, 2000).

Insertion refers to adding characteristics of arts disciplines into the curriculum whole. An example of insertion may include a lesson in science and language arts concerning facts about the sun (science content) and a cultural tale about the sun's existence using multicultural children's literature (language arts content), such as *Coyote and the Sky: How the Sun, Moon, and Stars Began* by Emmett Garcia (2006). In the lesson, the classroom teacher inserts visual art examples that depict the sun, such as *Le Soleil* by Vincent van Gogh (1888). The integrity of the science discipline is not disturbed, nor is the language arts focus changed concerning the cultural tale read to the children. The visual examples are merely offered to help children visualize the science concept in a superficial way. After teaching the science lesson, the teacher may show the painting and explain that it was painted by van Gogh in 1888. No other information is offered, nor do the children engage in discussion (art criticism, aesthetics, and art history) about the painting. The children do not paint or draw the sun (art making) to demonstrate understanding of science or language arts information. The focus remains on the science and language arts concepts, not on learning about the visual arts (Irwin & Reynolds, 1995).

Multidisciplinary instruction involves more than one subject area addressing the same theme, but the subjects generally are taught separately. Usually the classroom teacher collaborates with an arts specialist or another teacher to design a thematic unit of study. Multidisciplinary instruction may include learning about marine life in science class and writing a play on the theme of marine life in language arts with the classroom teacher. For language arts, the teacher and children may read books, such as *Dolphins at Daybreak* (Magic Tree House series) by Mary Pope Osborne (1997) or *National Geographic Little Kids First Big Book of the Ocean* by Catherine D. Hughes (2013). The arts specialist works with the children only to create costumes in visual arts class. Although the theme of marine life is addressed in each class, the children must make their own learning connections (Krug & Cohen-Evron, 2000).

Interdisciplinary approaches to arts integration advocate keeping the integrity of each art form. Authentic arts learning goals, as defined by national and state standards, are crucial in this approach. The arts disciplines are connected with other content areas, but a focus remains on arts learning. It is important to note that each possible discipline in an arts-integrated approach has a body of knowledge for study and practice. The integrity of this body of knowledge must be kept intact to promote arts integration practices. Before designing an interdisciplinary (arts-integrated) curriculum, educators should ask several questions, such as the following:

- What is the content to be taught (arts, science, language arts, math, social studies)?
- What is appropriate instruction (teaching strategies)?
- Who provides the instruction (classroom teacher and arts specialists)?
- How will children demonstrate understanding of all content (including arts)?
- How is children's comprehension assessed in all content areas?

arts integration Meaningful connections that emphasize the enduring knowledge inherent in each content or discipline that is taught in and through the arts.

insertion A type of miscue when a word(s) is added to the text.

multidisciplinary Instruction involves more than one subject area addressing the same theme, but the subjects generally are taught separately.

interdisciplinary Authentic arts learning goals, as defined by national and state standards, are connected with other content areas, with respect for each discipline's body of knowledge for study and practice.

Figure 10.2
*Continuum of Arts
Integration*

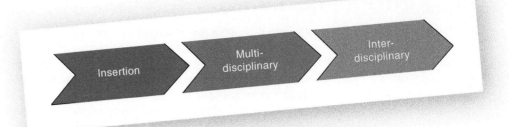

The questions educators ask concerning interdisciplinary instruction should address content, instruction, implementation, and assessment (Bresler, 1995; Roucher & Lovano-Kerr, 1995). An interdisciplinary curriculum example might include collaborative planning between classroom, visual arts, music, and physical education teachers at the elementary school level, focusing on the natural world and the children's sense of place. This interdisciplinary unit of study may include content from science, language arts, visual art, music, and dance. For example, initial planning for a unit began when the children were exploring the school garden, noticing butterflies and caterpillars on specific plants. The classroom teacher taught the life cycle of the butterfly during science class using books such as *National Geographic Kids: Caterpillar to Butterfly* by Laura Marsh (2012) and *From Caterpillar to Butterfly* (Let's Read and Find Out Science series) by Deborah Heiligman (1996). Caterpillars were placed in a screened container with specific plants and displayed in the classroom for children to observe and record data in their science journals. During language arts, the children and teacher discussed ideas about butterflies and wrote poems and short stories about their experiences in the school garden and with the classroom caterpillar display. Different children's books, such as *Butterfly, Butterfly: A Book of Colors* by Petr Horacek (2007), were read aloud by the teacher for group discussion. In visual arts class, the children further explored butterflies using the pop-up book, *In the Butterfly Garden* by Philippe Ug (2015). Children learned about the artist and his work through online research (art history) and discussed the pop-up illustrations (art criticism). Children created drawings while observing butterflies in the school garden and used these drawings in their own pop-up designs. A class pop-up book was made by binding together each child's pop-up illustration. The music and physical education teachers collaborated to create a dance and sound composition that the children performed in the school garden.

Active engagement of young children throughout the learning process is an important part of an arts-integrated approach for literacy development. There are a variety of styles and methods of arts integration, and the teaching process is constantly evolving. The insertion, multidisciplinary, and interdisciplinary approaches fall along a continuum of arts-integration practices that begin with minimal inclusion of the arts and end with a full focus on the arts in curriculum (see Figure 10.2). There are many entry points along this continuum of arts-integration practices. Teachers should consider how in-depth and meaningful interaction in the arts results in expressive demonstration of comprehension when developing arts-integrated literacy curriculum.

For young children, the active engagement that occurs when studying the art forms excites their imaginations. This process of active engagement is another key step to developing early literacy. Through their five senses, young children are engaged in the language arts curriculum. Imagine a class of young children dancing the alphabet or interpreting and creating visual images or sculpting letters of the alphabet with clay. Young children can describe how sounds of musical instruments relate to phonics. Understanding how sound is made through pitch and vibration in a musical instrument and relating this to vocal cords, breathing, and mouth position is enlightening for young children. The arts make the language arts curriculum come alive when designing activities for young children.

When engaging the whole child in the learning process, teachers must address the cognitive, socioemotional, and physical aspects of each child. The "head, heart, and hand" image evokes the concept that we are not filling their minds but rather the children are actively engaged in making connections that provide guidance for their lives. As shown by

Figure 10.3, there are areas of cognition that relate to or overlap the areas of the physical body and socioemotional self. This interrelationship provides excellent learning opportunities and relates to the holistic model of literacy. Creativity is fully engaged when cognitive, socioemotional, and physical parts of self are balanced.

Creativity in the arts is defined through playfulness. "A willingness to play is a sign of caring which in turn leads to trust, community building, and collaborative learning" (Szekely, 1990, p. 6). An example of integrating play into your literacy lesson can involve the concept of lines and line segments in writing the alphabet. The teacher begins by asking the children to imagine a circus, where the teacher is the circus ringmaster (the teacher can wear costumes, a top hat, and a black coat). The amazing stretch-a-line (yarn, cord, rope, etc.) is introduced with a "circus" flair by the ringmaster (teacher). The performer (child) stretches the yarn vertically, horizontally, diagonally, and so on, to demonstrate movement in line segments, which then magically form letters under the teacher's guidance. Children in the audience can draw the line segments during the performance in sketchbooks with crayons (Szekely, 1990). An arts-integrated literacy lesson engages all the senses and encourages participation to connect cognitive, socioemotional, and physical aspects of self.

Figure 10.3
Head, Heart, and Hand Venn Diagram

✔ **CONSIDER THIS...**

Consider how you can integrate the arts more fully into a literacy lesson. If you design a lesson that involves the arts at the insertion level, how can you add to the lesson to reach an interdisciplinary level?

10-4 Artistic Experiences for Early Literacy

In the language arts curriculum, the arts can connect in many areas of teaching and learning. Teachers considering the arts-integration approach toward literacy should represent each discipline with authenticity and integrity (Bresler, 1995). Understanding new vocabulary for each art form promotes integrity during literacy lessons. Vocabulary development is important for young children; therefore, introducing new vocabulary for visual arts, dance, drama, and music is crucial in an arts-integrated lesson. For example, the concept of movement and rhythm in each art form closely relates to reading and writing. There is an underlying energy to reading aloud that is guided by word choice and sentence structure during writing. This energy relates to rhythm and movement in visual images, music, a play, and choreography. Georgia O'Keeffe's paintings of New Mexico's landscapes can provide inspiration for children to explore rhythm and movement in their own natural environment. The children's book, *My Name is Georgia* by Jeanette Winter (2003), provides a look into the artist's life and motivations for painting. Reading children's literature that focuses on artists, dancers, actors, and musicians may inspire children to express their ideas through a variety of arts forms.

In support of arts integration within the American school system, the President's Committee on the Arts and Humanities (2011) published a report, *Reinvesting in Arts Education: Winning America's Future through Creative Schools*, which focused on the importance of children's artistic learning. Arts integration supports student learning, self-expression, and active engagement across the curriculum. Educators should embrace the following recommendations from this report:

1. Build collaboration between different approaches.
2. Develop the field of arts integration.
3. Expand in-school opportunities for teaching artists.

4. Utilize federal and state policies to reinforce the place of arts in K–12 education.
5. Widen the focus of evidence gathering about arts education. (President's Committee on the Arts and Humanities, 2011).

Cooperative learning and collaboration are important in early literacy to support confident readers and writers. For every artistic experience, there are connections between creating, discussing, and studying the arts. The "arts point to and help define meaning, truth, spirit, social values, religion, and other foundations of human culture" (Anderson, 1995, p. 10). Arts learning includes history, arts creation, arts criticism, and aesthetics (Hurwitz & Day, 2001).

Children benefit from studying historical and contemporary artistic works. Arts history includes information about the life of an artist/musician/dancer/actor/author and the time frame for the artistic work, including cultural and historical influences. The experiences children have when interacting with a visual artwork, music (vocal and instrumental), dance, or dramatic selection is guided by the senses. The children's reactions, while appreciating and studying an artistic experience, involve aesthetics (sense of beauty and philosophical value of the arts). What we find to be beautiful or wonderful in the world around us guides our aesthetic sensibilities. Young children easily discern what they like and dislike. This aesthetic sensibility guides them to select certain colored objects, toys, food items, and clothes. The senses guide young children through an aesthetic experience, a sense of awe and inspiration during artistic interaction. "The capacity for aesthetics is a fundamental human characteristic" (Mayesky, 2009, p. 37).

Dewey (1934) supported aesthetics as the foundation of experience. The aesthetic experience involves the physical senses and emotions to create a heightened awareness related to our sense of beauty. Young children experience wonder and delight, and their senses are enlivened, becoming keenly aware of their surroundings during the aesthetic experiences (Dewey, 1934). Providing an open learning environment, in which children can discuss their ideas freely and express their understanding in a variety of ways, promotes aesthetic development for young children. This type of encouraging learning environment allows each child to develop his or her own sense of aesthetics and see the beauty that surrounds us every day.

Having artistic discussions with children is an important part of the creative process. Children should have opportunities to talk about their artwork and the artwork of others. Thoughtful discussions about the arts engage children in the *art criticism model*. Arts criticism helps young children to comprehend and interpret the meaning of the artistic expression. Four basic steps are involved in arts criticism discussions:

1. Description (What do you see in the artistic work?)
2. Analysis (How is the artistic work put together?)
3. Interpretation (What is the artist/musician/dancer/actor saying?)
4. Evaluation (Do you like the artistic work? Why or Why not?)

Throughout the arts criticism process, children learn to think independently and use higher-order thinking skills to apply criteria to their reasoning (Feldman, 1993). This inquiry process promotes analysis and metacognition. Artistic experiences in literacy support a child's creative development. By discussing, studying, experiencing, and creating works of artistic expression, young children communicate their ideas through the arts.

10-4a Creating Books with Children

Bookmaking and storytelling are excellent instructional strategies for young children, especially for English language learners. When children act as authors and illustrators, they create meaning through art and language. Semiotics (Albers, 2007) is the term for this communication of meaning and exploration through the visual and performing arts. Semiotics is the study of how we utilize multiple sign systems (music, visual art, dance, drama, writing, and speaking) to comprehend underlying meanings or messages in text or imagery.

There are several approaches to making books with young children. Children can use their own words, language, and culture, making their learning meaningful and relevant. One way to begin the bookmaking process is to have children draw a series of illustrations. Sentences can be written or dictated for each illustration. Individual stories can be combined

arts history Information about the life of an artist/musician/dancer/actor/author and the time frame including cultural and historical influences for the artistic work.

aesthetics Sense of beauty and philosophical value of the arts.

aesthetic experience A sense of awe and inspiration during artistic interaction.

semiotics The study of how we utilize multiple sign systems (music, visual art, dance, drama, writing, and speaking) to comprehend underlying meanings or messages in text or imagery.

ASSESSING COMPREHENSION SKILLS THROUGH ART CRITICISM

Promoting oral language skills and metacognition is an important part of literacy instruction. Teachers can model the art criticism process to support deeper comprehension of artwork/illustrations. Through discussion guided by the teacher, children can analyze images/artwork using the art criticism model. For assessment purposes, the teacher considers whether or not the child is able to complete each part of the art criticism model and writes anecdotal notes for reflection.

Assessment Guide

Directions: Share a visual of an artwork (not a child's or a classmate's artwork) with a child and ask him or her to use the art criticism model to discuss the artwork. During the discussion, record notes in the appropriate columns.

Art Criticism Process	The child was able to	The child was not able to
Describe the use of: Line Shape Color Texture Space		
Analyze the use of: Balance Symmetry/Asymmetry Emphasis (focus of work)		
Interpretation (What is the story told by the artwork?)		
Evaluation (What does he/she like/dislike about the artwork? Explain why.)		

Think about It

When assessing young children, how can you encourage using new vocabulary to support oral language? For example, an anchor chart listing the art criticism vocabulary can be posted in the classroom. The teacher can refer to the chart and review vocabulary prior to modeling the art criticism process.

❯❯ **Professional Resource Download**

into a class book. Children can learn the different jobs (author, illustrator, editor) to create a book using puppets to role-play during a bookmaking project (see Photo 10.10).

With older children, teachers can emphasize the writing process in a writing workshop format (Calkins, 1986). After brainstorming writing ideas, children can complete a story map (graphic organizer) to plan their stories. A storyboard, which is a series of pages that includes sample illustrations and text, can be used to help children organize and sequence their story. Before illustrating the final drafts, the teacher could have a series of mini-lessons on different styles of artwork based on the work of famous artists, dancers, actors, musicians, and authors, such as Mozart, Monet, Baryshnikov, or Shakespeare. For example, children can learn how to use a hand-painted tissue paper collage in the style of Eric Carle, illustrated in *The Very Hungry Caterpillar* (1969). Pen and ink drawings by Nancy Ekholm Burkert can inspire illustrations that emphasize the characteristics of line, shape, and texture as illustrated in *James and the Giant Peach* by Roald Dahl (1961). Robert Sabuda is well known for his style of pop-up books that capture our imagination through movement as in the redesign of *The Wonderful Wizard of Oz* (2000), originally

storyboard A series of pages that includes sample illustrations and text; can be used to help children organize and sequence their story.

Table 10.1

How to Transform Fairy Tales

1. Change the style from traditional to modern language.

2. Change the details, sequence, or main plot event.

3. Change the time and place (setting), point of view, or characters.

4. Write a sequel to the original story.

5. Change the illustrations.

6. Change the culture (for example, characters, setting, events, language, or dialect).

7. Combine components of different tales.

8. Write the story in a different format, such as a play, poem, readers' theater, or song.

Apply & Reflect

Select a children's book, such as *The Very Lonely Firefly* by Eric Carle (1995). In a group of four create a dramatic interpretation of the story. Create masks or puppets, a poem or song, and a dance sequence (creative movement). Use rhythm instruments to enhance the story. Share your artistic performance with the class.

written by Frank Baum (1900). The whimsical simplicity of Rosemary Wells's illustrations in Ruby & Max (series) promote drawing skills that focus on story sequence.

Another technique for making books with children is creating altered books by reinventing existing books. Children begin with an old book that is no longer used, damaged, or discarded from the school library and use a variety of art materials to change or alter the original book to their artistic design. When creating unique books with children, remember there should be an emphasis on creativity and imagination.

A twist to the altered book is story transformations, which are alternative versions of familiar or traditional folk and fairy tales (Towell & Matanzo, 2010). The teacher could read several different versions of a fairy tale (for example, "Snow White," "The Three Little Pigs," "Little Red Riding Hood," or "Cinderella"). After comparing the different versions, the children write their own versions of fairy tales by changing different components (see Table 10.1).

Photo 10.10 *Illustrator and copy editor puppets for role-playing different careers in the publishing business*
Susannah Brown

PICTURE BOOKS AND WRITING: ACTIVITY FOR PRESERVICE TEACHERS TO DO WITH CHILDREN

Purpose: Practice writing skills using picture books. Children become active readers when asked to visualize or draw about text or when describing and writing about illustrations. Comprehension is improved by involving children through interpretation, prediction, and extension strategies. The wordless picture book, *The Journey* by Aaron Becker (2013), provides opportunities for children to imagine what can happen next. In this book, a young girl takes a journey around the world through her drawings with a red crayon. Good readers associate words with the senses of touch, sight, hearing, smell, and taste to enhance their understanding of text and illustrations. Relating prior experiences to text and illustrations supports comprehension.

Procedure: The teacher shares the cover illustration of *The Journey* to stimulate children's prior knowledge. The children describe what they see in the illustration and associate with personal experiences. Each time the page is turned, the children discuss what they see and predict the story events that will happen next. Because the picture book doesn't include text, the children can write the text or dictate for the teacher to record on the board or chart paper. When viewing the last few illustrations, the children identify the emotional connection between the boy and girl characters. After viewing and discussing the last illustration, the teacher returns to the first pages and asks the children to look more carefully at the illustration. Make sure the children notice the boy in the first illustration and the emotional situations occurring for the girl in the beginning of the story. In small groups, the children will identify how a selected page illustration excites the five senses. Each group writes a sentence or phrase to describe the illustration, which is shared with the whole class. Individually, children can illustrate or create a collage of places they would like to visit during a journey.

Teaching Analysis: Reflective practices are a necessary part of the *literacy assessment cycle* and are key components in preservice preparation and certification such as edTPA. Analyze the strengths and areas of improvement in this lesson idea. Answer the following:

- What is successful?
- What would you change to improve the lesson?
- What did you learn about teaching literacy?

Links: Making connections to technology and developmentally appropriate practices (DAP) supports lesson planning and literacy instruction. Adaptations of this lesson idea are provided through the following:

- **Technology Link:** Children can research a travel destination using online resources. Images and video of travel during vacations can be shared with the class.
- **DAP Link:** Children have opportunities to express their understanding through oral language and visual art.
- **Executive Function Link:** Creative play and active engagement during an interactive read-aloud develop children's self-regulation skills in social settings as reflected in the holistic model of literacy (cognitive, socioemotional, and physical).
- **Classroom Link:** Children ages 0 to 3 can play with small red plastic boats and soft purple feathers (stuffed bird toy) while the adult discusses the illustrations during a cuddle read.
- **Classroom Link:** Children ages 3 to 6 can use plastic boats in a bucket of water or sculpt purple birds using modeling clay and feathers to create their own imaginary journeys.
- **Classroom Link:** Children ages 6 to 9 can write and illustrate an extension of where the boy and girl ride their bicycle built for two (the next adventure).

 CONSIDER THIS...

Consider which type of book you would like to create with children. For example, simple pop-up books use movement to promote reader interaction, and a class big book created by children supports collaboration and teamwork.

10-5 Creativity in Literacy

Creativity involves all parts of the self (cognitive, socioemotional, and physical). Imagination, inspiration, and innovation are derived from experiences and guide the creative process. Children build schema (knowledge concepts) as they practice speaking, reading, and writing while connecting new knowledge to existing knowledge (Piaget, 1969). New experiences and learning scaffold into application, and the creative process continues (Robinson & Aronica, 2015).

altered books Books that are redesigned by using a variety of art materials to change or alter the original book.

schema Each child's unique understandings, knowledge, and interpretation of the world around them based on real-life experiences.

Brain Briefs

BRAIN RESEARCH CONNECTING MUSIC, DANCE, AND LITERACY

A young child's brain retains more information for longer periods of time when learning with music and creative movement. Music and creative movement experiences support the formation of important brain connections that are developed from birth to age 3 (Carlton, 2000). One study found that babies (5 months old) are able to discriminate between and respond to happy and sad musical selections (Flom, Gentile, & Pick 2008). This research supports the inclusion of music and movement to emphasize emotional understanding and develop social understandings.

Think about It

How can teachers help children develop emotional understanding through music and dance? For example, a listening center can be designed that features a variety of multicultural musical selections. Children can draw faces that express the emotion in the music and use whole-body movement to interpret the music. For example, *A Bad Case of the Stripes* by David Shannon (1998) can inspire children to write about their emotions and make connections between music, illustrations, and text. Younger children can use pattern writing and complete the sentence: The music we listened to made me feel _____.

In an arts-integrated approach to teaching and learning, meaningful expression of comprehension is closely aligned with the lesson's objectives. Arts integration involves creativity, imagination, flexibility, and purposive individual and group work, all focusing on the arts form and life connections. Along the way, children develop a deeper understanding of real-life experiences and apply this understanding to their individual literacy development.

Invented writing/spelling is an important part of the process of recognizing that the marks or symbols communicate meaning. Children combine letters using their knowledge of phonics to create words. The emphasis is on communication rather than correct spelling. Invented spelling is part of the spelling development process and is often referred to as letter-name spelling. Remember this process is unique to each child, and all children develop literacy skills at their own rate. This holds true for children's artistic learning as well.

The arts provide a foundation for the visualization system (mental images that emerge during and after reading from the readers' sensory experiences, emotional connections, and prior knowledge) (Keene & Zimmerman, 2007). The visualization system is key in literacy because all experiences are stored in memory and are used later on to formulate words and sentences, both verbally and in writing/reading. All images and experiences are organized in a child's memory, which is used when associating new words in a child's understanding. An example of the close relationship between literacy and artistic development is found in Aliki's *Marianthe's Story: Painted Words and Spoken Memories* (1998), a children's flip book that combines two stories in one and that tells the story of a young girl communicating through her paintings first and then through language. Marianthe, the young girl in the story, describes her first day at school.

Although Marianthe does not speak English, she communicates through her artwork until finally in the second story, *Spoken Memories*, she is able to verbalize her life story for the class. This children's book beautifully illustrates the connection between the arts and literacy.

Artwork that is discussed in class can provide the inspiration for designing small stages to encourage dramatic play. For example, Claude Monet's impressionistic painting of his garden and water lily pond inspired 3-year-old children to create a mini-Monet

visualization system Mental images that emerge during and after reading from the reader's sensory experiences, emotional connections, and prior knowledge.

garden using a shoe box and found objects. Reading *Linnea in Monet's Garden* by Cristina Bjork (1987) is a wonderful literacy connection to this project.

Young children benefit from discussions of their artwork and enjoy explaining their artwork, while the teacher records their responses. One example of this process includes drawing self-portraits and identifying the parts of the body that are illustrated by the child in writing. The child becomes aware of the visual representation as an image depicting the self and identifies the written word with an actual body part. The written word comes alive and the once unrecognized symbols (letters of the alphabet) are imbued with meaning.

Through the use of a variety of teaching and learning approaches, children can develop their language arts skills, such as speaking and visually representing. Through arts integration, teachers can celebrate the cultures and lives of children in the classroom. In today's society, being visually literate is imperative, and the use of technology in the classroom to meet the needs of this visual generation is important.

Communication and comprehension are the goals of literacy, and by carefully planning visually representing activities in their curriculum, teachers can assist children in developing their language arts skills. In addition, using multiple sign systems (different forms of expression) to communicate meaning helps children achieve their learning goals (Harste, Short, & Burke, 1988). Children can represent their understanding through visual art, music, dance, drama, writing, and speaking. The use of multiple sign systems promotes comprehension for diverse learners and broadens children's perspectives. For example, readers can learn to think like writers and writers can learn to think like readers. Authors can learn to think like artists and artists can learn to think like authors. The more children learn to think from different perspectives, the better they will be able to communicate and comprehend their world.

 CONSIDER THIS…

> Consider how different children's literature can focus a lesson toward arts integration. For example, reading books that feature artists as main characters can encourage modeling creative behaviors. A child may want to play the piano after reading *Who Was Wolfgang Amadeus Mozart?* by Carrie McDonough (2003).

10-6 Literacy Strategies and Practices for Arts Integration

Allowing children to share who they are and letting them experience the feeling of praise and acceptance gives them the incentive to continue developing their creative skills. Providing a safe learning environment with a variety of arts media enhances literacy development. Children should be able to explore different literacy centers depending upon their decisions for creative expression. A wide variety of materials should be available for children to select as described by James L. Hymes (1989), an early childhood researcher and advocate:

> A classroom for young children often looks for all the world like an artist's studio. The products that come out are children's products, but the process that goes on is the artist's process. The rich availability of easels, paints, brushes, paper, clay, and collage materials helps young children live like artists. (Hymes, 1989, p. 81).

Young children benefit from varied sensory experiences such as visiting the beach, swimming, and building sand castles. A stimulating environment beyond the classroom nurtures children's cognitive, socioemotional, and physical parts of self.

Table 10.2 offers artistic activities and literacy strategies related to arts integration for three age groups (0 to 3, 3 to 6, and 6 to 9). These strategies and practices reflect the parts of self that are integral to literacy development. Through creative action, children develop their existing knowledge to create new understandings.

multiple sign systems Different forms of expression to communicate meaning and to help children achieve their learning goals.

Table 10.2	Literacy Strategies and Practices Supporting Arts Integration	

Age Groups	Cognitive	Socioemotional
0 to 3	Use large bold lines and shapes to stimulate visual attention. Provide mark making experiences using safe textural materials (sand, clay, finger paint, shaving cream, and crayons). Use soft, pliable materials such as dough and fabric to sculpt objects. Discuss and question before, during, and after creative activities.	Make a variety of sounds to indicate emotion: laughter, giggles, gurgles, pops, gasps, and oohs/ahs related to the story line. Select and play music that relates to the emotion of the story. Exaggerate body gestures to emphasize emotion of characters.
3 to 6	Create artwork that represents a new ending to a story. Draw, paint, or sculpt a new character for a well-known story. Describe reasons why specific art media were selected. Express why an object, image, or performance is beautiful. Draw a line that interprets a dance or music selection.	Express opinions of their artwork and the artwork of others. Use vocalizations to depict emotions during storytelling. Create and use masks to depict different characters' emotions. Create a painting using colors that represent your emotions. Create a painting using dancing feet responding to music.
6 to 9	Critique artworks based upon the elements (arts vocabulary) using the arts criticism model: description, analysis, interpretation, and evaluation). Design a newspaper/ brochure with photographs of important news. Draw a cartoon illustrating a biography. Compare and contrast two books with different illustrators. Predict the story looking only at the illustrations. Create a photo collage illustrating text. Film a mini-movie that focuses on a character in the story.	Interview a musician/artist/actor/dancer, and share their motivation and inspiration with the class. Make a book that flips, pops, twists, or flies (moveable books) to represent a character's emotions. Use photography to depict various emotions (portraits). Discuss artwork and describe how an ant would feel when crawling through the art and what would they see (or an elephant, bird, or worm). Draw symbols representing the emotions of the characters and rewrite the story only using the drawn symbols (no text). Dance an emotional interpretation of a poem, song, or story.

Physical	Children's Books	Family Involvement
Clap hands/feet to a beat in poetry or song. Create physical response to a pattern of sound with repetition. Grasp simple instruments such as rattles, bells. and tambourines to create sound. Use puppetry, stuffed animals, props, facial expressions, and large gestures to dramatize a story and emphasize meaning. Develop small and large motor skills during movement that illustrates words or letters.	*Art for Baby* by Reed Business Information, Reed Elsevier Inc. *I Am an Artist* by P. L. Collins *Dance!* by Bill Jones and Susan Kuklin *Let's Be Animals* by Ann Warren Turner *Giraffes Can't Dance* by Giles Andreae *Baby Beluga* by Raffi	Family members and children create and use an area for artistic exploration that includes art materials, musical instruments (harmonica, tambourine, rattles, etc.), costumes (hats, scarves, colorful clothes), and props (puppets, stuffed animals). Move up/down/low/high/ big/small/turn around in front of a mirror. Act out nursery rhymes, dramatic play with props. Visit a children's museum to encourage sensory experiences.
Create and perform sound patterns/sound stories that illustrate the meaning, characters, settings, and events (e.g., "Old MacDonald Had a Farm"). Choreograph a simple movement sequence using props related to the text. Perform a dramatic scene that depicts the climax of the story using props. In a small group form statues or a tableau that depicts a scene in the story. Play an instrument that represents a descriptive word or phrase in text. Select an object in the class to create sound related to text.	*Roy Lichtenstein's ABC* by Bob Adelman *Annie's Gifts* by A. S. Medearis *Beautiful OOPS!* by Barney Saltzberg *A Day with No Crayons* by Elizabeth Rusch *When a Line Bends . . . A Shape Begins* by Rhonda Gowler Greene *How Can You Dance?* by Rick Walton	Write and perform a play of a favorite story, sing songs, and dance to music. Model writing name poems, and read during a family poetry slam. Hide an object (child) and describe the object and the hiding place for a parent to find it (Treasure Hunt). Use clay to model a character in the story and use during dramatic retelling of story. Draw shapes, letters, and numbers with chalk outside and read concept books (counting/ABCs/colors/shapes).
Create and perform a sound poem that depicts a current event. Choreograph a dance that uses elements of space (up/down/low/high), time (long/short), and repetition with pattern/sequence to depict a scene in a story or play. Create moveable artwork (pin wheels, sculpture with wheels). Compose and perform a musical rendition of a well-known story or poem. Connect literary genres with musical genres, such as a fable told as a rap song or a sonnet sung as an opera. Pantomime what will happen next in a story or current event. Write a script for a play using folktales or other literature as inspiration and cast classmates for the performance. Compare how different instruments are played (strings, brass, percussion). Conduct a musical selection, and write about the experience.	*Story Painter: The Life of Jacob Lawrence* by John Duggleby *Ludwig van Beethoven* (Getting to Know the World's Greatest Composers and Artists Series) by Mike Venezia *Vincent Van Gogh: Sunflowers and Swirly Stars* by Joan Holub *Stories of Women Composers for Young Musicians* by Catherine W. Kendall *Henri Matisse: Drawing with Scissors* by Jane O'Connor *Alvin Ailey* by Andrea Davis Pinkney and Brian Pinkney	Create a collaborative mural (painting or collage). Select favorite family photos and write short stories about the people and events featured. Watch family videos and write funny captions or jokes. Write and perform a play to celebrate a holiday or family tradition. Visit an art museum, performing arts center, and musical concert, and discuss ideas about what was seen. Create a shared drawing where the beginning is covered up with a blank sheet of paper. Each person adds to it, covers the new drawing, continues to the next person, and at the end the drawing is revealed.

Summary

Through arts integration in literacy lessons, young children have unique opportunities for creative expression. In this chapter, we discussed effective ways of teaching literacy through the arts. Children's understanding is enhanced through artistic and creative expression. Because children are unique individuals, teaching strategies need to appeal to diverse learning styles. To understand the arts and early literacy connections, emphasis should be placed on a process-based approach to promote exploration and active engagement. Teachers should provide opportunities for children to use their varied intelligences (Gardner, 1999a). Artistic experiences for early literacy, such as making artistic books, allow children to apply creativity. The artistic environment supports the holistic model of literacy (HML) through development of the cognitive, socioemotional, and physical parts of self. A passion for reading and writing is supported when children are actively engaged. The arts provide an avenue for creativity and expression, leading children to a lifelong love of literacy.

Chapter Exercises

1. Design an arts-integrated activity that celebrates children's imaginative and creative interpretation of a favorite children's book. Share your idea with a partner and expand the arts activities to include different forms of expression (dance, drama, music, and visual arts).
2. Plan a classroom center that encourages children's meaningful mark making experiences using a variety of media (for example, drawing, sculpting, and using fiber and textiles). Brainstorm with a partner how to share children's mark making success with peers, other teachers/classes/school, and family members.
3. Select a literacy skill (writing letters/words/sentences) and connect an arts activity that supports active engagement. Review activities with a small group of peers and identify types of arts integration (insertion, multidisciplinary, interdisciplinary) represented. Discuss how to expand activities to reach the interdisciplinary level of arts integration.
4. Write a mini-lesson that includes arts making and arts history activities. Share with a partner and consider integrating arts criticism and aesthetics activities to fully engage young children with the arts form (dance, drama, music, and visual arts) you selected.
5. Create a diorama using a shoe box and various art materials depicting a scene from a selected text (narrative or informational). Present information from the text to the class using your diorama to help students visualize the content.

Teacher Toolbox

MUSIC AND CHILDREN'S LITERATURE: TEACHING SENTENCE FLUENCY

Appropriate for Ages 4 to 9

Children's literature that features artists, musicians, dancers, and actors encourages children to be creative. Music can be integrated into a literacy lesson on sentence fluency using the book *Charlie Parker Played Be Bop* by Chris Raschka (1992). Children can imagine a musical instrument that they would like to play and write words associated with that instrument. Using a photograph of themselves, the children can collage pictures printed from online sources of their selected musical instruments to create illustrations to inspire the writing process. Rhymes and musical sound words are repeated throughout the book. *"Lollipop, Boomba, boomba, Bus stop. ZZnnzznn. Boppitty, bibbitty, bop. BANG!"* (pp. 11–16). Children can experiment making their own sound words to create rhymes about their musical instrument. Starting with their first and last names, children can write sentences about themselves playing the instrument and the different sounds it makes. Before sharing their sentences with a partner, children can use the sentence fluency checklist.

SENTENCE FLUENCY CHECKLIST

Did I use different words to start my sentences?
Did I construct my sentences differently?
Are my sentences different lengths?
Did I read my sentences aloud to check how they sound?

Adapted from Culham (2008).

Key Terms and Concepts

aesthetic experience	graphic symbol system	multiple sign systems
aesthetics	imagination	schema
altered books	insertion	semiotics
arts	interdisciplinary	storyboard
arts history	mark making	visualization system
arts integration	multidisciplinary	

Appendix: Integrated Lesson Plans

The following five sample lesson plans use the standards found in the Common Core State Standards for English Language Arts (CCSS), the National Association for the Education of Young Children (NAEYC), and the National Core Arts Standards (NCAS). We understand that each state has developed standards to guide teachers in lesson planning. We recommend that teachers use the state standards as required by their respective school districts to guide their lessons. Preservice teachers can use these five sample lesson plans as inspiration for developing their own future classroom lessons. **Developmentally appropriate practices (DAP)** are featured in these sample lesson plans and can be adapted for all children (birth to age 9). Each lesson provides opportunities and activities for teaching reading and writing skills through children's literature and artistic expression.

Lesson 1

Accepting Diversity and Self-Identity

Purpose

Children learn to read and write easily using diverse learning styles and active engagement. Imagination, creativity, and symbolism guide children to comprehend the emotional meaning embedded in text.

Literature Link

The Giving Tree by Shel Silverstein

Standards

Common Core State Standards for English Language Arts
Reading Standards for Literature K–5
Key Ideas and Details
Grade 3

3. Describe characters in a story (for example, their traits, motivations, or feelings), and explain how their actions contribute to the sequences of events.

The National Association for the Education of Young Children
NAEYC Early Childhood Program Standards and Accreditation Criteria

1. Relationships

    1.D.01 Indicator b)—Evidence for building positive self-identity and valuing differences includes materials and books that portray children as unique individuals and show different cultures, ethnicities, and backgrounds.

2. A Curriculum: Essential Characteristics

    2.A.1 1 and 12—Play is characterized by children's active engagement and enjoyment and their ability to determine how the activity is carried out. Teaching staff are expected to encourage and facilitate active play

involving physical movement as well as pretend or dramatic play. Children are expected to have opportunities to play individually and with peers.

2.D.07—Dramatic play props (telephones, dolls, clothes), puppets, flannel boards, language board games, and small animal figures are examples of materials that promote discussion when used.

National Core Arts Standards
Connecting
Anchor Standard 10: Synthesize and relate knowledge and personal experiences to make art.

Lesson Grade Level

This lesson is appropriate for third graders as it focuses on reading, comprehension, spelling, writing, and arts skills. This lesson can be modified for different age groups.

Suggested Time Frame for Lesson

This lesson may be completed over four days with 35-minute sessions each day.

Objectives

- Students will listen to *The Giving Tree* by Shel Silverstein as read by the teacher.
- Students will identify the main characters of the story and explain verbally the beginning, middle, and end of the story.
- Students will create costumes and scenery depicting the story.
- Students will dramatically act out the actions of the story using character voices, full body movements, and costumes.
- Students will use creative movement while the teacher is reading of the story acting out the characters.
- Students will write a new story including beginning, middle, and end paragraphs concerning the theme of respect and caring for others.

Instructional Activities

Day One: 35-minute session
1. The teacher begins the lesson by reading the book, *The Giving Tree* by Shel Silverstein.
2. The students identify the main characters of the story; the beginning, middle, and end of the story; and word choice, word patterns, and emotions of the characters of the story as depicted through the illustrations.
3. The students write down all the aspects of the story that are identified on a chart for reference throughout the lesson.

Day Two: 35-minute session
1. Students create sketches of costumes and scenery.
2. Children brainstorm in small groups about materials that could be used, such as paper, fabric, and recycled items. As directed by the teacher, students create the costumes and scenery.
3. The teacher reads the story aloud while the students act out the story in costume using full body movements.

Day Three: 35-minute session
1. The students brainstorm about story lines concerning respect and caring. Students begin to write their own stories based upon the theme. Students organize their ideas using graphic organizers (webs) for the beginning, middle, and end of their stories. They list the traits of each character and sketch a picture of each character.
2. The students write paragraphs for the beginning, middle, and end of their stories. These paragraphs are edited for word choice and sentence fluency.

3. After revision, the students share their stories in small groups. Each group of students provides feedback to improve the story using a worksheet provided by the teacher concerning word choice, word patterns, sequence, and theme. The teacher meets with students to review and revise their stories.
4. After final editing, the students write the final neat copy of their stories.

Day Four: 35-minute session

1. Students read their stories aloud to the class.
2. The teacher asks them to make connections between each story and the central theme.
   - What is the same about *The Giving Tree* and the student's story?
   - What is different?
   - Identify the main character in the story.
   - Explain the events in the beginning, middle, and end of the story.
3. The final written copies can be displayed on a bulletin board along with photographs of the students in costume during the dramatic play.

Assessment of Student Learning

The teacher assesses student learning informally throughout the lesson. While the students are sketching and creating costumes and scenery, writing, and participating in the dramatic play, the teacher asks each student questions to assess comprehension.

The following simple checklist provides a guide for teachers to assess each student:

Criteria	Satisfactory	Unsatisfactory
The student identifies the main characters of the story.	_____	_____
The student identifies the beginning, middle, and end of the story.	_____	_____
The student created costumes and scenery.	_____	_____
The student participated in the dramatic activity.	_____	_____
The student brainstormed ideas using graphic organizers.	_____	_____
The student drafted a first copy of the story and used peer and teacher feedback to revise the story.	_____	_____
The student completed final editing and wrote a final neat copy of the story.	_____	_____
The student read the story aloud to the class.	_____	_____

Sample List of Supplies

- *The Giving Tree* by Shel Silverstein
- Chart paper and markers for the teacher
- Paper, various types for student artwork
- Crayons and colored pencils
- Fabric
- Recycled items, such as plastic bottles, package wrapping, boxes

Resources

Silverstein, S. (1964). *The Giving Tree*. New York: HarperCollins.

Summary

This sample lesson plan provides children with the opportunity to demonstrate knowledge and comprehension in a variety of ways. All children should be actively engaged in the lesson. There may be children in your classroom who are more successful at the dramatic activity than the drawing activity or writing activity. By varying your teaching approach, you are allowing children to succeed depending upon their strengths and needs.

Planting the Seeds of Literacy

Purpose

Young children learn through their five senses (sight, hearing, taste, touch, and smell). The language experience approach (LEA) is important as children learn to read through their own words. During their experiences children access their own personal vocabulary that is meaningful and relevant to their lives.

Literature Link

Johnny Appleseed by Steven Kellogg

Standards

Common Core State Standards for English Language Arts
Reading Standards for Literature K–5
Integration of Knowledge and Ideas
Kindergarten

7. With prompting and support, describe the relationship between illustrations and the story in which they appear (for example, what moment in a story an illustration depicts).

The National Association for the Education of Young Children
NAEYC Early Childhood Program Standards and Accreditation Criteria

1. Relationships

   1.D.01 Indicator b)—Evidence for building positive self-identity and valuing differences includes materials and books that portray children as unique individuals and show different cultures, ethnicities, and backgrounds.

2. A Curriculum: Essential Characteristics

   2.A.1 1 and 12—Play is characterized by children's active engagement and enjoyment and their ability to determine how the activity is carried out. Teaching staff are expected to encourage and facilitate active play involving physical movement as well as pretend or dramatic play. Children are expected to have opportunities to play individually and with peers.

National Core Arts Standards
Creating
Anchor Standard 1: Generate and conceptualize artistic ideas and work.
Anchor Standard 3: Refine and complete artistic work.

Lesson Grade Level

This lesson is appropriate for preK and kindergarten children as it focuses on reading aloud, prereading and reading skills, storytelling, comprehension, prewriting and early writing skills, and arts skills. This lesson can be modified for different age groups.

Suggested Time Frame for Lesson

This lesson may be completed over two days with 35-minute sessions each day.

Objectives

- Students will listen to *Johnny Appleseed* by Steven Kellogg as read by the teacher.
- Students will identify the main character of the story and explain verbally the beginning, middle, and end of the story.

- Students will dictate the story in their own words for the teacher to write on sentence strips.
- Students will sing along in a group *Rain Makes Applesauce* by Julian Scheer.
- Students will help make applesauce as a class.
- Students will plant apple seeds and act out the movements of Johnny Appleseed from the story.
- Students will illustrate their favorite part of the story.

Instructional Activities

Day One: 35-minute session

1. The teacher begins the lesson with a sensory activity. Each student is given a felt bag (touch bag) with an apple inside. The students are not allowed to look inside the bag, but instead use their sense of touch to figure out the mystery object. Ask the students to verbalize what they think is inside their bags. When they guess the object is an apple, have the students visualize the color and kind of apple in their bags. Next, they close their eyes as they are asked to smell a freshly cut apple. Ask them what this smell reminds them of: Autumn, apple pie, apple slices with caramel sauce, or spending time with Grandma baking are possible answers. Finally, let the students look at their apples inside the bag. Have the children notice the differences in their apples. Make a list of the colors, types, and shapes. Make a list of the descriptive words for later use.

2. The teacher introduces *Johnny Appleseed* by Steven Kellogg by taking a picture walk through the book as the students make predictions about the story. The teacher reads the book aloud to the class. Next, the students identify the main characters of the story, the beginning, middle, and end of the story, word choice, word patterns, and emotions of the characters of the story as depicted through the illustrations. The teacher records their responses on a chart. In their own words, the students dictate to the teacher what the story is about. The teacher reminds the students to use their descriptive apple words. The teacher then writes students' exact words on sentence strips. Together the students and teacher read aloud the sentence strips. Next, students are selected to read aloud their own words on the sentence strips. The sentences will become part of the display board for student use.

3. The students gather props to use in re-creating the story. The teacher reads the story aloud while the students act out the story using the props, assuming the role of Johnny Appleseed and improvising using full body movements.

Day Two: 35-minute session

1. The teacher reviews the book by showing the students the illustrations and asking comprehension questions. The students work at their tables and illustrate their favorite part of the story. The illustrations are shared and students make positive comments using their visual art vocabulary about each other's artwork. The illustrations are displayed in the class along with the sentence strips. (Note: Students can create a class book.) An alternative to this would be to have the students draw their apples from the beginning of the lesson. Students could also cut apples from construction paper and use a hole punch to create wormholes in their apples. A pipe cleaner representing the worm can be inserted into the hole.

2. The teacher guides the students back to the whole group. The teacher introduces the book and song "Rain Makes Applesauce," by Julian Scheer. The students sing along with the teacher. The teacher emphasizes the repetitive parts of the song (chorus) for all to sing.

> *Oh, you're just talking silly talk*
> *Oh, you're just talking silly talk*
> *I know I'm talking silly talk . . . But*
> *Rain makes applesauce!*

3. Next the students make applesauce. Allow each child to do some part of this recipe (wash apples, pour in an ingredient, and so on), and ensure that adequate supervision is given during cooking with young children. Here is a sample recipe for applesauce:

> *Recipe:* In a 2-quart saucepan over medium heat, combine *6 cups of apples*—about 4 to 5 medium apples (washed, peeled, cored, and chopped—note: Students love to use the apple peeler, which has a hand crank on the side.), *3/4 cup water or apple juice/cider*, *1/8 teaspoon ground cinnamon* (optional), and *1/8 teaspoon ground cloves* (optional). Bring to a boil, reduce heat, and simmer 10 minutes. Stir in *1/2 cup sugar* (optional), and simmer 5 more minutes. Makes about 8 child-size servings. Serve and enjoy.

4. Students can save the seeds from the process and plant the seeds for future apple trees. During the closure the teacher can ask the following questions:
   - What was your favorite part of the lesson?
   - What did Johnny Appleseed do in the story? Beginning? Middle? End?
   - Did Johnny Appleseed help anyone in the story?
   - What can we do to help others?

Assessment of Student Learning

The teacher assesses student learning informally throughout the lesson. While the students are illustrating, singing, reading, and participating in the dramatic play, the teacher asks each student questions to assess comprehension.

The following simple checklist provides a guide for teachers to assess each student:

Criteria	Satisfactory	Unsatisfactory
The student participates in the touch and smell activity.	_____	_____
The student brainstorms descriptive words about apples.	_____	_____
The student identifies the main characters of the story.	_____	_____
The student identifies the beginning, middle, and end of the story.	_____	_____
The student creates at least one sentence strip (dictated to the teacher).	_____	_____
The student created illustrations of their favorite part of the story.	_____	_____
The student participated in the dramatic activity.	_____	_____
The student sang aloud with the group.	_____	_____
The student participated in making applesauce.	_____	_____

Sample List of Supplies

- Chart paper and markers for teacher
- Felt bags or touch bags
- Apples
- Sentences strips for teacher
- *Johnny Appleseed* by Steven Kellogg
- Props for story retelling, such as hats, bags, and costumes
- Paper and crayons for children
- Songbook *Rain Makes Applesauce*, by Julian Scheer
- Knife, cooking pot, measuring cup, and microwave or hot plate for teacher to cook applesauce
- Cooking ingredients for applesauce
- Plates, bowls, and plastic spoons for children to eat applesauce

Resources

Aliki, A. (1963). *The Story of Johnny Appleseed*. New York: The Trumpet Club,
Kellogg, S. (1988). *Johnny Appleseed*. New York: Scholastic, Inc.
Lindbergh, R. (1990). *Johnny Appleseed*. Boston, MA: Little, Brown & Co.
Gibbons, G. (1984). *The Seasons of Arnold's Apple Tree*. New York: Harcourt Brace Jovanovich.
Scheer, J. (1985). *Rain Makes Applesauce*. New York: Holiday House.

Summary

This lesson plan sample provides students with the opportunity to demonstrate knowledge and comprehension through music, reading, writing, dramatic play, group discussion, sensory experiences, and visual art. Children benefit from diverse learning strategies in a caring classroom environment.

Lesson 3

Expressing Ideas and Connecting with Others

Purpose

Young children learn through dramatic retelling of narratives, which promotes comprehension. Modeling the experiences featured in the text supports schema building and relates text to real-world application. During read-aloud activities, children relate vocabulary to meaningful and relevant personal experiences.

Literature Link

Mouse Paint by Ellen Stoll Walsh

Standards

Common Core State Standards for English Language Arts
Reading Standards for Literature K–5
Key Ideas and Details
Kindergarten
  2. With prompting and support, identify characters, settings, and major events in a story.
Range of Reading and Level of Text Complexity
  10. Actively engage in group reading activities with purpose and understanding.

The National Association for the Education of Young Children
NAEYC Early Childhood Program Standards and Accreditation Criteria
  1. Relationships
      1.D.01 Indicator b)—Evidence for building positive self-identity and valuing differences includes materials and books that portray children as unique individuals and show different cultures, ethnicities, and backgrounds.
  2. A Curriculum: Essential Characteristics
      2.A.1 1 and 12—Play is characterized by children's active engagement and enjoyment and their ability to determine how the activity is carried out. Teaching staff are expected to encourage and facilitate active play

involving physical movement as well as pretend or dramatic play. Children are expected to have opportunities to play individually and with peers.

2.D.07—Dramatic play props (telephones, dolls, clothes), puppets, flannel boards, language board games, and small animal figures are examples of materials that promote discussion when used.

3. Early Literacy

    2.E. Early Literacy

    2.E.01 and 02—Evidence of each type of book listed (picture books, wordless books, and books with rhymes) must be seen.

    "Wordless" books include books with few words in which information or narrative is conveyed primarily through imagery. Books, songs, and so on, should be linked to concrete objects and direct experiences in the home or learning environment.

National Standards for Arts Education
Presenting
Anchor Standard 6: Convey meaning through the presentation of artistic work.

Lesson Grade Level

This lesson is appropriate for pre-K, kindergarten, and first-grade children as it focuses on early reading, comprehension, and arts skills. This lesson can be modified for different age groups.

Suggested Time Frame for Lesson

This lesson may be completed over two days with 35-minute sessions each day.

Objectives

- Students will listen to *Mouse Paint* by Ellen Stoll Walsh as read by the teacher.
- Students will identify the main characters of the story and explain verbally the beginning, middle, and end of the story.
- Students will dramatically act out the actions of the story using character voices, full body movements, and puppets.
- Students will use creative movement during the initial reading by the teacher (with teacher's guidance), the dramatic retelling of the story, and while singing the primary and secondary color song.
- Students will sing along with others a song about primary and secondary colors.
- Students will mix primary colors to create secondary colors using tempera paint.
- Students will create a tempera painting using the primary and secondary colors.
- Students will identify one connection between the story and the arts forms.

Instructional Activities

Day One: 35-minute session

1. The teacher begins the lesson by introducing the book, *Mouse Paint* by Ellen Stoll Walsh. The students and teacher complete a picture walk through the story, while the students identify the main characters of the story, the beginning, middle, and end of the story, the primary and secondary colors, creative movement that occurs in the story, and emotions of the characters of the story as depicted through the illustrations. The teacher writes down all the aspects of the story that the children identified on a chart for reference throughout the lesson.

2. Next the teacher reads through the story while showing the pictures to the students. During the reading, the teacher indicates to the children which physical movement to re-create (hopping into the puddle, dancing around to mix the colors, washing in the water bowl, and so on). The teacher emphasized voice changes for various characters in the story depending upon the emotions reflected in the illustrations.

3. The teacher divides the students into groups of four and gives three students a mouse puppet and one student a cat puppet. The mouse characters have a white mouse puppet, a fully colored mouse puppet (primary colors), and a secondary/primary colored mouse puppet to match the story line. The teacher will indicate through the story line which puppet is to be used. The teacher reads the story aloud while the collaborative groups act out the story in sequence with the puppets and full body movements. When each mouse has a story line, the teacher directs the students to speak aloud in character voice. After the reenactment of the story, the teacher asks each group to identify the main characters and the beginning, middle, and end of the story. The teacher collects the puppets and brings the students back for a whole group closure.

Day Two: 35-minute session

1. The teacher has three clear cups filled with watercolor paint (red, yellow, blue) and three empty clear cups. The teacher sings the primary and secondary color song while mixing the colors to demonstrate the color changes that occur.

> ### *The Primary and Secondary Color Song*
> (To the tune of *Three Blind Mice*)
>
> *Red, Yellow, Blue*
> *Red, Yellow, Blue*
> *We are the primary colors*
> *We make all the other colors*
> *We're Red, Yellow, Blue*
> *Red, Yellow, Blue*
> *Orange, Green, Purple*
> *Orange, Green, Purple*
> *We are the secondary colors*
> *We are made from primary colors,*
> *We're Orange, Green, Purple*
> *Orange, Green, Purple*

After teaching the song, the teacher divides the students into groups of six. Students hold construction paper cards of the primary and secondary colors. While singing the song, the students hold their cards up to indicate whether the colors they are holding are primary or secondary.

2. The teacher dismisses the students to their tables and gives each student a paper plate with the primary colors, brushes, and water containers. The students, wearing smocks, begin to mix the primary colors to create the secondary colors on the paper plate.

3. The students create paintings using the mixed colors.

4. The teacher guides the cleanup procedures and brings the students back to whole group for closure. The teacher asks the students to make connections between the activities in the lesson.
   - What was the same about using the puppets and when you were painting?
   - What was the same about the creative movement and singing the song while using the color cards?
   - What was the storybook about?
   - Were any of the activities about the same ideas? Which ones?

The teacher allows the students to share their paintings with the class while explaining the colors they used and the subject matter of the painting.

Assessment of Student Learning

The teacher assesses student learning informally throughout the lesson. While the students are painting their pictures, the teacher checks to see if each student understands how to mix primary colors to make secondary colors and asks each student questions to assess comprehension.

The following simple checklist provides a guide for teachers to assess each student:

Criteria	Satisfactory	Unsatisfactory
The student identifies the main characters of the story.	_____	_____
The student identifies the beginning, middle, and end of the story.	_____	_____
The student was able to creatively move to the story line during the reading.	_____	_____
The student participated in the puppetry activity.	_____	_____
The student participated in the singing activity.	_____	_____
The student identifies primary and secondary colors.	_____	_____

Sample List of Supplies

- Chart paper and markers for teacher to record key ideas and details
- *Mouse Paint* by Ellen Stoll Walsh
- Mouse stick puppets (for each group to retell the story)
- Paper (suitable for tempera painting)
- Painting aprons/smocks/old T-shirts
- Tempera paint (red, yellow, blue), brushes, small water cups, paper plates (for color mixing palette), paper towels/sponges for cleanup

Students will need to wash their hands after painting so plan accordingly.

Resources

Stoll Walsh, E. (1995). *Mouse Paint.* New York, NY: Harcourt, Inc.

Summary

Teaching strategies should appeal to diverse students and learning styles. The lesson plan provides students with opportunities to demonstrate their knowledge and comprehension in a variety of ways. There may be children in your classroom that are more successful at the dramatic activity than the painting activity. The concept of color mixing remains the same, but the demonstration of comprehension is different. Integrating the arts with literacy is a powerful tool for creative, cognitive, socioemotional, and physical growth and development.

Lesson 4

Exploring Word Study

Purpose

Children are motivated to read chapter books through the imaginative adventures of *Henry and Mudge.* Word study promotes phonics and decoding of unknown words. Children learn strategies to unlock new words and become independent readers. Dramatic play and visual art activities guide children to explore story elements. Phonics skills are embedded throughout the lesson.

Literature Link

Henry and Mudge by Cynthia Rylant

Standards

Common Core State Standards for English Language Arts
Reading Standards for Literature K–5
Integration of Knowledge and Ideas
First Grade

7. Use illustrations and details in a story to describe its characters, setting, or events.

Second Grade

7. Use information gained from the illustrations and words in a print or digital text to demonstrate understanding of its characters, setting, or plot.

Third Grade

7. Explain how specific aspects of a text's illustrations contribute to what is conveyed by the words in a story (for example, create mood, emphasize aspects of a character or setting).

The National Association for the Education of Young Children
NAEYC Early Childhood Program Standards and Accreditation Criteria

1. Relationships

   1.D.01 Indicator b)—Evidence for building positive self-identity and valuing differences includes materials and books that portray children as unique individuals and show different cultures, ethnicities, and backgrounds.

2. A Curriculum: Essential Characteristics

   2.A.1 1 and 12—Play is characterized by children's active engagement and enjoyment and their ability to determine how the activity is carried out. Teaching staff are expected to encourage and facilitate active play involving physical movement as well as pretend or dramatic play. Children are expected to have opportunities to play individually and with peers.

   2.D.07—Dramatic play props (telephones, dolls, clothes), puppets, flannel boards, language board games, and small animal figures are examples of materials that promote discussion when used.

National Core Arts Standards
Creating
Anchor Standard 1: Generate and conceptualize artistic ideas and work.

Lesson Grade Level

This lesson is appropriate for first through third graders as it focuses on reading, word identification, and word sort skills, and arts skills. This lesson can be modified for different age groups.

Suggested Time Frame for Lesson

This lesson may be completed in a one-hour session.

Objectives

- Students will read a chapter book, *Henry and Mudge* by Cynthia Rylant, independently and as a group read-aloud.
- Students will identify the main characters of the story and predict what the story is about through the illustrations.
- Students will identify high-frequency words and unfamiliar words in the book.
- Students will identify word patterns, silent "e" letter, syllables, and meaning of the selected words from the book.
- Students will draw a comic strip that explains a selected word.
- Students will act out the characters of a selected comic strip with a small group of peers.

Instructional Activities

1. The teacher begins the lesson by introducing the book, *Henry and Mudge: The First Book* by Cynthia Rylant (Simon & Schuster, 1996). This delightful series captures an adventurous friendship of a boy and his dog. The teacher will start with a picture walk through the first chapter, asking the students to predict what the story is about and identifying the main characters. Students will then read a chapter on their own while the teacher circulates to check comprehension individually. Next, the students will practice by reading aloud the chapter by sections, allowing each child to have a chance to read aloud a few sentences. While reading, the teacher will identify high-frequency (sight words) words and unfamiliar words, which will be included on the class word wall. While reviewing the list of words, the teacher asks students to identify common spelling patterns such as the silent "e." They can identify the meaning of the words through the context clues and through the picture dictionaries. Students may be asked to sound out the syllables or spell new words aloud with the whole class.

2. Next, each student identifies and illustrates the meaning of the words, using crayons, pencils, colored pencils, and paper. Next, students design a comic strip that identifies the application of the new words with their own characters or characters in the book. The comic strips are shared in class and are used to create new story lines. Students can also act out and create a skit of the comic strips to better understand the applications of the new words.

Assessment of Student Learning

The teacher assesses student learning informally throughout the lesson. While the students are reading individually, the teacher will ask comprehension questions while circulating around the class. The teacher will assess the comic strips from each student to ensure that the new word's meaning is correctly illustrated. Each group will demonstrate their ability to act out the comic strip for the teacher and rest of class.

The following simple checklist provides a guide for teachers to assess each student:

Criteria	Satisfactory	Unsatisfactory
Student is able to identify high-frequency words and unfamiliar words in the book.	_____	_____
Student is able to use resources in the classroom to identify the meaning of selected words from the book.	_____	_____
Student is able to identify word patterns (spelling).	_____	_____
Student is able to identify silent letters within selected words.	_____	_____
Student is able to identify the base word, prefixes, and suffixes of a selected word.	_____	_____
Student completes a comic strip that explains the meaning of an unfamiliar word.	_____	_____
Student is able to act out the comic strip character with a small group of peers.	_____	_____

Sample List of Supplies

- *Henry and Mudge* by Cynthia Rylant
- Word wall displayed in class for teacher to add new words
- Paper, pencils, crayons, colored pencils for comic strips

Resources
Rylant, C. (1996). *Henry and Mudge: The First Book.* New York, NY: Simon & Schuster.

Summary

Integrating the arts into literacy lessons allows for multiple forms of knowledge expression. Children can apply comprehension through illustrations combined with text. Comic strips like sentence strips can be reorganized into passages that promote creativity and imagination. Dramatic skits provide opportunities for playful expression and promote interaction and collaboration.

Lesson 5

Thinking Creatively for Vocabulary Comprehension

Purpose

Expanding vocabulary through creative activities promotes comprehension and imagination. Using basic phonics and word decoding skills during reading and writing experiences encourages students to explore unfamiliar vocabulary.

Literature Link

Oh, the Thinks You Can Think! By Dr. Seuss

Standards

Common Core State Standards for English Language Arts
Reading Standards: Foundational Skills (K–5)
Phonics and Word Recognition
First Grade
3. Know and apply grade-level phonics and word analysis skills in decoding words.
   a. Know the spelling-sound correspondences for common consonant digraphs.
Second Grade
3. Know and apply grade-level phonics and word analysis skills in decoding words.
   b. Know spelling-sound correspondences for additional common vowel teams.
Third Grade
3. Know and apply grade-level phonics and word analysis skills in decoding words.
   c. Decode multisyllable words.

The National Association for the Education of Young Children
NAEYC Early Childhood Program Standards and Accreditation Criteria
1. Relationships
   1.D.01 Indicator b)—Evidence for building positive self-identity and valuing differences includes materials and books that portray children as unique individuals and show different cultures, ethnicities, and backgrounds.
2. A Curriculum: Essential Characteristics
   2.A.1 1 and 12—Play is characterized by children's active engagement and enjoyment and their ability to determine how the activity is carried out. Teaching staff are expected to encourage and facilitate active play

involving physical movement as well as pretend or dramatic play. Children are expected to have opportunities to play individually and with peers.

> **2.D.07**—Dramatic play props (telephones, dolls, clothes), puppets, flannel boards, language board games, and small animal figures are examples of materials that promote discussion when used.

3. Early Literacy

> **2.E.** Early Literacy

> **2.E.01 and 02**—Evidence of each type of book listed (picture books, wordless books and books with rhymes) must be seen.

National Standards for Arts Education
Creating
Anchor Standard 1: Generate and conceptualize artistic ideas and work.
Responding
Anchor Standard 7: Perceive and analyze artistic work.

Lesson Grade Level

This lesson is appropriate for first through third graders as it focuses on developing vocabulary, vocabulary comprehension, and arts skills. This lesson can be modified for different age groups.

Suggested Time Frame for Lesson

This lesson may be completed in three 45-minute sessions.

Objectives

- Students will identify known and unknown words within a story and use context clues to connect unfamiliar or inventive words to create meaning using context clues and illustrations.
- Students will invent a new word for an imaginary creature and use descriptive adjectives and illustration to create a story about the new word with teacher and classmate assistance.
- Students will dramatically act out the movements of their new creature using props and costumes and create a word song to describe the new creatures using rhyme.

Instructional Activities

Day One: 45-minute session

1. The teacher introduces and reads *Oh, the Thinks You Can Think!* by Dr. Seuss (1975). After reading through the book, the teacher and students identify the words that are known and unknown (invented by Dr. Seuss). The teacher writes the list of words on the board.
2. Students work in groups of four to identify the unfamiliar words using their own copy of the book. The groups use a sticky note to identify the page and unfamiliar words. For example, the words *guff, snuvs, bloogs, zong, rink-rinker-fink, jibboo, vipper of vip,* and *beft* are words Dr. Seuss invented for the story. Students write descriptive words on the sticky notes to help identify the unfamiliar words using context clues and illustrations. Students can use "vocabulators," clear tubes that contain objects pertaining to a theme, or texture boxes containing objects to promote sensory experiences. The teacher can create vocabulators and texture boxes in advance to help students brainstorm descriptive words.
3. The groups share their descriptive words and ideas with the whole class under the teacher's direction. Unfamiliar words are described and identified.

Day Two: 45-minute session

1. The students begin by reviewing the words from the last session. Then groups work together to create a new word of their own that identifies a new and imaginary creature. The children write descriptive words about their new creatures and create a group collaborative illustration.

2. Using the descriptive words and the Dr. Seuss book, students work together to create a two-line rhyme about their new imaginary creature. A student or teacher writes each group's two-line rhyme at the bottom of their illustrations.

3. The teacher leads the whole group to create a class rhyme by combining the shorter poems together. The teacher reads the whole class poem and then each group reads their two-line poems aloud as the teacher directs the performance. The teacher may use a small drum or tambourine to create a simple beat as the class *sings* the poem together.

Day Three: 45-minute session

1. After rereading the class poem aloud to music, students use props and costumes to dramatically create the movement of their new creature. For example, two students might cover themselves with a bed sheet or large piece of fabric to create a body for the creature. Another student can hold a box to represent the head of the creature, while the fourth student holds a rope or yarn for a tail. The students practice moving together to create actions for their new creature. The teacher uses a small drum or tambourine to create slow and fast beats while students practice their movements. By varying the tempo, students can imagine different situations that could involve the new imaginary creature. To encourage a variety of movements, the teacher asks the students how would their creature jump, run, roll over, crawl, walk, and shake.

2. The students put the costume aside and the teacher uses all the illustration pages with the two-line poems to create a class book of their work. The teacher reads the class book and celebrates their work by honoring each group with the class-decorated hula hoop. The teacher holds the hula hoop over the groups (one at a time), and the class thanks them for their excellent work. The class celebrates and honors their successes through this simple ceremony.

Assessment of Student Learning

The teacher assesses student learning informally throughout the lesson. While the students are illustrating their new imaginary creatures and writing their rhyming songs, the teacher checks to see if each student understands new and unfamiliar words and asks each student questions to assess comprehension.

The following simple checklist provides a guide for teachers to assess each student:

Criteria	Satisfactory	Unsatisfactory
The student identifies known and unknown key words of the story.	_____	_____
The student identifies the unfamiliar words through use of context clues and illustrations from the story.	_____	_____
The student was able to dramatically act out the movements of an imaginary creature using props and costumes.	_____	_____
The student created a rhyming song about the imaginary creature.	_____	_____
The student participated in the singing activity of the rhyming songs created by the class.	_____	_____

Sample List of Supplies

- *Oh, the Thinks You Can Think!* By Dr. Seuss
- Sticky notes, pencils
- Large drawing paper for collaborative drawing, crayons, colored pencils, markers
- Small drum or tambourine for musical beat
- Fabric, boxes, yarn, string, rope, and other textural materials for costume
- Hula hoop decorated for celebration ceremony

Resources

Seuss, T. (1975). *Oh, the Thinks You Can Think!* New York, NY: Random House Books for Young Readers.

Summary

Dance, music, and dramatic play encourage children to explore new ways of expressing their understandings. Creative rhyming text, such as books by Dr. Seuss, allow children opportunities to explore words and practice phonics skills. Collaborative poetry writing and drawing exercises support active engagement in literacy.

Glossary

A

accountable talk Discourse within a learning community that involves accurate and appropriate knowledge to promote critical thinking skills.

aesthetic experience A sense of awe and inspiration during artistic interaction.

aesthetics Sense of beauty and philosophical value of the arts.

alphabet knowledge Knowing the names and sounds of the English alphabet, including capital and lowercase letters as well as individual consonant and vowel sounds.

alphabetic principle Knowledge that letters represent sounds.

altered books Books that are redesigned by using a variety of art materials to change or alter the original book.

analytic phonics Beginning with sight words, teachers guide children to identify patterns in words and phonics generalizations.

antonyms Words that have opposite meanings, such as *wide* and *narrow*.

approximations Scribble writing and pretend reading, early stages in literacy development.

art criticism model To comprehend and interpret the meaning of artistic expression through four basic steps: description, analysis, interpretation, and evaluation.

arts A term that includes creative work in dance, drama/theater, music, and visual arts.

arts history Information about the life of an artist/musician/dancer/actor/author and the time frame including cultural and historical influences for the artistic work.

arts integration Meaningful connections that emphasize the enduring knowledge inherent in each content or discipline that is taught in and through the arts.

assessment The process of gathering information on student performance for instructional decision making.

attention deficit/hyperactive disorder (ADHD) A child who typically has problems sitting still (hyperactive) or concentrating on learning (attention deficit).

authentic assessment Assessment, quality teaching and learning are seamlessly bound, as one is connected to the other to ensure achievement.

author's chair A special chair where writers sit to share their work in front of a group of peers.

autism A spectrum of cognitive, socioemotional, and physical (neurological) disorders that usually occur when speaking or connecting with others.

autophotographies Visual autobiographies that incorporate photographs with captions to describe personal stories or memoirs.

B

basal readers Textbooks that teach children how to read using controlled vocabulary and leveled passages to learn specific skills.

beginning English language learners Children who have recently immigrated to the United States and are just starting to learn English.

blending Putting sounds together (phonemic awareness skill).

book talks Short previews of a book to provide interest or motivation.

bottom-up reading model A code-based approach to reading instruction.

breve A phonetic symbol for a short vowel sound.

C

character maps Graphic organizers with specific character traits and examples from the text to help readers understand character development.

children's languages Different ways that children communicate with each other, such as dramatic play, music, dance, art, and puppetry, usually associated with the Reggio Emilia approach.

choice boards A variety of extension activities or projects, based on the multiple intelligences that are related to a specific book, topic, or theme.

classroom libraries A collection of reading materials that includes a variety of genres for classroom use.

classroom management A set of techniques and skills that allow a teacher to maintain a positive learning environment for all students.

close reading An instructional strategy that requires students to read and critically examine the same text multiple times for different purposes.

cloze A reading comprehension assessment using passages with deleted words.

cognitive dialogue Discussions between students and teachers that encourage thinking.

compacting A process of varying instruction to allow for previous student mastery of learning objectives.

comprehensible input ELLs acquire language by listening and comprehending verbal communication at a higher level than their current speaking/reading/writing English language level.

comprehension The process of constructing meaning for a specific purpose that involves the reader's understanding of the author's text and his or her prior knowledge.

concept maps Graphic organizers that represent the relationships between concepts or ideas in text.

concepts about print An awareness of how print works (Clay, 2006).

consonant blends Letter combinations that retain their original sounds (two or three letters); sometimes called a consonant cluster.

consonant digraphs Two consonants that make one sound (i.e., *ch, th, sh, wh*).

constructivism Includes the idea that all learning should flow from the students' desires and connections to the real world.

creative classrooms Classrooms that engage students and allow opportunities for innovative problem solving.

creative learning spaces Provide support and active engagement for early literacy development.

creative literacy development Supporting children in the classroom by valuing their thoughts, personalities, emotions, intelligence, and imagination.

creativity The result of an active imagination and the capacity to form mental metaphors, new ideas, and fantasies.

cross-check Using multiple strategies for decoding unknown words.

criterion-referenced test Teacher-created assessments that measure student performance to determine learning mastery of specific content knowledge or skills.

cuddle read When a child snuggles in the adult reader's arms during read-aloud sessions.

cut-up sentences A decoding strategy where a sentence is written on a strip of paper, cut into words, and put back together.

decoding Reading or interpreting thoughts; pronouncing words in text.

developmentally appropriate practices (DAP) Involves an understanding of child development, the specific strengths and needs of a child, and the cultural context in which the child lives.

dialects Language variations within geographic regions.

dialogue journal Written conversation shared in a journal format.

differentiated instruction Tailoring instruction to the individual needs of students, either in small groups, or one-on-one instruction.

differentiated reading model A model of early literacy instruction that focuses on specific skills for different groups of children, according to their individual strengths and needs.

digraphs Two vowels that make one sound (vowels or consonants).

diphthongs Vowel combinations like *ou, ow, oi, oy* (two vowels make a new sound).

diversity The concept of diversity means accepting, valuing, and respecting the uniqueness of each child; recognizing differences and appreciating similarities.

effective classroom organization The arrangement of the physical environment to promote children's learning potential.

emergent curriculum Lessons that evolve from children's needs and interests.

emergent English readers Another term for beginning English learners.

emergent literacy Children learn to read and write gradually, as they progress in their literacy development (Clay, 1966).

encoding Writing to express thoughts.

entry points Accessible adaptations of curriculum.

environmental print Print that is found in the real world, such as street signs, billboards, restaurant signs, and labels on cereal boxes or other food products.

executive function A critical cognitive skill that includes self-regulation, which focuses attention, builds working memory, and controls socioemotional behaviors through creative play,

games, and active engagement (Kray & Ferdinand, 2013).

explicit instruction Systematic, explicit instructional strategies are used for teaching a variety of emergent literacy skills.

expressive language Communication involving speaking and writing.

eye anchors Objects, photos, or cards with written topics that help to keep children engaged and on task.

family dialogue journals Interactive writing notebooks that support the partnership between home and school.

family literacy Involves family members (immediate and extended) participating in literacy experiences at home and in their communities.

flexible grouping Allows for interchangeable skills groups based upon the content, purpose, and task.

fix-up strategies Strategies that are used when readers lose track of their reading, looking back to see what they missed or rereading a few pages if necessary.

formal assessments Tests that systematically measure how well students have mastered learning outcomes, such as standardized testing, norm-referenced tests, and placement criteria.

formative assessments Assessments that occur frequently and document a child's learning process.

freewriting Writing freely to focus on content (ideas) rather than format (mechanics).

genres Different types of children's literature: picture books, traditional literature, poetry, realistic fiction, historical fiction, fantasy, and informational books.

gifted and talented Gifted children are advanced intellectually and talented children excel in their creative skills. These children often have unique needs that require special teaching and learning accommodations.

grapheme The visual representation of a sound (letter or letters).

graphic organizers A visual map of concepts.

graphic symbol system Earliest marks made through creative expression in the emergent literacy process that are developed in written language.

graphophonic cueing system One of the language cueing systems that represents how a word looks (graphic symbols) and how a word sounds (phonics).

holistic model of literacy (HML) Becoming literate includes the cognitive, socioemotional, and physical aspects of self.

homophones Words that sound similar but have different meanings and spellings, like *two* and *too, knight* and *night,* or *hi* and *high.*

imagination Involves creating an idea or perception that has not yet been formed, such as a dream, story, or image that can be shared with others.

inclusion The Individuals with Disabilities Education Improvement Act (IDEIA) (U.S. Department of Education, 2004) ensured that all children are included in classes to the fullest extent possible.

informal assessments Frequent assessments, such as observation, anecdotal records, criterion-referenced tests, and portfolio assessment, that are tied to instruction.

informational text A type of nonfiction or expository text that contains information on one or more topics.

insertion A type of miscue when a word(s) is added to the text.

interdisciplinary Authentic arts learning goals, as defined by national and state standards, are connected with other content areas, with respect for each discipline's body of knowledge for study and practice.

interest centers or **interest groups** Organized for children to self-select learning experiences according to their preferences.

invented spelling Phonetic spelling.

J

jackdaws Collections of artifacts (concrete objects) that relate to a specific book, topic, or theme for the purpose of providing interest or background knowledge.

K

key word approach A form of the language experience approach that begins with a word and ends with a story (Ashton-Warner, 1963).

kid watching A naturalistic assessment technique, based on observation.

L

language cueing systems Systems of language that are used during the reading process: semantic, syntactic, graphophonic, and pragmatic.

language development The process through which a child learns expressive and receptive language.

language experience approach A method (consisting of dictated stories and word banks) for teaching children how to read that uses their own language as the primary text.

learning contracts Agreements between the teacher and student that set learning goals.

learning progression A standards-based pathway that learners travel as they progress toward mastery of skills.

letter identification task One of the emergent literacy assessments in Marie Clay's *Observation Survey* (1993) that tests recognition of capitals and lowercase letters.

lexile levels Lexile measures (reading levels) are based on two fairly reliable predictors of text difficulty, frequency of words, and sentence length.

literacy centers Designed learning spaces targeting specific reading, writing, and listening skills, based on different subject areas in the language arts curriculum.

literature circles A discussion group that reads the same book; the members usually reflect their thoughts in writing prior to each discussion.

long vowel A vowel that is pronounced the same as the name of the letter.

macron A phonetic symbol for a long vowel sound.

manipulating sounds Changing the first, middle, or final sound in a word to a different sound (phonemic awareness skill).

manipulatives Small objects that children move around during multisensory lessons to learn mathematical and other concepts.

mark making Scribble marks made with fingers (finger painting, drawing in the sand) and by holding a writing/drawing implement (crayon, marker, paint brush) to encourage the development of eye–hand motor skills and communication meaning.

maze A reading comprehension assessment using text with deleted words that includes word choices.

meaning vocabulary Key words that are important for comprehending the text.

mentor texts High-quality texts that illustrate specific skills or concepts for reading and/or writing instruction.

metacognition Understanding one's own thinking during the reading process.

metacognitive awareness Knowing or realizing why you think the way you do.

miscue A response during oral reading that is different from the actual text.

miscue analysis Analyzing miscues (substitutions) during oral reading to understand the reader's use of strategies (that is, language cueing systems) during the reading process.

multiculturalism A complex issue with the understanding that the various cultures in our society deserve an equal amount of respect.

multidisciplinary Instruction involves more than one subject area addressing the same theme, but the subjects generally are taught separately.

multiple intelligences A theory developed in 1983 by Dr. Howard Gardner that suggests there are eight different kinds of intelligence: linguistic, logical-mathematical, spatial, bodily-kinesthetic, musical, interpersonal, intrapersonal, and naturalist.

multiple sign systems Different forms of expression to communicate meaning and to help children achieve their learning goals.

N

norm-referenced test Standardized assessments that involve validity (Does the test measure what it is intended to measure?) and reliability (Are there consistent results over time?).

O

open mind portrait A drawing (facial portrait) of a character using textual clues for authenticity; the character's thoughts and/or feelings based on text evidence are included to support the reader's understanding of character development.

observational learning theory This theory (Bandura, 1986) states that behavior is imitated and learning occurs through the observation of role models.

onset The beginning part of the word before the first vowel.

P

performance assessment Timed writing prompts used for collecting writing samples at specific times throughout the year.

phoneme The smallest unit of sound in a word.

phonemic awareness An awareness of letters and sounds in spoken words.

phonics An awareness of letters and sounds in written words.

phonological awareness Ability to recognize and use units of sound in spoken words including syllables, onsets, and rimes.

phonology A branch of linguistics that encompasses the systematic organization of sounds.

picture and word sorts Games to learn spelling patterns where children sort words or pictures into categories according to vowel and consonant sounds.

pointer A wand used to indicate specific areas of the big book during shared reading.

portfolio assessment Planned continuous assessment that allows children to demonstrate their goals and skills in literacy development.

pragmatic cueing system One of the language cueing systems that deals with the social aspects of language use.

process-based approach The process of creating where children immerse themselves in the learning experience rather than the end result.

progressivism John Dewey's philosophy of education (1916) that consists of two essential elements: a respect for the diversity of children and the development of critical, socially engaged intelligence.

project-based learning A style of literacy learning (in three phases) that begins with the interests of the children in the classroom (preschool+). Concept webs for the unit of study are created with the guidance of the teacher, based on a specific theme or topic. *Phase One* includes the selection and introduction of the concept or theme that evolved from children's interests. In *Phase Two*, parents and community members who are experts in the field are invited to speak with the children about the topic. In *Phase Three* of the project-based approach, children participate in a culminating learning activity.

Q

quick draw A simple sketch a child creates and shares to show his or her understanding of a character, theme, plot, or topic during interactive read-alouds using fiction or nonfiction text.

quick write A brief piece of writing that children create and share to demonstrate what they know about a topic, theme, character, or plot during interactive read-louds using fiction or nonfiction text.

R

r-**controlled vowel** When the letter "r" follows a vowel, it changes the vowel sound.

reading behaviors Behaviors readers exhibit when they are reading orally, such as repetitions, self-corrections, and pauses that are not counted as reading errors.

Reading Recovery An intensive early intervention program for first graders that was designed by Marie Clay (2006).

realia Real-world objects that are used as a visual strategy during reading instruction with English language learners.

receptive language Involves listening and reading.

response to intervention (RTI) A method of differentiating instruction to meet the requirements of inclusion as defined in the Disabilities Education Improvement Act.

return sweep A concept of print when a child understands that the end of one line of text connects to the beginning of the next line on a page.

rime The part of the word that comes after the vowel (also called a phonogram).

rubrics Set criteria for measuring student learning.

running records An oral reading assessment that is used to determine if a child is reading on his or her correct instructional reading level, used in Marie Clay's *Observation Survey of Early Literacy Achievement* (1993).

S

scaffolding Assisted learning that links prior learning to new learning.

schema Each child's unique understandings, knowledge, and interpretation of the world around them based on real-life experiences.

schemata The plural form of schema.

schema theory The concept that readers or listeners construct meaning based on their background knowledge, connecting the unfamiliar to the familiar.

scientifically based reading research Reading skills, such as phonemic awareness, are taught through systematic, explicit instruction.

scribbling stage of spelling development The first stage of writing when children between one and three years of age experiment with lines and squiggles (Sulzby & Teale, 1985).

segmenting Breaking sounds apart (phonemic awareness skill).

self-actualization Reading one's potential, including aesthetic and intellectual achievement (Maslow, 1954).

semantic cueing system One of the language cueing systems that represents meaning.

semantic webs Graphic organizers that represent the meaning of text.

semiotics The study of how we utilize multiple sign systems (music, visual art, dance, drama, writing, and speaking) to comprehend underlying meanings or messages in text or imagery.

shared reading The teacher and children read together, typically using a big book, in a whole class setting.

shared writing An interactive writing experience when a teacher and students share the pen.

short vowels Vowel sounds that are found in words like *apple, elephant, inchworm, octopus,* and *umbrella.*

sight words High-frequency words that must be memorized for instant recognition.

social constructivism Knowledge can be mutually learned and constructed by young children in social contexts (Vygotsky, 1962).

specific academic praise This positive interaction promotes self-awareness and encourages repetition of successful literacy behaviors.

standardized test Administered by educators to measure student performance on a nationwide level.

storyboard A series of pages that includes sample illustrations and text; can be used to help children organize and sequence their story.

story pyramid A graphic organizer (type of story map) that consists of a formula for labeling parts of a story.

story grammar Components of a story and the relationship between the parts (setting, theme, plot, and resolution).

synonyms Words that have similar meanings, such as *pretty* and *beautiful.*

syntactic cueing system One of the language cueing systems that represents word order or sentence structure.

synthetic phonics Children blend letters and sounds to form words.

summative assessments Assessments are records of a child's mastery of specific skills.

systematic assessment Teachers help children to be aware of their own literacy skills, goals, and needs through a frequent, preplanned assessment cycle.

T

text complexity This term refers to characteristics of informational text, which are critical for reading comprehension including text structures (cause and effect, question and answer, main idea and details), text features (table of contents, index, maps, and charts), as well as illustrations, concepts, and key vocabulary.

text evidence Examples from the text to support the reader's interpretation.

text set A collection of books in different genres on the same theme or topic.

think-alouds Teachers verbalize their own thinking while reading orally in order to demonstrate how skilled readers construct meaning.

tier assignments Focus on essential literacy skills by varying levels of complexity depending upon the child's abilities or readiness.

top-down reading model A meaning-based approach to reading instruction.

V

visual literacy Using images to interpret and communicate meaning.

visual thinking skills (VTS) Focus on guiding students through the process of becoming visually literate and developing creative and critical thinking skills by viewing a variety of images from different cultures and discussing personal connections to these images.

visualization system Mental images that emerge during and after reading from the reader's sensory experiences, emotional connections, and prior knowledge.

vocabulary A collective sum of words and phrases arranged in the English language to communicate meaning.

vocabulary self-collection strategy Students self-select their new vocabulary words.

vowel digraphs Two vowels that only make one sound: "oa" in *boat* or "ea" in *meat;* the first vowel sound is long and the second is silent.

vowel generalizations Patterns of vowels and consonants that work approximately 50 percent of the time, such as CV, CVC, CVCV, and CVVC.

W

word callers Readers who can pronounce the words but do not understand the meaning.

word choice Vocabulary a writer uses to convey specific thoughts and ideas.

word study Effective instruction in phonics, spelling, and vocabulary focusing on specific words usually selected from text.

word wall Class display of key words.

writing vocabulary task One of the assessments on Clay's *Observation Survey* (1993) when students are asked to write as many words as they can during a 10-minute period.

writing workshop A block of time for writing instruction and practice, approximately 60 to 90 minutes three to five times a week.

Z

zone of proximal development (ZPD) The zone where a child learns best, with assistance from a peer or teacher (Vygotsky, 1962).

References for Children's Literature

A

Ada, A. F. (2001). *Gathering the sun: An alphabet in Spanish and English*. Simon Silva (Illus.). New York: Rayo of HarperCollins.

Adelman, B. (1991). *Roy Lichtenstein's ABC*. New York: Bullfinch.

Adler, D. (1990). *A picture book of Martin Luther King, Jr.* New York: Holiday House.

Adler, D. (1997). *Cam Jansen: The mystery of the dinosaur bones*. New York: Puffin.

Ahlberg, A. (2001). *The jolly postman*. Janet Ahlberg (Illus.). New York: LB Kids Publishers.

Aliki. (1998). *Marianthe's story: Painted words and spoken memories*. New York: Greenwillow Books.

Almada, A. A. (2013). *Walking through a world of aromas*. Madrid: Cuento de Luz.

Amery, H. (2001). *Stories from around the world*. Tulsa, OK: Educational Development Corporation.

Andreae, G. (2001). *Giraffes can't dance*. London, UK: Orchard Books.

Anholt, L. (1994). *Camille and the sunflowers*. New York: Barron's Educational Series.

Artell, M. (2001). *Petite rouge—A Cajun Red Riding Hood*. J. Harris (Illus.). New York: Dial Books for Young Readers.

Awdry, R. W. (2014). *Thomas and friends story time collection*. New York: Random House Books for Young Readers.

B

Bagert, B. (1992). *Let me be the boss . . . poems for kids to perform*. Honesdale, PA: Boyds Mills Press.

Bang, M. (2004). *When Sophie gets angry— really, really angry*. New York: Scholastic.

Banks, K. (2006). *Max's words*. Boris Kulikov (Illus.). New York: Farrar, Straus and Giroux.

Barnett, M. (2014). *Sam and Dave dig a hole*. Sommerville, MA: Candlewick Press.

Base, G. (1996). *Animalia*. New York: Puffin Books.

Bates, K. L. (1994). *O beautiful for spacious skies*. San Francisco, CA: Chronicle Books.

Baum, L. F., & Sabuda, R. (2001). *The wonderful Wizard of Oz: A commemorative pop-up*. New York: Simon and Schuster Books for Young Readers.

Becker, A. (2013). *Journey*. Sommerville, MA: Candlewick Press.

Bjork, C. (1987). *Linnea in Monet's garden*. New York: R & S Books.

Boynton, S. (2011). *Happy hippo, angry duck: A book of moods*. New York: Little Simon.

Bradley, D. (2013). *Alphabet book of animals*. Amazon Digital Service, Inc.

Brennan-Nelson, Denise. (2012). *Maestro Stu saves the zoo*. Tim Bowers (Illus.). Ann Arbor, MI: Sleeping Bear Press.

Brown, M. W. (1947). *Goodnight moon*. Clement Hurd (Illus.). New York: HarperCollins.

Brown, M. W. (1990). *The important book*. Leonard Weisgard (Illus.). New York: HarperTrophy.

Bryant, J. (2008). *A river of words: The story of William Carlos Williams*. Melissa Sweet (Illus.). Grand Rapids, MI: Eerdmans Books for Young Readers.

C

Campbell Ernst, L. (2004). *The turn-around, upside-down alphabet book*. New York: Simon & Schuster Children's Publishing.

Campoy, F. I. (2009). *Mi di de la A a la Z*. Tres Cantos, Madrid: Alfaguara Infantil.

Carle, E. (1969). *The very hungry caterpillar*. Cleveland, OH: World Publishing Company.

Carle, E. (1994). *The very lonely firefly*. New York: Philomel Books.

Carle, E. (2011). *The artist who painted a blue horse*. New York: Philomel Books.

Carle, E. (2013). *Friends*. New York: Philomel Books.

Castillo, L. (2014). *Nana in the city*. New York, NY: Clarion Books.

Cheney, L. (2002). *America: A patriotic primer*. Robin Preiss Glasser (Illus.). New York: Simon & Schuster Books for Young Readers.

Cherry, L. (1990). *The great kapok tree*. New York: Voyager Books.

Choi, Y. (2001). *The name jar*. New York: Dragonfly Books.

Clay, M. (1985). *Sand*. Portsmouth, NH: Heinemann.

Clay, M. (1985). *Stones*. Portsmouth, NH: Heinemann.

Clay, M. (2000). *Follow Me, Moon*. Portsmouth, NH: Heinemann.

Clements, A. (1997). *Big Al*. New York: Atheneum Books for Young Readers.

Cole, H. (2012). *Unspoken: A story from the underground railroad*. New York: Scholastic Press.

Cole, J. (1989). *Anna Banana: 101 Jump-rope rhymes*. Alan Tiegreen (Illus.). New York: HarperCollins.

Cole, J. The magic school bus (series). Bruce Degen (Illus.). New York: Scholastic.

Cole, J. (2010). *The magic school bus and the climate challenge*. Bruce Degen (Illus.). New York: Scholastic.

Collins, P. L. (1994). *I am an artist*. Brookfield, CT: Millbrook Press.

Couric, K. (2000). *The brand new kid*. Marjorie Priceman (Illus.). New York: Doubleday.

Cowen-Fletcher, J. (1999). *Mama zooms*. New York: Scholastic.

Cowley, J. (1999). *Red-eyed tree frog*. New York, NY: Scholastic.

Creech, S. (2003). *Granny Torrelli makes soup*. New York: HarperCollins.

Cronin, D. (2003). *Click, clack moo: Cows that type*. Betsy Lewin (Illus.). Weston, CT: Simon & Schuster Publishing.

Cronin, D. (2003). *Diary of a worm*. Harry Bliss (Illus.). New York: HarperCollins.

Cronin, D. (2007). *Diary of a fly*. Harry Bliss (Illus.). New York: HarperCollins.

Curtis, J. L. (2008). *Big words for little people*. Laura Cornell (Illus.). New York: Joanna Cotler Books/HarperCollins Publishers.

Curtis, J. L. (2012). *My brave year of firsts: Tries, sighs, and high fives*. Laura Cornell (Illus.). New York: HarperCollins.

D

Dahl, R. (1961). *James and the giant peach*. Quentin Blake (Illus.). New York: Puffin Books.

Daywalt, D. (2013). *The day the crayons quit*. New York: Philomel Books.

DePalma, M. N. (2005). *The grand old tree*. New York: Arthur A. Levine Books.

Dewdney, A. (2005). *Llama llama red pajama*. New York: Viking.

DiCamillo, K. (2009). *Because of Winn Dixie*. Somerville, MA: Candlewick Press.

DiCamillo, K., & McGhee, A. (2011). *Bink and Gollie*. Tony Fucile (Illus.). Somerville, MA: Candlewick Press.

Dorros, A. (1997). *Abuela*. Elisa Kleven (Illus.). New York: Puffin Books.

Duggleby, J. (1998). *Story painter: The life of Jacob Lawrence*. San Francisco, CA: Chronicle Books.

Dumont, J. F., (2005). *A blue so blue*. New York: Sterling.

Dunrea, O. (2002). *Gossie*. New York, NY: Houghton Mifflin Harcourt.

E

Eastman, P. D. (1960). *Are you my mother?* New York: Random House Children's Books.

Eastman, P. D. (1966). *Go, dog, go!* New York: Random House for Young Readers.

Edwards, P. D. (1998). *Warthogs in the kitchen: A sloppy counting book*. Henry Cole (Illus.). New York: Troll.

Ehlert, L. (2006). *In my world*. New York, NY: Houghton Mifflin Harcourt.

Elschner, G. (2014). *Funny machines for George the sheep: A children's book inspired by Leonardo da Vinci*. London, UK: Prestel Publishing, Ltd.

Ernst, L. C. (2004). *The turn-around, upside-down alphabet book*. New York, NY: Simon & Schuster.

F

Falconer, I. (2000). *Olivia*. New York: Atheneum Books for Young Readers.

Floca, B. (2013). *Locomotive*. New York: Atheneum/Richard Jackson Books.

Fox, M. (1986). *Hattie and the fox*. New York, NY: Simon & Schuster.

Fox, M. (1989). *Wilfred Gordon MacDonald Partridge*. La Jolla, CA: Kane Miller Books.

Fox, M. (1993). *Time for bed*. New York, NY: Houghton Mifflin Harcourt.

Fox, M. (2003). *Whoever you are*. Leslie Staub (Illus.). New York: Voyager Books.

Fox, M. (2004). *Where is the green sheep?* Judy Horacek (Illus.). New York: Harcourt Children's Books.

G

Garcia, E. (2006). *Coyote and the sky: How the sun, moon and stars began*. Albuquerque, NM: University of New Mexico Press.

Garza, C. L. (1996). *In my family*. San Francisco, CA: Children's Book Press.

Gehl, L., & Lichtenheld, T. (2014). *One big pair of underwear*. San Diego, CA: Beach Lane Books.

Global Fund for Children. (2007). *Global babies*. Watertown, MA: Charlesbridge.

Greenberg, J., & Jordan, S. (2009). *Vincent van Gogh: Portrait of an artist*. New York: Yearling.

Greene, R. G. (2001). *When a line bends . . . a shape begins*. James Kaczman (Illus.). Boston, MA: HMH Books for Young Readers.

Grimm, J., and Grimm, W. (1905). *Little Red Riding Hood*. In *Grimm's fairy tales*. New York: Maynard, Merrill, & Co.

Guthrie, W. (2000). *Bling blang*. Vladimir Radunsky (Illus.). Somerville, MA: Candlewick Press.

H

Harrison, D. L. (2012). *Cowboys*. Honesdale, PA: Wordsong.

Heiligman, D. (1996). *From caterpillar to butterfly*. Bari Weissman (Illus.). New York: HarperCollins.

Heller, R. (1991). *Kites sail high: A book about verbs*. New York: Grosset & Dunlap.

Heller, R. (2008). *A cache of jewels and other collective nouns*. New York: Putnam Juvenile.

Henkes, K. (1998). *Lily's purple plastic purse*. New York: Greenwillow.

Henkes, K. (2004). *Kitten's first full moon*. New York: Greenwillow Books.

Henkes, K. (2010). *Wemberly worried*. New York: Greenwillow Books.

Henkes, K. (2013). *The year of Billy Miller*. New York: Greenwillow Books.

Hesse, K. (1999). *Come on rain!* New York: Scholastic.

Hills, T. (2010). *How Rocket learned to read*. New York: Schwartz and Wade Publishing.

Hoberman, M. A. (2012). *You read to me, I'll to you: Very short fairy tales to read together*. New York, NY: Little Brown Books for Young Readers.

Hoffman, M. (1992). *Amazing Grace*. Caroline Binch (Illus.). New York: Dial Books.

Holub, J. (2001). *Vincent Van Gogh: Sunflowers and swirly stars (smart about art)*. New York: Grosset & Dunlap.

Horacek, P. (2007). *Butterfly, butterfly: A book of colors*. Sommerville, MA: Candlewick Press.

Hughes, C. D. (2013) *National Geographic kids first big book of the ocean*. Washington, DC: National Geographic Children's Books.

I

Idle, M. (2013). *Flora and the flamingo*. San Francisco, CA: Chronicle Books.

J

James, S. (1991). *Dear Mr. Blueberry*. New York, NY: Simon & Schuster.

Janeczko, P. B. (2005). *A kick in the head: An everyday guide to poetic forms*. Chris Raschka (Illus.). Sommerville, MA: Candlewick Press.

Jeffers, O. (2014). *Once upon an alphabet: short stories for all the teachers*. New York, NY: HarperCollins.

Jenkins, S., & Page, R. (2008). *What do you do with a tail like this?* Boston, MA: HMH Books for Young Readers.

Johnson, S. T. (2008). *A is for art: An abstract alphabet*. New York: Simon & Schuster/Paula Wiseman Books.

Johnston, T. (1994). *Amber on the mountain*. Robert Duncan (Illus.). New York: Dial Books for Young Readers.

Jones, B. T., & Kuklin, S. (1900). *Dance! With Bill T. Jones*. New York: Disney-Hyperion.

K

Katz, K. (2002). *The colors of us*. New York: Square Fish.

Kendall, C. W. (1993). *Stories of women composers for young musicians*. Tacoma Park, MD: Toadwood.

Klassen, J. (2011). *I want my hat back*. Somerville, MA: Candlewick Press.

Kraus, R. (1994). *Leo the late bloomer*. Jose Aruego (Illus.). New York: HarperCollins.

Kundardt, D. (2001). *Pat the bunny*. New York, NY: Golden Books.

L

Laden, N. (1998). *When Pigcasso met Moostisse*. San Francisco, CA: Chronicle Books.

Lears, L. (1998). *Ian's walk: A story about autism*. Park Ridge, IL: Albert Whitman & Co.

Lehman, B. (2004). *The red book*. Boston, MA: Houghton Mifflin Harcourt.

Levine, E. (2007). *Henry's freedom box*. Kadir Nelson (Illus.). New York: Scholastic Press.

Levine, R. (2000). *Story of the orchestra: Listen while you learn about the instruments, the music, and the composers who wrote the music!* New York: Black Dog & Leventhal.

Lewis, B. (2007). *In Jesse's shoes*. Laura Nikiel (Illus.). Grand Rapids, MI: Bethany House Publishers.

Lionni, L. (1973). *Frederick*. New York: Dragonfly Books.

Litwin, E. (2008). *Pete the cat* (series). James Dean (Illus.). New York: Scholastic.

Litwin, E. (2010). *Pete the cat: I love my white shoes*. James Dean (Illus.). New York: HarperCollins.

Lowry, L. *Anastasia* (series). New York: Yearling.

Lowry, L. (2009). *Crow call*. Bagram Ibatoulline (Illus.). New York: Scholastic Press.

Lowry, L. *Gooney bird* (series). New York: Yearling.

Lowry, L. *Sam Krupnik* (series). New York: Yearling.

Marsh, L. (2012). *National Geographic kids caterpillar to butterfly*. Washington, DC: National Geographic Children's Books.

Martin, B. Jr. (1992). *Brown bear, brown bear, what do you see?* Eric Carle (Illus.). New York: Henry Holt and Company.

Martin, W. (2014). *The train book: A kid's book about trains*. Amazon Digital Services.

Mayer, M. (1992). *Nightmare in my closet*. New York: Penguin Group.

McBratney, S. (2008). *Guess how much I love you*. Somerville, MA: Candlewick Press.

McCloskey, R. (1966). *Make way for ducklings*. New York: Puffin Books.

McDonough, Y. Z. (2003). *Who was Wolfgang Amadeus Mozart?* Carrie Robbins (Illus.). New York: Grosset & Dunlap.

McGee, A. (2007). *Someday*. New York: Atheneum Books for Young Readers.

McKissack, P. (1986). *Flossie and the fox*. Rachel Isadora (Illus.). New York: Dial Books for Young Readers.

Medearis, A. S. (1997). *Annie's gifts (Feeling good)*. Anna Rich (Illus.). East Orange, NJ: Just Us Books Inc.

Metropolitan Museum of Art. (2002). *Museum ABC*. New York: Little, Brown Books for Young Readers.

Millman, I. (2003). *Moses goes to the circus*. New York: Farrar, Straus, & Giroux.

Morales, Y. (2014). *Via Frida*. New York, NY: Roaring Brook Press.

Morrison, P., & Murakami, T. (2009). *Art for baby*. Dorking, UK: Templar Publishing.

Muth, J. J. (2002). *The three questions*. New York: Scholastic Press.

Numeroff, L. (1985). *If you give a mouse a cookie*. Felicia Bond (Illus.). New York: HarperCollins.

Numeroff, L. (1998). *If you give a pig a pancake*. Felicia Bond (Illus.). USA: HarperCollins Publishers.

Numeroff, L. (2008). *If you give a cat a cupcake*. Felicia Bond (Illus.). USA: HarperCollins Publishers.

Numeroff, L. (2011). *If you give a dog a doughnut*. Felicia Bond (Illus.). USA: HarperCollins Publishers.

O'Connor, J. (2002). *Henri Matisse: Drawing with scissors*. Jessie Hartland (Illus.). New York: Grosset & Dunlap.

Osborne, M. P. (1997). *Dolphins at daybreak*. New York: Learning Links.

Pallota, J. (1989). *The ocean alphabet book*. Watertown, MA: Charlesbridge.

Parish, P. *Amelia Bedelia* (series). Fritz Siebel (Illus.). New York: HarperCollins.

Parr, T. (2009). *The peace book*. New York, NY: Little, Brown Books for Young Readers.

Parr, T. (2010). *The earth book*. New York: Little, Brown Books for Young Readers.

Pett, M. (2014). *The girl and the bicycle*. New York: Simon and Schuster.

Pfister, M. (1999). *The rainbow fish*. J. Allison James (Illus.). New York: NorthSouth Books.

Pilkey, D. (2004). *Dog breath*. New York: Scholastic Paperbacks.

Pinkney, A. D. (1995). *Alvin Ailey*. Brian Pinkney (Illus.). New York: Disney-Hyperion.

Pinkney, J. (2009). *The lion and the mouse*. Boston, MA: Little, Brown & Company.

Polacco, P. (1998). *Thank you, Mr. Falker*. New York: Penguin Putnam Books for Young Readers.

Polacco, P. (2001). *The keeping quilt*. New York: Simon & Schuster.

Prelutsky, J. (2006). *Behold the bold umbrellaphant and other poems*. Carin Berger (Illus.). New York: Greenwillow Books.

Prelutsky, J., & Seuss, Dr. (1998). *Hooray for Diffendoofer day!* New York: Alfred A. Knopf Books for Young Readers.

Priddy, R. (2011). *My big animal book*. New York: Priddy Books/Macmillan Publishing.

Raffi. (1990). *Baby Beluga*. Ashley Wolff (Illus.). New York: Knopf Books for Young Readers.

Rankin, L. (1991). *The handmade alphabet*. New York: Dial Books.

Rappaport, D. (2007). *Martin's big words: The life of Dr. Martin Luther King, Jr.* Bryan Collier (Illus.). New York: Hyperion.

Raschka, C. (1992). *Charlie Parker played be bop*. New York: Scholastic.

Raschka, C. (2011). *A ball for Daisy*. New York: Schwartz & Wade.

Reynolds, P. (2003). *The dot*. Somerville, MA: Candlewick Press.

Reynolds, P. (2004). *Ish*. Somerville, MA: Candlewick Press.

Ringgold, F. (1991). *Tar beach*. New York: Dragonfly Books.

Roche, D. (2003). *The best class picture ever!* New York: Scholastic.

Rosenstock, B. (2014). *The noisy paint box: The colors and sounds of Kandinsky*. New York, NY: Knopf Books for Young Readers.

Rosenthal, A. K. (2006). *Cookies: Bite-size life lessons*. Jane Dyer (Illus.). New York: Harper-Collins Publishers.

Rusch, E. (2007). *A day with no crayons*. Chad Cameron (Illus.). New York: Cooper Square Publishing LLC.

Ryan, P. M. (2001). *Hello ocean*. Watertown, MA: Charlesbridge.

Rylant, C. (1998). *Tulip sees America*. New York: Scholastic.

Sabuda, R. (1999). *The movable mother goose*. New York: Little Simon.

Salley, C. (2002). *Epossumondas*. Janet Stevens (Illus.). San Diego, CA: Harcourt Children's Books.

Saltzberg, B. (2010). *Beautiful oops!* New York: Workman Publishing Company.

Santat, D. (2014). *The adventures of Beekle: The unimaginary friend*. New York: Little, Brown Books for Young Readers.

Scillian, D. (2010). *Memoirs of a goldfish*. Ann Arbor, MI: Sleeping Bear Press.

Seeger, L. V. (2007). *First the egg*. New York: Roaring Book Press.

Selznick, B. (2011). *Wonderstruck*. New York: Scholastic Press.

Sendak, M. (1988). *Where the wild things are*. Weston, CT: HarperTrophy.

Seuss, Dr. (1957). *Cat in the hat*. New York: Random House Books for Young Readers.

Seuss, Dr. (1960). *Green eggs and ham*. New York: Random House Books for Young Readers.

Seuss, Dr. (1963). *Dr. Seuss's ABC*. New York: Random House Books for Young Readers.

Seuss, Dr. (1990). *Oh the places you'll go!* New York: Random House Books for Young Readers.

Seuss, Dr. (1996). *My many colored days*. New York: Knopf Books for Young Readers.

Seuss, Dr., & Prelutsky, J. (1998). *Hooray for Diffendoofer Day!* New York: Alfred A. Knopf.

Shannon, D. (1998). *A bad case of stripes*. New York: Scholastic.

Shaw, N. E. (1997). *Sheep in a jeep*. New York: HMH Books for Young Readers.

Simon, S. (1998). *Wild babies*. Logan, IA: Perfection Learning.

Smith, C.R. Jr. (2003). *I am America and America is me!* New York: Cartwheel Books.

Smith, R. M. (2008). *An A to Z walk in the park*. Alexandria, VA: Clarence-Henry Books.

Snider, P. (2013). *My special family*. Oyster Bay, NY: Bish Bash Books.

Soto, G. (1993). *Too many tamales*. New York: Puffin Books.

Stead, P. (2010). *A sick day for Amos McGee*. Erin Stead (Illus.). New York: Neal Porter Books/Roaring Book Press.

Stockland, P. M. (2005). *Swing, slither, or swim: A book about animal movements.* Todd Irving Ouren (Illus.). Mankato, MN: Picture Window Books.

Sykorova-Pekarkova, E. (1996). *Caperucita Roja.* Madrid: Ediciones/Joaquin Turina.

Taback, S. (1999). *Joseph had a little overcoat.* Pine Plains, NY: Viking Books.

Tafolla, C. (2009). *What can you do with a paleta?* Magaly Morales (Illus.). Berkeley, CA: Tricycle Press.

Teague, M. (2002). *Dear Mrs. LaRue: Letters from obedience school.* New York: Scholastic.

Thomas, A. (1994). *Pearl paints.* New York, NY: Henry Holt & Company.

Turner, A.W. (1998). *Let's be animals.* Rick Brown (Illus.). New York: HarperFestival.

Ug, P. (2015). *In the butterfly garden.* New York: Prestel Publishing USA.

Van Allsburg, C. (1985). *The Polar Express.* Orlando, FL: Houghton Mifflin.

Van Allsburg, C. (1987). *The Z was zapped.* Orlando, FL: Houghton Mifflin.

Van Fleet, M. (2007). *Dog.* New York: Simon & Schuster.

Van Laan, N. (1990). *Possum come a-knockin'.* George Booth (Illus.). New York: Dragonfly Books.

Venezia M. (1994–2001). *Getting to know the world's greatest artists.* New York: Children's Press (series).

Venezia M. (1997). *Getting to know the world's greatest composers.* New York: Children's Press (series).

Walton, R. (2001). *How can you dance?* Ana Lopez-Escriva (Illus.). New York: Putnam Juvenile.

Wardlaw, L. (2011). *Won Ton: A cat tale in haiku.* New York, NY: Henry Holt & Company.

Weiss, G. D., & Thiele, B. (1995). *What a wonderful world.* New York: Atheneum Books for Young Readers.

Wells, R. (1989). *Max's chocolate chicken.* New York: Puffin.

Wells, R. (1998). *Yoko.* New York: Hyperion Books.

Wells, R. *Ruby and Max* (series). New York: Viking Juvenile.

Wells, R. (2004). *Max's breakfast.* New York: Viking Books for Young Readers.

Wiesner, D. (1980). *Tuesday.* Boston, MA: HMH Books for Young Readers.

Wiesner, D. (2006). *Flotsam.* New York: Clarion Books.

Wiesner, D. (2010). *Art and Max.* New York: Clarion Books.

Weiss, G. D., & Think, B. (1996). *What a wonderful world.* A. Bryan (Illus.). New York: Atheneum.

Wild, M. (2006). *Fox.* Tulsa, OK: Kane Miller Publications.

Wilder, C. (2014). *Sea turtles for kids.* Amazon Digital Services.

Williams, V. B. (1997). *More, more, more, said the baby.* New York: Greenwillow Books.

Willems, M. (2003). *Don't let the pigeon drive the bus.* New York: Hyperion Books.

Winter, J. (2003). *My name is Georgia.* Boston, MA: Houghton Mifflin Harcourt.

Winter, J. (2006). *Dizzy.* New York: Arthur A. Levine Books.

Winthrop, E. (2001). *Dumpy LaRue.* New York: Henry Holt & Company.

Wood, A. (2001). *Alphabet adventure.* Bruce Wood (Illus.). New York: Blue Sky Press.

Woodson, J. (2001). *The other side.* E. B. Lewis (Illus.). New York: Putnam Juvenile.

Yolen, J. (2006). *Fairy tale feasts: A literary cookbook for young readers and eaters.* Phillipe Be'ha (Illus.); recipes by Heidi Stemple. Northampton, MA: Crocodile Books.

Young, E. (2002). *Seven blind mice.* New York, NY: Puffin Books.

References

A

Adams, M. J. (1990). *Beginning to read: Thinking and learning about print.* Cambridge, MA: MIT Press.

Albers, P. (2007). *Finding the artist within: Creating and reading visual texts in the English language arts classroom.* International Reading Association.

Allen, R. V. (1964). The language experience approach. In W. G. Cutts (Ed.), *Teaching young children to read.* Washington: United States Office of Education.

Allington, R. L. (2006). *What really matters for struggling readers.* Boston: Pearson.

Allyn, P. (2009). *What to read when: The books and stories to read with your child and all the best times to read them.* New York: Avery Trade Books.

American Psychiatric Association. (2013). *Diagnostic and statistical manual of mental disorders* (5th ed.). Arlington, VA: American Psychiatric Publishing.

Anderson, T. (1995). Rediscovering the connection between the arts: Introduction to the symposium on interdisciplinary arts education. *Arts Education Policy Review, 96*(4), 10–12.

Anderson, C. (2000). *How's it going? A practical guide to conferring with student writers.* Portsmouth, NH: Heinemann.

Anderson, R. C., & Freebody, P. (1985). Vocabulary knowledge. In H. Singer & R. B. Ruddell (Eds.), *Theoretical models and processes of reading* (3rd ed., pp. 343–371). Newark, DE: International Reading Association.

Anderson, R. C., & Pearson, P. D. (1984). A schema-theoretic view of basic processing in reading. In P. D. Pearson (Ed.), *Handbook of Reading Research*, (pp. 255–292). New York: Longman.

Andress, B. L. (1973). *Music in early childhood.* Washington D.C.: Music Educators National Conference.

Armstrong, T. (2009). *Multiple intelligences in the classroom.* Alexandria, VA: Association for Supervision and Curriculum Development.

Ariza, E., Morales-Jones, C., Yahya, N., & Zainudden, H. (2010). *Why TESOL? Theories and issues in teaching English to speakers of other languages, K-12 classrooms.* Dubuque, IA: Kendall Hunt.

Ashton-Warner, S. (1963). *Teacher.* New York: Simon & Schuster.

B

Bandura, A. (1986). *Social foundations of thought and action: A social cognitive theory.* Englewood Cliffs, NJ: Prentice Hall, Inc.

Banks, J. (1993). *An introduction to multicultural education.* Needham Heights, MA: Allyn & Bacon.

Bauer, E. B., & Arazi, J. (2011). Promoting literacy development for beginning English learners. *The Reading Teacher, 64*(5), 383–386.

Beck, Isabel L., McKeown, M., & Kucan, L. (2002). Choosing words to teach. In *Bringing words to life: Robust vocabulary instruction* (pp. 15–30). New York, NY: Guilford Press.

Bear, D. R., Invernizzi, M., Templeton, S., & Johnston, F. (2015). *Words their way: Word study for phonics, vocabulary, and spelling instruction* (6th ed.). Upper Saddle River, NJ: Prentice Hall.

Bloom, B. (1956). *Taxonomy of educational objectives.* White Plains, NY: Longman.

Bodrova, E., & Leong, D. J. (2006). *Tools of the mind: The Vygotskian approach to early childhood education* (2nd ed.). London: Pearson.

Boushey, G., & Moser, J. (2006). *The daily 5: Fostering literacy independence in the elementary grades.* Portland, ME: Stenhouse Publishers.

Bresler, L. (1995). The subservient, co-equal, affective, and social integration styles and their implications for the arts. *Arts Education Policy Review, 96*(5), 31–37.

Bromley, H. (2006). *Making my own mark: Play and writing.* London: The British Association for Early Childhood Education.

Brown, S. (2012/2013). *Art integration in the schools.* Mason, Ohio: Cengage Learning.

C

Calkins, L. M. (1986). *The art of teaching writing.* Portsmouth, NH: Heinemann.

Calkins, L. M., & Harwayne, S. (1987). *The writing workshop: A world of difference.* Portsmouth, NH: Heinemann.

Calkins, L. M. (1994). *The art of teaching writing.* Portsmouth, NH: Heinemann.

Calkins, L. Ehrenworth, M., & Lehman, C. (2012). *Pathways to the common core.* Portsmouth, NH: Heinemann.

Calkins, L., Hohne, K., & Robb, A. (2015). *Writing pathways: Performance assessments and learning progressions.* Portsmouth, NH: Heinemann.

Cambourne, B. (1988). *The whole story: Natural learning and the acquisition of literacy in the classroom.* Auckland, New Zealand: Ashton Scholastic.

Carlton, E. B. (2000). Learning through music: The support of brain research. *Child Care Information Exchange, 133*(5), 53–56.

Cartwright , K. B. (Ed.). (2008). *Literacy processes: Cognitive flexibility in learning and teaching.* New York, NY: Guilford Press.

Cartwright, K. P., & Duke, N. K. (2010). *Word callers: Small-group one-to-one interventions for children who "read" but don't comprehend.* Portsmouth, NH: Hienemann.

Chopra D. & Tanzi R. (2013). *Super brain.* New York, NY: Harmony Books.

Clark, B. (2002). *Growing up gifted.* Columbus, OH: Merrill/Prentice Hall.

Clay, M. M. (1966). *Emergent reading behavior.* Doctoral dissertation, University of Auckland, New Zealand.

Clay, M. M. (1979). *The early detection of reading difficulties: A diagnostic survey with recovery procedures.* Auckland, NZ: Heinemann.

Clay, M. M. (1987). Implementing Reading Recovery: Systematic adaptations to an educational innovation. *New Zealand Journal of Educational Studies, 22,* 35–38.

Clay, M. M. (1991). *Becoming literate: The construction of inner control.* Portsmouth, NH: Heinemann.

Clay, M. M. (1993). *An observation survey of early literacy achievement* (3rd ed.). Ports-mouth, NH: Heinemann.

Codell, E. R. (2003). *How to get your child to love reading: For ravenous and reluctant readers alike.* Chapel Hill, N.C.: Alconquin.

Coleman, M. B., & Cramer, E. S. (2015). Creating meaningful art experiences with assistive technology for students with physical, visual, severe and multiple disabilities. *Art Education, 68*(2), 6–13.

Common Core State Standards Initiative. (2010). *English language arts common state standards.* www.corestandards.org /ELA-Literacy/.

Copple, C., & Bredekamp, S. (2009). *Developmentally appropriate practice in early childhood programs serving children from birth through age 8*. Washington, DC: National Association for the Education of Young Children.

Council for Exceptional Children. (2013). *Public policy agenda for the 113th United States Congress*. www.cec.sped.org/~/media/Files/Policy/Current%20Sped%20Issues%20Home/public%20policy%20agenda%20FINAL.pdf.

Craig, D., & Paraiso, J. (2008). Dual diaspora and barrio art: Art as an avenue for learning English. *Journal for Learning through the Arts, 4*(1).

Csikszentmihalyi, M. (1997). *Creativity flow and the psychology of discovery and invention*. New York: Harper Perennial.

Culham, R. (2004). *Using picture books to teach writing with the traits*. New York: Scholastic.

Culham, R. (2008). *The trait crate, Grades K, 1, 2 & 3*. New York: Scholastic Teaching Resources.

Cunningham, P. M. (2012). *Phonics they use: Words for reading and writing*. New York: Pearson.

Cunningham, P. M., & Hall, D. P. (1994). *Making words*. Greensboro, NC: Carson Delosa Publishing.

Cunningham, P. M., & Hall, D. P. (2001). *Making big words*. Greensboro, NC: Carson Delosa Publishing.

Cunningham, P. M., & Allington, R. L. (2015). *Classrooms that work: They can all read and write*. New York: Pearson.

D

Dale, E. (1965). Vocabulary measurement: Techniques and major findings. *Elementary English, 42*(8), 895–901.

Dallabrida, E. S. (2015). Back to school around the world: Painting a picture of global Educational and cultural traditions. *Literacy Today, 33*(1), 36–38.

Daniels, H. (2002). *Literature circles: Voice and choice in the student-centered classroom*. Portland, ME: Stenhouse.

Dashiell, J., & DeBruin-Parecki, A. (2014). Supporting young children's vocabulary growth using F.R.I.E.N.D.S model. *The Reading Teacher, 67*(7), 512–516.

The Department of Children, Schools and Families. (2008). *Marking making matters: Young children making meaning in all areas of learning and development*. Nottingham, UK: DCSF Publications.

D'Esposito, M., & Chen A. J. (2006). Neural mechanisms of prefrontal cortical function: Implications for cognitive rehabilitation. *Progress in Brain Research, 15*(7), 123–139.

DeVries, B. A. (2011). *Literacy assessment and intervention for classroom teachers.*

Scottsdale, AZ: Holocomb Hathaway, Publishers.

Dewey, J. (1934). *Art as experience*. New York: The Berkley Publishing Group.

Dewey, J. (1938). *Experience and education*. New York, NY: Macmillan Publishing Company.

Dewey, J. (1966). *Democracy and education*. New York: First Press.

Dolch, E. W. (1948). *Helping handicapped children in school*. London, UK: Garrard Press.

Dow, A. (1899). *Composition*. Berkley and Los Angeles, CA: University of California Press.

Duke, N. K., & Pearson, P. D. (2002). *Effective practices for developing reading comprehension*. In A. E. Farstrip & S. J. Samuels (Eds.). *What research has to say about reading instruction* (pp. 205–242). Newwark, DE: International Reading Association.

Durkin, D. (1966). *Children who read early: Two longitudinal studies*. New York: Teachers College Press.

E

Eisner, E. W. (2002). *The arts and the creation of mind*. New Haven, CT: Yale University Press.

Elbow, P. (1973). *Writing without teachers*. Oxford, England: Oxford University Press.

Engelmann, S., Haddox, P., & Bruner, E. (1983). *Teach your child to read in 100 easy lessons*. New York: Simon & Schuster.

F

Feldman, E. (1973). The teacher as model critic. *Journal of Aesthetic Education, 7*(1), 50–57.

Feldman, E. (1987). *Varieties of visual experiences* (3rd ed.). New York, NY: Harry N. Abrams, Inc.

Feldman, E. B. (1993). *Practical art criticism*. Upper Saddle River, NJ: Prentice Hall.

Fisher, P. J., & Blachowicz, C. L. (2005). Vocabulary instruction in a remedial setting. *Reading & Writing Quarterly, 21*(3), 281–300.

Fisher, D., & Frey, N. (2012). Close reading in elementary schools. *The Reading Teacher, 66*(3), 179–188.

Fisher, D., Frey, N., & Kroener, J. (2013). High quality supports for students with disabilities. *Principal Leadership, 14*(3), 56.

Fletcher, R. (1999). *Live writing: Breathing life into your words*. New York: HarperCollins.

Flint, A. S. (2008). *Literate lives: Teaching, reading, and writing in elementary classrooms*. Hoboken, NJ: John Wiley & Sons.

Flom, R., Gentile, D. A., & Pick, A. D. (2008). Infants' discrimination of happy and sad music. *Infant Behavior and Development, 31*(4), 716–728.

Forney, M. (2001). *Razzle dazzle writing—Achieving excellence through 50 target skills*. Gainesville, FL: Maupin House Books.

Forney, M. (2007). *Writing superstars*. Deland, FL: Buttery Moon Multimedia.

Fountas, I., & Pinnell, G. S. (2009). *The Fountas and Pinnell leveled book list, k-8+*. Portsmouth, NH: Heineman.

Fountas, I., & Pinnell, G. S. (2011). *The continuum of literacy learning, preK to 8: A guide to teaching* (2nd ed.). Portsmouth, NH: Heineman.

Fox, M. (2001). *Reading magic—Why your child can learn to read before school and other read-aloud miracles*. Fort Washington, PA: Harvest Books.

Frey, N., & Fisher, D. (2010). Reading and the brain: What early childhood educators need to know: *Early Childhood Education, 30*, 103–110.

Freire, P. (1993). *Pedagogy of the oppressed*. New York: Continuum Publishing Company.

Fromkin, V. A., Rodman, R., & Hyams, N. (2010). *An introduction to language*. Independence, KY: Wadsworth Cengage Learning.

G

Galda, L., Sipe, L. R., Liang, L. A., & Cullinan, B. E. (2013). *Literature and the child* (8th ed.). Belmont, CA: Wadsworth/Cengage.

Gambrell, L. B. (1996). Creating classroom cultures that foster reading motivation. *Reading Teacher, 50*, 14–25.

Gandini, L., Etheredge, S., & Hill, L. (2008). *Insights and inspirations from Reggio Emilia: Stories of teachers and children from North America*. Worcester, MA: Davis Publications.

Gardner, H. (1983). *Frames of mind: The theory of multiple intelligences*. New York: Basic Books.

Gardner, H. (1991). *The unschooled mind: How children think & how schools should teach*. New York: Basic Books.

Gardner, H. (1999a). *Intelligences reframed: Multiple intelligences for the 21st century*. New York: Basic Books.

Gardner, H. (1999b). *The disciplined mind: What all students should understand*. New York, NY: Simon & Schuster.

Gee, J. P. (2015). *Literacy and education*. New York: Routledge.

Gentry, J. R. (2010). *Raising confident readers: How to teach your child to read and write—from baby to age 7*. Cambridge, MA: Da Capo Lifelong Books.

Gipe, J. P. (2014). *Multiple paths to literacy: Assessment and differentiated instruction for diverse learners, K–12* (8th ed.). Boston: Pearson.

Glazer, S. (1998). *Assessment is instruction: Reading, writing, spelling and phonics for all learners*. Norwood, MA: Christopher-Gordon.

Goldstein, B. (2011). *Bilingual language development and disorders in Spanish-English speakers*. Baltimore, MD: Brookes Publishing.

Goodman, K. S., Bird, L. & Goodman, Y. (Eds.) (1982). Revaluing readers and reading: Topics in learning and learning disabilities. *The Whole Language Catalog*, 1(4), 87–93.

Goodman, K. S., Goodman, Y. M., & Hood, W. J. (1988). *The whole language evaluation book*. Portsmouth, NH: Heinemann.

Goodman, Y., & Owocki, G. (2002). *Kidwatching: Documenting children's literacy development*. Portsmouth, NH: Heinemann.

Goodman, Y. M., Watson, D. J., & Burke, C. L. (2005). *Reading miscue inventory: From evaluation to instruction*. Somers, NY: Richard C. Owen Publishing.

Graves, D. H. (1983). *Writing: Teachers and children at work*. Exeter, NH: Heinemann.

Greene, M. F. (2014, October). *What do all babies need, yet aren't getting equally?* NY: Reader's Digest Magazine.

H

Hall, T., Strangman, N., & Meyer, A. (2003). Differentiated instruction and implications for universal design for learning implementation. *National Center on Accessing the General Curriculum: Effective Classroom Practices Report*, 2–24.

Hallanhan, D. P., Kauffman, J. M., & Pullen, P. C. (2011). *Exceptional learners: An introduction to special education*. Boston, MA: Pearson Education.

Halliday, M. A. K. (1978). *Language as social semiotic: The social interpretation of language and meaning*. Baltimore, MD: University Park Press.

Harris, A. J., & Sipay, E. R. (1990). *How to increase reading ability: A guide to development and remedial methods*. Boston: Longman.

Harste, J. C., Short, K. G., & Burke, C. (1988). *Creating classrooms for authors: The reading-writing connection*. Portsmouth, NH: Heinemann.

Heard, G. (1998). *Awakening the heart: Exploring poetry in elementary and middle school*. Portsmouth, NH: Heinemann.

Hoover-Dempsey, K. V., Walker, J. M. T., Sandler, H. M., Whetsel, D., Green, C. L., Wilkins, A. S., & Closson, K. E. (2005). Why do parents become involved? Research findings and implications. *Elementary School Journal*, 106(2); 105–130.

Housen, A. (2000). Art viewing and aesthetic development: Designing for the viewer. In P. Villenueve (Ed.), *From periphery to center: Art museum education in the century* (pp. 172–179). Reston, VA: The National Art Education Association.

Hurwitz, A., & Day, M. (2001). *Children and their art: Methods for the elementary school*. Orlando, FL: Harcourt College Publishers.

Hymes, J. L. (1989). *Teaching the child under six*. Minneapolis, MN: Consortium Publishing.

I

International Literacy Association. (2006). *New roles in response to intervention: Creating success for schools and children*. International Reading Association. www.literacyworldwide.org.

Irwin, R., & Reynolds, J. (1995). Integration as a strategy for teaching the arts as disciplines. *Arts Education Policy Review*, 96(4), 13–19.

Ivey, G., & Johnston, P. H. (2013). Engagement with young adult literature: Outcomes and processes. *Reading Research Quarterly*, 48(3), 255–275.

J

Jacobs C., & Wendel I. (2010). *The everything parents guide to ADHD in children*. Avon, MA: Adams Media.

Johns, J. L. (2012). *Basic reading inventory*. Dubuque, IA: Kendall Hunt.

Johns, J. L., & Lenski, S. D. (2010). *Improving reading: Interventions, strategies, and resources*. Dubuque, IA: Kendall Hunt.

Johns, J. L., & Lenski, S. D. (2014). *Improving reading: Strategies, resources and common core connections*. Dubuque, IA: Kendall Hunt.

K

Katz, L. G., & Chard, S. C. (1989). *Engaging children's minds: The project approach*. New York: Ablex Publishing.

Kasten, W. C., Kristo, J. V., & McClure, A. A. (2005). *Living literature: Using children's literature to support reading and language arts*. Upper Saddle River, NJ: Pearson.

Keehn, S., Harmon, J., & Shoho, A. (2008). A study of readers theater in eighth grade: issues of fluency, comprehension, and vocabulary. *Reading & Writing Quarterly*, 24, 335–362.

Keene, E. O., & Zimmerman, S. (2007). *Mosaic of thought: The power of comprehension strategy instruction*. Portsmouth, NH: Heinemann.

Keifer, B., & Tyson, C. (2009). *Charlotte Huck's children's literature: A brief guide*. New York, NY: McGraw-Hill.

Klein, J., & Stuart, E. (2012). *Using art to teach reading comprehension strategies: Lesson plans for teachers*. Lanhan, MD: Rowman & Littlefield Education.

Kluth, P. (2010). *"You're gonna love this kid!" Teaching students with autism in the inclusive classroom*. Baltimore, MD: Brookes Publishing.

Kohl, M. A. (1994). *Preschool art: It's the process, not the product*. Beltsville, MD: Gryphon House Publishing.

Koralek, D., Charner, K., Malstrom, E. C., Jaffe, M., Bohart, H., Dombrink-Green, M., Wegner, W., & Baker, L. (2015). *Expressing creativity in preschool*. Washington, DC: The National Association for the Education of Young Children.

Koster, J. B. (2009). *Growing artists: Teaching the arts to young children*. San Francisco, CA: Cengage Learning.

Krashen, S. (1993). *The power of reading*. Portsmouth, NH: Heinemann.

Krashen, S. (2004). *The power of reading: Insights from the research* (2nd ed.). Ports-mouth, NH: Heinemann.

Krashen, S. (1982). *Principles and practices in second language acquisition*. Oxford, UK: Trentham Books.

Kray, J., & Ferdinand, N. K. (2013). How to improve cognitive control in development during childhood: Potentials and limits of cognitive interventions. *Child Development Perspectives*, 7(2), 121–125.

Krug, D., & Cohen-Evron, N. (2000). Curriculum integration positions and practices in art education. *Studies in Art Education, 41*(3), 2–5.

L

La Pray, M., & Ross, R. (1969). The graded word list: Quick gauge of reading ability. *Journal of Reading*, 12(4), 305–307.

Layne, S. L. (2005). *Igniting a passion for reading*. Portland, ME: Stenhouse Publishers.

Leslie, L., & Caldwell, J. S. (2010). *Qualitative reading inventory 5*. Upper Saddle River, NJ: Allyn & Bacon.

Levine, M. (2002). *A mind at a time*. New York: Simon & Schuster.

Li, F., Cao, B., Cai, X., & Li, H. (2011) Similar Brain Mechanism of Hypothesis-Testing between Children and Adults. *Developmental Neuropsychology, 36*, 957–970.

Louie, B., & Sierschynski, J. (2015). Enhancing English learners' language development using wordless picture books. *The Reading Teacher, 69*(1), 103–111.

Lowenfeld, V., & Brittain, W. (1987). *Creative and mental growth*. New York: Macmillan.

Lowenfeld, V. (1968). *Viktor Lowenfeld speaks on art and creativity*. Reston, VA: National Art Education Association.

Marohn S. (2002). *The natural medicine guide to autism*, Charlottesville VA: Hampton Roads Publishing Co. Inc.

Martinez, U., & Nolte-Yupari, S. (2015). Story bound, map bround: Stories, life, and learning. *Art Education, 68*(1), 12.

Maslow, A. H. (1954). *Motivation and personality*. New York, NY: Viking Press.

Mayesky, M. (2009). *Creative activities for young children*. Boston, MA: Wadsworth Publishing.

McGee, L. M., & Richgels, D. J. (2011). *Literacy's beginnings: Supporting young readers and writers* (6th ed.). Needham, MA: Allyn & Bacon.

McGregor, T. (2007). *Comprehension connections: Bridges to strategic reading*. Portsmouth, NH: Heinnemann.

McKenna, M. C., & Kear, D. J. (1990). *Elementary reading attitude survey*. In J. L. Johns & S. D. Lenski (Eds.), *Improving reading: Interventions, strategies, and resources*. Dubuque, IA: Kendall Hunt.

Miller, D. (2013). *Reading with meaning: Teaching comprehension in the primary grades*. Portland, ME: Stenhouse Publishers.

Miller, D. (2009). *The book whisperer: Awakening the inner reader in every child*. San Francisco, CA: Jossey Bass Publishing Company.

Moll, L. C., (2015). Tapping into the "hidden" home and community resources of students. *Kappa Delta Pi Record, 51*(3), 114–117.

Montessori, M. (1914). *Dr. Montessori's own handbook*. New York: Frederick A. Stokes Company.

Montessori, M. (1936). *The secret of childhood*. New York: Frederick A. Stokes Company.

Morrow, L. M. (2009). *Literacy development in the early years: Helping children read and write*. Boston: Pearson.

Moses, L., Ogden, M., & Kelly, B. L. (2015). Facilitating meaningful discussion groups in the primary grades. *The Reading Teacher, 69*(2), 233–237.

Murphy, S. (2012). Reclaiming pleasure in the teaching of reading. *Language Arts, 89*(5), 318–328.

Nagy, W. E. (1988). *Teaching vocabulary to improve reading comprehension*. Available from National Council of Teachers of English, Urbana, IL and International Reading Association, Newark, DE.

National Association for the Education of Young Children and National Association of Early Childhood Specialists in State Departments of Education. (2003). *Early childhood curriculum, assessment, and program evaluation: Building an effective, accountable system in programs for children birth through age 8*. Washington, DC: Authors. www.naeyc.org/files/naeyc/file/positions/pscape.pdf.

National Coalition for Core Arts Standards. (2014). *National core arts standards: Dance, media arts, music, theatre and visual arts*. http://www.nationalartsstandards.org/

National Council of Teachers of English & International Reading Association. (2010). *Standards for the assessment of reading and writing* (rev. ed.; pp. 11–31). Copyright 2010 by the NCTE/IRA.

National Council of Teachers of English & International Reading Association. (2012). *Standards for the English language arts*. www.ncte.org/standards/ncte-ira.

National Dance Association. (1990). *Guide to creative dance for the young child*. Reston, VA: National Dance Association.

National Early Literacy Panel. (2008). *Developing early literacy: Report of the National Early Literacy Panel*. Washington, DC: National Institute for Literacy.

National Reading Panel. (2000). *Teaching children to read: An evidence-based assessment of the scientific research literature on reading and its implications for reading instruction*. Washington, DC: National Institute of Child Health and Human Development, National Institutes of Health.

Nieto, Sonia. (2010). *Language, culture, and teaching: Critical perspectives* (2nd ed.). New York: Routledge.

Nieto, Sonia. (2003). *What keeps teachers going?* NY: Teachers College Press.

Nell, M. L., Drew, W. F., & Bush, D. E. (2013). *From play to practice: Connecting teachers' play to children's learning*. National Association for the Education of Young Children.

Northrop, L., & Killeen, E. (2013). A framework for using Ipads to build early literacy skills. *The Reading Teacher, 66*(7), 531–537.

Oczkus, L. D. (2012). *Best ever literacy survival tips: 72 Lessons you can't teach without*. Newark, DE: International Reading Association.

Parsons, S. A., Malloy, J. A., Parsons, A. W., & Burrowbridge, S. C. (2015). Students'engagement in literacy tasks. *The Reading Teacher, 69*(7), 223–231.

Pashler, H., Bain, P. M., Bottge, B. A., Grasser, A., Koedinger, K., McDaniel, M., & Metcalfe, J. (2007). *Organizing instruction and study to improve student learning: IES practice guide*. Washington D.C.: National Center for Educational Research.

Perfetti, C. A. (1985). *Reading ability*. London, UK: Oxford University Press.

Piaget, J. (1953). *The origins of intelligence in children*. New York, NY: Basic Books.

Piaget, J. (1964). *The moral judgment of the child*. New York, NY: Free Press.

Piaget, J. (1969). *The psychology of the child*. New York: Basic Books.

Pinnell, G. S., & Fountas, I. (2011). *Literacy beginnings: A prekindergarten handbook*. Portsmouth, NH: Heinemann.

Pitri, E. (2001). The role of artistic play in problem solving. *Art Education, 54*(3), 46.

Pole, K. (2015). "Why downt you riyt back to me?" Family letter writing in kindergarten. *The Reading Teacher, 69*(1), 119–128.

Powell, K. C. (2012). *Educational psychology of the self and learning*. Boston, MA: Pearson.

Powell, K. C. (2006). *Educational psychology of the self*. Dubuque, IA: Kendall Hunt.

Powell, K. C. & Kalina, C. J. (2009). Cognitive and social constructivism: Developing tools for an effective classroom. *Education*. 130(2), 241–250.

President's Committee on the Arts and the Humanities. (2011). *Reinvesting in arts education: Winning America's future through creative schools*. Washington, DC. www.pcah.gov.

Ramirez, K. (2006). *What good is accountable talk if you can't understand it? The importance of teaching kids to be clear, effective speakers*. http://teachersnetwork.org/tnli/research/achieve/Ramirez.pdf.

Rasinski, T. V., & Padak, N. D. (2001). *From phonics to fluency: Effective teaching of decoding and reading fluency in the elementary school*. New York: Longman.

Rasinski, T., Padak, N. D., & Fawcett, G. (2010). *Teaching children who find reading difficult*. Boston: Allyn & Bacon.

Ray, K. W., & Laminack, L. L. (2001). *The writing workshop: Working through the hard parts (and they're all hard parts)*. Urbana, IL: National Council of Teachers of English.

Ray, K., & Smith, M. C. (2010). The kindergarten child: What teachers and administrators need to know to promote academic success in all children. *Early Childhood Education Journal, 38*(5), 5–18.

Reutzel, D. R. (2015). Early literacy research: Findings primary grade teachers will want to know. *The Reading Teacher, 69*(1), 14–24.

Riccio, L. L., Rollins, J., & Morton, K. (2003). *The sail effect*. Washington, DC: WVSA Arts Connection.

Rieger, A., & McGrail, E. (2015). Exploring children's literature with authentic representations of disabilities. *Kappa Delta Pi Record, 51*(1), 18–23.

Robinson, K., & Aronica, L. (2015). *Creative schools: Revolutionizing education from the ground up.* London, UK: Penguin UK.

Rosenblatt, L. (1978). *The reader, the text, the poem.* Carbondale, IL: Southern Illinois University Press.

Roucher, N., & Lovano-Kerr, J. (1995). Can the arts maintain integrity interdisciplinary learning? *Arts Education Policy Review, 96*(4), 20–25.

Routman, R. (1994). *Invitations: Changing as teachers and learners, K–12.* Portsmouth, NH: Heinemann.

Routman, R. (2002). *Reading essentials: The specifics you need to teach reading well.* Portsmouth, NH: Heinemann.

Rushton, S. P., Eitelgeorge, J., & Zickafoose, R. (2003). Connecting Brian Cambourne's conditions of learning theory to brain/mind principles: Implications for early childhood educators. *Early Childhood Education Journal, 31,* 11–21.

S

Samuels, S. J., & Flor, R. F. (1997). The importance of automaticity for developing expertise in reading. *Reading & Writing Quarterly, 13,* 107–121.

Schickendanz, J. A. (1999). *Much more than the ABCs: The early stages of reading and writing.* Washington, DC: National Association for the Education of Young Children.

Schwartz, K. (2015). *Why kids need to move, touch and experience to learn.* ww2.kqed .org/mindshift/2015/03/26/why-kids-need -to-move-touch-and-experience-to-learn/.

Serafini, F. (2001). *The reading workshop: Creating space for readers.* Portsmouth, NH: Heinemann.

Serafini, F., & Youngs, S. (2013). *Reading workshop 2.0: Children's literature in the digital age. The Reading Teacher, 66*(5), 401–414.

Snow, C. E., Burns, M. S., & Griffin, P. (Eds.) (1998). *Preventing reading difficulties in young children.* Washington, DC: National Academy Press.

Soundy, C. S., & Lee, Y. H. (2013). A medley of pictures and patterns in children's drawings. *Young Children, 68*(2), 70.

Stahl, S. A. (1992). Saying the "p" word: Nine guidelines for exemplary phonics instruction. *The Reading Teacher, 45*(8), 618–625.

Stahl, S. A. (1999). *Vocabulary development.* Brookline, MA: Brookline Booksmith.

Stauffer, R. (1970). *The language experience approach to the teaching of reading.* New York: Harper & Row.

Stephens, D, Cox, C., Downs, A., et. al. (2012). There ain't NO PIGS with WIGS: Challenges of Tier 2 intervention. *The Reading Teacher, 66*(3), 93–103.

Sternberg, R. (1990). *Metaphors of mind: Conceptions of the nature of intelligence.* New York, NY: Cambridge University Press.

Sulzby, E. (1985). Children's emergent reading of favorite storybooks: A developmental study. *Reading Research Quarterly, 20,* 458–481.

Sulzby, E. (1990). Assessment of emergent writing and children's language while writing. In L. M. Morrow & Smith, J. (Eds.). *Assessment for instruction in early literacy* (pp. 83–109). Englewood Cliffs, NJ: Prentice Hall.

Sulzby, E., & Teale, W. H. (1985). Writing development in early childhood. *Educational Horizons, 64,* 8–12.

Szekely, G. (1990). The teaching of art as performance. *Art Education, 43*(3), 6–17.

T

Taba, H. (1967). Implementing thinking as an objective in social studies. *Effective Thinking in the Social Studies,* 25–49.

Tabors, P. (1997). *One child, two languages: A guide for early childhood educators of children learning English as a second language.* Towson, MD: Brookes Publishing.

Teachers College Reading and Writing Project. (2009). *High frequency word assessment (Grades 3-8).* Retrieved from http: //readingandwritingproject.com/public /resources/assessments/spelling/spelling _word_list_directions.pdf.

The Department of Children, Schools and Families. (2008). *Marking making matters: Young children making meaning in all areas of learning and development.* Nottingham, UK: DCSF Publications.

Tompkins, G. E. (2013). *Literacy for the 21st century: A balanced approach* (6th ed.). Upper Saddle River, NJ: Pearson.

Towell, J. (2013). *Hooked on books: Language and literature in elementary classrooms.* Dubuque, IA: Kendal Hunt.

Towell, J., & Matanzo, J. B. (2010). Children as authors and illustrators: A demonstration of the writing process. *The College Reading Association Yearbook, 31,* 375–389.

Trelease, J. (2013). *The read-aloud handbook.* New York: Penguin Books.

Tyner, B. (2004). *Small-group reading instruction: A differentiated teaching model for beginning and struggling readers.* Newark, NJ: International Reading Association.

U

United States Department of Education. (1965). *Elementary and secondary education act.* Washington, DC: U.S. Government Printing Office.

United States Department of Education. (1993). *Gifted and talented act.* Washington, DC: U.S. Government Printing Office.

United States Department of Education. (2002). *No child left behind act.* Washington, DC: U.S. Government Printing Office.

United States Department of Education. (2004). *Individuals with disabilities education improvement act.* Washington, DC: U.S. Government Printing Office.

V

Vecchi, V. (2010). *Art and creativity in Reggio Emilia: Exploring the role and potential of ateliers in early childhood education.* New York: Routledge.

Very Special Arts. (2012). *The intersection of arts education and special education: Exemplary programs and approaches.* Washington D.C.: The John F. Kennedy Center for the Performing Arts.

Vukelich, D., & Christie, J. (2009). *Building a foundation for preschool literacy: Effective instruction for children's reading and writing development.* Newark, DE: International Reading Association.

Vukelich, C., Christie, J., & Enz, B. J. (2011). *Helping young children learn language and literacy: Birth through kindergarten.* New York: Pearson.

Vygotsky, L. S. (1962). *Thought and Language.* Cambridge, MA: MIT Press (original work published in 1934).

Vygotsky, L. S. (1978). *Mind in society: The development of psychological processes.* Cambridge, MA: Harvard University Press.

W

Wardle, F. (2003). *Introduction to early childhood education: A multidimensional approach to child-centered care and learning.* Boston, MA: Allyn & Bacon.

Weaver, C. (2002). *Reading process and practice.* Portsmouth, NH: Heinemann.

Willems, P. P., & Gonzalez-DeHass, A. R. (2006). *Educational psychology casebook.* New York: Pearson/Allyn & Bacon.

Woolfolk, A. (2011). *Educational psychology.* Boston, MA: Allyn & Bacon.

Y

Yopp, R. H., & Yopp, H. K. (2007). Ten important words plus: A strategy for building word knowledge. *The Reading Teacher, 61*(2), 157–160.

Yopp, R. H., & Yopp, H. K. (2010). *Literature-based reading activities.* Boston: Allyn & Bacon.

D

2010 NAEYC STANDARDS
Initial and Advanced Early Childhood Professional Preparation Programs
Correlating the Standards with Chapters in **CREATIVE LITERACY IN ACTION**

These NAEYC Standards provide the foundation for accreditation of early childhood programs in higher education.

Standards	Chapters
Standard 1: Promoting Child Development and Learning	1, 2, 4, 5, 7, 9
Standard 2: Building Family and Community Relationships	8
Standard 3: Observing, Documenting, and Assessing to Support Young Children and Families	3
Standard 4: Using Developmentally Effective Approaches	6, 9, 10
Standard 5: Using Content Knowledge to Build Meaningful Curriculum	4, 5, 6

NAEYC STANDARDS
Early Childhood Program Standards and Accreditation Criteria
Correlating the Standards with Chapters in **CREATIVE LITERACY IN ACTION**

These NAEYC Early Childhood Program Standards reflect current best practices in early childhood programs.

Standards	Chapters
Standard 1: Relationships	1, 9
Standard 2: Curriculum	2, 4, 5, 6, 7, 9, 10
Standard 3: Teaching	2, 4, 5, 6, 7, 9
Standard 4: Assessment	3
Standard 7: Families	8
Standard 8: Community Relationships	8